DOROTHY THOMPSON

DOROTHY

A Legend

THOMPSON
in Her Time ❧ ❧

Marion K. Sanders

Illustrated with Photographs and Drawings

1973

HOUGHTON MIFFLIN COMPANY BOSTON

ISBN: 0-395-15467-7
Library of Congress Catalog Card Number: 72-9013
Printed in the United States of America

To my friend and peerless editor Joyce Hartman

Foreword

A BIOGRAPHY entails much research which is said to be a lonely business. Yet in the case of this book, strenuous would be a more appropriate description. My memory of the past two years is less of long hours in libraries than those spent in pursuit of Dorothy Thompson's friends and associates, scattered over two continents. To the many who shared their recollections and insights with me, I am deeply grateful. Their names are listed on pages 375–376.

The large collection of Thompson papers in the George Arents Research Library at Syracuse University has been a priceless resource. Dorothy saved much of her correspondence and diaries after she met Sinclair Lewis, whom she married in 1928, and even more after 1936 when she became a celebrity in her own right as a columnist, radio commentator, and lecturer. She was then in her forties, served by three secretaries, and had ample file-space in two large homes. Earlier, as a peripatetic foreign correspondent, she had neither a place to store her memorabilia nor the expectation that they would be of lasting interest. She did, however, preserve her early love letters. In her papers there is little documentation of her years abroad in the 1920s and almost none from 1914, when she graduated from Syracuse University, until 1920, when she went overseas for the first time.

Filling in these gaps has been a challenging task and I am immensely grateful to those who made it possible, particularly Barbara De Porte Grossman, Mrs. Henry Goddard Leach, and Beatrice Sorchan Binger. I wish also to thank those who gave me access to other unique material: Whitelaw Reid, for allowing me to go through the Helen Rogers Reid papers before they were consigned to the Library of Congress; my daughter, Mary von Euler, for preserving the Frances Gunther papers and Marcia Wilson for cataloguing them; and Dale Warren of Houghton Mifflin Company.

I am grateful, too, for the help of Carolyn Ann Davis and Stacy Ulisano of the Syracuse University Library, John R. Payne of the University of Texas Library, Maureen Coutts of the Illinois Institute of Technology, Donald Gallup of the Beinecke Library at Yale, and Morton Yarmon of the American Jewish Committee.

In addition, I must mention the forbearing friends who furnished suggestions, clues, and spiritual and logistical support, especially: Elizabeth Eagan, Morris L. Ernst, Ruth Heller, Katya and John Jacobs, Nancy and Theodore Kaghan, Harold Manheim, Mary Presper, Melanie and Roman Totenberg, and — not least — Shirley Baker, a manuscript typist undaunted by the most disheveled copy.

The dedication of this book is a minimal expression of my debt to my editor, Joyce Hartman. Her unstinting encouragement and her sage annotations on early drafts are shining examples of what a good editor really does.

Finally, to Dorothy Thompson: I believe you would have approved the principle that has guided me in drawing on your papers; that is, to include any material if — and only if — it casts light on your character and times. For the past two years you have been a fascinating, often infuriating presence in my life but always — as your friend Dame Rebecca West put it — "rattling good company." I shall miss you.

Marion K. Sanders

October 24, 1972
New York City

Contents

Illustrations

(Following page 208)

Dorothy with her mother, father, and favorite aunt (*Willard Thompson*)

Church and parsonage in Hamburg, New York (*Willard Thompson and the Historical Society of the Hamburg Methodist Church*)

Dorothy acquires a stepmother, 1903 (*Willard Thompson and the Historical Society of the Hamburg Methodist Church*)

On the Lewis Institute Basketball Team, 1911 (*Illinois Institute of Technology*)

Dorothy with Aunts Margaret and Hetty, 1912 (*Syracuse University Library*)

Gertrude Tone (*Niagara Falls Gazette, Niagara Falls, New York*)

Barbara De Porte (*Barbara De Porte Grossman*)

Page of a travel journal, 1920 (*Barbara De Porte Grossman*)

In Rome, 1920 (*Barbara De Porte Grossman*)

Holiday in the Bavarian Alps, 1921 (*Beatrice Sorchan Binger*)

Dorothy at twenty-eight (*Syracuse University Library*)

Rose Wilder Lane (*Wide World Photos*)

Paul Scott Mowrer (*Wide World Photos*)

Marcel Fodor (*Wide World Photos*)

Dorothy and Josef Bard (*Syracuse University Library*)

Edna St. Vincent Millay (*Photo by Eugene Jan Boissevain. Courtesy of Dale Warren*)

Phyllis Bottome (*Wide World Photos*)

Louis Untermeyer (*Wide World Photos*)

Eugenia Schwarzwald (*Syracuse University Library*)

An ovation for Eleanor Roosevelt (*Whitelaw Reid*)

Morris L. Ernst (*The Bettmann Archive*)

Gustav Stolper (*Wide World Photos*)

Max Ascoli (*Black Star*)

Hamilton Fish Armstrong (*Wide World Photos*)

David L. Cohn (*Lillian Cohn*)

Alexander Sachs (*Underwood & Underwood*)

Cartoon by Gardner Rea

The "big house" at Twin Farms (*Previews, Inc.*)

Michael and Wells Lewis (*Dale Warren*)

Dorothy, Michael, and Herman Budzislawski (*Madeline Shaw Green*)

Alexander Woollcott (*Photoworld*)

Vincent and Diana Sheean (*Wide World Photos*)

Hilda, Baroness Louis de Rothschild (*Photo by Engeborg de Beausacq. Courtesy of Baroness de Rothschild*)

Dame Rebecca West (*Black Star*)

A note to Helen Rogers Reid (*Whitelaw Reid*)

Dorothy in her Turtle Bay home (*Ralph Crane from Black Star*)

Madeline Shaw at the command post (*Ralph Crane from Black Star*)

Dorothy marries Maxim Kopf (*Elli Marcus*)

Wedding guests (*Madeline Shaw Green*)

Dorothy's bookplate (*John S. Mayfield*)

Dale Warren and Esther Root Adams (*Elli Marcus*)

Dorothy in her fifties (*Syracuse University Library*)

Notes for an autobiography (*Syracuse University Library*)

In her garden (*Dale Warren*)

PART I

THE GIRL FROM SYRACUSE

🦋 1
"God was everywhere"

IF YOU WERE TO DRIVE TODAY from the Genesee valley through the small segment of western New York State where Dorothy Thompson spent her childhood, you might imagine yourself in Ohio or Indiana. Here the Midwestern plains begin, and in spirit as well as topography the region is more closely akin to the farmlands on the far shore of Lake Erie than cosmopolitan New York City some 400 miles to the south and east. The first white settlers were westward-bound New Englanders; a small influx of Germans from Pennsylvania followed, but the heterogeneous immigrant tides of later years flowed elsewhere. Rutted country roads have been replaced by broad ribbons of concrete lined with motels, pennant-decked gas stations, and shopping centers. However, when you turn off the main highways you find tranquil, tree-shaded village streets and venerable frame houses with pillared front porches and wide lawns. Life still centers around the churches whose spires dominate the landscape. Few are Catholic; there are no synagogues and one seldom encounters a dark skin. This is white Protestant America.

"God was everywhere," Dorothy wrote in a reminiscence of her youth, part of a never-completed autobiography. "Jesus was father's personal friend . . . and the Thompson family was under special protection."

Dorothy was a restless, sometimes wayward child given at an early age to running away from home in search of adventure or escape from an oppressive situation. "I ran a long, long way in space, time and my own mind," she wrote, "following my own will and passions. But I could not break the slender evanescent tie to my father."

Father, whose idealized image pervaded her life, was the Reverend Peter Thompson. Born in County Durham in the English North Country, he grew up as a poor orphan in the home of a prosperous uncle. Though the Thompsons were Anglicans, Peter responded to a "call" from the evangelical faith of John Wesley. He was an ordained Methodist preacher in 1890 when, at the age of twenty-eight, he visited relatives in Chicago. There he met and fell in love with eighteen-year-old Margaret Grierson, the slim, dark-haired daughter of a genteel Anglo-Irish mother. Mrs. Grierson had married "beneath her" — a socialist railroad worker who deserted her to return to his native Scotland and was never mentioned in the family.

After their marriage Margaret and Peter headed back for England, with a honeymoon stop at Niagara Falls. There, a chance encounter led to a "charge" — as a Methodist parish is known — in Lancaster, an industrial town near Buffalo, and a subsequent decision to stay in America. Reverend Peter was a short wiry man, dubbed "the little minister" by parishioners who had read J. M. Barrie's popular novel of that name. Mild-mannered, with a high-domed forehead and a bristling mustache, he had compensated for a meager formal education by a passion for reading. His benevolence and the elegance of his British-accented diction inspired admiration, as did the fine clear tenor voice in which he led the hymn-singing.*

In the tradition of its early circuit riders, the Methodist Church required mobility of its pastors, who were assigned to new parishes every few years. Dorothy was born in Lancaster on July 9, 1893. When she was three months old, the family moved

---

* As a fifteen-year-old boy, Harry Emerson Fosdick, who would become one of the nation's most celebrated liberal churchmen, divided his worship between the Methodists and Presbyterians since there was no church of his own Baptist faith in Lancaster. "The best remembered minister was Reverend Peter Thompson . . . he was kindness itself," he wrote in his autobiography, *The Living of These Days* (Harper, New York, 1956).

to Clarence, a village a few miles to the north, where her brother Peter Willard and her sister Margaret arrived at two-year intervals. After a short tour in Tonawanda, midway between Buffalo and Niagara Falls, the Thompsons were transferred in 1900 to Hamburg, some twelve miles south of Buffalo, for the longest stay of Dorothy's childhood.

"The piano was crated," she recalled. "Mama's china, Father's books and the Mason jars full of food from the cellar were packed and moved for the third time in my brief lifetime. I was a big girl now, going on for seven and the second grade in school, a 'carefully brought up' parsonage child." The white clapboard church on Union Street with its tall spire was the largest over which Reverend Peter had yet presided. Like all the previous Thompson dwellings, the parsonage across the lawn lacked such amenities as a bathroom and was furnished with castoffs from the attics of church ladies banded together as "willing workers." On the walls of the front parlor hung portraits of John Wesley and Frances Willard, the temperance leader after whom Dorothy's brother had been named. Illuminated by kerosene lamps* and dependent in winter on the heat of a basement furnace and floor registers, the house boasted a large, cozy kitchen warmed by a wood-burning range. Here after morning prayers, breakfast was eaten and "high tea" in the evening — later Americanized to supper. The children's favorite playgrounds were an apple orchard behind the parsonage and an empty gray weathered barn where Dorothy and her friends set up a trapeze, practiced circus gymnastics, and plotted assorted "deviltry." As punishment for minor misdeeds, Dorothy was required to memorize choice passages from the considerable library her father accumulated from traveling booksellers. "By the time I was twelve I had memorized reams of poetry, some fifty psalms and several chapters of the Bible," she wrote. "To this day I can recite most of Shelley's 'Ode to the

* "Modern gas lighting" was installed shortly after the Thompsons moved in.

West Wind' entirely because it struck my fancy to let the horses out of the church stables during a pause between church and Sunday school."

A collaborator in these pranks was her friend Marguerite Jarvis, who recalls lingering after the church service with Dorothy to crawl through the pews in the hope of salvaging pennies dropped from the collection plate. Pennies were important since the minister's salary was never more than $1000 a year, some of it paid in farm produce. A tenth was regularly set aside as a tithe for the church missions and a few dollars were banked every month for the children's college education. Marguerite's father commuted to his optical store in Buffalo, but Dorothy could afford the nickel fare on the interurban trolley only two or three times during her five years in Hamburg.

Sundays the faithful trooped to the morning church service, Bibles in hand. Sunday school began at noon and was followed after dinner by a Junior League meeting at 3:30, the Epworth League at 6:30, and a vesper service at 7:30. There were Wednesday prayer meetings and an abundance of church work in a parish always painfully short of funds. The joys of Christian fellowship — which can be sensed in the exuberant hymn-singing at a Methodist service, apparently compensated for the stern discipline of a creed that forbade drinking, dancing, playing cards, or attendance at the theater except for a great classic. There were no movies, and Dorothy's chief diversion was reading; at an early age she had graduated from *St. Nicholas* magazine and insipid children's books to Dickens, Thackeray, Scott, George Eliot, Hawthorne, Emerson, Mark Twain, Shakespeare, Victor Hugo, Palgrave's *Golden Treasury,* and, of course, the Bible, which was compulsory.

In church Dorothy might fidget during sermons but she was awed by her father's mystical relationship to the Almighty. "He was accompanied by an 'Unseen Presence,'" she wrote, "the Holy Spirit of Jesus Christ. When he prayed he talked to Him as if He was in the room and his face looked shining and listening, as though he heard Him reply . . ."

Reverend Peter was a genial as well as a saintly father, who loved gardening, found time to play with his children, and encouraged them to read anything that gave them pleasure. For his oldest daughter he had great, if undefined, aspirations. So, too, did her young playmates. "Dorothy, even as a little child, stood out among the rest of us," Marguerite Jarvis said. "She was very bright, very independent, extremely devoted to her family and also, I'd say, very sensitive though she covered it with bravado." The happiest days of Dorothy's childhood were spent in the gently rolling hills and wide pastures that surround Hamburg — still today a picture-book town with quiet streets radiating out from an abandoned cemetery that has been converted into a village green. "I cannot recall ever having been bored or at a loss for something to do," Dorothy wrote. "Some of my playmates lived in larger houses but our pleasures were the same, and in our home there were more festivities, I think, than in most. Every birthday, Thanksgiving, Christmas, the New Year and Easter were celebrated. So was every day that I, and later my brother and sister, brought home an 'A' report in all subjects." *

In her memoir, Dorothy recalled in loving detail the menus of these gala occasions — homemade ice cream and pies, boiled onions in cream sauce, "parsnips parboiled and delicately fried," a plump roast turkey or porklet. Except for these great occasions, the chief fare was homemade bread, milk, potatoes, apples, pancakes with blackjack molasses, vegetables — fresh or home-preserved — and "occasional benefactions of chickens and hog-meat from a farmer parishioner." Oranges were a once-a-year treat in the Christmas stocking. Dorothy was a skinny,

---

* She developed a charming children's book out of her recollections of these Yuletide festivities, *Once on Christmas* (Oxford University Press, New York and London, 1939).

hungry little girl who grew up with an enthusiasm for good food that resulted in a never-conquered weight problem.

An imaginative child, she was given, as she would always be, to romantic fantasies about herself. In these daydreams sometimes "Dorothy" was on a big steamer sailing to foreign lands. Or she might be wandering alone in a mysterious walled garden surrounding her unknown great uncle's English mansion where a dining room table groaned with joints of beef and luscious puddings. This "Dorothy" was "tall and slender with raven black hair, large, thickly fringed violet-blue eyes and a skin like a rose in the snow . . . People stood transfixed at her appearance, and talked of her incredible, unbelievable beauty. No one praised her cleverness."

This was, of course, the antithesis of the real Dorothy with her skimpy dark-brown braids, gray-blue eyes, and freckled nose, who was admired for her intelligence and her remarkable memory.

Peter and Margaret Thompson's American relatives had settled in Illinois. The only one who paid frequent visits was Grandma Grierson. "She would clasp us all to her capacious but by no means tender bosom and proceed to make the fur fly. She knew better than anyone about everything," Dorothy wrote. "My mother was working too hard, the children's manners needed improving, father's income wouldn't support a church mouse and nothing in America was as good as in England."

Grandma Grierson was in residence in the spring of 1901 when, just before Easter, Margaret Thompson suddenly took to her bed, gravely ill. To the children, it was an unbelievable occurrence. The family had always worried about Peter's health. He was tireless in his pastoral duties, but winters for him were a misery of recurring colds and pleurisy. Margaret, slightly built though she was, cooked, baked, made and mended clothes, cleaned, scrubbed, did the laundry for a family of five, and still found time and strength for church work, for studying and learning to play the piano. At her bedside Dorothy prayed to — or rather bargained with — God: she would be good forever if He would spare her mother. Two days later she was dead. "I felt no grief, only a crushing pain in my chest, a queer undefinable feeling of guilt . . ." Dorothy wrote.

Later she learned that her young, strong mother "had perished of what nobody ever dies of, or so they say, a miscarriage, or rather the doctor's failure to recognize what was happening. In attempting to halt the hemorrhage he had sealed in the poisons and she died of general septicemia — 'blood poisoning.' " Family intimates whispered that the doctor had erred in his treatment because he was not told that the cause of the hemorrhage was a bungled abortion performed by his patient's mother, Grandma Grierson. The remembered experience left Dorothy with a deepened aversion for her grandmother and may have helped shape the concern for women that would one day find expression in the suffrage movement and in her writings.

Outwardly, Dorothy's spirits were restored by a summer spent with her brother on a parishioner's farm, where she reveled in the bucolic pleasures of barns and stables and in the gigantic meals served three times a day. But the early loss of her mother, the feeling that she had been deserted and that it was somehow her fault, left a deep scar. One immediate consequence was to heighten her identification with her father. She began to play the role of little wife, accompanying him on his pastoral rounds in a rented horse-drawn buggy, warming his slippers before the fire as she had seen her mother do — more companion than daughter. The household ran smoothly, for Peter had installed as mother-substitute his widowed sister, Elizabeth Hill, who had brought up ten children of her own and proved a capable and loving manager. Her regime lasted only two years.

At her mother's funeral Dorothy had taken note of the church organist, Miss Eliza Abbott, a formidably plain, bespectacled spinster of forty, looking "unpleasantly solemn" as she patted the heads of the motherless Thompson children. Presently, Reverend Peter was seen Sunday afternoons riding in the buggy owned by the Abbotts — one of Hamburg's first families — to preach in the nearby village of Armor, where the Methodists could no longer afford a full-time minister. Recognizing Eliza as a rival, Dorothy attacked with the only weapons at her command — heated argument and calculated rudeness. But to no avail. Aunt Lizzie departed in 1903 and Peter and Eliza were married. In the wedding photograph taken outside the church, ten-year-old Dorothy wears a look of fierce defiance.

❧ 2
Advantages

TWO YEARS LATER, in 1905, the Thompson family was again on
the move, this time some twenty miles southward to the village
of Gowanda. Though the church was not large, the parsonage
was new and boasted a real bathroom. For the first time Dorothy had a room all to herself. But her delight in these luxuries
was short-lived. She soon discovered that this was not the
egalitarian farming community to which she was accustomed,
where everybody's houses and habits were much the same and
the Methodist minister was a leading citizen despite his meager
income and shabby Prince Albert coat. Gowanda's elite —
thanks to industrial and banking connections — were not merely
"well off" but rich. Visiting a school friend, Fanchon Arthur,
she was dazzled by parquet floors, oriental rugs, a butler, a
French maid, and filmy batiste lingerie, handmade in Paris. She
came home consumed with envy. Vigorously abetted by her
father, she grappled with this sinful state of mind and promised
him to count her own blessings. But privately she still aspired
to worldly pleasures and comforts.

The drabness of her life was, of course, accented by the irksome presence of Reverend Peter's second wife. In her written
recollections of these years, Dorothy adopted a jocular tone,
describing Eliza as "a dour stepmother, a self-pitying hypochon-
driac bravely but futilely struggling against an allergy to children." * Curiously, she placed no blame on Peter for choosing

---

* According to Dorothy the sole benefit that accrued to her from the marriage
was access to the medical library of Eliza's father, Dr. George Abbott (uncle of

this singular mate. However, her sense of betrayal by her father may have contributed to the hostility to males in general that she first expressed in satirical childish poems. One titled "Just Martyn" holds up to scorn girls who were smitten with a handsome but, in her eyes, insignificant boy. Another derisive verse featured an unflattering caricature of one of her male teachers. And in one ditty she went so far as to make fun of the Methodist Church, where she had recently undergone a spectacular conversion at the hands of a visiting evangelist.

She particularly resented what she regarded as Eliza's hypocritical piety. Father well understood the uses of guilt feelings in changing evil ways, but it was Eliza who introduced the element of shame for which Dorothy never forgave her. "If you broke one of God's comandments," she wrote, "it was up to you and God. You would be isolated in your room to think and pray 'Please God, forgive me, and I will never do it again.' After this you came back into the sitting room red-eyed, father smiled a little as he said gravely, 'I know you are sorry.' Just like God. *And nobody in the family ever spoke of it again.* Not until Mother Eliza came into the family — the stepmother who was a scolder and kept prying into your soul and your motives and getting between you and your own conscience . . . Once she even tried to make me pray out loud in the presence of the family, but father stopped it . . ."

Dorothy was still a mischievous tomboy at fourteen when she entered Gowanda High School. She was devoted to her brother and sister and even more attached to Fanchon Arthur. "It was one of those passionate, faintly erotic friendships which adolescent girls have for each other," she wrote in her diary years later.* However, the guerrilla war between Dorothy and Eliza

---

his namesake, the future Broadway playwright-producer). There she surreptitiously acquainted herself with the facts of human anatomy, procreation, and birth that were decorously deleted from the school physiology texts of her day.
* This entry was made in 1935. Fanchon during her first year at Smith College was converted to Catholicism and became a nun; Dorothy visited her at the convent, which Fanchon eventually left.

had reached an impasse. Since separation seemed the only solution, Reverend Peter decided to send Dorothy to Chicago to live temporarily with her Aunt Margaret Heming and her spinster sister Hetty Thompson.

Dorothy bade a tearful farewell to Fanchon. The sorrow of exile from her family was mitigated by release from Eliza's yoke and the prospect of exploring the wide world of her dreams. She had, in any event, learned to mask painful feelings. Her brother Willard remembers the parting as cheerful. Dorothy was on her way to bigger things and God would look after her.

To save face, Eliza spread the word that the brainy but difficult older Thompson girl was going to Chicago because she merited "advantages" beyond the scope of the Gowanda High School. Though this was scarcely the motive, it became the result. Her aunts enrolled her in Lewis Institute, a school noted for educational excellence and such innovations as a two-year junior college and evening classes for adults. It had been endowed by Allen Cleveland Lewis, a nineteenth-century philanthropist who saw a need for training young men of modest means in the liberal arts and in useful scientific and technological skills and also affording like opportunities to "respectable females." The tuition, in 1908, was twenty dollars a quarter.*

In a starched, high-collared white blouse, with her skirt swirling at her shoe tops and her hair pinned up in a tidy bun, Dorothy roller-skated to and from school on Washington Boulevard, filled with a new zest for learning. She had always been an omnivorous but undiscriminating reader. Now she discovered the satisfaction of serious, purposeful study and developed the disciplined work habits that were to be one of her greatest professional assets. These were, she said, the happiest years of her school life, when wide vistas were opened to her by gifted teachers. Outstanding among them was Dr. Edwin Herbert Lewis,

---

* The founding Lewis was no kin of Dorothy's favorite teacher, Dr. Edwin Herbert Lewis, nor of her future husband, Sinclair Lewis. After World War I Lewis Institute became a four-year college. Subsequently it was merged with Armour Institute to become the Illinois Institute of Technology.

whose scholarship an earlier Lewis graduate, the journalist Arthur Krock, had called "one of the richest experiences of my life." "Dr. Lewis seemed to think that the preservation of the English language, in all its purity, had been exclusively entrusted to his care," Dorothy wrote, "that, for instance, to split an infinitive was some form of juvenile delinquency. He could flare into tempers. Once, in a class in Elizabethan poetry he suddenly pounded the table and cried to an inattentive class, all girls, 'Here I try to introduce you to sheer magic, but all you will ever be good for is to rustle pots and pans.'

" 'No, I won't,' my mind responded indignantly, but I also became determined to prove it to him." According to her classmates, Dorothy, who had become a proficient debater, would sometimes march up the aisle toward Dr. Lewis' desk in the course of a heated discussion.

Another English teacher, Kate B. Miller, took her to see the celebrated Shakespearean actors E. H. Sothern and his wife Julia Marlowe in *The Tempest*. "I had never been to theatre before and was spellbound," Dorothy wrote. "To show my gratitude I learned the loveliest of the lyrics by heart and the next day stayed after school more than an hour to discuss with her the inner meaning of Shakespeare's mysterious and magical play."

Dorothy's school record was brilliant in English, history, and Latin and respectable in French and German. But she barely achieved passing grades in mathematics. "Is very neglectful of the written work," her math teacher noted sternly on her report card. "Does and hands in only part of what is expected." During a vacation visit to her home, brother Willard, for once superior to his clever older sister, undertook to coach her in algebra, which he, a future engineer, had easily mastered.

The family was now living in Spencerport. They found Dorothy considerably changed, as did her friends. Her aunts had bought her the first clothes she had owned, which were becoming as well as practical. They had also told her she was pretty, a verdict confirmed by her yearbook photograph. She was more self-confident and articulate than ever. On one Sunday when her father was ill, she preached the sermon in his place, proving herself fully equal to the Methodist role of a "godly layman possessing the gift of exhortation." Nor was she any longer the meek subservient daughter in her father's presence. At a church social, Reverend Peter reprimanded her for disappearing for what he suspected was a moonlight tryst. It had been, in fact, an innocent stroll with another girl, Frances Moore, who was nonetheless humiliated by the preacher's reproaches. But Dorothy, according to Frances, "just listened perfectly quietly, kind of politely but absent-mindedly" and then said in the sweetest voice, "And now, Father, could we have some ice cream?"

This was, presumably, a display of independence from the husband of Eliza Abbott. Perhaps, too, it was a reflection of a new mood. Her crowning academic achievement at Lewis had been a translation of Horace's Ode IX in an approximation of the original meter:

> Hence with cold! Build high the hearth
> For youth is thine.
> We must laughter have and mirth
> Life, jest and song with never dearth
> Of Sabine wine!

Novel sentiments for a Methodist minister's daughter.

roommate. The Hooples too were the children of a Methodist minister. But they were prosperous city folk living in New York City in what impressed Dorothy, on her occasional visits, as urban luxury. To Ruth, Dorothy was an exciting companion destined, she was confident, for a great literary future. She hoped one day to have her as a sister-in-law. Gordon — then a premedical student — obligingly served as escort for his sister's chum, whom he found entertaining but somehow unfeminine. Indeed he was uneasy about what seemed to him Dorothy's excessive emotional dependence on his sister and was relieved when, a few years after college, Ruth departed for missionary work in China.

Of her own feelings in her college days, Dorothy wrote, "I liked boys well enough and they did not dislike me, but they often bored me with their damp hands and shy callow advances and I frightened them off with my rather high-falutin speech. Sexually, even for those times I was retarded rather than precocious. I did not know what I wanted to do with my life but I knew that I did not want to marry until much later, and unless one desired marriage one did not flirt around. And besides I was carrying too heavy a schedule to permit of it. I found excitement in the classrooms and lecture halls."

Dorothy's classmates were impressed with her versatility. She could compose a poem to order, deliver an eloquent sermon at vespers, and also run up a handsome party dress out of a bargain remnant. But she was not always lovable. Some called her an intellectual snob, particularly when a group gathered for an evening with their revered English teacher, Jean Marie Richards, who was also Dean of Women. She was a Smith graduate who spoke in the cultivated accents of Boston. Dorothy would blissfully monopolize the conversation as though no one else was present — a lifelong habit that would discomfit many future companions.

As at Lewis, Dorothy's marks were excellent in her major

subjects, English and European and American history. But required courses in physics and higher algebra again proved her nemesis and she was graduated with only a *cum laude.** Many of her extracurricular activities were merely extensions of her religious childhood — the Young Women's Christian Association, the Silver Bay Club, the Epworth League, and the Student Band, which was devoted not to music but to the service of overseas missions. There was, however, one exciting new challenge — the women's rights movement.

A feminist tradition had always flourished at Syracuse, where, in Dorothy's time, half of the 3000 students were women. As early as 1832, when it was founded as Genesee Seminary, a woman was admitted to the first class. (Oberlin would follow suit the next year.) Subsequently renamed Geneva College, it established a faculty of medicine that in 1849 conferred the first M.D. degree on an American woman, Dr. Elizabeth Blackwell.

In 1912 the women's suffrage movement, after years of discouraging defeats and internecine wars, began to gain fresh momentum. Dorothy was an active member of the Syracuse Equal Suffrage Club. She composed a hymn, "Glad in Maytime," which would be sung for years at the Women's Day pageant on May 12, "the one day in the year when Syracuse University is under the rule of the co-eds." She peddled chocolate bars and sandals to help raise funds for a women's building that finally rose long after her graduation.

Dorothy vaguely hoped to become a writer but had no notion of how to go about it and at the same time earn a living. During vacations she worked in a candy factory, waited on table in restaurants, and peddled encyclopedias door to door. She also did a stint in the university's settlement house in the Fifteenth Ward. But although Methodism strongly emphasized the "social gospel," Dorothy had no calling for good works. "I felt pity for

* In 1940 she was awarded a Phi Beta Kappa key *honoris causa.*

the unfortunate," she wrote, "but I did not love them as my father did. I loved those whom it is easy to love: the beautiful, the strong, the good and the truly free who never do anything just for money."

Reverend Peter had now been transferred to the Sumner Place Church in Buffalo, where Dorothy, after graduating from Syracuse, was offered a job at suffrage headquarters. She could live at home, receive free board from hospitable sympathizers when she was on the road, and thus eke out a living on a salary of eight dollars a week. Obviously she could not yet contribute to the college education of her brother and sister. But there were not, in the summer of 1914, any more lucrative alternatives at hand.

✺ 4
For Love of the Cause

DOROTHY'S TERRITORY as a suffrage organizer was the cradle of the women's rights movement. Here in western New York in 1848, Elizabeth Cady Stanton and Lucretia Mott had presided over the first women's rights convention at Seneca Falls. In later years Susan B. Anthony of Rochester had trudged through these same villages, farms, and cities urging women to "agitate, educate, organize." Headed by one of Miss Anthony's protégées, Carrie Chapman Catt — probably the ablest organizer the movement produced — the New York State Suffrage Association in 1914 had achieved a new level of efficiency and dedication. In addition to forceful leadership and an inspiring tradition, upstate suffragists had the stimulus of a choice villain close at hand, Mrs. James W. Wadsworth, the wife of their own United States senator, who was president of the National Anti-Suffrage Association.

Through the nineteenth and early twentieth centuries, suffragists had forged strong ties with the temperance movement and Protestant churches. As Dorothy barnstormed through the towns where she had spent her childhood and through others nearby — Medina, Geneseo, Batavia — Methodist churches opened their doors to meetings; she could count on childhood friends to swell the crowd at outdoor gatherings and to march in suffrage parades. These expeditions on the old Erie Railroad compensated for days and nights at Buffalo headquarters spent in such tedious political chores as compiling lists and stuffing envelopes. After a year, her prowess as a soapbox orator and street-corner fund raiser was rewarded with a raise in salary to seventy-five dollars a month. She worked with such enthusiasm and energy that her friends would have been surprised to know that she later said she hated organizing work and stayed with it only "for love of the cause."

Another inducement perhaps was the opportunity the movement afforded for meeting important and glamorous people. The tragic Triangle Factory fire of 1911 had stirred the social conscience of some of the wealthiest ladies of New York society, who began now to contribute money and spirited leadership to the suffrage association as well as other reform movements. Among them was Mrs. Charles L. Tiffany, President of the College Equal Suffrage League, who would in the near future become one of Dorothy's influential friends along with her sisters, Gertrude and Henrietta Ely of Philadelphia's Main Line, and her sister-in-law, Dorothy Tiffany Burlingham.

Chairman of the campaign district where Dorothy worked was Gertrude Tone of Niagara Falls, wife of the president of the Carborundum Company and daughter of Stanislas Pascal Franchot, state senator from Niagara and Orleans Counties. Though they would doubtless have met in due course, Dorothy did not rely on chance to bring a lowly foot soldier to the attention of the commanding officer. On summer weekends in a rented boat, she rowed back and forth near the dock of the Tone summer cottage on the Canadian shore of Lake Erie, the very picture of romantic melancholy solitude. Gertrude was touched and amused. Presently Dorothy was a frequent visitor at the Tone mansion on Buffalo Avenue, where all the best families lived in spacious elegance with wide lawns sloping down to a park, in earshot of the falls. "How much that family meant to me," she wrote, recalling evenings spent with Gertrude, her husband, Dr. Frank, and their two small sons, Ned and Franchot, the future stage and screen actor. She was, she said, secretly in love with Gertrude's handsome young brother, Ned Franchot.

Gertrude is described by her sister-in-law, Maude (Mrs. Ned) Franchot, as "very handsome with *piercing* dark eyes and almost beetling brows." A portrait painted in the first years of her marriage shows her as a wasp-waisted Gibson girl in a Madame Récamier pose. In later photographs she wears pince-nez glasses and her wide mouth is curved in an enigmatic smile. "Gertrude was a *true* intellectual," Mrs. Franchot wrote, "with a vast range of interests from religion (mostly eastern) through philosophy and politics. She was an iconoclast in the religious field." Married to a conservative upstate Republican she was, according to Mrs. Franchot, "as far left as she could get politically without being a card-carrying Communist. She had a horrible inferiority complex because she lacked a college education — that went to her brothers — one older and two younger. She was *just* a female and God! how she resented it and her father's generation's attitudes. She did everything that was modern, new and frowned upon. She had an early analysis in the twenties . . ."

Gertrude became, for Dorothy, an idealized mother figure, the first in a series of older women to whom she became deeply attached. "I was twenty and G was 37," she wrote in her diary, "and I see her still quite vividly. She wore a black broadcloth tailored suit with white frills and a *jabot* and a big hat. She was handsome, full-figured and womanly, and I wanted to be close to her, to be like her. I took my fortnight's free vacations and went all the way to Northern Canada to be with her — she was at Gerryowen [the Franchot family's summer "camp"] just in order to, while exploring in a canoe, say 'Why it's you — so near!' Just to be near her . . . Sometimes I think I love her better than anyone . . ." *

"Gertrude found in Dorothy a young woman — attractive and brilliant and broke," Mrs. Franchot wrote. "So she took her

* The entry was made in 1932, at the onset of a similar relationship. Gertrude's influence survived in the severely tailored suits and frilly blouses that Dorothy favored all her life.

under her generous but demanding wing, supplied her with money to live on and plenty of nourishing encouragement." She was also cordial to two of Dorothy's coworkers in the suffrage ranks. One was Mary Gawthorpe, who had come from England with stirring tidings of Emmeline Pankhurst's militant tactics. The other was Barbara De Porte, who volunteered her service in the summer of 1917 after graduating from Cornell and became one of Dorothy's most devoted friends. The sisterly affection that developed between the two surprised them both. Though they shared an enthusiasm for the cause and literary ambitions, they were by heredity opposites. Barbara was Russian-born, descended from cultivated and prosperous Sephardic Jewish families. The Portuguese surname Deporto was miswritten as De Porte by an immigration officer when her two older brothers, Ossip and Yasha, came to America. They had established themselves comfortably here when Barbara, at sixteen, joined them following the death of her parents.

At the age of twenty-four, Dorothy had never known a Jew. She had met none at college (nor any Catholics, either). Her father had taught her that some day the Jews would accept Christ and together they prayed that this prophecy would be fulfilled. Meanwhile, though they were in error, he said, one must never forget what Israel, the people of the Book, had given to the world and one must never persecute a Jew. Living in a totally Christian society, she had not been exposed to anti-Semitism and her encounter with Barbara made her an instant semitophile. Barbara — a diminutive girl with soulful dark eyes, a round cherubic face, and a heavy Slavic accent — was *exotic,* for she was not only Jewish but Russian. In the spring and summer of 1917, Americans were exhilarated by the news that their allies under the democratic Kerensky government were launching a new offensive against the Austro-Hungarian armies. Barbara became a novelty attraction at suffrage meetings where she brought greetings from the heroic soldiers on the eastern front who, she said, longed to know that America was a true democracy where women were no longer disfranchised. By November, when the Bolsheviks triumphed in Russia, suffragists in New York were celebrating their own victory. It had been a long time in coming. Frustrated for half a century in attempts to secure passage of the amendment through Congress, the movement had adopted a state-by-state strategy. New York, with its large representation in Washington, was a key state. However, suffrage work was virtually suspended in the early months of 1917 as the organization conducted a military census and concentrated on other activities attuned to the martial spirit that followed America's entrance into World War I.

A major political drive got under way during the summer. More than a million signatures on petitions were collected and every voter in the state was circularized at least once. On Election Day, with more than 6000 women serving as poll watchers, the amendment passed, a huge plurality in New York City outbalancing the negative vote upstate. The Eighth — Dorothy and her friends proudly noted — was the only district outside the metropolitan area that carried. American women would not vote in a national election until 1920, following final ratification of the Nineteenth Amendment. But the battle in New York State was over.

Dorothy may have been tempted to settle down in Buffalo. After stepmother Eliza had departed this earth in 1916, the Thompsons were once again a harmonious family. Willard had enlisted and was overseas with the AEF but hoped to go to engineering school after the war. With Peggy in college, it was imperative to add to the family income. Barbara and Dorothy decided to join forces and forge ahead on their now chosen careers in journalism. The place to do this, they were certain, was New York City. Happily, Gertrude Tone, who found the atmosphere of Niagara Falls "suffocating," invited them to share her charming duplex apartment at 125 East 16th Street.

🥀 5
Useful Friends

THE PATRIOTIC FERVOR of World War I was at its height when Dorothy and Barbara arrived in New York in December 1917. Fifth Avenue resounded with martial tunes as dense crowds cheered parading doughboys proudly marching in leggings and felt hats, confident that, in the words of a popular song, "Just like Washington crossed the Delaware, General Pershing will cross the Rhine." Zealous orators and writer implored those who could not fight to buy Liberty Bonds, roll bandages, knit socks for the boys in the trenches, and conserve meat by learning to make tasty hamburgers of soy beans. Nightclub audiences sighed as tenors reminded them that "Mid the war's dread curse, stands the Red Cross nurse, She's the rose of no man's land."

Much as she yearned for a heroic role in the crusade that, in President Wilson's words, would "make the world safe for democracy," Dorothy's primary responsibility was to earn a living. This was proving far from easy. Barbara acquired a lowly job in the city room of the New York *Evening Post* through the intercession of its literary editor, Russian-born Simeon Strunsky, whom she met via a mutual friend. But Dorothy had as yet no helpful connections in the newspaper and magazine worlds, which seemed unanimously inhospitable to an unknown young woman from the hinterland with no journalistic credentials. Several editors encouraged her to submit feature stories to their Sunday supplements. As New York then boasted more than a dozen dailies, this was a considerable market; but the rewards of free-lancing, she discovered, were chiefly the honor and satisfaction of seeing one's name and copy in print. As a stopgap, Dorothy went to work as a publicist for a Bible publishing society. The handsome salary of fifty dollars a week did not compensate for a dreary, dead-end job that she hoped to leave before long. The opportunity came within a few months. Mrs. Charles Tiffany was one of the backers of an experimental program known as the Social Unit. Dorothy was interviewed by its administrator, Wilbur Phillips, and hired as publicity director. The novelty of the scheme attracted Dorothy as did the personality of Mr. Phillips, who combined a reformist zeal with a dignified poise and quiet wit that reminded her of her favorite college professors.

The Social Unit proposed to establish a social laboratory in an urban neighborhood. To this end, Phillips had circularized a number of city mayors and finally secured consent to launch the plan in the Mohawk-Brighton District of Cincinnati. Eminences of the liberal-philanthropic establishment agreed to sponsor the organization, among them Dr. Richard C. Cabot, Mrs. J. Borden Harriman, Miss Margaret Woodrow Wilson, Mrs. Willard Straight, Gifford Pinchot, Mrs. Daniel Guggenheim, Adolph Lewisohn, Lillian Wald, John Collier, and John Lovejoy Elliot. For Dorothy, the new job involved a cut in salary, down to thirty dollars a week, and a move to Cincinnati, but it promised to be more exciting than peddling scriptures.

The project was a small-scale prototype of the poverty programs of the 1960s and stirred up similar antagonisms when community organizers encouraged the poor to articulate their grievances. Dorothy enjoyed doing battle with local politicians, made a spirited defense of the program in brochures and on the lecture platform, and inspired glowing accounts of the project in leading magazines. Life was pleasant in Cincinnati where the Social Unit had attracted a group of idealistic young people who enjoyed working together and spent happy Sundays on long walks into the nearby Kentucky hills. Particular friends were

Mary and Peter Burnett. The latter was the first intellectual man she had met who shared her passion for sitting up far into the night to discuss "ourselves, what the world needed and philosophy and ethics." Another intimate was Regina Kronacher, daughter of a well-to-do Cincinnati family whose hospitality rescued Dorothy from the rigors of a boarding house where she had acquired the reputation of being "very demanding of the maids." This was odd behavior for a young woman who had never employed a servant. Singular too was her breezy statement to Regina, "I never save money. When I need more money I just go out and look for another job."

In fact, Dorothy was stinting herself in order to send every penny she could spare to her family, who were still very much on her mind. She found time to collaborate with Peggy in preparing a newsletter for doughboy Willard. Typed in two columns, it was a parody of a small-town weekly. The one copy that Willard eventually brought back with him from France consists of jokes, poems, and a mix of national, world, and family news and gossip, written in a style that reflects Peggy's wry wit and Dorothy's élan. Among other items, the *Home Fire News* carried the tidings that

> Woodrow Wilson, candidate of this paper for President of the U.S. in 1920 and whenever else he wants to serve, at last came out unequivocally in favor of the Woman Suffrage Amendment . . . Latest developments indicate that the rider of the agricultural bill, carrying with it a bone-dry total wartime prohibition, will go through . . . Great sorrow is being felt over the untimely death of John Purroy Mitchel, the former Mayor of New York, who was killed in a fall from an airplane . . .
>
> Ye editor of H.F.N., it was announced today, has changed her address from Miss Craven's Boarding House to 765 Greenwood Ave., Avondale. This change was effected through the Christian spirit of Miss Regina Kronacher, w.k.* human being of Cincinnati

---

* A spoof on a familiar cliché of small-town journalism; almost everyone mentioned was characterized as "well known."

who is taking a pre-medical course this summer and remains in the city. This change carries with it a sleeping porch, real food and a garden to grub in . . . Miss D. Thompson and Miss Kronacher ate chicken and watermelon at the Zoo last night for the Fatherless Children of France. Great Patriotism . . . Rev. Peter Thompson officiated recently at the marriage of Miss Marguerite Jarvis to Mr. Thomas Bourne of Hamburg. It was a swell affair and added not only to the Social Column of the Buffalo papers,

Under our tender care the
crops Grow   and Grow   and Grow

So do the Weeds.

our esteemed contemps, but added to the family income. Rev.
Peter Thompson has bought him a new panama offen the proceeds.

Peter Thompson, Eminent Buffalo Divine, will be in Silver Lake
in August where he will conduct a course at the Epworth League
Institute. He will be joined by the w.k. editor, D. Thompson and
the w.k. general of the Farm Army, Gen'l. Peg Thompson . . .

This holiday in the summer of 1919 was the last Dorothy
would spend in the staid Methodist scenes of her childhood. In
the fall, Phillips decided to leave the Cincinnati project in local
hands and devote himself to stimulating similar ventures elsewhere from a national office in the Metropolitan Tower in New
York. Miss Thompson would join him there as National Publicity Director. "Around this time I fell in love with W," Dorothy
wrote in her diary. "W" was Wilbur Phillips who, unfortunately, already had a wife, Elsie. To make matters more difficult, she was a friend and active associate in the Social Unit.

✺ 6
"hectic, lovely, exciting"

THE ARMISTICE signed on November 11, 1918, marked not only the end of an era abroad, but the beginning of a new epoch in manners and morals in America. Assessing the startling changes in sexual attitudes and behavior that took place in the 1920s, Dr. Alfred C. Kinsey attributed them in part to the homecoming of millions of young soldiers who had been exposed to love European-style. Not until the 1960s would there be a comparable cleavage in standards between the generations. It was at precisely this time that Dorothy, still at twenty-five "a carefully brought up parsonage child," found herself on her own in New York and romantically entangled with a married man eighteen years her senior.

She was also, for the first time, plunged into a politically alien world. Middle America, where she had been reared, was gripped by hysterical panic lest Bolshevism, which had triumphed in Russia and seemed to be engulfing Europe, might invade America. Responding to the public mood, in the closing days of the Wilson administration, Attorney General A. Mitchell Palmer rounded up and deported alleged anarchists on the flimsiest of evidence. Like all political liberals, Wilbur and Elsie Phillips were surely appalled by this witch hunt. So, too, were Barbara De Porte's friends — socialist-oriented Zionists, labor leaders she had met during a summer spent as a volunteer worker during a prolonged strike, Russian-born artists and writers in a state of euphoric optimism about the exciting changes in their homeland. They came to impromptu parties in Gertrude Tone's apartment, and a lion among them was Louise Bryant, who had actually visited the Socialist Paradise. When Gertrude was in town, she added to the group all manner of surprising people — black jazz musicians from Harlem, eastern swamis, psychoanalysts, actors, playwrights — anyone whose ideas and life-style were the cultural antithesis of Niagara Falls.

But life for Dorothy was more than parties. In addition to her regular job, she was beginning to sell articles to the *Times,* *Tribune,* and *Sun,* and to magazines — the *Outlook* and *Leslie's* *Weekly.* In the course of her publicity work, she had come to know a number of editors and had impressed them with her competence. When a young Bryn Mawr graduate, Beatrice Sorchan, went job hunting, Charles Merz of the *New Republic* sent her to Dorothy, who hired her as an assistant. "I adored her from the first instant," Beatrice said. "She was hectic, lovely, exciting." Dorothy enjoyed being an object of worship and was impressed by Beatrice's milieu. Her mother, Mrs. Walton Martin, was the originator of Turtle Bay Gardens, a unique group of renovated town houses, in East 48th and 49th Streets, sharing beautifully landscaped parklike backyards. Beatrice recalled that on her first visit, Dorothy drank in every detail and said, "Some day I'm going to own one of these houses." The prophecy would be fulfilled in two decades. Beatrice was also a friend of Wilbur and Elsie's and fascinated by her first glimpse of a clandestine "affair," which in fact was never consummated.*
Wilbur, at forty-three, was no jazz-age playboy, but a rather strait-laced, very Christian gentleman and a social worker by profession. There were tender scenes and many introspective and, no doubt, guilt-laden conversations. The relationship came to an abrupt end in early 1920 when Elsie Phillips at thirty-nine became pregnant for the first time. In later years Dorothy rarely spoke of this romance, though she was fond of recalling an eve-

---

* Dorothy's first husband and her closest friend, Barbara, bear convincing witness on this point.

ning when, she said, she sat on a bench in Washington Square Park weeping for her lost love. A prostitute passing by glanced at Dorothy's shabby pumps, patted her shoulder, and said comfortingly, "Cheer up, dearie, it's just your shoes."

At the time, however, she and her friends saw nothing comic in the situation. And none was more concerned than Barbara, whose standards of sexual morality were less advanced than her political views. "I felt Dorothy must get away, change her surroundings, forget the whole thing," she wrote. "This was the impetus that pushed me toward beginning to do something about my hitherto dim vision of a trip abroad. I persuaded Dorothy that it was possible to organize such a trip, that we might scrape enough money together if we got chores to perform, that we could really go to Europe."

The "chores" in prospect were tenuous. The New York *Evening Post* would consider their contributions. Dorothy had a vague commitment from the Buffalo *Evening News* and an introduction to the American Red Cross in Paris where she might be hired as a publicity writer. She and Barbara, after paying for their steamship tickets, had a nest egg of $500 between them — some of it borrowed — which they pooled in a joint bank account. Dorothy provided herself with an escape hatch by applying for a publicity job in Baltimore in the fall. "I know my job," she wrote on June 11, 1920, to her prospective employer — a relative of Natalie De Witt Clinton Wright, a grande dame of the suffrage movement. "I have really studied newspapers and studied the public. I have done a great deal of pamphlet work, prepared speakers' manuals, edited reports, staged photographs, worked up lantern lectures, staged events for filming and written quantities of newspaper material of all kinds . . . My plans for going abroad are just now very much upset, because of the difficulty my travelling companion is encountering in getting a passport. I hope very much that they will adjust themselves, so that I may sail on the 19th, as I had planned . . ."

Barbara's passport troubles, caused by a missing birth certificate, were ironed out and the two would-be journalists boarded the S.S. *Finland* on schedule. The wide Atlantic ahead was bracing. Dorothy was also sustained — as she would be in future romantic defeats — by a triumvirate of her own sex. There was Gertrude Tone, the mother figure, and Beatrice Sorchan, the acolyte, who would both share her adventures by letter. And at her side was Barbara De Porte, the ideal sister-comrade. Presently, she would be seeking out a male to add to the picture — not a husband, for there was much to be done before she settled into marriage, if she ever did — but a dashing lover, suited to the needs of the truly free "modern" woman she felt she had now become.

PART II

COMING OF AGE IN
THE TWENTIES

🎋 1
An Amazing Voyage

As THE S.S. *Finland* steamed out of New York harbor on June 19, 1920, Dorothy was too keyed up to write the notes she had planned to send to her dearest friends via the pilot boat. A week had passed before she composed a letter to Beatrice Sorchan, telling her that her spirits were soaring, that she had put on at least five pounds, had not been seasick a moment, and that also on board were Marilyn Miller of the Ziegfeld Follies, President John Grier Hibben of Princeton, and the British poet Alfred Noyes. But these were by no means the most interesting passengers.

"It's been an amazing experience," she wrote. "The ship is crowded with Zionists whose presence in the first cabin has led to our being extended all the privileges of the place except meals."

It was, of course, through Barbara De Porte that Dorothy met this remarkable group who were en route to a World Zionist Conference in London, the first such gathering since Britain in 1917 had, through the Balfour Declaration, announced its support for "the establishment of a national home in Palestine for the Jewish people."

"To an anti-Semite, the trip would be a torture probably," Dorothy wrote to Beatrice, whose father was Jewish, "but to me, to whom an alien temperament is always stimulating, it has been altogether amusing. The delegation numbers several extraordinary people, notably Max Radin of the University of California, Dr. David de Sola Pool (without exception the handsomest man I *ever* laid eyes on), a Portuguese Jew and a radical rabbi . . . With Max Radin and Dr. Pool I have had a *delightful* time to the scandal of the ship's Jewry. It has become known that he chose a particularly delightful moonlit spot in which to recite to me in impassioned tones his own dramatic and original translation of the 'Song of Songs which is Solomon's!' We have flirted, in other words, quite and wholly outrageously, the whole episode enhanced by his rabbinical character. Besides this we've had seemingly endless discussions of Zionism . . . I think I shall perhaps become the leading Gentile authority on Judaism . . . I have, as you know, a very real admiration for this extraordinary race, and an appreciation of qualities in them . . ."

According to Barbara, the admiration was mutual. "Dorothy met the leaders of the movement on shipboard and its poets," she wrote. "She won their interest and their hearts. She listened to them debating and discussing. She questioned them far into the night. She was a very charming, interested person with an immense talent for making and keeping friends. In those years she was also gentle, curious about everything — about life, people, places. What the ancients called 'curiosita divina' was hers to an unusual degree."

The trip was marred for Dorothy only by the presence on board of Barbara's importunate suitor, Meir Grossman, an enterprising young Russian journalist and a dedicated Zionist. Dorothy found nothing attractive about this unimpressive young man who spoke only halting English and threatened to disrupt her plans by marrying her traveling companion. For the moment, at least, Barbara was firmly saying no.

The *Finland* reached England on June 30. Next day Barbara hurried to the office of Earl Reeves, chief of the International News Service in London, and persuaded him to let her cover the Zionist Conference. Dorothy lingered for a few farewell gatherings with her Zionist friends, which provided an opportunity to shake the hand of the august leader of the movement, Dr. Chaim Weizmann. She replenished her capital by pawning an elaborate dressing case Mrs. Tiffany had given her as a farewell gift. "Why in the world didn't she give me the money?" she ruminated later. "I suppose she thought I would have been insulted. Little did she know how open to insults I was!"

Dorothy departed for Ireland, where she had promised to look up some of her father's relatives. It was a propitious trip. This was the time of bloody combat between the Sinn Fein and Britain's Royal Irish Constabulary, reinforced by hastily recruited auxiliaries known as the Black and Tans because they wore dark trousers and khaki tunics. Whether Dorothy found any long-lost cousins we do not know. She did, however, gather excellent material, including an interview with Terence MacSwiney, Lord Mayor of Cork, just before he began a fatal hunger strike in company with two other Irish patriots, Michael Fitzgerald and Joseph Murphy.

"When she returned to London, a week or so later," Barbara wrote, "she brought five wonderful stories from Ireland with her. I marched her with these stories to Mr. Reeves. He sent them on to the New York office of INS."

They arrived at an opportune moment, when interest in the Irish rebellion was at a high pitch in America. Alfred E. Smith and other Irish-American politicians were giving a warm welcome to Eamon de Valera, hero of the 1916 Easter Rebellion and first president of Eire, who was in the United States on a fund-raising drive. Like many young radicals, the future novelist Kay Boyle, then a seventeen-year-old fledgling poet, longed to join the battle for Irish freedom and carried with her everywhere a copy of a letter MacSwiney wrote in Brixton Prison on the forty-sixth day of his hunger strike.

Dorothy's performance in Ireland and Barbara's expert coverage of the Zionist Conference persuaded Reeves to make them INS string correspondents. Though no income was assured, they now possessed credentials. As professional journalists they set out on a journey they hoped would eventually lead to the mysterious new world of Russia.

🦋 2
"how much lay ahead and beyond!"

DURING HER FIRST MONTHS on the continent, Dorothy kept several journals, which she subsequently entrusted for safe keeping to Barbara, who, in due course, returned two. Dorothy either lost or destroyed them, for they are not among her papers. Barbara had mislaid a third diary and forgotten its existence until the spring of 1971 when she and I began to correspond. When we met that fall in London, she handed me a battered notebook, written in Dorothy's unmistakable hand. This — the longest consecutive record of her personal life she ever kept — had been buried in an old trunk among a miscellany of photographs and clippings.

After she became a celebrity, Dorothy regaled interviewers with dramatic anecdotes about her solitary adventures in Europe. Barbara's name was never mentioned and the sole reference to an anonymous "travelling companion" among her papers is in the letter applying for a job in Baltimore on her return. Why she expunged this particular chapter from her story is puzzling, since it contains nothing discreditable. On the other hand, it might have been an embarrassment because it contradicts accounts of her youthful exploits published after she achieved fame. Among them were the stories that she covered the Zionist Conference in London for INS (she was in Ireland; it was Barbara who reported that meeting); and that she developed pneumonia in Milan in the course of a hazardous assignment, somehow made her way to Vienna, and after a month in the hospital returned to Paris to learn of her father's death (she had nothing worse than a severe cold and her father lived till the following year). Corroborating the diary are letters to Beatrice Sorchan. It would seem that Dorothy, who longed to write a novel, produced only one successful work of fiction — her own legend.*

Far from being the self-sufficient Valkyrie described in articles about her, Dorothy appears in her journal as an adventuresome but also insecure and surprisingly girlish woman of twenty-seven, clinging to Barbara, whom she usually calls by her Russian names, Varvara, the contraction, Varya, or a childhood nickname, Assya. Some passages are written in a self-consciously "literary" style and were apparently copied from notes or earlier drafts. Others are spontaneous emotional outbursts in which her usually neat hand becomes a scrawl. It seems clear that dates and sideheadings were inserted in the margins after the original entries. The voice throughout is that of a determined feminist who is also an incurable romantic, peculiarly susceptible to tall, dark, and dashing men. A born reporter, with an insatiable appetite for information, a sharp eye for the relevant detail, and a determination to understand as well as observe, she reacted in a very personal way to people, places, and events. The result, as the following excerpts show, is a poignant account of what it was like to be young, poor, ambitious, and female on a first trip abroad in the 1920s.

Sept. 1st   I shall never forget this first evening in France, in Rouen . . . where long ago "the maid" was burned at the stake. It lured us so en route to Paris we stopped off to spend a day and a night. At the hotel we struggled with our rudimentary *At Rouen*   French. "Une chambre, pour deux avec l'eau froid et chaud, comfortable mais bon marchè." We mut-

---

* Among these fantasies was a biographical sketch published with one of her *Saturday Evening Post* articles, which includes the statement that she went to Vienna to do graduate work and was there in time to watch the closing days of the (First World) War.

tered the phrase over and over on our way to the
"Hotel Dieppe." Then it was Assya who assayed
the assault on the maitre d'Hotel — Assya with her
amazing facility with any tongue . . . we have a
room broad and wide with two super beds, comfortable and commodius, a night table on either
side and "l'eau chaud" when we demand it. All
for 18 francs, which at the present rate of exchange
is about $1.75. At seven, having bathed and
dressed we wandered out. The sense of adventure
was strong in us, again. Did we not still have the
charmed $500? Had not the Cheval glass in our
more or less sumptuous abode shown us pink
cheeks and shiny eyes? Did we not have roses in
our belts from admirers in England? . . .
Such a dinner! And for 8 Frs. That is to say
about 50 cents! Soup! Mackerel with an enchanting sauce. Veal. Salade! A carafe of "vin blanc"
and so on through to coffee and benedictine that
was like flowers in our nostrils . . . We talked of
how wonderful everything was, how expansive life!
How good it had been to us . . .
In the spring we would go to Russia. We *would*
write — a novel perhaps. Women *could* be friends,
couldn't they? Didn't we prove it? Here we were:
racially different, brought up under the most opposite conditions and environment — now casting
our lots together under the most trying circumstances — so intimate, so difficult, yet loving and
appreciating each other more and more every day
. . . How beautiful and good everything was —
how heavenly to be alive — how much lay ahead
and beyond! Thus our first night in France!

Sept. 2   After travelling around Paris in a taxi-cab for an
hour, stopping at one hotel after another and always being turned away, we landed at last among
the South Americans at the Hotel de Bresil et
Portugal in the Square Montholon, where we got
a room (very decent) for 14 frs. a day. The first

thing we did was to unpack, wash our faces, call a taxi and drive to the Champs Elysees. There sitting under the trees at a little restaurant we ate our first dinner in Paris, Varya was so excited she could hardly talk — and I was more so. Walking from the Etoile to the Place de la Concorde simply took away our breath . . .

Sept. 8

At the Red Cross headquarters in the Rue Chevreaux this afternoon we met an old friend, Mrs. Kudlicka, from Buffalo. She has just gotten back from Poland . . . She's pro-Pole; anti-Bolshevik and anti-semitic. At Underwoods, where I was trying to rent a typewriter, ran into a very young American from N. Carolina . . . who is working for a few weeks on the Paris edition of the N.Y. Herald . . . We talked about journalism, I very loftily giving him advice . . .

Sept. 9
in the
Luxembourg
Gardens

The
Opera

We sat in the gardens all afternoon. I lining Varya's jacket with a recut pongee dress. She writing a story and asking me about it . . . now scribbling a paragraph, reading it aloud, re-scribbling it . . . And tonight the opera. Samson and Dalila . . . We sat in the topmost loge in the 6 Fr. seats but the music was divine and if we had to lean over the rail to see the stage, we had a magnificent view of the great theatre . . . A wonderful place to stage a scene in a novel. Something tragic and lofty — like a magnificent suicide . . . A memorable day — not space to record a very human conversation at dejeuner with Madame Charvoz [their French teacher].

Sept. 10

Reaction, I suppose, anyway a sombre day. We finished lining the coat and had an absurd quarrel over it. At dejeuner we were both dull and the lesson didn't go very well. We wasted a glorious afternoon mending clothes in our room.

The following day a momentous telegram from Reeves of INS arrived. The New York office was well pleased with Doro-

thy's Irish stories and suggested that she go to Austria for a
month to survey the situation there. After a festive *déjeuner*
with Mme Charvoz, Dorothy and Barbara interviewed two
leading women syndicalists but were too elated to do any more
work that afternoon. Their jubilation was short-lived.

Sept. 16 *Bad* *news* *The Day's* *Work*	Another telegram from Reeves received this morning says "New York now wires 'Cancel Thompson Austria.'" We have spent a gloomy day. Barbara went out after information . . . for a trade story for the NY Eve Post, but I stayed in all day and wrote vociferously. Then this evening under a horrible light concocted a chemise, because our communal underwear is going the way of all flesh and even in France they are too expensive for us to buy! . . . This existence of ours is highly precarious — I wonder why I seem driven to stick it out. Several nice safe jobs with regular stipends await me in NY, but as the days pass that life seems farther and farther away.
We make *the* *Front* *Page*	Peggy sent me two copies of the Pittsburgh Leader. They arrived this morning. My first Irish story — the conversation with MacSwiney had made the front page and so had Varya's interview with Madame Polovtzeva [member of a Soviet purchasing commission].

The diary was neglected for several days, following a chance
meeting with a friend of Barbara's, Joseph Schlossberg, a fellow
Zionist and Secretary-Treasurer of the Amalgamated Clothing
Workers of America. He was on his way to Italy, where he had
excellent connections with labor leaders. Barbara was armed
with a letter of introduction from George Lansbury, the intrepid British Socialist-Labour leader and editor of the *Daily
Herald*. The two young reporters seized the opportunity to
join Schlossberg and to cover, under ideal auspices, what might
well be the biggest news story in Europe: Italy's apparently imminent revolution. The last week in Paris was filled with fran-

tic sightseeing and enlivened by an encounter with the director of a Russian relief organization. "He offered me a job as his secretary," Dorothy confided in a letter to Beatrice. "Of course I accepted. Everything was very frank and friendly and I was simply thrilled to death. Well — quite 'out of the blue' he invited me to dinner one night and I accepted. We drove to a gay restaurant in the Bois de Bologne, ate a long dinner and then took a taxi home. And suddenly, quite without warning, he made *violent* love to me.

"I was simply furious. You know how I hate scenes. I would have slapped his face had I been three years younger. Of course he protested he adored me. Told me the story of his unhappy married life, offered to divorce his wife and marry me. Ugh — ! I told him that if he were the last man on earth I wouldn't marry him. And of course, I wouldn't go to Russia with him after that. I wish I were a man."

The trip to Rome strained the Thompson–De Porte budget since Schlossberg, traveling on an expense account, insisted on riding first-class. However, the journey proved worthwhile. In northern Italy, for more than a month, workers in the metallurgical industry, organized by left-wing leaders, had occupied factories in what was, in effect, the world's first large-scale sit-down strike. Thanks to their introductions from trade unionists, Dorothy and Barbara were admitted to the Fiat factory in Rome, were photographed eating minestrone with the strikers and their families, and sent off to INS their first major news story from the continent. The antiquities of Rome and the company of lively Italian socialists filled the rest of the week. On October 7, they took the train for Florence and had what Dorothy called an "extraordinary experience" en route.

> There was only one other man in our compartment if you exclude the morose old gentleman who snoozed in the corner, and he was a gross-looking Italian, about fifty years old, who quickly

revealed his identity — president of the Court of Appeals of Florence . . . He opened a conversation and we replied — first because these conversations enroute furnish the most valuable kind of uncolored information about the state of affairs, and second because not to do so would be pure posing on our part. Nevertheless both Varya and I felt uncomfortable under his gaze which was distinctly sensual and "turkish" and under his questions which became more and more personal. Where were we going? Were we alone? Who was the gentleman travelling with us? etc. etc. (Varya says I made an awful faux pas by explaining that J.S. [Joseph Schlossberg] was "un ami." I spent the rest of my trip trying to explain him as an old "ami de mon pere.")

The conversation was in French which neither Varya nor I know well. The compartment was stifling and the morose old gent wouldn't have the window open so Varya, who had a headache went into the corridor and opened a window there. The Deputy Chief Justice followed her and there ensued a remarkable conversation as follows

"Etes vous mariè?"

"Non, monsieur."

"Mais — vous *connaissez* les hommes."

"Pardon" — perplexed.

"Je dis — vous *connaissez* les hommes" — boldly. "Etes vous *vergine?"*

Varya — scarcely believing her ears — "Je ne comprend pas."

He: "Parceque — nous somme sympathetic — Vous et moi, et j'esper peutetre vous — mois — nous embrason —"

Varya, peremptorily, with flashing eyes, *"M'sieur,* il n'est pas comme il faut, s'il vous *plais."*

Whereupon he shrugged his shoulders and begged her pardon. But what a revelation of the Latin point of view toward women, two women, mod-

erately attractive, willing to talk with strange men
(in a railroad compartment) — and *still* virgin at
27! *

* Dorothy's spelling, even in her native tongue, was unreliable, and in foreign
languages wildly erratic. Where her own writings are quoted, throughout this
book, only obvious slips in her typing have been corrected.

❧ 3
Reluctant Virgin

"I WANT TO STAY FOREVER under these gleaming skies," Dorothy wrote to Beatrice. "The only thing I miss in Italy is a lover. To be twenty-seven and loverless in Italy is a crime against God and man."

Barbara, though equally bereft, was comforted by a torrent of mail from her suitor in London. But Dorothy had only the memory of Wilbur. She no longer, she said, cried herself to sleep but "my heart aches whenever I think of him." Her diary suggests that she did not spend much time repining but was, on the contrary, actively in search of a new object for her affections. She had met so far a number of American and British journalists and an assortment of French and Italian Socialists whom she found amusing but eminently resistible.

The party broke up temporarily on October 10 when Barbara accepted an invitation to visit Signora Argentina Altobelli, general secretary of the syndicate of Agricultural Workers in Bologna. Schlossberg was off to a conference in Milan where they all agreed to meet on October 26, a commitment Dorothy was to regret. Meanwhile, Dorothy headed for Genoa, hoping to interview Captain Giuseppe Giulietti, the colorful forty-one-year-old chief of the left-wing-maritime union who had participated in the adventuresome seizure of Fiume led by the poet Gabriele d'Annunzio in 1919.

Oct. 11   Well I emancipated myself from the bourgois taste of J.S. and rode to Genoa third class — eight hours ride for thirty lira! Without question the most interesting — and in its way — delightful journey I have had in Italy. The people were delicious. Tickled to death to have an American! Insisted on giving me the best seat (hardly anyone had a seat at all) Offered me cakes (which I took; they were delicious; flavored with arrow-root) and talked to me through two youths in a patois of mixed French, German and English. But we understood each other. And a fat old Italian with a bold eye tickled me (and himself) to death by calling me a "Schöne Fraulein" all the way. I have an idea it wasn't because he *thought* me so, but because he wanted to show off his German.

We all took turns at standing and holding the babies (there were a raft of them) and I got into Genoa feeling dreadfully tired — but what of it?

Hotel
Genoa

Caroti [a young socialist she had met in Florence] had engaged a room for me. Damn these labor leaders. It was magnificent — to the tune of 25L and nothing else to be had. Two washbowls, eight chairs, five mirrors, *no* desk, damask sheets and — bedbugs! I changed in the morning. For 10L I get a desk, only one chair and a sofa, one washbowl and — I imagine — the bedbugs just the same . . .

It's not fashionable to like Genoa. People (tourists) stick up their noses at you when you praise it and I haven't *dared* to *whisper* that I like it far better than Florence. But I do. It is such a gay city and in its streets one feels the heritage of generations of bold sailors who went to far lands and came back with strange cargoes . . . Wasn't it the home of Christofer Colombo, whose statue adorns the square across from the "Statione Centrale" — and in 1920 of Giulietti — pirate of the seamen's union? . . . Giulietti was out of town and I shall have to wait until Thursday so I "saw" the town. Young Caroti was my guide and he's a fascinating lad . . .

On board
one of the
"Seized Ships"

We went on board the Andrea Costa — one of the ships which was seized by Giulietti and now belongs to the Garibaldi cooperative. It was flying the Italian flag on the poop and the Red flag with black letters GARIBALDI from a mast. The Andrea Costa was named for the Karl Marx of Italy. It had made one trip to New York and the crew had had a wonderful reception from the Italian labor temple. On the prow was a bas relief (medal) presented to them by the Italian-American workers. A head of Garibaldi with the Soviet coat of arms in the corner.

Awaiting Giulietti's return, Dorothy went on "long poking walks" in the city and worked on a magazine piece she was trying to develop out of her Irish interviews. Wearing a hammer-and-sickle lapel pin that had been given her by young Caroti, she walked into a typewriter establishment to rent a machine. To her surprise the proprietor told her that as a "comrade" she could use it for nothing. The interview with Giulietti finally took place on October 14 with Caroti acting as interpreter.

I fall in
love

There were already a half dozen people waiting in the outer room of his offices in the great modern building owned by the Workers of the Sea, when I was ushered in to see him. He had his back to the door as I entered, and I got a very pleasant impression of tallness. (Most Italians are so short!) Then he turned around suddenly — and I fell in love with him! I mean it literally. I found myself delighting, physically, in his warm clasp of my hand. "I am *very* happy to meet you," I said warmly, then, more daringly — "Papa Giulietti" He laughed at this, still holding my hand, his eyes taking me in boldly, but with a flattering appreciativeness. He's *terribly* handsome. A very clear, "fit" color, a fine head, but not too heavy; very black "snapping" eyes, and a brilliant, flashing, fascinating smile . . . I have never been so stimulated and magnetized by any man in my life. As we talked we constantly broke into laughter and his eyes watched me with the most expressive, the most inviting, the most *speaking* expression. Every once in a while he would flash a smile at Caroti and say something (I wormed it out of Caroti afterward. He had said: "Oh, she's *nice* — very nice — I like her — I should like to be with her etc. etc.") Anyway, he kept me there two hours, to the rage of his secretary and the waiting crowd. He started to shake hands at the table and held mine all the way to the door. We were obviously delighted and charmed with each other. "Adio, *Cara,*" he finally said, looking right into my eyes with that delicious smile still on his lips.

Caroti says his personal fastidiousness is famous

He was dressed, by the way, with the most meticulous care. His linen was perfect, his black suit pressed, his nails manicured. Caroti said he was 45, never smokes, hardly ever even drinks wine. There is not a line in his face except around his eyes. They are surrounded by tiny wrinkles that even stretch across his straight, rather small nose, and that evidently come from laughter. He's incredibly vital and young and egotistical. When he laughs it is deep and throaty. He throws his head back and flashes his teeth and his eyes simply dance.

The "Joie de vivre" of Giulietti

I was tremendously aware of him physically every moment I was with him and felt that he wanted me to be. I noticed every detail of his person. The way his hair grows, like a small boy's, all over his head in great hyacinth locks, curling from the center. His soft, round impulsive chin — the jaw, which is very muscular and manly, redeems it; even his lower lip, very full and red and half pouting, and the lines that deepen engagingly in his cheeks when he laughs. He wears a short, close-clipped moustache — dark, of course. His mouth is really beautiful.

The next afternoon — her last day in Genoa — Dorothy was at work in the typewriting establishment when the lights suddenly went out, the result of a two-hour general strike. She followed a red flag to an arcade where a crowd had gathered.

I hear
him
speak

We have a
few moments
in the dark

An
intimate
chronicle

The arcade was jammed and Giulietti was speaking. His hair was down over his eyes and he was clawing the air and rolling out great sonorous sentences in a gorgeous baritone. I went closer to the ladder on which he was speaking. I suppose my unconscious was urging me on. Anyway in descending he saw me. The same delighted smile flashed across his face. He came to me and led me into a room behind the ladder — a vacant store I think it must have been in the Arcade. Anyway it was dark and there were only a few people there. But I could see his teeth flashing and I could *feel* him. I was actually trembling a little. We talked about the meeting and he was polite and explanatory in his absurd English (this English may be one reason why he seems so naif and childlike) — but all the time I could feel his look caressing me, with the little laughter wrinkles deepening around his eyes. I felt just a little tipsy and warm as if with wine. When I gestured with one hand he caught it — just for the briefest second, but it was an indescribable caress.

"When you go?" he whispered. (We were talking sotto voce not to disturb the meeting at the door) "Tonight," I replied. "I go to Milan."

His face fell so frankly that I laughed.

"I waited for you for three days," I said. "Now I have seen you, I depart."

He was enveloping me with his personality.

"But I do not want you to go. I want to be with you. Is it possible?" he asked. "Is it possible?" he repeated very softly.

"I'm afraid not," I said. I was trying to be matter of fact, but I was simply flaming.

"Will you not stay with me — two-three days?" (he was whispering again.) "I do not want you should go —" He wasn't touching me but I might have been in his arms! "Do you not desire also?" — he went on whispering and I could see his tantalizing head and even the little dents on each side of his mouth. I didn't dare to trust myself and fortunately someone came up at that moment and dragged him away. "I desire greatly to stay with you. Surely you desire also to stay with me." Those were his last words. And there was a little more in this strain. Then the meeting broke up and I had to go. I had just time to catch my train. We said another adio in the street and kissed each other with our eyes.

Enroute to Milan in a Third class Carriage

This may be disgusting but it is a true chronicle. It is distinctly fortunate for my virtue that I'm committed to Varya to be in Milan tonight. I know that I should not have resisted him. Himself, my mood, and Genoa — that wonderful shore — those dim romantic streets — I'm not even glad to be saved . . . I still have an accelerated pulse . . . I certainly wouldn't want to marry him, and he is quite evidently against matrimony. But it would have been such a smashingly thrilling episode . . .

✺ 4
Journey's End

MOST OF THE BOLD REVOLUTIONARIES Dorothy and Barbara met in Italy would, within two years, be dead, exiled, or undergoing the castor oil torture in fascist jails while the one-time socialist Benito Mussolini boasted that he had made the trains run on time. With the country close to civil war, in the autumn of 1920, travel was rugged.

Leaving Genoa two hours late, Dorothy's train pulled into Milan in a wet and chilly dawn. When the hotel room she had reserved proved nonexistent, she spent the night huddled on a restaurant table. Schlossberg provided a steamer rug but could not offer her a bed in the room he was sharing with another man. "I thought of Eugene Debs and all other people in prison," she wrote of this dreary experience. Milan seemed even gloomier next day when she lost a precious working notebook to a pickpocket as she waited in the station for Barbara to arrive from Bologna.

"We are staying here to write because we aren't attracted to do anything else," Dorothy wrote to Beatrice. "We've met everyone who is concerned in the present revolutionary situation — that is to say everyone on the labor side: [Giacinto Menotti] Serrati, the editor of *Avanti!*, Giulietti, the piratical leader of the Seamen's Federation (and incidentally, one of the most interesting and fascinating human beings I have ever met. I positively fell in love with him . . .)

"Also, we discovered an extraordinary woman in this land of wretched women (I am certainly more of a feminist than ever — !) Mm. Altobelli, the General Secretary, organizer and founder of the Peasants' Trade Union — an organization with a million members, simply magnificent . . ."

Days and nights of steady labor resulted in a long magazine piece, "The Last Day," an account of the factory sit-in strike under the joint Thompson–De Porte byline. "We have been in the most heavenly mood toward each other ever since our brief separation," Dorothy wrote in her diary. "We had a long talk about my feeling in regard to Giulietti and about Meyer and W.P. . . . J.S. returned and we again have that frightful married feeling . . ."

Although they were bored with their forty-four-year-old escort and pained by his extravagant travel tastes, they followed him to Venice and luxuriated for a night at the Danieli. The skies were blue again; palaces, gondolas, canals, and San Marco moved Dorothy to lyrical rhapsodies. Their next goal was Vienna since Reeves had again expressed interest in the Austrian situation. En route they stopped off in Trieste, where Barbara wanted to meet with a group of young Zionists bound for Palestine. She found them destitute, housed in bleak barracks. The two were so moved by their plight that Barbara gave them her sealskin coat and Dorothy sold her gold watch and contributed the proceeds along with her few spare articles of clothing to the young pioneers. Dorothy called Trieste — imperial Austria's seaport that was annexed by Italy after World War I — a "dead grey city." It suited her mood. She had just received word from her Cincinnati friend, Mary Burnett, of the untimely death of her husband Peter, whose wit and idealism had endeared him to Dorothy. She was further dejected by the realization that she was about to lose her traveling companion. A dozen letters and three telegrams from Meir had awaited Barbara in Venice. At the same time Reeves decided that the long-planned trip to the USSR must be postponed. He still liked their proposal to enter Russia from the south and work their way north, reporting on the provinces and on what was happening to the "little" people rather than Moscow and Petrograd officialdom. But November was no time to undertake such a journey. After Vienna there would be few further assignments in Europe, and the practical solution would be to go home over the winter. Under the circumstances, Barbara felt free to marry. Then in April, she reasoned, Dorothy could come back to London, and they could go to Russia together as planned. "This understandably upset Dorothy very much," Barbara wrote. "For one thing she had no wish to return to the States; for another, she was sure that when spring came I would not be in a position to undertake such a journey; there might even be a baby on the way. Besides, she did not like Meir. She said the marriage would not last three months (it lasted 44 years)."

In the account book that she kept in the back of her journal, Dorothy recorded their fiscal as well as her emotional predicament. After paying for the Trieste-Vienna-Paris trip and Barbara's fare to London, the nest egg would be down to 2674 lire (about $130). With stringent economies it might last thirty-three days. Grim though the prospect seemed, she was determined to stay abroad. To leave would be an admission of failure. Nor could she harbor any lasting resentment against Barbara. Instead, she went to London for the wedding.

"By the way, Barbara is to be married Thursday," she wrote cheerfully to Beatrice. "Mark is a dear . . . and adores her. [Perhaps because it seemed less alien, she had rechristened Meir, Mark.] They are postponing their honeymoon until January and they are going to *Egypt*. Lucky dogs! He has a nice little house in the west end, and we two, properly chaperoned, are *staying* in it. (He's with a friend.)"

On the wedding day, November 18, Dorothy marched alongside of Barbara under the Khuppa — the canopy beneath which bride and groom stand with their witnesses at orthodox ceremonies. Distressed to learn that she was not Jewish, the rabbi was further upset when Dorothy informed him she was a minister's daughter. But Barbara, who did not take religious rites seriously, was amused and happy because Dorothy, as she put it, "behaved like the dear friend she was."

🦋 5
"yet I believe in myself . . ."

BACK IN PARIS ten days after Barbara's wedding, Dorothy confided in her diary.

Paris
November
27

Not until I went to the R.C. [Red Cross] and attempted to resume my life as a manufacturer of publicity did I realize what the past five months have done to me. I can never go back to it — never. I wonder if I shall be able to stick out the winter. Oh I wish that I were either talented or less intelligent. The whole place is cluttered up with almost successful people. Senario writers, magazine writers, photographers. They know their job well. Do it. Make a "good living." But, oh, their shallowness. Appalling. Rose Wilder Lane, their chiefest writer with her sob stuff . . . Oh, I hate them! Hate them! . . . I am more intelligent than they are. And less successful. I could weep because I cannot express how I feel and make it count. How unhappy I am . . . I feel all alone, quite. I even want to be alone . . . Oh why, why, why haven't I talent.

All day I work. How I have worked this week. How much I have written. Most of it trash. Except the four Vienna stories for Reeves. They were sincere and honest anyway. I felt them. I *wanted* to make the people whom I wrote for feel for Vienna . . . I am lonely, too lonely to care about seeing people I don't care about. The thought of Peter's death depresses me. Nobody cares for me except the people for whom I do not

deeply care. I want to write to Gertrude whom I
love as I do the best in myself, but she does not respond. I will not let myself think that she does not
care for me as deeply as I love her, but why should
she? She knows that I am vain, and often untruth-
ful, and fond of praise and cowardly in the face of
censure, that I am a snob, and am really awed by
nice manners and nice clothes. I think she does
not write because she is bored with me. It is horrible to be intelligent but uncreative. To be des-
picable and mean and always want to be good.

This lament echoes the self-reproaches of the small girl convinced that those she loved best deserted her because of her own
wickedness. It is also the voice of a frustrated writer. Two
months earlier in Italy she had sketched out the plot of a novel.
"I have almost reached the decision," she then wrote in her
diary, "to finish this trip as quickly as possible and return to
Paris, take a little room in the Quartier Latin, take a job writing on space for the A.R.C. — I can earn a living there in four
hours a day and settle down to using the rest of my time until
spring in writing . . ."

Now in the autumn of 1920 she was in a position to do precisely this. For a facile writer, it was possible to eke out a living
at the Red Cross rate of ten francs a hundred lines and still have
time left over for more serious work. She had found a small
but cozy room on the top floor of the Hotel Cayré near the
Boulevard Raspail where she had privacy and even central heat-
ing and hot and cold running water. This was the moment to
apply for membership in the circle of literary expatriates who,
in Kay Boyle's and Robert McAlmon's words, were blissfully
"being geniuses together." But Dorothy, alas, lacked the credentials. "All that I have written on my novel, I have destroyed.
It was awful and I knew it," she wrote to Beatrice on December
9. "Perhaps I can never make a go of writing. I wonder — And
yet I believe in myself — why?"

Dorothy had seldom doubted her own abilities, but she needed emotional support to sustain her self-confidence. In Paris, before long, she found it in the person of Rose Wilder Lane, whose "sob stuff" she had denigrated when she first went to work for the Red Cross. Rose was, in fact, a versatile professional writer who made a good living out of articles and stories, novels and biographies that, while seldom distinguished, were always publishable. Lean and energetic, she was imbued with the restless adventuresome spirit of her pioneer forebears. A brief marriage had ended in divorce and even the men who found her attractive sensed that she was somehow a woman's woman.*

Rose — six years her senior — replaced Gertrude Tone as Dorothy's temporary mother on whom she could lean in periods of stress. In Rose's comfortable apartment and on weekend excursions to an inn in the valley of the Loire, the two talked far into the night about life, love, politics, philosophy, and the literary marketplace. Dorothy abandoned the novel, accepting journalism as her natural vocation. Though she regarded much of her output as trivial, it was satisfying to sell almost any feature story she wrote to the New York *Post,* the *Christian Science Monitor,* or even to the "pestiferous Hearst" — as she characterized her least favorite publisher. The problem was to find some more dependable source of income and status than freelancing.

Making the rounds of newspaper offices in Paris, she met Paul Scott Mowrer, chief of the Chicago *Daily News* service, who found her "brighter and more attractive" than most of the young Americans who were then competing for the few badly paid jobs at European bureaus and the Paris edition of the New York *Herald.* He urged her to leave France and set up shop in another good news center — perhaps Vienna.

Dorothy liked the idea. Presently she persuaded the chief of

* Professionally she was always overshadowed by her mother, Laura Ingalls Wilder, author of the perennially best-selling *Little House Books* for children. Rose's most memorable work was *Let the Hurricane Roar,* a moving tale based on her grandparents' life in the early days of the Dakota Territory. It was reissued thirty years after its first publication in 1933.

the Philadelphia *Public Ledger*'s Paris bureau, Wythe Williams, to make her his unsalaried correspondent in Austria. The Red Cross also agreed that her talents could well be used in publicizing its large-scale relief program based in Budapest under the direction of Captain James Pedlow, a veteran of "Wild Bill" Donovan's World War I Rainbow Division. Since express trains made the trip from Vienna to Budapest in less than four hours, Dorothy was confident that she could manage both assignments.

Early in 1921, she packed her meager belongings, counted her savings, and figured that her luck and talents would somehow enable her to survive. She might have been describing herself in a story she later wrote about a group of American girls who remained in Paris after their war work — for the Red Cross or the Salvation Army — was finished. "They were held," she said, "by some inexplicable lure, some invisible romance . . . They were types of the American garçonne . . . What set them apart from other people was their gallantry . . ."

PART III

"A BLUE-EYED TORNADO"

1
"Mein Goldenes Wien"

"Two THINGS HAPPENED to central Europe during the decade of the 20s, people in Vienna still say — the world economic crisis and Dorothy Thompson," John Gunther wrote in an admiring essay titled "A Blue-Eyed Tornado." "She was brimful of excitement and freshness and saw stories that were not stories to more experienced correspondents . . ."

Since her first visit a year earlier, she had felt a warm sympathy for defeated Austria. The country was, in 1921, merely the German remnant of the dismembered Hapsburg empire that had for centuries provided an economically viable free trade area for a population of 50 million. Under the terms of the treaty signed at Saint-Germain in 1919, the territory was sliced up — some to form the new succession states of Yugoslavia and Czechoslovakia, other portions going to Italy, Poland, and the now independent kingdom of Hungary. What remained as Austria was the once imperial city surrounded by mountains and lakes, a few industries and farms that could nourish only a fraction of its 6 million people at the expense of near starvation for the 2 million who lived in Vienna. Black markets flourished in a city reduced to destitution by a ruinous currency inflation while the newborn League of Nations debated whether and when to bolster a defunct economy by an infusion of foreign credits.

Yet the hungry Viennese still flocked to the opera, theater, and concerts, whimsically characterized their plight as "desperate but not serious," dawdled in cafés and forgot the grim present when a violinist played such nostalgic tunes as *"Mein Goldenes Wien."*

For Dorothy, Vienna was to prove a place of golden opportunity.

She was captivated by the charm of a city whose baroque architecture is elegant rather than imposing, where wide avenues are lined with noble chestnut trees, a short ride on a trolley car or bus brings you to vine-covered hills, gracefully landscaped parks are adorned with monuments honoring Goethe and Mozart as well as martial heroes, and where the standard greeting to females is *"Küss die Hand."* Her writing reflected the zest and warmth of what was to become a lifelong love affair with Vienna. Never having worked in a newspaper office, hers was not city-desk prose. Her style was vivid and free-flowing, filled with the concrete details through which the written word breathed life into distant scenes before the days of radio and television.

"Coffee in Vienna is more than a national drink," she wrote in one of her Sunday pieces. "It is a national cult. Palaces have been built for it; palaces where there are satin-brocaded walls, deep divans, onyx-topped tables, great windows curtained in gold-colored silk. These palaces are the center of Vienna's social, intellectual and spiritual life." After spelling out the recipes for a dozen varieties of Viennese coffee ranging from thick Turkish mocha to *Capuciner* and *Melange Schlag,* she continued, "You cannot buy a railroad ticket or post a letter or register in a hotel in Vienna without being reduced to tears or profanity as your temperament leads you, by the red tape and inefficiency involved. But you can go into a Vienna cafe and order a 'Capuciner' and ask for your favorite newspaper and they will be set before you instanter. For the price of a coffee you have a whole library at your disposal. And a fortnight later you can go into the same cafe and sit down and a Vienna waiter will look at you for a second, with one clairvoyant glance, and without your saying a single word he will lay before you a 'Capuciner' and the *Berliner Tageblatt,* the *Manchester Guardian, Le Temps,* the *New York Herald* and *Simplicissimus* . . ."

In a more earnest vein, she reported at length on the accomplishments of Vienna's Social Democratic city government, which despite economic stringencies was using its independent taxing power to construct low-cost housing and to finance an extensive welfare program. Living in a tiny flat at Rainergasse 5 in the Margareten District, a working-class neighborhood, she was impressed by the courage and idealism of the Viennese socialists who were her neighbors. A sure instinct seems to have told her that her future as a journalist lay in the German-speaking world, and she set about mastering the language with the help of a teacher who charged a dollar for three lessons a week. She came to feel completely at home in German, though its syntax always eluded her. "I never knew anyone to speak German so fluently and so ungrammatically" was a typical verdict of the natives.

Although there was no dearth of stories in Vienna, her duties for the Red Cross required frequent trips to Budapest. There she demonstrated her virtuosity as a publicist. A roundup of social and economic conditions in Hungary, for example, in the *Christian Science Monitor* included an adroit puff for her client:

"The first anniversary in Budapest of Captain James Pedlow, the American Red Cross Commissioner, was celebrated last week by pilgrimages to his rooms of rich and poor who came to tender and express affection. 'Pedlow Kapitan' is a name to conjure with in Budapest. People laughingly say that the restoration of the monarchy is almost certain, but no one knows who the king will be — Karl [Charles] or Captain Pedlow . . ."

Pedlow introduced Dorothy to the man who would become her chief journalistic mentor, Marcel Fodor, the Hungarian-born correspondent of the Manchester *Guardian*. A short, round, thirty-year-old bachelor, he preferred to be called Mike or Fodor because, as he put it, "Marcel is a name for a tall dark handsome chap not a little roly-poly like me." Educated in England and schooled in British socialism, Fodor had a working knowledge of a half-dozen languages and an encyclopedic memory packed with the intricacies of Central European politics. Captivated by Dorothy's vivacity, quick intelligence, and the beauty of her "tender skin," he promptly invited her to dinner.

"This was not a simple matter," he recalled. "This was a starving city where the regular restaurant fare was sauerkraut with garlic or spinach with garlic and bread which in America would have been considered cattle-feed. We went to one of the better black market places."

Over an illicit goulash what was to become a lifelong collaboration began. Fodor happily accepted the role of guide and political counselor.* With Fodor as her escort, Dorothy regularly covered dress rehearsals at the State Opera and the Volksopera and wrote glowing accounts of such notable events as the Vienna premiere of *Der Rosenkavalier* with Lotte Lehmann and Elisabeth Schwarzkopf and the matchless performances of Maria Jeritza. These pieces may well have brought her by-line to the attention of the Philadelphia *Ledger's* music-loving publisher, Cyrus Curtis. But her main interest — like Fodor's — was in politics. Shortly after their meeting, he was on the scent of what he believed to be a major news break that she would share. At issue was the future of the Hapsburg dynasty, a subject of worldwide interest in an age still bemused by royalty with or without thrones.

When Emperor Franz Josef's long reign ended with his death in 1916, he had no direct successor. His son Rudolf had died in the romantic double suicide at Mayerling nearly thirty years earlier. His nephew Franz Ferdinand, assassinated at Sarajevo in June 1914, left no legitimate heir since his marriage to a woman of nonroyal blood was rated as morganatic. Thus the Hapsburg crown fell to Franz Josef's grandnephew Charles. A benign but feckless monarch, Charles had made a belated attempt to preserve the empire as a federation of nationalities.

---

* A few years later he performed a like service for John Gunther, who wrote, "He educated Dorothy Thompson and me practically from the cradle."

Married to Zita, Princess of Bourbon-Parma, he tried and failed in the spring of 1917 to negotiate a separate peace with the Allies, using her brothers as intermediaries. After the war, the peace treaties firmly established Austria as a republic. But in Hungary, "legitimists" plotted Charles's return from his exile in Switzerland, where he had gone shortly after his forced abdication in 1918. Following the brief socialist regime of Count Michael Karolyi and a Communist interlude under Béla Kun, Admiral Nikolaus Horthy seized power in 1920 and declared Hungary a kingdom with the throne vacant.

On March 27, 1921, the would-be ruler left Switzerland, arriving at an unscheduled stop of the Orient Express near the Hungarian border. Thanks to a tip from one of his scouts, Fodor and Dorothy arrived at the spot almost simultaneously with Charles. They interviewed his entourage and observed the monarch's hasty departure. The plot failed, but Dorothy scored her first exclusive story for the *Ledger*.

Shortly afterward, she followed Fodor to Prague, where his credentials as a regular correspondent enabled her, though still a mere free lance, to visit President Thomas G. Masaryk at his country home and to attend a press conference of Foreign Minister Eduard Beneš. The latter, according to Fodor, was startled by the searching, even impudent questions asked by this "charming, innocent looking" lady. The *Ledger* was pleased to publish the resulting articles.

After only a few months in Austria and Hungary, the sheer volume of Dorothy's output was so great that, on space rates, she was earning as much if not more than a correspondent's salary. It seemed a good moment to try for a spot on the regular staff. The possibility justified the thirty-six-hour train ride to Paris and Fodor willingly accompanied her. After a joyful reunion with Rose Lane, Dorothy, wearing her most becoming blue hat and a new camel's-hair coat, called on Wythe Williams in the *Ledger* office.

While this momentous interview was in progress, Fodor and Rose awaited the outcome in Petty's Tea Shop on the Place de la Madeleine. Dorothy emerged running and shouting, "I got it! I got it!" She was now the salaried Vienna correspondent of the Philadelphia *Ledger*. Her journalistic empire would include not only Austria and Hungary but also Czechoslovakia, Yugoslavia, Albania, Rumania, Bulgaria, Greece, and Turkey. The pay would be the far from princely sum of fifty dollars a week but there would be a modest expense account. And she would now be privileged to join — as a legitimate member — the court of the dean of the foreign press corps, A.P.'s Frederick Kuh, at the Café Herrenhof; to eavesdrop along with other journalists on the whores and black marketeers — the latter known as *Schieber* — at the Café Atlantis, Vienna's chief rumor mill. Above all, instead of mailing her copy and praying that it be accepted, she could from now on compose daily cables and at the post office mark them PRESS COLLECT LEDGER PHILA PA USA. This happy prospect called for a champagne celebration at the Café de la Paix followed by a gala dinner at Rose's apartment.

Late that night when Dorothy returned to her room at the Hotel Cayré, a Red Cross colleague, Ruth Horton, was waiting for her with a telegram that had been forwarded from the Red Cross office in Budapest. The next day she wrote in the diary that she had neglected for nearly six months:

May 7   The telegram said my father had died on the 4th of May and was signed Margaret [her sister Peggy]. There was no other word from home excepting a letter from father himself, dated April 15, in answer to a very racy one which I had written him from Budapest . . . That then is the last word from my father. My last sight of him was on the dock where he stood beside my brother and Gertrude Tone, shorter than they, incredibly innocent, and childlike in his face, waving farewell.

Though there were still many empty pages in this journal, no more would be filled. She paid a visit to Barbara Grossman in London and found her pregnant and living what Dorothy later called "a drab little life with a cook general." Perhaps as a gesture of farewell, she left all the records of their joint adventures with Barbara. Dorothy did not learn, for many months, that her father — true to a promise made to his second wife — was buried in Hamburg in the Abbott plot next to Eliza and that her mother's grave was isolated in the Thompson plot under a stone marked only: "Margaret, wife of Rev. P. Thompson 1873–1901."

2
"Vivimus, vivamus"

"Exceptionally pretty," "lovely," "a typical American girl" — so is Dorothy described by those who met her during her first year in Vienna. They recall her as tall and slim with a delicate pink-and-white complexion commonly reserved for blondes. In photographs taken at this time, her short hair falls carelessly over her forehead, her mouth is sensuous, the chin rounded, and her eyes blaze with a fanatical intensity. "I am at this moment very happy," she wrote to Rose Lane ". . . *'Vivimus vivamus'* was my class motto at prep school — let us live while we live. I still feel in my heart the inexhaustible, fascinating romance of life. I look ahead with interest to my own life, most of the time, feeling something of that detached yet engrossed interest which one feels at reading an exciting novel . . ."

Vienna seemed to surround her with warmth and affection. She was made welcome by the small circle of journalists, visiting experts, and Anglo-American diplomats that included the novelist Phyllis Bottome, wife of Captain Ernan Forbes-Dennis, who was attached to the British legation. Her New York friend, Dorothy Burlingham, had become a semipermanent resident while she and her children underwent psychoanalysis at the hands of Sigmund Freud and his daughter Anna. Fodor was in constant attendance. If there was an empty evening, she could spend it with one of her Viennese acquaintances — perhaps the economist Gustav Stolper, who with his wife Toni edited an important journal, the *Oesterreichische Volkswirt*, equivalent in content and caliber to the London *Economist*. Frequently, she took advantage of a standing invitation to the home of Frau Doktor Eugenia Schwarzwald in the Josefstadt Strasse, where one was always assured an excellent dinner and the company of ministers of state, bankers, students, politicians of all persuasions, and such artistic notables as the painter Oskar Kokoschka, composer Arnold Schönberg, or the avant-garde architect Adolf Loos. Director of a progressive and fashionable girls' school, and a philanthropist of formidable energy and expansive generosity, Genia's lasting memorial is a chain of nonprofit temperance restaurants, established in the years of Vienna's desperate hunger. (The *Wiener Öffentlicher Küche* marked by the sign WOK would — more than fifty years later — still be serving thrifty natives and tourists.) In Genia, a short, stocky woman with a mop of curly gray hair, Dorothy found yet another mother figure.

Although she was by no means rich, Dorothy could now afford some professional enhancements for her looks, including the twice-a-week ministrations of Vienna's justly renowned hairdressers. A few American dollars could also buy the services of expert milliners, seamstresses, tailors, and furriers. "I have a new fur coat," she wrote to Rose Lane, "not at all elegant but smart; of wild-cat; soft yellowy-gray, with stripes on it; short and loose with a voluminous chinny collar, and an impertinent little turban with a green feather. Then I have a suit; olive green with a lovely silvery haze in it — duvetine. There's a frock, first, cut Russian style, with a high collar and a side fastening, its only trimming a narrow band of beaver down the side. It has a knee-length coat, straight-cut, with a loose back, and a high rolling collar of beaver and therewith a tiny, tight little muff. And the suit has its own hat, likewise of the green-gray duvetine, with a tiny rim of beaver" — an impressive wardrobe for a young woman who only a few months earlier was patching the lining of the coat she shared with an equally threadbare companion. In a long self-analytical paragraph in this letter she buried the most electrifying of her tidings. She had, she said, lost her "virginity outside of marriage with equanimity."

It happened in the spring of 1921. She had gone with Fodor to a party at the Budapest home of Rustem Vambery, a one-time professor of law at the university who had been ousted by the Horthy regime and was now legal adviser to the British legation. There she met his former assistant, Josef Bard, also a doctor of law but now bent on a literary career. Josef was tall, slender — not yet thirty — and handsome in the rather saturnine style of Rudolph Valentino and other film idols of the period, and Dorothy saw in him the dark eyes of Giulietti and a Slavic version of Wilbur Phillips' intellectual grace and idealism. Josef was an accomplished linguist, a writer and philosopher of promise, and, incidentally, Jewish. She found him irresistible. Josef in turn was charmed by Dorothy's American good looks, her gaiety and verve. His childhood had been melancholy and his adolescence scarred by Hungary's humiliating defeat in World War I. He yearned to leave his native land where anti-Semitism had long been endemic but was now the official policy of the Horthy dictatorship. (Horthy's anti-Semitism was, however, selective; very rich Jews were not molested. One of this privileged group was Josef's friend Baron Ladislas — known to his intimates as Laci — Hatvany, who continued to luxuriate in his immense estate near Budapest.) When she was in Budapest, Dorothy and Josef met at the Ritz Hotel. In Vienna she welcomed him at her new flat at Rechte Wienzeile 31 in an unfashionable but pleasant neighborhood overlooking the open markets on the Wien River; there were occasional weekends at an inn in Semmering. Dorothy's circle liked Josef who, in general, found Americans delightful, though there were exceptions. Among them was a feminist group that gathered in Vienna for an international peace conference in July 1921. Like many beleaguered males who feel threatened by women en masse he chose to believe that most of "those suffragettes" were lesbians. He was offended by their breezy, practical approach to the mysteries of love and horrified when one caller exhibited a purseful of what he called "sexual objects."

Dorothy was also pained. "I can't be like Doris Stevens — or Jane Burr —" she wrote, "discussing my life's intimacies." * Although she now had a lover, she had by no means forgotten the proprieties learned in Hamburg, New York. "My dear, you *should* see the Austrian beaches," she wrote to Rose, describing an outing on which she had taken one of the peace delegates, Maud Swartz, Secretary of the Women's Trade Union League. "As my little sister would say, 'These women ain't got no shame.'

This (see sketch) is the maximum clothing ever worn by a Viennese. Anyhow Maud enjoyed it and chortled with glee, swearing to drag Mrs. Henry Villard thither if it cost her her life. I said it would because the lady was a non-resistant. I'd heard her say so that afternoon."

Absorbed in her new romance, Dorothy, the one-time suffrage worker, now found a large aggregation of women "hideously depressing." Even the great Jane Addams — founder of Hull House — had lost her glamour. She was bored by the banal oratory of Rosika Schwimmer, the flamboyant pacifist who had persuaded Henry Ford to finance a peace ship in 1916. The visiting peace ladies further irked her by gossiping about her apparent intimacy with two men, Josef and Fodor, refusing to believe that the latter was merely a dear friend and collaborator. (He had once proposed marriage but took her refusal philosophically and later rejoiced that he had not become the "slave of a human dynamo.") Ignoring malicious tongues, Dorothy went off with Josef for a long weekend

---

* The women's rights, birth control, and peace movements had interlocking directorates. Doris Stevens had been a prominent member of the militant National Women's Party led by Alice Paul. The "sexual objects" were probably contraceptive diaphragms, which were still illegal in the United States.

at Plattensee — a lake on the Hungarian plains — acquired a blistering sunburn, and in August decided to escape from the unusually torrid climate and her fevered emotions by joining Beatrice Sorchan and a Bryn Mawr classmate, Louise Wood, on a walking tour in the Bavarian Alps.

A week with these innocent companions reminded Dorothy that she too was a *nice* American girl. "If I were more courageous I suppose I would live with Josef openly," she wrote to Rose in September, "but I'm frankly *not* courageous enough. Vienna isn't big. All the American colony would know, because, with my unfortunate talent for making friends, I know most of them . . . To go to Budapest would be even worse, for Budapest is only a village, really. So it's either a clandestine and intermittent relationship or it's marriage, or it's the end. And the first won't do — it isn't what I want and he wants."

Dorothy weighed her desire for the security of marriage against a recurrent urge to "throw my things in a suitcase, take the only hundred dollars I have in the world and start away for another city and a new environment — maybe China — I want so to be free."

Economically too, it was an impossible match. "Here we are, both poor as Job's turkey. Josef who is a clever boy, is educated to be a lawyer. He won't practise law in Hungary, because he hates the damned country and wants to get out of it and a law practise would tie him there for good. On the other hand, law is the *hardest* profession to take to another country — to England or America. He's the correspondent now of the A.P. in Hungary, and perhaps eventually journalism will let him out . . ." It was an unlikely prospect, since Josef, by his own account, detested journalism, had no news sense, and had set his heart on writing an ambitious philosophical work, tentatively titled "The Mind of Europe." *

* The book was never completed. However a segment of it became a magazine piece titled "Why Europe Hates the Jews," which appeared in *Harper's Magazine* in March 1927.

There was also the vexing problem of Dorothy's nationality. Under United States law at that time she would lose her citizenship if she married a foreigner. Lack of an American passport might be a serious handicap to a journalist whose livelihood depended on freedom to travel under the protection of a powerful and stable government.

Rose shared all of Dorothy's misgivings and strenuously opposed the match. But in the end love triumphed over logic. Dorothy and Josef were married early in 1922.* With Dr. Vambery acting as best man, the ceremony took place in the city hall of Budapest's eighth district, a locale dictated by the fact that civil marriages were permitted in Catholic Austria only if both participants professed to be atheists, an impossible condition for Dorothy. A few days later in Vienna there was a wedding party in the Bristol Hotel apartment of one of Dorothy's elderly admirers, Colonel William B. Causey, an American adviser to the Austrian government.

The acquisition of a husband solved one pressing problem for Dorothy, the matter of a permanent roof over her head. She had been periodically threatened with eviction by the *Wohnungsamt* — the bureaucracy that controlled Vienna's scarce housing and gave a low priority to the needs of unattached women. As a legally united couple, the Bards were privileged to lease a spacious flat at Prinz Eugenstrasse 58, in one of the city's smartest neighborhoods. A balcony overlooked the Belvedere Palace and its superb gardens. This was Dorothy's first chance to furnish a sizable home of her own — and she made the most of the furniture bargains to be found in the Spiegelgasse and the antique shops in the Doroteergasse. She indulged in quantities of kitchenware, an old cherry table with spindly legs, a Baroque wooden angel minus a hand and foot, a secondhand piano, and an antique bronze clock. She painted her own bedroom an ethereal blue, curtained Josef's bedroom-study in chintzes, and

---

* Neither Dorothy's papers nor Josef's memory nor the municipal records of Budapest yielded the precise date.

found a place of honor for Gertrude Tone's wedding gift —
a handsome oriental rug.

To Mary Gawthorpe, her friend of suffrage days, she sent a
sketch of the apartment and its furnishings and assured her, "I
like marriage. I find it the most satisfactory institution which I
have yet encountered."

Mary forwarded the letter to Gertrude, who wrote to Dorothy,
"I note that the institution functions to your satisfaction. Josef,
bottled up away from kitchen noises, without the separate entrance for his comings and goings is evidently not the Josef who
would a roving go, as per premarital plans. This is a wonderful
step forward. The whole place must be charming and I con-
gratulate you . . . I have the picture of you — a complete one,
certain, clear — not a nuance to darken it . . ."

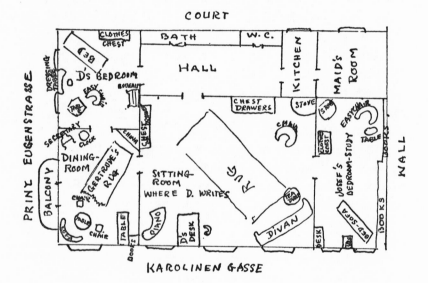

🎄 3
Star Reporter

"I THOUGHT my newspaper would fire me learning I was marrying," Dorothy wrote to Mary Gawthorpe. "But with proper feministic impulse they gave me a raise."

The increase in pay was well-earned. In the preceding six months her daily cabled dispatches, which had regularly made the front page, were followed by a stream of lively Sunday features. She had even, in the autumn of 1921, scored a worldwide scoop.

Half a century later, the heavy lenses of Fodor's eyeglasses were misted over as he proudly recalled his protégée's exploit. "Nobody but Dorothy could have done it," he said, modestly minimizing his own role. "I was on the Budapest-Vienna train when I noticed a tall fellow with a Van Dyke beard getting off at a small station in the Burgenland. It wasn't a regular stop. I recognized him as Count Apponyi, an important Hungarian politician and a great royalist. As soon as I got to Vienna, I hurried to Dorothy's flat. As we were trying to figure out what this meant, one of my men phoned to say that King Charles had — for the second time — arrived from Switzerland and was going to make another try for the Hungarian throne. He was now at Count Apponyi's estate. We took the next train to Budapest."

Every other journalist in the area did the same. But there was little of consequence to report, for the coup had again failed when Admiral Horthy, who had promised Charles his support, had a change of heart. Instead of marching triumphantly tc Budapest without opposition, as he had been led to expect,

Charles's *opéra bouffe* army was ignominiously routed. Now he and his wife Zita were held incommunicado in the Eszterhazy castle in Tata and all requests for interviews with them were flatly refused. Leaving their colleagues, Dorothy and Fodor went to the Red Cross office where she persuaded Captain Pedlow that the road between Budapest and Tata was strewn with wounded soldiers in desperate need of medical services. Dorothy donned a nurse's uniform; Fodor was given a Red Cross badge and in a car flying the American flag they managed with Pedlow to reach Tata by nightfall. Dorothy insisted that as part of their mission they must try to insure the safety of the royal captives. For this humanitarian purpose they were admitted to the castle where Dorothy interviewed Charles and Zita at length. When the three visitors left, Charles entrusted them with a telegram addressed to the oldest of his seven children: *"Seiner Kaiserliche Hoheit Erzherzog Otto, Pragins, Schweiz: Mama und ich wohl. Sei nicht besorgt. Küsse. Vater and Mutter"* (Mama and I are well. Don't worry. Kisses. Father and Mother).

With communications in Hungary disrupted, Fodor hastened back to Vienna to put his and Dorothy's story on the wire. It would appear on the front page of the Manchester *Guardian* and the Philadelphia *Ledger* a day ahead of any other paper and at least twenty-four hours before Prince Otto received the parental message.

Dorothy remained in Budapest with Josef. He had arranged an interview for her with Ferenc Molnár, whose play *Liliom* was a current Broadway hit but who preferred the pleasures of "a little flat, a strong cognac and a good black coffee" in his native city to the bright lights of New York. With Josef serving as interpreter Dorothy gathered the components of a "personality" piece for the theater page.

When she mailed it to Beach Conger, who directed the *Ledger*'s Central European operations from Berlin, she wrote,

"I think Molnár has never before been interviewed, although his plays have an enormous vogue in the U.S. and a new one is to appear shortly. I hope you'll like it . . . a local newspaper asked him for an interview later, and he gave them my questions and his answers and the interview was printed in three Budapest papers, as from the Philadelphia *Ledger.* Then a Hungarian paper in Vienna copied it . . ."

Later she spun a 7000-word feature article out of the Charles-Zita episode. In this account, Pedlow and Fodor vanished from the script. "The writer is able to reproduce the story of the mad adventure as it was recounted to her by the adventurers themselves, gathered around the teatable in the Esterhazy Castle in Tata where King Karl and Queen Zita were first taken prisoners, thus bringing their dash for the throne to an inglorious conclusion . . ." she wrote. "Not even the knowledge of personal danger incurred by stealing through government lines and into the castle under false pretenses could dissipate the unreality which clothed the story, as it unfolded like some thrilling tale of fiction rather than an episode from contemporary history . . ."

This was the beginning of the Thompson legend in which the intrepid girl reporter, braving unimaginable perils to get the news, becomes as much a part of the story as the events she is covering. Within a month, there would be a similar opportunity to appear as a participant in, rather than a mere observer of stirring events.

In Vienna on December 1, 1921, hungry mobs rioted and looted fashionable hotels and shops, in a most un-Viennese show of violence. Fodor and Dorothy rushed to the Ringstrasse as word of the disorders reached them in the café where they were dining with Whitney Shepardson, member of an American trade mission, and his wife. Dorothy was wearing her cherished wildcat coat. To her surprise, a woman stepped out of the mob and warned Dorothy that she would be safer if she were clothed in a less luxurious garment. Moments later a cobblestone crashed through the plate-glass window of the Hotel Sacher. With Shepardson, a towering six-footer, acting as bodyguard, the group retreated to the relative safety of a balcony in the Hotel Bristol. A number of other journalists had gathered there, including Toni Stolper. "Dorothy was in a state of wild excitement," Toni recalled. "She felt she was witnessing a revolution though really it was a minor incident which ended quite peaceably."

"I was down in the midst of it," Dorothy wrote in her follow-up account of the experience, which became even more dramatic in a third version in which she described herself as "caught in the midst of the crowd . . . in a state of almost ecstatic excitement . . ." In later years, when the story was told and retold to interviewers, the cast of characters was changed and her companions became Morris Ernst and Walter Lippmann, whom she did not know at the time and who in December 1921 were not in Vienna.

Distorted though the anecdotes were in the retelling, Dorothy rightly won a name for managing to be on the scene whenever dramatic events were taking place and for pursuing the news without regard to the effort or perils involved. Her Spartan childhood and the rigorous years in the suffrage movement had inured her to the discomforts of travel in the pre-jet age. In fact she loved nothing more than an impromptu journey to an unlikely or hazardous spot. And her energy and initiative were limitless.

"Things were rather exciting last week but are completely quiet now," she wrote to Beach Conger a few days after the Vienna riots. "What would you think of a series on European personalities? I think I could get up a good one, if you'd let me go outside my territory a bit. Arthur Griffith [a leader of the Irish Free State], Richard Strauss, Arthur Schnitzler, Argentina Altobelli (one of the most interesting women I have ever met in my life . . .), Horthy, Ludendorff — mix'em up soldiers, poets, musicians etc. Polovtzeva, a member of the Soviet economic mission in London . . . and a charmer . . . That is in case a revolution doesn't break out here to keep me busy . . ."

Dorothy's office was in her living room, where a steady stream of copy poured from her typewriter without benefit of secretaries. To cover her large territory she had to rely on part-time local correspondents who were unaccustomed to digging for news beyond the periodic tidings that a wolf had eaten a thirteen-year-old child in Herzegovina. If a coup or a revolution seemed imminent, Dorothy dashed off in person to Prague, Sofia, or Salonika. Such impromptu trips became increasingly urgent in 1922 and 1923 as an ominous wave of violence convulsed Europe. Within twelve months, German nationalists assassinated Walter Rathenau, a liberal Jewish cabinet minister, Mussolini assumed dictatorial powers in Rome, and his thugs murdered the Socialist deputy Giacomo Matteotti, who had dared write a book titled *The Fascisti Exposed.*

In the summer of 1922, Dorothy was offered an ideal opportunity to prove her professional mettle when Conger, planning to go on home leave, invited her to fill in for him as acting chief of the *Ledger*'s bureau in Berlin. This was the time of the astronomical currency inflation when the German mark plummeted from its prewar rate of 4.20 to the dollar to billions and even trillions. It was also a time of revolutionary social and political ferment when the mass insanity that had seized the city found expression in the anarchist absurdity of the Dada movement. By comparison Vienna seemed a quiet backwater.

To comprehend and report on the chaos of Berlin was the most challenging assignment that had ever come Dorothy's way and it taxed her energies to the full. When Josef paid her a brief visit, he felt that she scarcely noticed his presence. Back in Vienna, he gave vent to his wounded feelings in affectionately reproachful letters.

"My love," he wrote, "you told me once you would be satisfied with a very simple life, a little house, garden, friends, books, work you like. But as a matter of fact you want much more from life, you are drunken with life, you would grab everything, live in a wild flush and besides — write thoughtful books . . . Something is wrong with us . . ."

4
Exuberant Bride

MANY OF THE TRANSPLANTED MALES who were foreign correspondents had escaped from home ties and responsibilities.
Some acquired local mistresses who were charming bedfellows
and ever-solicitous companions as well as translators and knowledgeable sources of political gossip. Those who were married
were usually blessed with highly functional wives who ran the
household and also typed, clipped newspapers, kept the files in
order, and took telephone messages. A correspondent who happened to be a woman enjoyed no such supporting services.
Josef's wide connections in the literary and artistic worlds of
Budapest and Vienna were helpful. But it was unthinkable for a
European husband to share in domestic chores, particularly
when they had mutually agreed that he was to be sheltered from
any intrusions that would interfere with his own writing. Nonetheless it was her work that paid the bills and had to take priority
over other claims. Although she must have been aware that
Josef bridled at his subordinate role, Dorothy admitted to no
misgivings about her marriage. When her temporary Berlin
assignment ended in early 1923 she returned to the Prinz Eugenstrasse flat ready for uxorious joys and eager to share with her
husband a growing circle of interesting friends. Newcomers to
the group were the poet Louis Untermeyer and his first wife,
Jean Starr, from whom he was later divorced and of whom he
was already weary. Untermeyer was charmed by the Bards.

"Wholesome, hearty, vibrant, apple-cheeked, good-hearted,
open handed were the words Dorothy immediately suggested,"

Untermeyer wrote in his memoir. "She was nearly thirty, a successful journalist and an exuberant bride. At our first meeting she would not discuss anything political. She wanted to talk about her husband . . . [He was] Hungarian-Jewish, suave, slender, black haired and strikingly handsome . . . a delightful companion, a stimulating conversationalist and a brilliantly spontaneous reconteur. Moreover, he was a writer. When we first became acquainted he was preparing a mammoth work on European culture. As I remember it, he was writing it simultaneously in three languages, using three different colored inks, black for German, blue for English and red for French . . . According to the gossips he was also, true to the mid-European bohemian tradition, casually unfaithful. He and Dorothy formed the center of an attractive circle which included not only journalists and authors but artists, actors, opera stars and the prettiest women in Vienna. Few of them could resist Josef; few indeed troubled to make more than the most perfunctory show of resistance. Even Dorothy's best friends succumbed to him, the irresistible embodiment of the romantically susceptible and ever-ready lover."

Since Untermeyer was himself straying from the domestic hearth, he had a natural empathy for Josef's philanderings. But they were not easy for a minister's daughter to accept.

A particularly painful episode occurred when Edna St. Vincent Millay unexpectedly appeared in Vienna. Dorothy adored her sonnets, knew many by heart, and imitated them in her own attempts at poetry. She was delighted when Edna agreed to rework, in verse form, Josef's translations of Hungary's leading poet, Andrew Ady. The collaboration, however, turned out to be more than literary. The three had gone together to Budapest where the hotels were crowded and Dorothy and Edna were forced to share a room. Dorothy recalled the incident years later in her diary.

"She was a little bitch, a genius, a cross between a gamin and an angel. In Budapest she had two lovers . . . both from the embassy. Keeping them apart was a *kunst* [an art]. And we sharing a room . . . She sat before the glass and combed her lovely hair, over and over. Narcissan. She really never loved anyone except herself. Very beautiful with her little white body and her green-gold eyes. 'Dotty, do you think I am a nymphomaniac?' she had asked. Then she comes in a Grecian robe and reads aloud to the Ladies Club, 'Such lips my lips have kissed . . .' And what a sonnet that one was.

"I had to go back to Vienna and I left her the toast of half the town . . . Handed her all I had because she was an angel. A bright angel. She might have left Josef alone, but not that, either. When she came back to Vienna, she twisted a little green ring on her finger. 'Josef gave it to me,' she said absolutely brutally. 'But he really cares for you.' 'It's all right Edna,' I said, 'I know he does.' And I was full of furious tears."

Though she wept in private, she held to the view that Josef's peccadilloes were irrelevant to the grand passion she was experiencing. Others might interpret his infidelity as a revolt against his unmasculine role in the marriage. Dorothy saw herself not as the dominant partner but as a hardworking handmaiden enabling a husband of far greater gifts to do truly creative work.

The tensions in their relationship were, however, apparent even to a casual acquaintance, John Nef, a young American economist who visited Vienna on his honeymoon in 1924. He recalled a lively gathering at the Bards' that included the novelist Ludwig Lewisohn and his pretty young wife and the American Minister Albert Henry and Mrs. Washburn. "Dorothy was attractive but to me there was something hard about her," Nef said. "Suddenly, in the midst of a conversation she said, 'Excuse me for a few minutes, I've got to get an article done.' She disappeared and we could hear her typewriter clacking away. In about a half hour she was back and picked up the thread of the conversation. She was a great talker. Josef was a witty fellow but she dominated the room when she was there. It wasn't comfortable."

5
Dateline Berlin

IF DOROTHY was more than ever absorbed in her work in 1924 there was a good reason for it: she was after a major prize. Conger had decided to return permanently to the United States and one of the choicest posts in Europe was up for grabs. A number of well-qualified correspondents might have succeeded him. A leading candidate was Raymond Gram Swing, the Curtis man in London who had previously spent six years in Berlin for the Chicago *Daily News* and the New York *Herald.* (Following his marriage to Betty Gram in 1920, he had added her maiden name to his and thenceforth became Raymond Gram Swing.) At twenty-six, red-haired, Texas-born Hubert Renfro (known always as H.R. or Knick) Knickerbocker, representing Hearst's INS in Berlin, had already made a name for his political acumen and knowledge of Germany. An old hand in Berlin was George Seldes of the Chicago *Daily News.* Jay Allen, who would subsequently be acclaimed for his brilliant reportage of the Spanish Civil War, was in Paris, working for the local edition of the *Tribune.* Something of a folk hero to American newspaper readers was dashing Floyd Gibbons, who had roamed Mexico with the bandit-revolutionary Pancho Villa in 1915 and accompanied General John J. Pershing on his punitive expedition the following year. Aboard the S.S. *Laconia* in 1917 when it was torpedoed and sunk by a German U-boat off the Irish coast, he managed, after a night in a small boat, to reach shore and cable a 4000-word eyewitness report of the disaster. A battlefront correspondent in World War I, he had lost an eye

at Château-Thierry and thereafter covered it with a patch —
black by day, white in the evening — which became his trade-
mark and badge of valor (as would happen in the 1960s with
Israeli general Moshe Dayan).

When Dorothy was chosen for the Berlin post she was the first
woman to head a major American news bureau overseas, but no
one questioned her qualifications. Her competitors accepted
her as a peer and became her staunch friends as did the remarkable group of young reporters who subsequently arrived to
create what John Gunther called "the bubbling, blazing days
of American correspondence in Europe." Never before had
there been such an influx of journalistic talent.

Paul Mowrer of the Chicago *Daily News,* when he visited his
home office in the mid-twenties, was astounded to discover that
a foreign post, which only a few years earlier had been considered a risky and unprofitable assignment, was now regarded as a
plum. "So great was the glamour of foreign work," he wrote,
"that half our reporters were bent on appointments in Paris,
London or Rome. Negley Farson got into the service by suggesting a romantic trip by canal and river from Holland to Ro-
mania . . . Bill Stoneman took a room with a Swedish family
in Chicago and then hurried to Stockholm. Another reporter,
John Gunther, impressed by Stoneman's success, saved money
and went to London. As we couldn't just let our people go on
appointing themselves in this way, we held John off for a while,
but to tide him over found him a place with UP and presently
weakened and took him on as a roving correspondent." The
journalists of this period not only covered the news with enthusiasm but also turned out books at an amazing rate. Although few had literary merit, they enjoyed a considerable
vogue and helped make their authors' personalities far better
known to their readers than any prior or subsequent reporters
for the "print media," as they would be classed in the age of
radio and TV. (One of the most successful was Negley Farson's

The Way of a Transgressor, which was a Literary Guild Selection in 1936. However, the only ones destined to stand the test of time were Vincent Sheean's *Personal History* and John Gunther's *Inside* books.) There was an easy camaraderie among the group who, as Gunther put it, "travelled steadily, met constantly, exchanged information, caroused, took in each other's washing and even when most fiercely competitive were devoted friends." Dorothy fitted comfortably in this fraternity whose members were largely her own kind. (Stoneman and Knickerbocker were both Methodist ministers' sons.)

When she went to work in Berlin in early 1925, Dorothy was the Central European representative of two major papers, the Philadelphia *Ledger* and the New York *Evening Post,* which Curtis had bought from Oswald Garrison Villard. Her employers had expressed their confidence with an ample salary and an unusually generous expense account. She hired as her assistant Margaret Goldsmith, a young writer who had recently been displaced by a man at the American Embassy, established Fodor as her representative in Vienna, and set about mastering the complex German situation. There was much to be learned; she agreed with A.P.'s Frederick Kuh, who had also moved from Vienna to Berlin, predicting that "Germany will give us more surprises than Russia."

Berlin was still a bizarre city, renowned for its homosexual and lesbian cafés, for its booted prostitutes of both sexes, and for a profusion of strange cults. But the special madness of the inflation was over. Almost by fiat, a financial genius, Hjalmar Schacht, had stabilized the currency by calling in the old marks — no longer worth the paper they were printed on — and issuing a new mark pegged at 4.20 to the dollar. In the same year, 1924, the Dawes Plan fixed German reparations at what seemed a reasonable level and American loans began to pour in. Spectacular new factories, schools, theaters, and public buildings rose, many designed by the architectural innovators of the Bauhaus School — Ludwig Mies van der Rohe, Le Corbusier, and Walter Gropius (whose wife, Alma Mahler, the champion collector of celebrated husbands, had recently left him to marry the novelist Franz Werfel). Dire unemployment, hunger, and tuberculosis continued to plague slum dwellers. Middle-class Berliners, however, looked the other way. Resigned to the loss of their lifetime savings, they were earning real money again and determined to enjoy the good life while it lasted. Capacity crowds at concert halls applauded Rudolf Serkin, Vladimir Horowitz, and the child prodigy Yehudi Menuhin, playing not only the great classics but the jolting works of Stravinsky, Ravel, Bartok, and Prokofiev. For playwrights, directors, and producers in search of novelty, Berlin was the mecca where Bertolt Brecht and Kurt Weill were collaborating on *The Threepenny Opera* and Max Reinhardt was giving a new dimension to Shakespeare at his Deutsches Theater, with Elisabeth Bergner as Juliet and Fritz Kortner starring as Shylock or Richard III. Those with more daring tastes cheered the songs and gyrations of topless black entertainer Josephine Baker. Berliners also talked proudly of the eminent scientists at their university, particularly of Albert Einstein, whose theory of relativity everyone discussed and no one understood.

Berlin's surface gaiety and prosperity were, in fact, as insubstantial as the mirage of political stability. Loans from abroad would one day fall due. The feeble, unpopular Weimar Republic had been merely shored up by a figurehead president, the aged field marshal Paul von Hindenburg. An illusion of lasting peace rested on the Locarno Pact, which, in 1925, guaranteed the existing borders of Czechoslovakia and Poland, reinforced by the fact that France had begun construction on her German frontier of what was believed an impregnable defense against future aggression — the Maginot Line. The French scheme to foment a separatist movement in the Rhineland had been thwarted as had her effort to speed up reparations payments by occupying the Ruhr. An apparently peaceful and united Germany would soon be admitted to the League of Nations.

But in prison, following the failure of his attempt to seize control of the Bavarian government in collaboration with General Erich von Ludendorff in 1923, Adolf Hitler had written *Mein Kampf,* his blueprint for a very different German future. Released from jail in 1924, he was energetically rebuilding his shattered National Socialist Party. His *Gauleiter* (leader of the district — *Gau*) in Berlin was Joseph Goebbels, the crippled future propaganda chief whose fierce nationalism and loathing for "rootless international Jews" rivaled his chief's. Thousands of unemployed young men were soon persuaded to don brown shirts and were equipped with clubs and spiked rings for use in future street battles.

An enterprising journalist like Dorothy found enough happening in Germany culturally and politically to keep her busy day and night. She made friends in the many layers of Berlin's bureaucracy and cultural life, journeyed to the Ruhr and Rhineland to do a series of firsthand reports, and swapped tips at the Adlon Bar with her journalistic colleagues. A valued instructor in the intricacies of German economics and politics was Edgar Ansel Mowrer, the handsome, scholarly Chicago *Daily News* correspondent and brother of Paul. His witty English-born wife, Lilian, had been trained as an actress. She was now mainly occupied with her small daughter and a lively social life but kept her hand in professionally by reporting on the Berlin stage for a London weekly and occasionally, after the advent of sound films, dubbing English-language dialogue at the UFA studios — where Marlene Dietrich would leap to fame starring with Emil Jannings in *The Blue Angel* under Josef von Sternberg's brilliant direction. Lilian provided Dorothy with an entrée — and frequent free passes — to the fascinating world of the Berlin theater.

The Mowrers, like all her Berlin friends, were aware that Dorothy had a husband though he was seldom seen. During his few visits he took less pleasure than ever in Berlin where his wife was now a considerable personage, spent most of her time dashing between chancelleries and press conferences in pursuit of news, and often filed two stories a day before and after an evening at the theater. With housing in even shorter supply than in Vienna, Dorothy had been unable after many months to find a permanent home and was living in makeshift quarters in a flat at Schiffbauerdamm 28, which the Congers had vacated. It was not a place where Josef could settle down to the life of contemplative writing he said he craved. Dorothy was grieved by his absence and disturbed by rumors about his amorous adventures that reached her via friends in Vienna and Budapest. Yet she continued to assure him when they met that she did not "particularly mind little affairs, if they are discreet, spontaneous and don't influence your feeling toward me . . ."

In December 1925 she went alone to the theater to see the opening of a boisterous new play, *Die Fröhliche Weinberg* (The Merry Vineyard). She described it as "an orgy of sunshine, harvest, love, lewdness, tenderness, satire and gargantuan mirth." Afterward she interviewed the twenty-nine-year-old playwright, sturdy, blue-eyed Carl Zuckmayer, who looked more like the peasants of his native Rhineland than a literary man. That night brought him instant fame and also marked the beginning of a lifelong friendship with Dorothy. "She couldn't have understood much of the language," Zuckmayer said, recalling their meeting, "because most of it was dialect. Still she roared with laughter and I guess the high spirits of the audience were contagious. Later she told me that it had been her first really happy evening for a long time."

This melancholy statement was something of an exaggeration; Dorothy found vast satisfaction in her journalistic adventures and even greater pleasure in recounting them afterward with imaginative embellishments. There was, for instance, the often told tale of the night in May 1926 when she was said to have walked alone in an evening dress and satin slippers through miles of Polish mud to report the military coup masterminded by right-wing general Joseph Pilsudski in Warsaw. Though this was not precisely what happened, the incident was a conspicuous example of her penchant for pursuing the news despite all rigors.

She had gone from Berlin to Vienna for the weekend, possibly in search of Josef or for a visit with Genia Schwarzwald. Saturday night she was at the State Opera with Fodor when they somehow got word of stirring events in Warsaw. Neither had much cash on hand and the banks were, of course, closed. Dorothy had interviewed Sigmund Freud and knew that he generally kept his fees from American patients in currency. She telephoned him and he obliged with a substantial loan. After going back to her hotel to change her clothes, she joined a group of correspondents that included A. R. Decker of the Chicago *Daily News* and Floyd Gibbons. The train came to a halt some fifteen miles from Warsaw, where the reporters managed to hire a ramshackle bus. It overturned en route, spilling out, among other things, the wardrobe trunk Gibbons had brought along since he was not only covering a revolution but planning a permanent escape from the unwelcome attentions of a Viennese lady. The bus was righted in due course and the entire group made it into Warsaw together, Dorothy wearing a tailored suit and flat-heeled shoes.

"We were all working for different papers," Decker said. "Generally we cooperated and most of us thought the idea of scooping each other pretty silly. Even though she made up some of these stories about herself afterward, Dorothy was a lovely girl and a great reporter."

This too was the view of her Berlin colleague George Seldes. "The usual female correspondents relied a great deal on sex attraction," he said. "They got to interview Mussolini via the famous Palazzo Chigi couch. Some of them boasted about it.

Dorothy was different. She was the only woman 'newspaper man' of our time. That was a very high compliment in the pre-women's lib days."

🕸 6
"I think I've died . . ."

PERHAPS BECAUSE OF the nomadic life she had led, Dorothy had an abiding faith in the healing powers of a "real home." She was, accordingly, elated in the spring of 1926 when she finally found a place of her own in Berlin — a sunny duplex at Händelstrasse 8, overlooking the Tiergarten in an elegant and convenient neighborhood. The Mowrers agreed to take the lower floor and Dorothy prepared to move into the upper one. Finally she would be able to play hostess to her growing Berlin circle. She also had renewed hopes for her marriage. In these pleasant surroundings she could surely provide Josef with the serenity he needed. Her Biedermeier furniture, china, and kitchenware, Gertrude's rug, and the antique clock were shipped from Vienna. She splurged on new draperies for Josef's study and a majestic armoire for his wardrobe.

"There was a big chintz couch — rather Victorian and informal," Lilian Mowrer said. "Dorothy had a good maid — Hedwig — and was very chummy with her — she gave a wedding party for her as I remember." Lilian, who was something of a stickler for British formality, found German domestics clumsy. "Their method of waiting on table was to stagger around with everything stacked on a huge tray and load and unload dishes. Dorothy didn't seem to mind their peculiar, rather conceited manners. In fact she took to German ways far more easily than I did," Lilian recalled. "For instance if you had German guests for tea — this was before we had cocktail parties — you always ran out of food. This wasn't because they were *that* hungry. They just couldn't eat standing up. They pulled up chairs to the buffet table and kept their plates full. Dorothy didn't mind. She just sent Hedwig out for more *kalte Aufschnitt* [cold cuts] and cake."

All this *gemütlichkeit,* alas, had no great appeal for Josef. "He was very attractive," Lilian said, "and must have been a rather splendid first lover for Dorothy. But as a husband — well, he just didn't seem to belong in the picture."

Dorothy was off at work most of the day. When she had a free evening the house was filled with guests, including frequent visitors from America. Josef formed a particular aversion for Dorothy's old friend Gertrude Ely, an energetic Philadelphia spinster who was becoming something of a figure in the Pennsylvania Democratic Party and fitted his stereotype of the "suffragette."

In the autumn of 1926, after a far from contented summer, he was off to London to stay with an American artist, Warren Vinton, while Vinton's future wife Helen paid an exchange visit to Dorothy in Berlin. At Vinton's home, Josef met and was much attracted to Eileen Agar, a petite blonde in her early twenties. A painter of some talent and the daughter of a socially prominent British family, she had eloped with a fellow art student. A divorce was imminent. Though her aura and manners were genteel, she had emancipated herself from the formal Mayfair world in which she had been reared and hungered for the cultural riches that Josef seemed to embody. She found his continental charm irresistible and the two were soon lovers.

In early November they went off together for a discreet holiday in the Tyrol. Josef took with him the unfinished manuscript of a novel and assured his wife by letter that he was making excellent progress on it. There are two versions of what followed. According to Fodor, he was in Berlin and declined

Dorothy's invitation to spend the night on the ground that he was eager to get home to Marta. "Thinking about my happy marriage, Dorothy started worrying about her own," Fodor said. "She got Josef on the phone and told him she was going to join him. He told her not to come because he needed to be alone to finish his book. I begged her not to go but she wouldn't listen. She threw things into a suitcase and caught the next train."

In Josef's account, Dorothy discovered that he had a companion through a postcard Eileen sent to the Vintons, who relayed the information. Whichever is the case, when Dorothy arrived at the mountain retreat she learned that Eileen was no passing fancy but a determined young woman who intended to make the relationship permanent. Dorothy returned to Berlin in a state of shock. Lacking a sympathetic female shoulder to weep on, she spent a hard-drinking evening with the first available male, who happened to be the amorous Floyd Gibbons. Reenacting her childhood scenes of guilt and punishment, she made a full confession to Josef when he returned to Berlin. He responded with anger and disgust. Recalling this odd reaction on the part of an admittedly wayward husband, Eileen commented, "The double standards, you know. What a man did in those days didn't matter. But for a woman of Dorothy's high moral standards — shocking!"

Dorothy herself was dismayed by her own wickedness. "I am ashamed of the incident with Floyd, ashamed of the drinking and everything," she wrote to Josef afterward. She saw herself as "a woman who had been absolutely innerly and outwardly loyal to her first love for six years . . . and then suddenly flung herself into the arms of the first wayfarer who not having a prostitute handy happened to want her — into the arms of someone she didn't in the least love, and whom she hopes and prays she'll never see again."

Josef departed for Paris to give the finishing touches to his novel,* hoping Dorothy would come to terms with reality. Instead she continued to dream that their marriage could somehow be patched up. ". . . I say over and over again: 'Josef does not love you; Josef finds you sexually unattractive; Josef has never been true to you; Josef has systematically sought for two years to find another woman who would give him more satisfactory love and a little financial assistance and make him free of you,' " she wrote. "You were just a bridge to Josef. Just a tool. And now it's over, it's all over . . .

"And my stubborn, stubborn, arrogant heart cries: No! No! You are *the* wife, *the* friend, *the* sweetheart-mother for Josef. Silly to treat him as a man. Silly Eileen treating him as a man. She will not love him in the end — only some one can love Josef who is so much stronger than he that his weakness cannot hurt her. Only someone can love Josef who can hold him against her breast . . . Silly Josef to say he must get away from his mother. No man ever cuts the umbilical cord completely. Silly Josef. He sought in me a new mother who should have born him over into a new race . . .

"And when this endless debate has squeezed the blood from my heart and set my temples pounding then I go to a mirror and say, 'And you, Dorothy?' And then I like myself, my body that is sturdy and strong, my head which is high again and free, and my eyes that have the sea in them. And I say, 'You Dorothy have gone straight ways in your stupidities and in your sins. You, Dorothy be proud. You, Dorothy, be a *mensch*.' "

Emotional stress produced physical symptoms that her Berlin doctor diagnosed as the possible onset of a serious cardiac ailment. Genia Schwarzwald was alarmed by Dorothy's appearance and mental state when she came to Vienna over Christmas. She sank into an almost suicidal depression when Josef used Genia as an intermediary to break the news that he wanted not a mere separation but a divorce. At Genia's urging she consulted Dr.

* *Shipwreck in Europe* (Harper, New York, 1928).

Theodor Reik, one of the city's leading Freudian psychoanalysts. The experience brought to the surface but did little to resolve painful doubts about her own sexuality.

"If you're going to be a novelist why not analyze what happened to a girl who became all woman in your arms," she wrote to Josef, "and was then thrown back into a semi-homosexual state by Budapest eroticism? . . . Why did you teach me all those tricks, throwing me back into infantile narcissism, into an adolescent homosexuality which would have been completely overcome? Which *was* overcome?" *

Back in Berlin, Dorothy was distressed to find that the news of her broken marriage was common gossip although she herself had not fully accepted it. Josef had gone to London to join Eileen, leaving behind his books, his Airedale, Rolf, and — quite heartlessly it seemed — all his letters from Dorothy. Nonetheless she continued to write, telling him, after an evening at a concert, "I came home. There was a bottle of Burgundy, some cold meat and apples; but emptiness is everywhere, and I did not uncover the plates, so nicely set by Hedwig. In all Berlin, amongst all friends, Hedwig is my only *trost* [solace]. *'Der Herr Doktor,' sie sagt, 'Hat die Gnadige Frau schrecklich gern, und ich glaube er wird bald zurich kommen'* ['The doctor,' she says, 'is terribly fond of the gracious lady, and I believe he will come back soon.'] . . . The house is empty Josef. Such a nice little flat made for you. Almost all the bills are paid . . . I wonder what I shall do with this career which was made to build a home, to help create a mutual life! Curious how I believed in our marriage. As in God . . . Every day I must say over to myself: You aren't married any more . . . It is worn out and over. Even the little fur coat which I bought before our marriage isn't worn out. Curious that a marriage

---

* In a diary that she kept in 1932 at the time of a similar episode there is a reference to a brief "sapphic" relationship with a woman identified only as F that took place in Berlin at Schiffbauerdamm 28 in 1925 or 1926.

should not survive a dead catskin . . . In all the world only I whom you have hurt most cruelly can smile and forgive you. And only you can see that I'm not a successful journalist but just a little wilful girl ready to fight for her playmate . . . I don't think you love Eileen so much, I think you love me . . ."

Friends from Vienna rallied to lend moral support, among them Dorothy Burlingham, Phyllis Bottome, the ever-kindly Genia, the painter Oskar Kokoschka, and surprisingly Karlie Geyersbach, a young opera singer, understudy to Jeritza, and a one-time flame of Josef's. Dorothy also picked up the threads of correspondence that had lapsed during her preoccupation with Josef. To Rose Lane, who had gone in search of adventure to the Albanian capital, Tirana, she wrote: "Nights now for me are terrors toward which I look through dully aching days. And so, to ease the terror I looked through old letters and manuscripts and found amongst them a letter from you . . . on the subject of marriage. And fascinated I read it through wondering at how little impression it had made upon me in those heydays of love, wondering at how illuminating your analysis was and how bitter the prediction. For here I stand, dear Rose, thirty-two years old, and alone. Josef has gone. Just like that — gone. He did not take even my photograph,* not any of the little things I gave him . . . and something queer has happened to me. I think I've died . . . there are his shirts back from the laundry which I ought to pack up and send to him in London, and the bathrobe smelling of him, and the flat just furnished small, and intimate, with an office for me in town so I wouldn't disturb him."

In reply, Rose urged Dorothy to visit her in Albania, which had just been proclaimed a republic and whose first president, Ahmed Zogu, would shortly be crowned King Zog. But Dorothy, for the moment, had lost her appetite for strange people

---

* She was wrong on this point. Josef kept a considerable collection of photographs of Dorothy.

and places; she needed companions in sorrow. One such was Gertrude Tone, who still considered herself Dorothy's "sister, mother, guide, philosopher and friend" despite a long hiatus in their correspondence. "I am miserable too," Gertrude wrote, offering her distillation of Freudian balm. ". . . Miserable indeed is she whose transference refuses dissolution and whose love and hate, ego strivings and deflations attach themselves . . . where they can be directed around one person and situation. With which sententious confession of a common slavery with you, I should say no more . . . *Why, why* don't you learn from me? Though Josef and you, and Frank and I in the details of the picture are as wide apart as you wish, the mechanisms are the same . . . in your last letter when you wrote of divorce, I was glad; but you don't speak of it in this. Why?"

Dorothy had often assured Josef that she would gladly give him his freedom whenever he really wanted it. But it proved hard to let go. "We were just about to file the final petition for divorce this morning when your letter arrived," Dr. Vambery wrote from Budapest on April 30, 1927. "I do not feel authorized to disentangle the wires conducting to the secret places of your heart . . . It cannot be my business to analyze your or Joseph's feelings . . . I take the matter from the lawyer's point of view and do my best to follow your instructions. As matters stand this petition can be kept in abeyance until you wish."

Only a few weeks earlier Dorothy had told Josef, "I know how to let go. That's the gentleman in me, if you like. I'm no Jeannie Untermeyer. You're as free as air, Josef."

Now Dorothy found herself a sister in sorrow of poor, clinging Jeannie, who had been again forsaken by the errant Louis. In the plaintive accents of the German *lieder* she still hoped to sing on the concert stage, even though her blunt husband insisted that she had "everything but a voice." Jeannie wrote from New York:

"Oh Dorothy — *Nur wer die Sehnsucht kennt* . . . I take

you mentally in my arms and speak tenderly to you . . . My
darling child I know your every pain . . . Oh darling Dorothy
you are so full of richness in yourself — you are — Louis and
I agreed — like the heroine of a book we just read. You have
the 'honey of life in your heart.' "

7

"Die Zeit Eilt, Die Zeit Heilt"

IN A MOSAIC over the front door of the Händelstrasse apartment was a motto that would prove appropriate: "Time flies, time heals." Her intimates found Dorothy still disconsolate but socially and professionally she seemed as ebullient as ever. She was the center of much flattering attention as, for instance, when a German diplomat, Baron Adolf von Maltzan addressed a meeting of the American Club and opened his remarks with the salutation, "Excellency, Gentlemen, and Dorothy." *

A variety of agreeable young men were ready to console a heartbroken but attractive and important American correspondent. Among them was a young scientist, Berthold Wiesner and a musician, Richard Bühlig. Count Karolyi of Hungary was in Berlin and a frequent guest at Dorothy's dinner table. Most charming of all was Count Helmuth von Moltke, great-grandnephew of the famous field marshal whose armies had defeated France in 1870. "I saw him often at Dorothy's," Lilian Mowrer said. "He was a handsome lad with very dark hair and eyes and very tall — he must have been 6 foot 7 or so. I think Dorothy first met him at Genia's country place, Grundelsee — she took in very select paying guests after the Schwarzwalds lost their money in the inflation. Helmuth had a delightful sense of humor which is rare in a German, a Prus-

---

* Von Maltzan, chief architect of the Russo-German pact signed at Rapallo in 1922, was characterized as "shifty-eyed and cynical" by Edgar Mowrer. When he was killed in a plane accident in 1927, Dorothy, who had a much greater empathy for Germans, described him as "a clever man and a good hearted soul."

sian." In other respects, too, he was the antithesis of the stereotype of a Junker — idealistic, international-minded, and attracted to Christian socialism. At twenty, he had shouldered
responsibility for the bankrupt family estate at Kreisau, and in
his personality and character he epitomized for Dorothy all
that was admirable in the German character.

She developed lasting relationships with other remarkable
men and women, some of whom would form the nucleus of a
private international intelligence network, others destined to
become ornaments of the salons she would one day establish
in New York and Vermont. Among them were Baroness Moura
Budberg (the great love of Maxim Gorki and later of H. G.
Wells), who was often in Berlin in the twenties; Harold Nicolson, who had joined the British Embassy staff; Shepard Morgan
(right-hand man to Parker Gilbert, the all-powerful reparations
commissioner) and his wife Barbara. Her Vienna acquaintances
Gustav and Toni Stolper had transplanted their economic journal to Berlin. And at the Adlon Bar she first met a writer six
years her junior who would play a unique role in her life,
James Vincent Sheean. Known to his friends as Jimmy, he was
then midway in the reportorial travels that would bring
him fame as the author of *Personal History*. He was immediately interested and amused by this very self-assured and
pretty woman. They had a long talk — the forerunner of many
such dialogues — about politics, world affairs, and cultural
differences. Sheean was taken aback when Dorothy wound up
the conversation with the comment: "Well, from the point of
view of God, I suppose all human differences are insignificant."
Though this pious statement seemed out of character, Dorothy,
who rarely attended church, always had God very much on
her mind. A project close to her heart — but never fulfilled —
was a book she hoped to write, based on interviews with the
world's leading statesmen about their concept of the Deity.

It was not, however, her faith in the Almighty nor the distractions of social life but the stern discipline of her job that in due course restored her emotional equilibrium. "Good old work," she wrote to Josef. "I hated it so, and nagged at it, and felt it kept me from higher things, and despised it in comparison with yours: in fact I was thoroughly treacherous to my work — but it stood by and doesn't let me down. Good old routine, good old head that functions automatically at the sight of a newspaper, fills up hours of my day with forgetfulness . . ."

In May 1927 Dorothy went to Geneva, where representatives of fifty nations had gathered for an economic conference. Around this time, Eileen was growing weary of being portrayed by Dorothy and her friends as the scheming "other woman" and having Josef condemned as a heartless philanderer. A face-to-face talk with the "wronged wife" seemed in order. "I liked and admired Dorothy," Eileen said. "I had to convince her I was no husband stealer."

The confrontation that took place in Dorothy's Geneva hotel room was handled with surprising aplomb by both participants. "We got along very well," Eileen said. "In fact Josef was a bit worried because we became so friendly. Dorothy told him I was just as much a career woman as she."

This was not quite the case. By Eileen's standards, cosseting a male ego had a higher priority than exhibiting her paintings, though, over the years, she managed to do both. A contented Josef, it turned out, could also be a faithful husband.*

There is no mention of this encounter in Dorothy's papers. Later she described Eileen as a "charming and sensitive" woman and maintained an amiable social relationship with the Bards throughout her life. Dorothy was incapable of vindictiveness. Bitter though her letters to Josef might be, at the same time she wrote magnanimously to Phyllis Bottome: "I cannot hate Josef. I cannot get over my queer feeling of responsi-

* They were married in due course and were enjoying domestic felicity in London when I visited them there in 1971.

bility for him . . . The death of a love is a very slow cruci-
fixion, and mine was a very full-blooded love. And somehow,
I am also to blame . . . I would not be happy if I felt that
Josef would lose any friends through me . . ."

In late May she experienced an unexpected change in mood
of which she later wrote to Rose Lane, "I think I was in the
worst and lowest state of mind that I have ever been in. I was
coming back to Berlin from Geneva . . . The thought of the
office and the job, the senseless circularness of life and its emptiness; the feeling of eternal repetition, and the chains of the
emotional state I was in, and could not break, were almost
driving me mad. At midnight we reached Basel, and without
knowing how or why, I threw my bags out of the window and
got out, leaving the train on which I had a sleeper and a ticket.
In the morning I took a tiny train and went to Bodensee, down
along the Rhine. It was the jolliest, gayest morning, with the
sun glinting on the stream, and all the tiny, ancient villages
crowding to its waters, and suddenly, quite incomprehensibly,
I felt happy . . ."

Filled with a new sense that "the world is wide and beautiful," she composed a sonnet.

> How grand it is this falling out of love —
> This falling out of you into the world!
> I had forgotten how the rivers move,
> I had forgotten how a leaf is curled,
> I think I had forgotten that the sun
> Is warmer than the beaming of your eyes,
> And that the inmost soul of anyone
> Is not the sum of all the mysteries.
> Now I can celebrate again the rites
> Of the world's loving; share its ecstacies;
> Melt to the phallic strength of Dolomites,
> Warm to the manly tenderness of trees.
> Even for you my love may yet revive,
> Seeing you part of everything alive.

PART IV

NEW HORIZONS

🌀 1
"He opens a future for me . . ."

SINCE HER CHILDHOOD, birthdays had been important occasions to Dorothy. She had seldom been in the mood for festivities during her marriage to Josef, but in the summer of 1927, as July 9 neared and she was about to turn thirty-four, she was resigned to the divorce and a celebration seemed in order. She liked best a dinner party for eight or ten and loved working out the details of a gala menu with her cook — a beautifully clear consommé or potage? Roast veal or venison? An interesting salad — perhaps a rémoulade of celery root? Rhine wine or burgundy? With these questions nicely settled, she assembled a guest list of matching international distinction: two Hungarians, Baron Hatvany and Count Karolyi, the Prussian Helmuth von Moltke and his distinguished mother, English-born Countess Dorothy, and three American colleagues — her neighbors, the Mowrers, and red-headed H. R. Knickerbocker, whose wife Laura was in Moscow on a journalistic assignment of her own.

Dorothy was indebted to Knick for producing the most valued guest — the novelist Sinclair Lewis. He had recently introduced them at a foreign office press conference, Dorothy had afterward interviewed Lewis, and they had dined together at the Adlon. Throughout the birthday party, which lasted far into the night, Lewis gazed at her with open rapture. Next morning, Dorothy told Lilian Mowrer that after the other guests had left Lewis had asked her to marry him. She was amazed and, naturally, flattered. For Harry Sinclair Lewis —

known to most of his friends as Red but usually called Hal by Dorothy — at the age of forty-two occupied a unique position in the literary world.

Main Street, published in 1920, had touched a contemporary American nerve as no novel had done before and probably none has since. It was withering satire documented with photographic realism that brought into question the whole value system of traditional rural America. The same technique won brilliant success for the books that followed — *Babbitt* in 1922, *Arrowsmith* in 1925. Carol Kennicott, George F. Babbitt, and Martin Arrowsmith became living characters in a new, self-doubting American folklore. Translated into many languages, the books were widely read throughout Europe. *Elmer Gantry,* which had just appeared in 1927, also caused a furor.

To meet the author in person was a memorable experience. Some were repelled by his gaunt frame, his carrot-colored hair, and his beet-red face pitted by precancerous lesions. But others were enchanted by his wit, his sympathetic concern for anyone who interested him, and his talent for mimicry. He could be a boorish monster during periodic drinking bouts and the most delightful and considerate of companions when sober. Though his writings caricatured his native Middle West and he had traveled widely abroad, his more sophisticated fellow writers thought him, at heart, provincial. "He really *was* Babbitt," Anita Loos said. "Mencken and I used to laugh about him. He was so *square*." One element in the affinity between Lewis and Dorothy may have been their common background in small-town America.

When they met, Lewis was seeking a divorce from his first wife, Grace Hegger, whose social and intellectual snobbery he had come to detest. In contrast, Dorothy's style was simple, direct, and unaffected; she was formidably self-confident but also free of vanity and pretense.

It was a whirlwind courtship sometimes conducted in public.

At a dinner in his honor, Lewis startled his audience with a one-sentence speech: "Dorothy, will you marry me?" A week after the birthday he had a foretaste of the rigors facing the suitor of an energetic foreign correspondent. Fodor had telephoned from Vienna with news of an ominous mass demonstration that had followed the acquittal of three Nationalists accused of murdering two socialist deputies. Incited by militant and probably Communist leaders, the rioters set fire to the magnificent palace of justice and the police, for the first time in Vienna's history, fired on the mob. Nearly a hundred fatalities resulted. A general strike was called, and further clashes seemed imminent, both contenders in this civil strife having organized private armies — the Christian Socialists' *Heimwehr* (which would one day help deliver Austria to Hitler) and the Social Democrats' *Schutzbund*.

It was a story Dorothy could not bear to miss. She chartered a plane and John and Frances Gunther came to the airport to see her off as did Lewis. At the last moment he decided to join her, though he had never flown before and was terrified by the prospect. Frances Gunther went along — as chaperone it was said — an odd precaution, for Dorothy and Lewis shared a suite at Sacher's and all Vienna was aware that she was embarking on a new romance. A large part of the world was let in on the secret when the eminent novelist, as a gesture of love, filed four stories at space rates for Dorothy's papers. They were mainly encomiums to the beautiful, blue-eyed Curtis correspondent; he did, however, produce one memorable report of the moonlit mass funeral of the dead policemen and workers. Fodor, Marta, and Genia Schwarzwald were overjoyed to find that her distinguished suitor had restored Dorothy's joie de vivre; if there were misgivings about his nightly drinking bouts, they were not mentioned.

Dorothy returned to Berlin in high spirits. Sigrid Schultz, who had been George Seldes' assistant and succeeded him as chief of the Chicago *Tribune*'s bureau when he was transferred to Rome, has vivid memories of an afternoon when they met in the Adlon Bar. Sigrid, who lived in maidenly propriety with her mother, sipped a "Schultz special" — grenadine-tinted orange juice — while Dorothy downed beer or schnapps. Two men, she told Sigrid, wanted to marry her — the first was contemplating divorce, the second had not yet decided. Sigrid cast her vote in favor of number one who was, of course, Lewis. The other, she guessed, was Knickerbocker, whose wife was unhappy about his attentions to Dorothy. "We must all pull together to make this work," Laura said when she learned of the Lewis-Thompson romance.

Dorothy agreed to spend her August vacation with Lewis on a walking tour in Shropshire and Cornwall. But he was not mentioned in a letter to her sister Peggy Wilson on August 1, in which she rhapsodized over a recently received photo of her new niece, Pamela, and urged Peggy to visit her in Berlin since she had no plans to return to the States. "Just now I begin to live again," she wrote. "I have a nice life, and work and interests . . . Everybody has been heavenly to me. I never knew I had so many friends; even two or three nice men have wanted to marry me . . ."

Josef, however, who had been kept posted about the new suitor and was properly awed by his renown, urged Dorothy to visit him at his rural retreat near Eastbourne when they came to England. "And bring Sinclair along," he suggested. Eileen, equally cordial, offered the loan of her London flat complete with "a decrepit old Italian maid, rather inclined to drip salt tears into the soup, but otherwise quite a good cook — I would love to think of you there . . ."

Whether or not the invitation was accepted there was an amicable meeting between current swain, ex-husband, and his lady. And the walking trip proved a happy experience. Lewis was romantically attached to England, loved walking, drank no hard liquor, and proved himself a marvelous companion. He extended the tour into the Rhineland and persuaded his good friends, the poet Ramon Guthrie and his wife Marguerite, to keep him company when Dorothy had to return to her job.

Early in September Lewis and Guthrie were back in Berlin and found quarters in Herkules Haus in Charlottenburg. In her diary, which she resumed, Dorothy wrote: "He occupies my mind continuously . . . since my return from England, he and he alone intervenes in my dreams . . . J. never took me wholly — he knew he couldn't digest me. That was both wise and magnanimous . . . Anyway I love Hal and belong to him."

There was a succession of dinner parties in Händelstrasse where, with Lewis as a special attraction, the guest lists included such visiting celebrities as Lady Diana Manners, star of Reinhardt's production *The Miracle,* the English novelist Arnold Bennett, and Lord Beaverbrook, the most powerful of British newspaper publishers in the years between the two wars. Unfortunately Lewis was drinking heavily again. In painful detail Dorothy recorded in her diary an evening when he was too unsteady to escort her to a very grand party and she was forced to spend a harrowing night in his apartment. A few days later, however, she persuaded herself that he had hit bottom and that this was the beginning of reform. "H. has kept his word since that day," she wrote. "God, how I adore him for it."

She described Lewis as not only intellectually but physically appealing, referring to his "long figure, leaning a little to the wind, the narrow face with its wound of a mouth, its jutting nose, its furroughs like red earth disturbed by an inner volcano, its shining eyes, blue as colorless water, with their changing pupils, the gestures of his tender, long-fingered hands . . ."

Her tone was less lyrical when she wrote to Rose Lane, comparing her current emotions with her feelings for Josef. "It isn't quite the same. I approach life with more humor. This is a gain and a loss. I cannot ever again reach into that transcendental state of feeling myself one, flesh of flesh and eyes of eyes of another individual. I am not nearly so much 'in love' — whatever that may mean. I cannot stretch my imagination to believe that SL is the most beautiful person in the world. I know him to be compounded of bad habits, weaknesses, irritabilities, irritancies. But he pleases me. He is a superb comrade. He amuses me: first requirement in a husband. He heightens my sense of life. He opens a future for me, so that for the first time in years, I dream of tomorrow, as well as enjoy today. Thus he gives me back the gift of youth."

2
Moscow, at Last

WHATEVER MISGIVINGS Dorothy may have had about Lewis as a husband were laid to rest in the autumn of 1927, when she agreed to marry him. No date could be set for the wedding and the engagement was, in theory, secret since he was not yet divorced. Dorothy was about to undertake a coveted assignment — a trip to the Soviet Union to report on the tenth anniversary of the Bolshevik Revolution on November 7. Leaving Lewis in Berlin, where he had begun work on *Dodsworth,* she was off in late October to fulfill the dream she and Barbara De Porte had nurtured when they boarded the S.S. *Finland* in 1920. The perspective would, to be sure, be quite different from the one they had planned, a fresh look at the "little people" by two obscure, wide-eyed young reporters. Dorothy was now a major journalist, living in such elegance as Moscow could offer at the Grand Hotel. She had no Russian-speaking companion to serve as her independent eyes and ears but had to rely on interpreters, official handouts, and conducted tours. But she had an undiminished curiosity about what she called "that stupendous drama of which the ten long years since the revolution have been but the prologue."

That decade had witnessed the great famine of 1920–1921, followed by the New Economic Policy, which had brought with it an improvement in living standards still evident in 1927. Lenin's death in 1924 had triggered the power struggle between Stalin and Trotsky that would be resolved at the year's end with the former's triumph and the latter's exile. The rigors of Stalinist purges, of successive five-year plans, and the collectivization of farms were still in the future. Soviet leaders were eager to display their accomplishments to the world press and an abundance of American experts were ready to advise and explain. On the one hand were such enthusiasts as Scott Nearing, Henry Longfellow Dana, and Anna Louise Strong, who saw the Soviet Union as a showplace for the most advanced European ideas, where impressive experiments in education and the treatment of criminals were under way, where divorce was obtainable by mutual consent (a measure that anti-Bolsheviks denounced as the "nationalization of women"), where the theater of Meyerhold, the films of Eisenstein and Pudovkin, and superb ballet and opera flourished. Others found these achievements outbalanced by the harsh realities of a dictatorial police state and a relentless propaganda machine. This was the view of Junius Wood, resident correspondent of the Chicago *Daily News,* and Paul Scheffer, the cynical correspondent of the *Berliner Tageblatt.* Dorothy listened to all, made the most of every opportunity to see for herself, took voluminous notes, and produced a series of articles for the New York *Evening Post* (later expanded into a book, *The New Russia*) that gave her readers the sense of sharing an exciting trip as seen through the very American eyes of a keen observer who made no claim to infallibility.

"The first Soviet celebration which I attended reminded me of nothing so much as the end of a sleighride party arranged by the Ladies' Aid of the church, as I remember it from my childhood," she wrote. ". . . one had more the feeling of returning to the old home town after a long absence than of entering the land which is the home of the World Revolution . . . the porters on the trains, in blouses and boots are extremely kind. 'Could I have some tea, comrade,' one asks and the comrade brings the tea. He is not tipped. I can remember such conductors on branch lines in up-state New York, not long ago . . . At the opera, the audience is dressed much as a Middle Western small town audience at a church festival might be garbed; modestly but decently." Ever food-conscious, she shared with her public the gustatory pleasures of a supper at a foreign office reception, "Red pyramids of crab, three sorts of caviar, delicious salads, roasted snipes and partridges; hot dishes of cabbage and pork in savory sauces brought in smoking casseroles; magnificent fruits, fresh and in sirups, foreign wines and wines of the sunny Crimea; sixty year old vodka with something of the aroma of old cognac . . ."

Life was strenuous but rewarding. "Such days!" she wrote to Lewis. "Yesterday, for instance. In the morning foreign office trying to get interviews with Tchicherin [the foreign minister] and Rykov [an old Bolshevik executed as a Trotskyite in 1938]. Then to the Pedagogical Seminar for a list of schools to visit. Then to an exhibition of the art of the Russian nationalities . . . then to an ancient monastery . . . Then to lunch — or whatever one may call this extraordinary meal which one eats between four and six and which is the only meal of the day . . . Then an opera — the Love for the Three Oranges, and before that an international congress of the Friends of Russia and at midnight to an artist's club in Moscow's Greenwich village . . ."

"You go gallivanting to strange lands and I sit home nursing the baby," Lewis replied. "T'aint right! But it's such a good baby — i.e. the planning is done and I'm actually writing the novel itself . . . The Nation just came with your Hindenburg birthday article. It's superb . . . Dear Waffle [a private nickname], there isn't an hour when I don't miss you. Du, *du* — I kiss you." He was bored by an evening with Frank Harris, author of a spicy memoir of Oscar Wilde and a sexually explicit autobiography, *My Life and Loves*. However, Lewis liked Dorothy's friend Count Max von Montgelas, editor of the Berlin tabloid *Zeitung am Mittag*, who had once worked for

Hearst in America. By way of souvenirs, Lewis asked Dorothy to collect Russian stamps for his seven-year-old son Wells and vodka labels for H. L. Mencken.

"Hal, I miss you so," she replied. "There is more company good and bad here than one needs, and more to see than I ever did find, and more to think about and talk about than in most places — why do I have these wistful moments when I feel like taking the next train home? The experience is so unique for me, I wish you were sharing it, as I wish for your sharing everything which is beautiful or stimulating . . . I shall snatch labels off all the vodka bottles that come my way and pilfer stamps . . . My love to the 'good baby' . . . This being morning, and I being energetic, I give you a tiny and very fast little kiss; on the nose . . ."

Lewis' wife Grace was depressed by the prospect of Reno. "Anyway, at least we've accomplished this, this past year, she and I," Lewis wrote to Dorothy, "come to realize definitely that we can not, never, by any possibility, get along together, live together; that there is no use in trying, that there would be no use trying even *were* there no Dorothy to give me life . . ." He parodied their mutual preoccupation with past loves:

" 'Curious how dull we are in realizing our own relations to people . . .'

" 'Yes — now with Joseph —'

" 'Now you look here. It's *my* day to talk about Gracie.'

" 'All right, sweet, I won't mention Joseph. I was merely going to say about Joseph —'

" 'Ah gee, let's talk about ourselves . . . Funny — we born Puritans, how hard it is for us to take the happiness we have.'

" 'I'm *not* a Puritan, not by a long shot. But you are. You bet I'm going to take my happiness. Where shall we go to dinner? What do you think of a nice bottlewine at Turk's?'

" 'You lamb!' "

He had dinner with the historians Charles and Mary Beard

and proudly reported their eagerness to meet the distinguished Miss Thompson. Loyally, he belittled the only professional rival of her own sex on the Berlin scene. Reporting on a wine-drinking evening with Ramon Guthrie, he wrote: "Talked with Guido [Enderis, correspondent of A.P. and later the *New York Times*] and with Sigrid Schultz — a dull woman — says Ramon 'She's the girl from back home.' That's it exactly; she's Main Street not one tiny bit changed by artist father, by correspondence, by furrintongues. And then who shd come in but John Drinkwater [the British poet and dramatist best known in America for his historical play *Abraham Lincoln*] . . . I've known him for years. He *looks* so nice and intelligent and when I meet him it's always a quarter of an hour before I remember that he's a pompous and brainless ass. Schluss . . . I'd rather have Guido than six dozen Sigrids and Drinkwaters put together . . ."

Ben Huebsch of Viking turned up in Berlin looking, among other things, for someone to translate *PEP,* an amusing little book of satirical verse that had made a considerable local stir. Subtitled *An American Song Book* by J. L. Wetcheek, it was actually a spoof by the German novelist Lion Feuchtwanger (the pseudonym being an English translation of his own name).

"Ben Huebsch *very* much wants you to translate PEP," Lewis wrote. "Can't you work it in, say in February." Much as he yearned to see her, he hesitated to join her because, he said, "I'd cramp your style in viewing the country horribly if I were there — you'd want to show me what you've already seen, instead of going to new things. Get it done and come to me —"

He urged her to shorten her stay but Dorothy rejoined, "Russia is stirring: I am working awfully hard, eating, thinking and breathing Russia — am more confused, more questioning, more doubtful of the verity of any impression, any sound. I find myself caring very much that this work should be good; and I'm desperately afraid it won't be. Terribly as I want to see you, too, I think two weeks' stay is much too little to be worth the journey . . .

"I want to come home. I am homesick. I am Hal-sick . . . I think all the time back in my mind, while I am visiting schools and talking to concessionaires all the time about us. Hal, I feel very humble. If I can ever be to you just a fraction of what I want to be, you will have a good wife. I love to work honeyest — only this separation is really too long. Even though you're so vividly with me. I bought some more linen, for the house, for our house . . ."

Lewis replied, "You speak of buying linens for OUR HOUSE — yes! it will be and before not long . . . God how I would love it! To walk, to fuss about a steamy barn, to look from clear windows at the curving frosted hills, to taste the sweet cold air, then to run away, but only for a hectic week, to New York! with plays in some known language . . . I enclose another *Nation* ad indicating that for even less than thirty thousand we shall probably be able to get a duck of a place. It's almost funny the excited way in which I look at these ads now . . ."

When Dorothy had been gone a month, Lewis could bear her absence no longer. On November 27 he telegraphed: "Fifty thousand words done and cannot endure longer without you leaving for Moskau tomorrow . . ."

Lewis did not share Dorothy's enthusiasm for the Soviet scene although his works were popular in Russia and he was greeted at the station by a delegation from the Soviet Society for Cultural Relations. When asked why he had come to Moscow, he is said to have replied, "To see Dorothy, just Dorothy."

It is unlikely that he saw a great deal of her during his ten-day stay. She was in the throes of assimilating her voluminous notes. She had accumulated a host of new friends, among them Theodore Dreiser, whose novel *An American Tragedy* had achieved immense success two years earlier. He was, Dorothy

said, "quite a gay dog . . . with a genuine — if rather elephantine — sense of humor." Vincent Sheean, in contrast,
found Dreiser at fifty-six "a pompous old bore." Sheean had
come to Moscow to rejoin Rayna Prohme, the young American
radical whom he had met earlier that year in China and who
had, in his words, "become all important to me, not only in the
personal sense . . . but in every convolution of thought, every
pulse of being . . ." Rayna had escaped to Moscow with Madame Sun Yat-sen, widow of the founder of the Chinese Republic, when the Nationalists drove the left forces out of the Kuo-
mintang. Rayna had made up her mind to join the Communist
Party, a step Sheean dreaded and from which he hoped to dis-
suade her. The argument was tragically ended by Rayna's brief
illness and sudden death. It was during this harrowing ordeal
that Sheean became aware of Dorothy's "indomitable courage
. . . the grain and texture of her character . . . the heights to
which she could rise, not by mind or heart alone but by some
other quality containing both but containing also something
else . . . that extra quality — something of a Christian con-
figuration — that led me in later decades to call her my 'Protestant sister.'"

In the funeral procession, he recalled, "Dorothy walked every
inch of the way, as did Madame Sun Yat-sen . . . Both could
have gone in government cars . . . they insisted on walking —
on and on and on for what seemed a space and time everlast-
ing, while the snow fell thicker and faster and the early darkness gathered . . ."

❦ 3
Prothalamion

LEWIS HAD PERSUADED DOROTHY to quit her job as soon as possible after returning to Berlin and then spend whatever time remained before his divorce with him in some balmy climate. Oddly, complete solitude did not seem essential to this premarital interlude. In January, Dorothy wrote to Rose Lane, who had decided to leave Albania after it became a vassal state of Mussolini's, inviting her to stop for a visit on her way home to America.

"No, darling, I shan't meet you — in the plural — in Sicily. No indeed," Rose replied. ". . . It isn't, you know, that I wouldn't love to know Sinclair Lewis, who is to me only a legendary figure. I'm sure he's interesting and amusing and everything I'd love to go farther than Sicily to know. But not now . . . It's Dorothy I want, though that doesn't say that I won't love Mrs. Lewis . . . I can't — as you're perfectly aware — help low growls in the throat whenever I think of your embarking in love again . . . I shall always, I suspect, a little hate the husband for having that part of the world, of living what's only yours. But then I always have a bit of a growl in my throat for men, all men in general . . ."

Dorothy wound up her affairs in Berlin and persuaded her employers to hire her favorite, H. R. Knickerbocker, as her successor. In early March 1928 she headed southward to Italy, the enchanted land where eight years earlier she had lamented that it "was a crime against man and God to be loverless."

While she searched for the perfect house, she took a room at the Bertolini Palace in Naples and reflected about this second marriage, which she seems to have anticipated with more hope than confidence. "I feel humble toward you, who feel humble toward no other living human being," she wrote to Lewis, "in that I must take what you give me, and be grateful for it. For I have no measuring rod for justice or generosity between you and me. So if by standards I apply to others you are unjust to me, my heart chides not you, but myself for having failed to call more forth — And yet I am imperious toward you as toward no one else, and ask from you, proudly, what no person has the right to ask from anyone . . . Yet loving you is not a simple thing, for thinking: He loves me! I am immeasurably raised in my self esteem; yet thinking: I love him! I am enraged at myself for being so round-faced and ever so faintly — please agree faintly — sear. I am enraged, and sometimes shake a fist at myself in the glass — that is why I would like to have a daughter for you; I feel, somehow, that I would make you a girl more worthy of being loved, for you see, in her case, I would know from the beginning that you were to love her, and in mine — I was already finished when you came along . . ."

This daughter — for unexplained reasons named Lesbia — became a character in a fanciful world she and Lewis invented.* It was populated by tiny creatures called Minnikins who figure in a kind of nonsensical fun that she and Lewis relished. Lewis seems to have had literary ambitions for Lesbia, expressed in a sketch attached to one of his letters:

---

* It is likely that Dorothy frankly discussed with Lewis her relationships with women, including what she called her "adolescent homosexuality." Her reputation had been somewhat ambiguous in Berlin where erotic aberrations were commonplace. Lesbianism, overt and suppressed, is a major theme of *Ann Vickers*, the novel Lewis wrote in 1932 that was based in large part on Dorothy's recollections of her years in the suffrage movement.

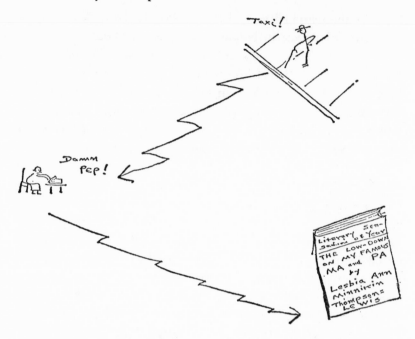

Dorothy rejoined: "Lesbia will *not* be a writer. I won't *have* it. She's going to be a lady farmer fruit-grower. Somebody *has* to be."

By mid-March she had found what she called "a friendly little villa; people say I have luck with houses and — I somehow think it will just do. Incidentally, Mussolini having stabilized the lira by decree around eighteen to the dollar which it ain't worth, and this being the season, and people wanting to rent villas for the WHOLE season of six months, prices for six weeks or so are prodigious. Therefore I consider that I am a good bargainer for having gotten this one for $270 for the whole six weeks . . ."

Under oath of secrecy, Dorothy had confided her plans to Peggy before her Russian journey. On March 21 she wrote to her again: "I am no longer correspondent of the New York Eve

Post and the Philadelphia Public Ledger in Berlin. I resigned
on the first of this month. Hal — that's Sinclair Lewis — insisted; I was so tired; he wanted me to have six weeks or a
month of sheer rest before we should marry. Grace, his wife,
is getting a divorce which ought to be granted about the middle of April and then we shall be married immediately. Meanwhile we are living in the most enchanted place in the world,
and in the most enchanting little house. It is a former guest
house in the gardens of the villa Galotti; once one of the great
houses of Naples, it is now pretty well decayed although the
King comes here to stay occasionally, still. The whole Villa,
which consists of a great Chateau-like house and a half a dozen
little 'dependances' in the gardens, lies on the Posillipo Cape,
jutting out into the Bay of Naples, opposite Vesuvius. And our
little house is nothing except a crenallated tower which rises
sheer above the Mediterranean . . . on the top floor there is a
bedroom for Hal, looking eastward to Naples and southward to
Vesuvius, and a little sitting-room workroom for him with nothing much in it except a cretonne sofa, a big writing table and a
little typewriter table, an easy chair, and a teatable. Outside of
it though is a big terrace on which one can pace up and down
and regard the sea and Naples — a sort of roof garden, with
palms in pots and wicker chairs. And there's my bedroom —
down the steps — and a tiny little bath with a stove which ex-
plodes every once in a while, and a little wine cellar — with
wine in it in immense straw-covered flasks. And then down the
stairs is a kitchen . . . and in the kitchen is a fat chef in a high
hat who makes the most delicious and, alas, fattening things to
eat . . . And then there's this room where I am writing you.
I think in all the world there isn't a lovelier room . . . it looks
over the sea, over the bay, with its pumice rocks, off to the
promontory, jutting into the sea, crowded with pink and ma-
genta and white buildings, and great dark patches which are
gardens. In the afternoon the sun shines on this promontory

and it is all gold and rose colored. It is the city of Naples . . ."

One could scarcely picture a more ideal setting for Dorothy and her creative mate. The only problem, she said, was the unseasonably cold weather in a house with stone floors and no fireplaces. "Hal and I wear winter woolies all day, and all the lovely things I brought to dress for dinner in — fancying myself in black lace and a Venetian shawl, sitting in a high-backed chair — don't be funny. I appear at dinner, as at all meals, in a woolen skirt, a pullover, a sweater-jacket, woolen stockings, my heaviest shoes and not infrequently, a hat! . . . often the wind blows out a cigarette match . . . But one gets used to anything — with woolens enough. I sleep in my shimmy, which I haven't done since Gowanda!"

Unfortunately, more ominous problems than the sirocco marred this blissful scene. Dorothy was hard at work on her Russian book and the translation of *PEP*. Lewis was writing at a ferocious pace, using the Villa Galotti as the setting for some of the most charming episodes in *Dodsworth*. But, as often happened, he found relief from the tension of work in sustained drinking afterward.

Josef Bard had come to Italy with Eileen chiefly to make the acquaintance of the poet Ezra Pound, whom he admired vastly. They were staying not far from Posillipo, and often strolled past the Villa Galotti where typewriters seemed to be clacking away all day. When they called one evening, Dorothy was storming about the house, hunting for a missing page of one of her manuscripts. Lewis, very drunk, launched a tirade of which the gist was that he had written a few books himself that were somewhat more important than her manuscripts. In her diary a year later Dorothy recalled the incident as "the night Hal denounced me to Josef." Also living nearby with the Gorki family was Baroness Moura Budberg, who was distressed by the frequent spectacle of Lewis lurching drunkenly along the road. Recalling the experience long years later, she remarked, "Dorothy once said to me, 'When reality is unsatisfac-

tory, imagination must substitute.' Her marriage to Lewis was
a sensible move from a practical point of view. But her love
for him — all those love letters — they were works of the imagination."

On April 16 Grace Lewis obtained her divorce in Reno.
Three days later Vambery mailed a copy of Dorothy's final
decree from Budapest and on April 23 Lewis, en route to London, informed the press that he and Miss Dorothy Thompson
were engaged, that they would be married in London, and that
they would spend their honeymoon touring the English coun-
tryside in a motor caravan. Dorothy sent the news simultaneously to her friends in Berlin. Knickerbocker wired in reply:

"YOUR LETTER TELEGRAM RECEIVED STOP
THANKS STOP ENTIRE CROWD BURST STORY
WITH DETONATION YOU SHOULD ABLE PERCEIVE
STOP EYE CABLED 800 WORDS STOP BEST REGARDS
FROM EVERYBODY ESPECIALLY FROM KECSKEMETI
[Paul Kecskemeti, Knickerbocker's assistant, a Hungarian jour-
nalist who later escaped Hitler's Europe to become a psycholog-
ical warrior in the U.S. Office of War Information] ME AND
BEST WISHES FOR PUNCTURELESS HONEYMOON
STOP CONGRATULATIONS BOTH OF YOU DOUBLE
ONES FOR LEWIS."

In the interest of decorum, Dorothy and Lewis had decided
to arrive separately in London, where their presence was likely
to attract public notice. While she waited to join him, Dorothy, plugging away at her work, wrote to him in a lighthearted
vein: "Well, I have finished eight of Mr. Wetcheek's twenty-
eight American ballads. Some of the rhymes are astonishing; in
fact in one case I had to use an Anglo-Saxon monosyllable,
which just shows that you never can tell when something will
come in handy; it was very apropos. In fact an adequate preface
to the entire volume would be the couplet:

> This book as art
> Ain't worth a —

"Wrangel [probably a White Russian friend from Berlin] turned up again on the way back from Capri, and wanted to know who was coming to our wedding party. I told him Princess Mary was to be chief bridesmaid and the Duke of York your best man. Queen Marie train-bearer. Kindly arrange this otherwise I will look funny telling him it in advance . . . I really only *want* Raymond and Betty Swing, Tommie [Ybarra of the New York *World*] and Berthold [Wiesner] . . . I adore you . . ."

PART V

MRS. SINCLAIR LEWIS

ꙮ 1
Into the Footlights

"I HOPE HAL got someone to arrange the wedding for him instead of trying to do it himself," Junius Wood wrote to Dorothy from Moscow.

Lewis would not have heeded this advice even if it had been passed on to him. He attacked the details of the nuptial plans with excited zest, determined that the celebration should fittingly mark the union of two eminent Americans, eager to advertise his romantic success. He would have liked the pomp of a church wedding. But it would have to be in the Savoy Chapel, he wrote on April 28, because "that's the only place in the diocese of London where marriage of divorced persons is permitted (except 'innocent party in case of adultery') — that and registry office. What we'll have to do is to be married at registrar's office, a very brief service with just two witnesses present, and then be married churchishly again, right after, at Savoy Chapel, which proves to be a charming old place, tiny and tranquil, tucked under the blatant walls of Hotel Savoy . . . You must be here not later than Thursday May 10, as on Friday we go to the registrar's office. I've been there once and left your copy of divorce decree together with mine, which arrived today. I've talked to the verger and one of the clergy at the Savoy Chapel, and Monday I see 'em again and try to fix an hour for the marriage, then begin to invite any kings and queens who are in town. So everything goes apace . . ."

Lewis, who had ordered a splendid Savile Row suit for the occasion, was concerned that his bride also be elegantly turned out. "Dora Miller [probably the wife of Webb Miller, a British journalist] said she'd be enchanted to take you to proper dressmakers," he wrote, "and I think I'd have her do it — she has expert knowledge."

Dorothy had planned to shop in Paris for her trousseau, but on May 2 she changed her mind.

"I think I ought to help a little on this wedding," she wrote. "So when I found today I could get a charming dress from Chanel right here in Naples, and that a crack dressmaker would finish it for me tomorrow night, I ordered it, decided to cut out Paris, and come straight to London. I leave here Friday — regretfully; it grows more beautiful daily, and only you could drag me away from it — stay Saturday and Sunday in Rome and leave Rome Sunday night, getting to London Tuesday. This is a longer route — over Switzerland and Ostend — but much cheaper because it has a second class . . .* Why do you seem so far from me? I am vaguely distressed, and cannot to save my life, see why? Is it just sheer homesickness for you? Good heavens, Hal, I am horribly afraid I am in love with you! !"

Lewis greeted her, when she reached London, with a guest list that he had carefully coded: invited–X; accepted–√; wrote–w; ask D–ad. Of the last group, Dorothy apparently vetoed Josef Bard and Eileen. Her former assistant Margaret Goldsmith, now married to Frederick Voigt of the Manchester *Guardian*, was out of town. So too, Lewis regretfully noted, were Nancy Astor, Noel Coward, Arnold Bennett, and H. G. Wells. The check list indicates that Rebecca West accepted, but Miss West was not in London and says she would not have attended anyhow for she was irked with Lewis at the time and had a premonition that the marriage would turn out badly.

In the end, most of the guests were friends of the bride-

---

* Dorothy had qualms about accepting money from a man who was not yet her husband. She kept a meticulous account of their shared expenses before the marriage.

groom's. There was a gratifying sprinkling of titles and British and American literary stars, including Lord C. B. Thomson (a Labour M.P. and Minister of Air who died in a plane crash in 1930), Viscount Castlerosse (Director of the London *Evening Standard* and *Sunday Express*), Sir Thomas and Lady Cunningham, Bertrand Russell's wife Dora, Lord and Lady Sackville (parents of Vita Sackville-West, Harold Nicolson's wife), Anita Loos and her husband John Emerson, Mercedes de Acosta (a New York social and literary light and a close friend of Greta Garbo's); and Crosby Gaige (New York theatrical producer and bon vivant). On the bride's side were Mrs. Pethick Lawrence (a grande dame of the British suffrage movement) and her husband, Henrietta Ely and two English relatives of Dorothy's father, Mesdames Arthur and Leslie Walton. (Dorothy's oldest friend in London, Barbara De Porte Grossman, was not invited. Lewis probably was unaware of her existence; if Dorothy thought of her, she may have decided that Barbara and her Zionist husband would not fit well in this very Protestant gathering.)

Lewis' English publisher, Jonathan Cape, and his wife were witnesses at the registry at noon on May 14, 1928. The rest of the party gathered in the chapel and at a luncheon that followed in the Savoy's Pinafore Room. Anita Loos, the only surviving wedding guest, recalls that during the chapel service her husband, who had studied for the ministry, whispered to her, "What's going on? This isn't an Episcopal service." Apparently, the preacher, officiating in the heart of London's theatrical district, was stagestruck himself. "He was a ham actor," Miss Loos said. "I guess he and Red cooked up this peculiar ceremony as a publicity stunt for both of them. It was a rigamarole, a lot of hocus pocus, all done in deadly earnest, with the preacher shouting at the top of his lungs to drown out the starlings who were making an ungodly racket on the Thames embankment. When I told Mencken about it afterward he thought it very funny and just like Red."

The reaction of the Methodist minister's daughter to this

parody of a religious rite is not recorded. In the wedding photograph, Lewis, wearing a pin-stripe suit and wing collar, looks urbane and poised. But the camera, which was seldom kind to Dorothy, portrays her as slightly dowdy, clinging to the arm of the gaunt, angular husband who towers a head over her. Though she had been on a Spartan diet of eggs, spinach, orange juice, and veal, she was still rather round of face and figure. The creator of her Neapolitan Chanel costume had swathed her in a nondescript silk dress with a fluffy white collar and billowing coat rather than one of the skimpy sheaths considered chic in the age of the flat-chested flapper. If Dorothy's eyes sparkled, they were almost invisible under one of the deep-crowned brimmed hats that were a fashion monstrosity of the period.

To Lewis' satisfaction, accounts of the wedding were featured in the press on both sides of the Atlantic. H. R. Knickerbocker forwarded a batch of clippings on May 27 with the comment, "For two pronounced social rebels you certainly met all the requirements. Savoy Chapel, the Rev. Hugh B. Chapman! . . . Every letter I get from the office has something in it about 'our Dorothy.' Do you know a fellow named E. J. Lewis, telegraph editor? He wrote me recalling the series of articles about German industry etc. which 'our Dorothy' had written and recommended the example.

"I am slaving along, enjoying the job . . . ordered . . . to cover the Olympics. It will be a lot of work but good fun . . . Junius Wood blew through on his way to America to cover the conventions . . . Gunther is going in to cover Russia, but has been delayed by the necessity for making preparations to become a father. Dorothy do you remember what you did with all the back expense accounts? We have never been able to find a trace of them . . ."

Within a few months Dorothy would be hungering for this kind of gossip from the world of journalism. But at this moment she was, as Vincent Sheean put it, "entering upon the phase known as celebrity . . . every flashbulb must have been in some respect like a notification of things to come . . . as if she had suddenly stepped up from the audience into the footlights . . ."

The day after the wedding, she hastened to the American consulate to have her citizenship — in limbo for six years — officially reaffirmed. Then the Lewises were off for a tour of England by car, hauling a house trailer (known in Britain as a caravan). It was an odd choice of honeymoons since Dorothy did not drive, Lewis was a menace at the wheel, and neither had any recent experience of camping out. But it was a newsworthy stunt. They described it as a gypsy adventure, although they spent fewer nights in the mobile home than in comfortable inns or the stately mansions of hospitable friends. From one of the latter Dorothy wrote to her sister:

> LONG BARN
> WEALD
> SEVENOAKS

DEAREST PEGGY:
. . . We are staying with the Nicolsons [Sir Harold and Vita Sackville-West] having caravanned in here in front of their house some time yesterday afternoon. I never believed such a house as this existed in the world . . . Once the mistress of this house lived as a spoiled little girl at Knole, the greatest house in England . . . But when Vita Sackville-West was a young woman her cousin, Sir Charles Sackville inherited, so she moved here; and to this house she added an ancient barn. I think I like it even better than 'Knole'! . . . I sleep in a great fourposter bed, its carved posts and headboards painted in blues, reds and gold and write at an oaken table three centuries old. But yet off my bedroom is a beautiful and quite modern bath, with six verses in the handwriting of Oscar Wilde framed above the W.C. Everyone who amounts to anything has visited in this house whose host and hostess are beautiful & simple people — Harold a damned good writer — if you want to know more about him read his book 'Some People' which is out in America. He's Counsellor of the British Embassy in Berlin . . .

"And the caravan, oh Peggy dear, the caravan it looks like this

Oh, Peggy, dear, the Caravan.
It looks like this:

Leaded windows.

Lockers under beds for bedding, over beds for coals, shoes, suitcases,

With two portable typewriters in the trailer, a news camera-
man photographed both writers pounding away. Lewis was reporting on the trip for the New York *Herald Tribune* while
Dorothy was finishing her Russian book and *PEP* and turning
out an occasional commentary on European affairs for the Curtis papers. She also kept a diary, in format resembling her
1920 journal with dates and sideheadings in the margins.
The tone and content, however, are very different. There are
few introspective passages; instead the emphasis is on encounters with newsworthy personalities and picturesque scenes with
an eye to future publication. (She used the diary as lecture material upon her return to America.)

Since Lewis was reporting the same events she developed the
"woman's angle" and a very housewifely image results:

> What can you carry in a caravan? Bacon and but-
> ter, beer and wine, oranges and bread, cakes and
> beans, olives and jam, honey and eggs, jugs and
> plates, cups and forks . . . everything which a civ-
> ilized human being wants, if his wife knows how
> to cook, to make a bed, and to wash dishes with-
> out afterward smelling of them. And is that pos-
> sible? But of course! Out of that little oaken chest
> of drawers, she takes a white pot of cold cream
> with a French mark. She rubs it thick on her
> hands and pulls on rubber gloves over them. That
> is all. And back goes the pot and shut goes the
> drawer. Everything is possible if you only keep
> ship-shape . . . In the fireplace is a little oil-stove,
> big enough for stews and steaks, puddings and
> roasts, and if you want them soufflés and crêpes-
> suzettes. Under that upholstered seat another zinc-
> lined box with an outlet to the ground — for ice;
> for milk & butter & wine . . .

Whether she actually produced this gourmet fare is unknown; however, her delight in the minutiae of housekeep-

ing was genuine. Highlights of the trip were the visits with the Nicolsons and Arnold Bennett. Afterward Dorothy went to London for a day to see Margaret Goldsmith, Oskar Kokoschka, and other friends. Presumably she also had business errands that justified a furlough from the honeymoon. Or possibly the close quarters were proving a strain. A few days earlier, in one of the rare personal entries in this journal, she had cryptically noted, "It was a nice day. Hal didn't lose his temper with me once." There were various sources of friction as, for example, when in Southwick they encountered a young man attempting to start a literary magazine.

> Hal spent an hour writing down addresses for the youth — Where to send the magazine for favorable comment. H. is too absurd! He combines contemptuousness with naive good-heartedness to an incredible degree. An anaemic magazine with a most anaemic young editor: better left to perish my own Nietzchean brutality advised . . .

The balmy weather was punctuated by a cloudburst on July 26, their final night in the trailer.

> To celebrate the last dinner, we opened half a dozen tins; a Cross & Blackwell Hare Soup, clams which I creamed, a bottle of Chambertin, and for sweet, an omelette with maple sirup. Both Hal and I were in mellow and exalted moods, and talked much about the books he was going to write and about the high estimate we have of the other. But at ten we were so sleepy, that Hal suggested a nap before we tackled the dishes. He promptly fell into unconsciousness, and I, though sleeping fitfully could not rouse myself until one-thirty, when I became aware that the caravan, which was practically sealed against the rain, was stinking horribly of left-over dinner. I tried to rouse Hal to help with the washing up, but it was no good. He merely grunted. I washed the grease into the dishwater — horrid is the smell of soup & soap in com-

bination — and was tidy by three. When I lay
down, in Hal's pyjamas — he was sleeping on my
bed & I couldn't get at my own night clothes —
and wound myself up in a down quilt, the corners
of which were dripping. I opened the window &
rain blew on my face but I let it blow. The reward
of virtue was that Hal brought coffee which he had
made himself to my bedside . . .

Next morning a team of horses towed the trailer out of a sea
of mud and it was hauled off to Oxford. The Lewises, having
had their fill of roughing it, luxuriated in the hospitality of
Hugh Walpole, who also loaned them his chauffeur to pilot the
Lewis car on their subsequent tours, which included a visit to
Dorothy's friend the biologist Berthold Wiesner, now based in
a laboratory in Edinburgh.

The diary ends August 2 on a melancholy note:

> Bad temper is the most destructive of human
> faults. It supplants trust with fear; it poisons love;
> it breeds aversion or indifference; it sterilizes emo-
> tion. Unless he stops taking me on or casting me
> off as the mood suits him I shall eventually cease
> to love H. Tonight because I disagreed with him
> in an argument he got up and left me, sitting alone
> in a public restaurant.

To outward appearance, however, it was a radiant couple
that sailed for America on the *Hamburg* on August 22. Nor, it
seems, had any danger signals reached Dorothy's friends. "We
have all followed the photographic and paragraphic accounts of
your honeymoon with bated breath," Knickerbocker wrote,
"but never have had more than scraps to feed upon. I read
your masterly contribution upon the death of Raditch with interest. [Stephen Raditch, leader of the Croatian peasant party
in Yugoslavia, had died August 8.] . . . The old town has not
yet recovered from your departure. Händelstrasse 8 looks very
lonesome . . . I hope Sinclair Lewis is as happy as he is fortunate . . ."

🌿 2
"incredibly strange . . ."

LOOKING BACK on the emotional seesaw of her first two years as Mrs. Lewis, Dorothy described it as "less an authentic experience than something read . . . a fantastic movie . . . incredibly strange . . ." Their life together in America, however, began auspiciously. Arriving in New York on August 28, they promptly drove off to hunt for the dream house, joined by Dorothy's sister Peggy. She was enchanted with her famous brother-in-law who, in turn, was drawn to this gentle self-effacing woman, the antithesis of his lusty, effervescent wife. His researches in the *Nation*'s real estate columns led them after several weeks to Barnard, Vermont, where they found 300 rolling acres and two venerable houses with a breathtaking view of Mount Ascutney. "You girls go and look the place over," said Lewis. "I'll sit right here and write out a check." In that pre-ski era, Vermont farmland was going begging; he paid only $10,000 for "Twin Farms." Insofar as the Thompson-Lewis marriage ever had roots, they were here, in this earthy setting that they both came to love and that evoked nostalgic memories of the rural background they shared.

Beguiled by the gold and crimson Vermont autumn, they moved at once into the smaller house that, though run-down, was habitable, and began reconstruction of the larger one, higher up on the hill. Lewis insisted on installing a huge window in the barn, which eventually became a studio–living room, commanding a spectacular sweep of valley and mountains. He also demanded plenty of bathrooms but otherwise relegated to

Dorothy the task of coping with New England carpenters, plumbers, upholsterers, and gardeners, whose individualistic ways proved trying in comparison with their obsequious European counterparts.

The first guest at Twin Farms was Vincent Sheean — one of their few genuinely mutual friends. All three spent much of the day writing; both Sheean and Dorothy were awed by Lewis' virtuosity as he forged ahead on the final draft of *Dodsworth*, ruthlessly cutting, throwing away thousands of words without a qualm.

"But it was not all work in Vermont," Sheean wrote. "Meals were hilarious and talk was mostly nonsense . . . Red could make up ten short stories before breakfast and invent a novel before lunch. Occasionally he made up a short story and presented it to me. The first short story of a more or less professional cast that I ever wrote was one of his, concocted in the midst of general laughter at the breakfast table . . ."

Lewis' eleven-year-old son Wells, a handsome, sensitive, fair-haired boy who came for a visit, took an immediate liking to his "Aunt Dorothy" but seemed intimidated by his father's unpredictable temper. Sheean recalls two outbursts, but on the whole, he writes, "I saw between Dorothy and Red a genuine affection . . . She was never sharp to him and he was never harsh to her."

They spent some uproarious evenings listening to the radio — then still a novelty — and laughing at the rhetoric of the presidential candidates, Herbert Hoover and Alfred E. Smith. Another diversion shared by Dorothy and her husband was doing crossword puzzles, which had recently become a national fad. The Lewises must have been a formidable team.

All that was best in the relationship between Dorothy and Lewis was realized in those first weeks in Vermont in the autumn of 1928. She summed it up on the title page of her translation of *PEP*, which she dedicated to "that good American Sinclair Lewis, in admiration and comradeship."

When the snows came to Vermont they moved to a duplex apartment at 37 West 10th Street in New York. Dorothy had imported her devoted German couple — eager to serve the *gnädige Frau* and her new husband. But it was a strange household. Lewis, drinking heavily again, filled the house with his cronies, who might or might not stay for meals. He rented a room in the nearby Lafayette Hotel to serve as an "office" where he could write free of distractions. Since he was not working, it was used chiefly for rendezvous with his bootlegger and random naps.

In January 1929 Dorothy left for Canada to report the impact of prohibition there. As often happened when they were separated, they corresponded in a tone of affectionate banter.

But this lighthearted mood did not survive the chaos of life in New York, as she sadly noted in her diary on February 13:

> Such a long time has elapsed — and so much has happened. We have bought the Vermont farm after nearly a month of motoring, looking for it; then New York, the flat here with my furniture from the Berlin flat & what we bought in Exeter; Christmas at Virginia Hot Springs (inexpressible boredom sustained only by my love for Hal) Now, tomoro we are to go to Southern Florida . . . because Hal is "tired." I agree because he has been drinking terribly again and only some such trip will make him stop it, but my heart is heavy & rebellious. My God — Florida mud flats, and all next summer Vermont! Not one enjoyable dinner party the whole winter; not one evening at the opera; not one concert, not a single human relationship — (can't bear it. I *won't* bear it. I had rather go & work in someone's kitchen than lead this sort of life, chased, pursued, harassed by fear's fear.)
>
> Tonight Hal invited the Perkins [probably Maxwell Perkins, the Scribners editor] to dinner — he

never asked me first — collapsed after it & went to
bed leaving me to carry the party. He does this
regularly. I told him I didn't want to go to Florida
because of my lecture date on the 21st. He then
got angry & sneered at me. "You with your important little lectures — You, with your brilliant
people — *You* want to talk about foreign politics
which *I* am too ignorant to understand." When
he talks so my heart freezes up. And then, in a
minute he is very sweet again . . .

To live with this mercurial, restless, unpredictable, brilliant,
and sometimes brutal man would have been a daunting assignment for any wife. Probably none was less likely to succeed than
a woman with a powerful ego of her own, whose need for admiration and attention was as intense as her husband's. Such
was the reaction of Lewis' sardonic friend H. L. Mencken when
they called on him in Baltimore in the summer of 1929. Menck-
en's future biographer Sara Mayfield, who was also present,
recorded her impressions of Dorothy in her memoir *The Constant Circle:*

There was still something of the Amazon, the Valkyrie about
her — something of a formidable Brunhilde turned Cassandra.
All the adjectives that applied to her seemed to begin with
B — big, blonde,* brown-eyed, brilliant, brash, beguiling — but
by that I do not mean to say that she was a seductive woman; had
she been she would soon have talked her seductiveness to death,
for no woman can be vociferous and charming . . .

Mencken when asked to forecast the outlook for the marriage is
said to have replied, "No telling. Red will drink and Dorothy
will talk until they both go *mashuggah.*"

According to Miss Mayfield, there was even less rapport when
Mencken with the bride he had married at the age of fifty, the
former Sara Haardt, subsequently visited the Lewises at Twin

* Miss Mayfield, it seems, was carried away by her alliterations. Dorothy's eyes
were blue and she was not blond.

Farms: "By her own admission, Dorothy Thompson's affections sometimes veered to the distaff side," Miss Mayfield wrote. "And if Henry had an aversion to such aberrations, Sara, if possible had a more intense one." *

Dorothy's book *The New Russia* was published in the autumn of 1928. Shortly afterward, Theodore Dreiser's account of his simultaneous stay in the USSR, *Dreiser Looks at Russia,* appeared. Careful readers noted a strange similarity between certain passages in the two books. Dorothy wrote indignantly to Rose Lane:

"Really it is too irritating. The old beast simply lifted paragraph after paragraph from my articles; I'm not speaking of material — we all got that where we could — but purely literary expressions. And, of course, ideas as well, because it never occurred to anyone else, for instance, to write about the social life in Moscow . . . Well that is bad enough. But when I came out and accused him of it, he started a whispering campaign to the effect that I was on intimate enough terms with him that I may have gone into his room and purloined his *notes! . . .*"

Old friends rose to Dorothy's defense. John Gunther wrote: "In England I got my first word of the Dreiser business. My dear, I formally and informally here & now & forever reiterate my faith in you. If you want character witnesses (!) cable me and I'll come with a shipload tomorrow. Rebecca West and the Swings are among ever so many people who agree with you on this — our love to you . . ."

The affair blew over but not before it had reached the front page after Lewis, at the Metropolitan Club, publicly accused Dreiser of plagiarizing his wife's work and a physical brawl resulted.†

---

* I queried Miss Mayfield about this statement. In reply, she wrote: "Dorothy Thompson's affections had been the subject of speculation among her journalistic colleagues and among the literati for some years . . ."

† Vincent Sheean offers the sensible theory that Dreiser's original manuscript was probably too short and a research assistant filled it out with excerpts adapted from Dorothy's *Evening Post* articles — a not unusual form of literary cannibalism.

This spirited defense was characteristic of Lewis. Often irascible in her presence and irked by her preoccupation with world politics, he was nonetheless zealous in advancing her career. He took pride in her successes, helped polish and sharpen her literary style, and introduced her to important editors, notably Thomas Costain of the *Saturday Evening Post,* the best-paying American periodical of the day, which over the next few years would be the major outlet for her writings. But this comradely relationship was not enough to make life serene.

In the spring of 1929 Dorothy went alone to Vermont to open the house and wrote in her diary on May 16:

> I feel that I must earn money. Our first wedding anniversary has passed — in the even[ing], when it was over Hal telephoned me. He gave me a lot of instructions about the place. Afterward, just as he was hanging up, I spoke of it. We were not together. I hate spring. All my springs have been full of inner wretchedness. Only the last one — it was beautiful — and the only one before that when I was happy was in 1921.

All summer the house would be filled with visitors, some of them experts on trade unionism whom Lewis had collected in the course of his research for *Frontier,* a monumental novel on the American labor movement with which he was struggling. As a countervailing force, Dorothy tried to assemble old journalistic colleagues. She wrote to John and Frances Gunther, who were grieving over the death of their baby daughter: "Is there anything on earth that Hal and I can do for you darlings . . . We both wish enormously that you could come & stay with us for as long as you wish — all summer if you like . . ." This visit, so far as we know, did not materialize. She was also disappointed when Floyd Gibbons failed to arrive on schedule. "I had no idea you were expecting me 'that' Thursday," he wrote, "and am hoping you will let me come up some subsequent Thursday . . . if you can't think of a more suitable punishment, I will accept sentence to spend my nights at Twin Farms without sheets, and make up for those you laid out for me . . ." Gibbons, whose book *The Red Napoleon* had just been published, was hunting for laudatory comments. His suggestion for Mrs. Lewis was: " 'Gibbons' complete knowledge of Russia makes him a master of his subject. Dreiser could not have done it better' — Dorothy Thompson."

Finally in the early autumn Vincent Sheean arrived, and Dorothy at last had a companion who shared her passion for debating and analyzing events on the far side of the Atlantic. Lewis liked nothing better than goading a younger writer into productive labor. Sheean remembers it as a happy time. "Red was not drinking much alcohol," he wrote, "and his nerves always benefited by a diet of beer or water. We walked quite a lot and he seemed in high spirits . . . I do not believe that any observer would have said, after a visit to Vermont, that Dorothy and Red could not make a permanent marriage; I doubt if any premonition afflicted their friends, even though the preceding winter in New York had not been all it might have been . . ."

Rose Lane when she visited the Lewises soon afterward also found the outlook promising. "Darling, you are going to affront all the literature of the ages," she wrote to Dorothy, "by triumphantly combining great beauty with a happy ending. Your husband's unintentional conquest was complete. I will now confess that I was prepared to dislike him intensely . . . I wanted you to be forevermore the Dorothy of 1920 — a song, a poem, a flame in the sunlight . . . it isn't so usual for admirable women to love, or to be loved by men who are worth the trouble . . . My objections to this marriage are hereby withdrawn in toto; I'm *for* it! . . ."

Lewis was, no doubt, at his best on this occasion. He liked offering helpful advice to fellow writers and probably made a special effort to charm Rose since he seemed to find Dorothy's possessive women friends an amusing challenge. Despite the fact that the labor novel was proving refractory, he had cause for relative contentment in the summer of 1929. Though the stock-market crash — which he had forecast a year earlier — was imminent, his own finances were in admirable shape. *Dodsworth* had been published in March and was reaping fine royalties.* He had also sold some short stories at top prices to *Cosmopolitan*. And in the fall, when Dorothy found she was pregnant, both looked forward with wistful hopes to the effect of parenthood on their volatile marriage.

* For the year 1929, Lewis paid an income tax of $14,533.10.

3
The "boredom of childbirth"

PLEASED THOUGH SHE WAS by the prospect of motherhood, Dorothy was in no mood to spend nine months in the 10th Street apartment knitting booties and studying the literature on the care and feeding of infants. Indeed, on several counts, it was an ill-timed pregnancy. At thirty-six, she was classed medically as an "elderly primipara" for whom a first childbirth entailed special risks. She had become convinced that life with Lewis would be tolerable only if she could achieve a measure of independence from his unpredictable whims; to do this she would need an income of her own. But she had pulled up stakes in foreign journalism and was only beginning to build a name for herself as a magazine writer and lecturer. She faced the prospect of starting a new career rather than simply continuing an established one after a brief interruption for childbearing.

Emotionally she was adrift, lacking a woman friend on whom to lean for counsel. Rose Lane had moved back to her native Ozarks. Beatrice Sorchan, now Mrs. Walter Binger, was busy with her own growing family. Gertrude Tone, separated from her husband, had become increasingly eccentric. Living at the Ritz-Carlton, she seldom emerged before dark, when she could wear a skirt long enough to conceal an elephantine swelling of her ankles, believed to be caused by a glandular ailment. Still seeking salvation through the Freudian gospel, she had allowed her psychiatrist, Dr. J. L. Moreno, to involve her in his pet project — a "therapeutic theater" where both players and audience acted out their neuroses. But peace of mind eluded her. On her nightly forays in search of pleasure she was drinking to such excess that her favorite son, Franchot, could not endure her presence in the same restaurant and they had reached an agreement dividing New York's speakeasies between them.

Dorothy, to be sure, had never had trouble making new friends. She was soon on an easy footing with most of New York's writers and editors — whom Lewis had known for years — among them Alexander Woollcott, Heywood Broun, and Harold Ross. A few became close friends — Wallace Irwin, a popular fiction writer best known for his "Mr. Togo" stories, and his wife Letitia, a novelist and playwright of modest talent; W. E. Woodward, whose life of George Washington had launched a vogue for "debunking" biographies, and his wife, who as Helen Rosen before her marriage had been a successful advertising executive for women's magazines; and Esther Root Adams and her husband Franklin P., whose column "The Conning Tower," signed F.P.A., was a showplace for contemporary wit and light verse and served as a kind of house organ for the Algonquin clique. Outgoing though she was, Dorothy had no intimates in this group in whom she could confide her anxieties about a marriage which she prized but in which she also felt trapped.

It was a relief, accordingly, when her lecture agent, William B. Feakins, arranged a Midwestern tour and she escaped in October from the chaos of her New York life. "I've been wondering how I might establish some contact with that truly cosmopolitan group at the opera in N.Y.," she wrote to Lewis from Terre Haute. "Hal, darling, I *ache* for a society in which I feel at home. The evening at von Tippelskirch's* was like a draught of champagne to me. But what shall I do this winter in N.Y. with you not there & Gertrude always there, and no contacts at all! Neither personal nor professional. You see, I'm in a depressed mood . . . You seem so far away, darling, so far away. In fact all of my life seems far away . . ."

---

* Von Tippelskirch was a German diplomat. Christa von Tippelskirch became the second wife of Hamilton Fish Armstrong.

She was troubled not only by her husband's remoteness but by the distance from Europe whence came the substance of her lectures and writings. For fresh information she was now dependent on European friends and old colleagues. On a stop in Grand Rapids she wrote to Lewis: "Beach & Lucille Conger captured me & I was glad. Fun to sit among familiar things; I had their flat & furniture a whole year in Berlin. And to talk Germany — Russia — politics on & on with Beach." A trip abroad in early 1930 that she had planned was postponed by her pregnancy. "We had so hoped to see you in Berlin," Lilian Mowrer wrote. "But when we knew the reason which was keeping you in America we were delighted for your sake & now we look forward with added pleasure to welcoming the new member of the family next winter . . ."

As always when they dealt with each other by letter, Dorothy and Hal found each other lovable and amusing. From the Palmer House in Chicago, she wrote: "It's nice here in this hotel. If only you were to come in in the morning in your woolly dressing gown & sit on the edge of the bed."

Lewis who, when he was at home writing, wore a shabby bathrobe all day, rejoined, "Woman, I'll have you to understand that I am *never* seen in the morning by any eye save God's till I have bathed, shaved, put on my riding clothes, read a chapter of the Good Book and written to my mother. We Lewises of Sauk Centre feel our obligation to the family tradition."

Having been warned of the hazards of a late-in-life first pregnancy, she was anxious about her health:

"I feel very wobbly," she wrote from Detroit. "Not actually sick but as though I might be any moment. Last night I dreamed I was on the farm and was driving a wagon load of beans into town down a hill. When I got to the bottom of the hill I found that the descent had jolted them all out of the wagon & I was terribly dismayed. This is a swell symbolic dream because when I awoke I could explain it immediately. The night before, in the sleeping car, the train had jolted so that I feared it would bring on a miscarriage . . ."

Home would at least mean an escape from jolting trains. She began to look forward to lazy days in bed reading and writing, with her own doctor nearby if anything went wrong. But when she returned to New York Lewis greeted her with the news that he must go to Reno to petition for a reduction in his alimony payments. Dorothy was to come with him and from Nevada they would proceed to California where they would spend the winter.

She acquiesced reluctantly. Reaching the West Coast, she found a temporary home that seemed ideally suited to their needs. "Hal & I have taken a delightful little house in Monterey," she wrote to Bill and Helen Woodward. "It has a writing room for Hal, a little sitting room, a dining room & kitchen, two charming bedrooms, and a lovely garden, full of roses, mimosa, blossoming quinces, forgetmenots, narciss, etc. Our nearest neighbor is Gouverneur Morris [grandson of the Revolutionary statesman and a prolific novelist] who turns out to be a peach as is his funny, clever, fantastic & delightful wife, Ruth. There is a good crowd in Pebble Beach & Carmel, but we are happily removed enough not to have to see anyone all the time. Both of us are loafing shamefully.

"Looking down upon myself the other day I decided I should be snow-capped if this kept up — so I've gone on a diet of 1500 calories a day to keep myself from becoming too like the High Sierras. I adore California — loved San Francisco — on the whole I think this is the best part of the U.S. . . . Red won his case at Reno 100% — but Grace is appealing, so it's still unsettled . . . Look up my friend Richard Bühlig [a one-time Berlin beau who was now in Hollywood]."

Within a few weeks California had lost its charm. Loafing was not a good way of life for Lewis. She sensed that their neighbors were bored with his clowning and was not enjoying her own role as the very pregnant Mrs. Lewis. In March after a brief stay with the Woodwards in Hollywood she left Lewis and took a train for Mansfield, Missouri, to visit Rose Lane at her home, Rocky Ridge Farm. She had certainly a need for the tenderness Rose provided.

Dorothy went to Vermont in April to supervise the opening of the farm and then returned to New York to await with her husband the birth of her child. Jimmy Sheean, who had spent most of the winter in Jerusalem (where he had become implacably aligned against political Zionism), had found an apartment near the Lewises and saw a great deal of them. "They were not quiet weeks," he wrote, "and as a matter of fact quarrels between Dorothy and Red became frequent and, as it seemed to me, utterly unreasonable. She was nervous over her pregnancy and he was drinking: that was enough. Any tiny thing would be enough to cause a quarrel under those conditions . . .

"There was actually a moment not very long before the baby's birth when Dorothy felt she could no longer endure life with Red and asked me to drive her to the Roosevelt Hotel where she could take refuge while she worked out plans for a separation. This was at about midnight or afterwards, when Red had gone into his periodic coma . . . I did as she asked. At the Roosevelt Hotel . . . she was in fact registering when she came to the signature and realized what it might mean. Red was at the height of his fame and she was at the peak of her pregnancy. It would have been a dreadful little item for the gutter press, which at that period paid a good deal of attention to the Lewis family. She put down the pen, apologized to the night clerk of the hotel, and asked me to take her back to Tenth Street, which I did . . ."

Both Dorothy and Red had confidently expected a daughter. But the infant who arrived on June 20, 1930, was a boy,

Michael. When Sheean called on Dorothy the next day at Woman's Hospital, he found her sitting up in bed in a becoming pink nightgown, looking radiant. Her labor had been easy, she said; none of the anticipated difficulties had occurred. But she was shocked that modern medical science had done nothing to mitigate the tedium of the long months of gestation — the "boredom of childbirth."

"She rang a bell. A nurse came in," Sheean wrote. "Dorothy lifted an imperious and well arched eyebrow . . . 'Bring in the child,' she said."

It was a characteristic gesture. Dorothy loved babies, from what might be called a grandmotherly elevation. That is to say, the little creature was an adorable object to be fondled at intervals so long as someone else changed the diapers, prepared the formulas, and walked the floors during colicky nights. This was precisely what she arranged when she departed for Vermont with a small retinue of servants. On the ground that his father could not endure an infant's squalling, Michael and his entourage were settled in the farmhouse while his parents moved into the newly refurbished "big house" a quarter of a mile away. While babies did indeed irritate Lewis, Dorothy too had little patience with infants or small children. Her mind was usually elsewhere, and in large doses they bored her. She was not even much interested in twelve-year-old Wells although a warm affection developed between them later when he was old enough for communication on an adult level. Yet her self-image was of a supremely devoted mother.

"Here I am," Dorothy wrote to Helen Woodward in October, "with restored and all too blooming health and my boy who is appallingly dear to me. He is such a funny little boy. (No one would think of calling him other than 'the boy.') . . . The summer's gone in getting well, taking care of Wells who was with us all summer & who is a child I am intensely sorry for & don't much like — and trying to keep him from getting on his

father's nerves to the point of exacerbation — & failing . . .
Our plans: We are not (as we had planned) going abroad for
six months with Michael. Nor are we returning to NY. We
have taken Frank & Esther Adams' house in Westport for the
winter. This is partly for the baby, partly for Red — partly for
me. For I should like to spend a winter in the snowy country;
Esther's house has an oil-burning furnace & is easily accessible
to N.Y. — either or both of us can run in for three-four days at
a time & still be in touch with the baby . . .

"I want to go abroad during the winter and may do so. I have
an excellent (trained) nurse for my boy who combines skill with
a most happy, calm, poised and professional personality (professional in the best sense of the word) . . . so if I can tear myself
from him I shall go to Germany & Russia on a fast trip — perhaps two months . . .

"Gertrude Tone has been taking thyroid and it's made a new
woman of her. I'd like to take it for my hips; *my* brain has gone
phut but that's due to domesticity — (which is unavoidable).
Show me a woman married to an artist who can succeed in her
marriage without making a full-time profession out of it. Oh,
Jesus God!! . . .

"As for my problems: a couple of months by myself seems
necessary and desirable — a couple of months away from my
very little boy — ten or twelve days journey away — seems
brutal. Brutal, I mean to me. He is the most lovely thing that
ever happened to me . . .

"Red, by the way, is crazy about him . . ."

Over the years, Dorothy would repeatedly refer to "my son
who is very dear to me," particularly during her many prolonged separations from him. And if Red was "crazy about" the
baby, he seldom relished his company. Within a month, the
Lewises would, in fact, be en route to Europe. Before leaving,
Dorothy made elaborate plans for her son's custody in the event
shipwreck or other natural disasters overtook his parents. In

a letter to Letitia Irwin that is strangely oblivious to the needs of a small infant, she spelled out a grandiose vision of her son's future. One is reminded of her girlhood fantasies about an imaginary "Dorothy."

"Dearest Tish" she wrote. "I honestly can think of no one else — or certainly of only one or two other people or families — to whom I could entrust, with any equanimity, the guardianship of our boy. Some of my oldest and most intimate friends are professional women, either unmarried, widowed or divorced, and to an extent, at least homeless. Among our other friends, many are unhappily married, or ill-adjusted in their marriages. Phyllis [Bottome] and Ernan Forbes-Dennis are a man and his wife, old friends, to whom I could entrust Michael confident that he would be brought up in a cultivated atmosphere, and in a way which we, Hal and I, could both approve, but they are English, and Phyllis has been ill for years with tuberculosis. My friends, the Schwarzwalds, in Vienna, love and understand children and have standards similar to our own, but they are Austrian. And our boy, after all, is an American. I love my sister, dearly, and admire her character, but I should like my boy to be brought up in a little more worldly way than she could show him, and the same is true of Hal's nearest relatives . . .

"You are that rare apparition: people both simple and worldly. I want my boy to grow up, at home in the great world, not over-impressed by famous names or grand houses or family traditions, but not sneering at them, either, merely out of a sense of inferiority. I don't want him to adore money, and neither do I want him brought up, as I was, to think that money is something disgraceful — again a compensation for a sense of inferiority — but to realize that it is power. Where that power ought to reside, and how be wielded, his generation will decide for itself . . . And teach him, Tish, if he ever comes into your hands, that no social, economic or political system is eternal or

worthy of profound reverence; that reverence should be preserved for life itself . . . Tell my boy, if you have the opportunity, that this is a grand world, and that his mother never for
an instant apologized for putting him into it . . .

"All this, darling, seems ridiculously remote; I intend to live
as long as humanly possible, and would greatly like to see the
possibilities extended. But ships do sink, though only occasionally, and there are always banana peelings . . ."

🎀 4
"former newspaperwoman . . ."

THE TRIP ABROAD in 1930 was no ordinary voyage. Lewis had won the Nobel Prize for Literature, the first American to be so honored. It was an electrifying event. When he was notified by phone in Vermont where he had lingered that fall, he suspected a practical joke. Similarly, Dorothy, when he called her in New York, is said to have rejoined, "Great, I just received the Order of the Garter." But it was true. Amid a flurry of press conferences, exploding flash bulbs, and congratulatory calls, preparations for the journey to Sweden proceeded. Rose Lane was summoned from Missouri to take charge of the Westport household, where the "very professional" Fraulein Rosa Haemmerli would minister to Michael. Lewis underwent the painful ordeal of having the pustules that marred his face removed by an electric needle treatment.

They sailed on the *Drottingholm* on November 29, reaching Stockholm during the luminous Santa Lucia festival. Contrary to expectations, Lewis behaved decorously throughout the round of Nobel banquets, receptions, and ceremonies and delivered an address that delighted his audience. (The honor accorded him evoked a few sour reactions at home from those who resented the presentation of the award to an author who ridiculed sacred American values and others who did not consider Lewis a novelist of the first rank.)

Dorothy, for the first time in her life, was seasick during the crossing and ran a fever in Stockholm. On December 21, when they reached Berlin where her former colleagues had planned a round of parties, she was seriously ill. On Christmas night she was operated on for acute appendicitis. INS cabled the news to America, identifying her as "Mrs. Sinclair Lewis, former newspaperwoman, whose husband recently won the Nobel prize for literature" — a somewhat demeaning designation for Dorothy. In fact, although she had published nothing for a year, she had brought with her to Europe several firm commissions from the *Saturday Evening Post.* She spent ten days convalescing in Thüringen with her husband. Then Lewis left for London, where he planned to negotiate a contract with a new publisher, having decided to sever his connection with Harcourt, Brace.*

Bent on demonstrating that she was still a very current figure in the world of journalism, Dorothy's first concern was her major *Post* assignment, an interview with ex-Emperor Charles's widow Zita. With her eight children she had vanished from public view and proved elusive. She was finally tracked down in southern France, ill and for the present incommunicado. The delay proved useful to Dorothy since there was no dearth of news in Germany.

It was the twilight of the Weimar Republic. The alliance of democratic parties in the Reichstag had collapsed with the resignation of Hermann Müller, head of the coalition government, in March 1930. He was succeeded by Heinrich Brüning, whom Dorothy greatly admired and described as having "the head of an eighteenth century cardinal-statesman." (He was a guest of honor at her Vermont home during his last years of exile, which were spent in nearby Hanover, New Hampshire.) When Brüning rashly called an election in September 1930, the Nazi Party, which in 1928 had polled only 800,000 votes, garnered more than 6 million, thus becoming the second largest

---

* Dorothy had encouraged the break, agreeing with Lewis that Harcourt had inadequately promoted his books and had failed to exploit the Nobel award. She also resented the share of his foreign earnings that went to the publisher.

bloc in parliament. The Communists also gained while the Social Democrats and other moderates lost over a million votes.

No country had been more vulnerable than Germany to the worldwide depression that followed the 1929 crash. As foreign investors called in their loans and export markets vanished, industries closed down and millions were thrown out of work. Chancellor Brüning's efforts to cope with the ailing economy paralleled those of President Herbert Hoover in Washington and proved equally futile. In America, a despairing nation would respond by giving Franklin D. Roosevelt an overwhelming electoral victory in November 1932. But in Germany, only Adolf Hitler offered hope, irrational though his program might be: he would repudiate the Versailles treaty, revive the traditions of early Teutonic heroism, provide work and bread for all, make Germany once again a great and proud nation. It was not only the hungry and unemployed who responded to this rhetoric. Generals of the regular army were no longer contemptuous of the vulgar Austrian corporal who promised to restore military might and glory. Seeing Nazism as a bulwark against communism, German industrialists poured funds into the Nazi treasury. The steel magnate Fritz Thyssen, for example, among other benefactions financed the return to Berlin of the future air marshal Herman Göring, who had been a fugitive in Sweden since the unsuccessful 1923 putsch. Middle-class Germans, who had little enthusiasm for the Weimar government, also saw Hitler as their defender against radicals, and if not all shared his virulent anti-Semitism they ignored it as the passing aberration of a true patriot. With Jewish businesses and individuals openly harassed, the realists among them who could afford to do so were making plans to leave the country. Yet a degree of optimism still prevailed among some thoroughly "German" Jews — themselves anti-Semitic in their disdain for the hordes of "Eastern" Jews who had swarmed into Germany and Austria after the pogroms that broke out in Poland and the Baltic countries at the end of World War I. Ironically, the Nazis were secretly supported by some Communists on the theory that they would take over after Hitler destroyed German democracy.

Hitler had mobilized a private army, the SA (*Sturm-abteilung*), which presently outnumbered the government's *Reichswehr*. Subsisting on a miserable dole (which Chancellor Brüning reduced in an attempt to balance his budget), thousands of unemployed young men gained a sense of purpose and fraternity when they donned the storm troopers' brown uniforms and paraded through the streets behind a squad leader in high boots armed with a horse whip. Small shopkeepers and a good many other Berliners found the spectacle edifying. "They were suddenly proud of being blond," Christopher Isherwood wrote. "And they thrilled with a furtive, sensual pleasure, because the Jews, their business rivals and the Marxists, a vaguely defined minority of people who didn't concern them, had been satisfactorily found guilty of the defeat and the inflation, and were going to catch it."

When the storm troopers invaded working-class neighborhoods, there were bloody clashes with Communist residents and a daily death toll that provided propagandist Joseph Goebbels with a ready supply of martyrs. (The most celebrated was storm trooper Horst Wessel, composer of the National Socialist anthem. Living on the earnings of a prostitute, he was murdered by another pimp who, fortuitously, was a Communist.)

Germany's future was being decided in the streets. Correspondents who had been continuously on the scene predicted that Hitler would soon triumph. But to Dorothy the contrast with the highly civilized Berlin she had known in the 1920s was a nightmare not quite to be believed. Unwilling to accept the gloomy prognostications of her colleagues, Mowrer, Knickerbocker, and Sigrid Schultz, she sought out German friends, American and British diplomats, interviewed Reichsbank president Hjalmar Schacht and such prominent Nazis as were accessible. Hitler was not yet talking to foreign reporters.

Dorothy's ambivalence about the National Socialist movement at this time and the intensely personal nature of her reactions to its leaders is reflected in a diary entry characterizing
Adolf Wagner, the future *Gauleiter* of Bavaria, as

> . . . attractive looking, obviously with a good
> *kinderstube* [well-bred], brutal, intelligent, un-
> subtle, un-intellectual, un-imaginative, provincial
> (and would remain so if he travelled the world
> around, like some Americans who insist on eating
> canned corn & buckwheat pancakes in Paris) brave,
> and, I confess it, not to me unsympathetic (because
> I am also arrogant, brave, and impertinent, and,
> like him, think myself, on the whole, superior, so
> that although I fought him on every point, he felt,
> somehow, that I liked him and left me convinced
> that even if I wrote against him my heart would
> be for him) . . .

Meanwhile, in London, Lewis, though doubtless glad to be
far from his professionally preoccupied wife, was solicitous, as
always, for her career. "Oswald Villard wants you to consider
being managing editor of the *Nation* beginning next fall," he
wrote. "He is also considering Raymond [Gram] Swing. [Henry
Raymond] Mussey has resigned as m.e., though he will stay on
the staff. Frieda [Kirchway, a *Nation* editor] has been all busted
up by the death of a child. Villard is crazy about you . . . I
take it from what he says he'll pay $7,500 a year, top-notch.
Might be worth considering; certainly it would link you to
America if later you wanted to do articles there & give you
grand American political dope while, perforce, keeping you in
touch with European politics . . . Mick & me could live on
Long Island."

For a small-circulation liberal periodical in a depression year
this was a handsome offer. Dorothy would have seized it ten
years earlier when her model of success was Signe Tocswig, an

associate editor of the *New Republic*. But in 1931, she had been a star of the foreign press corps and was the wife of a celebrated author. As a lecturer she had learned to enlighten and move audiences, in the style of her evangelist father. Her sights were set higher than mere editorial work.

"How *can* I take the *Nation?*" she wrote. "What about Vermont? Europe? You? I *see* you staying home & minding the baby. Du!"

In early February she decided to take a look at Austria and Upper Silesia, where trouble was expected along the Polish frontier. Also, for unexplained reasons, she was anxious to communicate with her first husband.

"Little Dotty, pretending to be a real grown-up journalist and going off to Upper Silesia," Lewis responded. ". . . I too have lost Josef's address! It must, as you suggest, be Freudian. Nor has he called me up . . . I adore you, think of you every minute."

Except for an opportunity to visit the Moltke family in Kreisau, her trip proved disappointing. "I found things about twenty times quieter than in Berlin . . ." she wrote Lewis from Silesia, "I feel a strange ache and emptiness — can it be that I *miss* you? Can it be that I want Mickey? But that would be absurd in a *Saturday Eve Post* reporter! Can it be that I don't think it's very *important* to be a Satevepost reporter? I'm afraid I think it isn't . . ."

It was important enough, however, to linger in Europe for the Zita interview, which finally took place in Brussels on March 23. Laden with raw material for a dozen major magazine pieces she came home in April and within a month moved the family to Twin Farms. Wells Lewis, now thirteen, who had come to look on Twin Farms as a real home, was disappointed when his mother decided to take him abroad in June. "Dear Aunt Dorothy," he wrote from Phillips Academy, Andover, on May 27, "I can't possibly come to Twin Farms until September. I feel horribly about it . . . How are you and Father and Michael. Praise be the Lord on high that Michael escaped the measles. Is he much bigger now? I will hate missing the farm, especially now when it is at its best, but perhaps I can spend all next summer there. So much love from Wells."

Peggy Wilson and her daughter Pamela came, as usual, for a long stay and there was a succession of interesting visitors including Dean Christian Gauss of Princeton and Mrs. Gauss, the poet Robert Hillyer, Louis Adamic, a young Yugoslav-born author who had written a study of class violence in America, and Wallace and Tish Irwin.

In her diary on August 25, Dorothy wrote:

> These days are beautiful. Hal on the water waggon for the last five days, and, as always, never more charming, brilliant or good tempered. It is already autumn. The trees are turning, and the blue and gold days have begun . . .

She had received from Warren Vinton (the friend who had introduced Josef and Eileen) a copy of *The Island,* a short-lived, very highbrow quarterly that Josef had edited and that featured Henry Moore's woodcuts and Ezra Pound's poetry as well as his own writings. Dorothy found it

> terribly disappointing. His own stuff is all that has any distinction . . . That strange, quick almost hurting sense of disappointment which I had all my life in Josef came back again sharply. I had a bad evening. This morning, however, when I went over to the old house to see Micky and the Irwins, I found them (not Micky) engaged in getting out their own Island. I also contributed a poem, and we had great fun, Tish and Peggy did drawings for woodcuts. We managed quite good parodies, remembering to be obscure, full of literary references in several languages, and always, underneath, rather dirty. In the evening we played Poker,

> cheating allowed, and were uproarious . . . Josef
> Bard ought to keep away from those Engish goys.
> He likes the way they dress, their complexions, and
> their simplicity. He is a good Jew-boy, really, and
> his great quality is intellectual hardness and lucid-
> ity. He's no Irish mystic . . .

The last observations (which were not, of course, intended
for publication) would surely have shocked Dorothy's Jewish
audiences. Although those of us who are Jewish often talk in
precisely this way about each other, the same words on Gentile
lips are grating. Innocent, in her own mind, of any tinge of
anti-Semitism, Dorothy never grasped the distinction.

In November she was again off for Europe — this time assigned by *Cosmopolitan* to interview Hitler. With soaring self-
confidence, he had received several foreign reporters including
Edgar Mowrer and Sigrid Schultz, who assured Dorothy that an
audience could readily be arranged for the distinguished Mrs.
Dorothy Thompson Lewis, known as a devoted friend of Germany if not the Nazis.

Checking in at the Adlon in Berlin she met the publisher
John Farrar, a friend and admirer of both Lewises. He suggested that if the interview went well she round it out into a
book by including background material on the Nazi movement.
She agreed and signed up with Farrar & Rinehart on the spot.
The book, titled *"I Saw Hitler!"* is a vivid exercise in "personal"
journalism.

"For seven years I have been trying to see Adolph Hitler,"
she wrote. "The first time I looked for him in the house of an
American woman, married and naturalized in Germany: Frau
Hanfstaengel [née Sedgewick, the mother of Hitler's press
chief] . . . Years ago, during the New York State Woman Suffrage Campaign, she had come over from Germany as a speaker
hired by the Woman Suffrage Party to advocate votes for
women. She made us a great deal of trouble: 'Ladies and gen-

tlemen,' she would say, 'I hope you will all vote for the woman suffrage amendment. And now let us pass to a consideration of why the *Lusitania* should not constitute a reason for war.' . . . Frau Hanfstaengel, as it turned out, was a German propagandist . . . Hitler had taken shelter elsewhere . . . during those years I tried, now and then to see him. He was lofty and remote from foreigners . . . But . . . things have changed . . . Hitler is coming into power . . . now he is prepared to address the world. And so he granted me an interview . . . [Though he had similarly favored others, Dorothy was confident that hers was the voice the world would heed.]

"I was a little nervous. I considered taking smelling salts. And Hitler was late. An hour late. Waiting upstairs in the foyer of the Kaiserhof Hotel I saw him shoot by, on the way to his rooms, accompanied by a body-guard who looked like Al Capone. Minutes pass. Half an hour. I go around to the room of the press chief: Ernest Hanfstaengel . . . Harvard graduate, famous among his classmates for his piano playing and his eccentricities. Fussy. Amusing. The oddest imaginable press chief for a dictator . . ."

Building up suspense, Dorothy makes the occasion not a mere interview but a dramatic confrontation. She also shares with the reader what turned out to be a monumental blunder. "When finally I walked into Adolph Hitler's salon in the Kaiserhof Hotel, I was convinced that I was meeting the future dictator of Germany. In something less than fifty seconds I was quite sure that I was not. It took just that time to measure the startling insignificance of this man who has set the whole world agog." Such was her self-assurance that she used these sentences as the headnote for her book's opening chapter. Hitler would soon be Chancellor of Germany and by March 1933 the Nazi dictatorship would be firmly established.

Fellow journalists were to twit her for years about this historic miss. She took their jibes good-naturedly, saying she had erred in failing to trust her first intuitive reaction. Throughout her career, she continued to make equally bold prognostications and to tot up her score in print a few months later. If, as often happened, her prophetic batting average was less than perfect, her readers were undismayed. The intensity of her emotional involvement gave her writing its glow, though it sometimes warped her judgment. At the time of her first look at Hitler, she still found it unlikely that the *gemütlich* and talented German people could be held in thrall by a demagogue whom she described as "formless, almost faceless, a man whose countenance is a caricature, a man whose framework seems cartilaginous, without bones. He is inconsequent and voluble, ill-poised, insecure. He is the very prototype of the Little Man."

Wrong though she was in her conclusion, her book provided a memorable portrait of the führer, a lucid and concise analysis and history of the Nazi movement, and a fine collection of pertinent photographs. Probably due to the haste with which it was published, identifying captions were lacking, to Lewis' annoyance.

"I butted in today, on receiving advance copy of your 'I Saw Hitler!' " he wrote to her, "(a nice book, and doesn't look a bit short) and told Ted Rinehart on the long distance phone (John [Farrar] and Stanley [Rinehart] being weg) that there should be titles under such photographs . . . doesn't say who the old general is; I suppose Ludendorff but don't know. I should? Is zat so! Who suggested the book in the first place! I ought to know.* Well *I* do, but the vulgus who read it won't. Oh. Oh so you don't have any vulguses among your readers. Aw gwan!"

---

* Lewis may have suggested a magazine piece. But according to Farrar, the book resulted from the encounter at the Adlon.

5

"out of a maelstrom . . ."

SINCE THE ADAMSES had reclaimed their Westport house, Dorothy before going abroad in the autumn of 1931 moved her family to an apartment at 21 East 90th Street. It boasted — among other amenities — two living rooms where Mr. and Mrs. Lewis could entertain their often incompatible guests; hers were increasingly experts in foreign affairs while Lewis continued to attract a wide assortment of fellow writers and convivial companions. The two, however, were seldom simultaneously in residence. In her diary Dorothy wrote:

> Whenever I separate from Hal it is as though I came out of a delirium into sanity, out of a maelstrom into a quiet place. And yet my heart goes rushing after him as he careens his way outward, restless, driven, ranting, panting, febrile — and electric.

This "electric" quality of Lewis' mind had always been his chief attraction for her. She had also, from the first, felt that he needed her to protect him from the painful consequences of his own follies. But if the marriage was to survive she knew that they must spend much of their time apart, perhaps in separate households, each paying his own way. Financially, however, this was not yet feasible.

She had become accustomed to an expensive way of life, with two well-staffed homes where she could be generously and continuously hospitable to friends who lived on a similar scale.

Some were successful authors and playwrights whose royalties were largely unaffected by the Depression or possessors of inherited wealth who still had ample capital to tap though their incomes dwindled. The Lewises themselves during the thirties suffered no more stringent economies than taking a tax loss by selling some "cats and dogs" among their stock holdings and seeking a substitute for the very expensive Fraulein Haemmerli,* who, as a specialized "infant's nurse," commanded the then astronomical wage of $250 a month.

But in 1931 Dorothy's own income was under $12,000. This included a $5000 "salary" from her husband — presumably so listed for tax purposes. She had been well paid for her articles in the *Saturday Evening Post, Pictorial Review,* and *Cosmopolitan* — $6500 in all. But *PEP* had yielded only $400 and royalties from *The New Russia* had dropped to a mere $47. Out of these earnings she had paid heavy expenses for travel, secretaries, and miscellaneous assistants amounting to more than $5000.†

As she had written to Tish Irwin in spelling out her hopes for her son, Dorothy recognized that "money is power," and she intended to have plenty of it. She had shown herself a tough businesswoman when she encouraged her husband to break his long-standing association with his publishers and sign what promised to be a more profitable contract with Doubleday, Doran. Lewis recognized this shrewd side of her character. He had a whimsical habit of signing his letters with fictitious names; in one note, discussing finances, he assumed the role of Becky Sharp's feckless and much exploited spouse — signing himself, "Your own Rawdon Crawley."

In her own mind, Dorothy justified her drive to earn money

---

* Rosa Haemmerli was replaced in due course by her younger, less "professional," and hence less expensive sister.

† In 1932 her magazine earnings climbed substantially and she added some $2000 in receipts from lectures — at an average of $150 per appearance. But there were again heavy travel expenses and a 25 per cent fee to her lecture agent.

by the need to escape from the day-to-day tensions of her marriage. It is unlikely, however, that she would have retired into domesticity even if her home life had been idyllic. (The proposition was never tested since Lewis was the only one of her three husbands who could afford to support her.) Although she enjoyed her status as Mrs. Sinclair Lewis, her restless, ambitious nature could not be satisfied by the reflected glory that came to her as the wife of a famous man. Nor could personal obligations take precedence over her consuming concern with developments in Europe.

Her frequent travels, of course, involved parting from her son as well as her husband. These separations worried her only sporadically. In her travel diaries, almost as afterthoughts, there are a few references to Michael, such as: "I am terribly homesick. I want my little boy, my tiny son." These pangs did not deter her from spending seven months abroad during the first two years of his life and accepting as many lecture appearances as her agent could arrange.

During her absences, Dorothy salved her conscience by making elaborate arrangements for the physical comfort of her family, hiring the most competent of domestics, and typing up detailed instructions for them. Although he would soon rebel at being left to tend the home fires — and indeed was much more prone than his wife to depart on short notice for distant places — Lewis seemed temporarily to enjoy looking after Dorothy's friends as well as her household while she was abroad in pursuit of Hitler.

"I have reached Phyllis Bottome on the phone . . . she will dine with me here the 24th . . ." he wrote, "and I have paid the rent. And I have today sent a check to Howard and Peggy for $150 — I can think of no way of spending money that better pleases me . . . The household runs like silk; you picked a swell staff — and one that seems all at peace within itself; Miss Haemmerli the Rk of Ages as ever — wouldn't one have thought that back here in NY, with things outside to do, with termination of the job in sight, she might have slipped just the tiniest bit? — well, she hasn't; Mrs. Currie always so solicitous, so delighted when I especially like some dish and eat a lot of it; Mrs. Cullen [a secretary] efficient and not a bit intrusive; the washerwoman as ever — Lord, the house might have been organized for years . . ."

There were several reasons for Lewis' benign mood. A gala Broadway première was in prospect for the film version of *Arrowsmith* starring Helen Hayes and Ronald Colman. And he had abandoned the frustrating labor novel. On November 21, 1931, he wrote to Dorothy:

"I am going to do something that is important and that, so far as I can remember, has scarcely been touched in all fiction, and has never been adequately done except perhaps in the case of Mr. Shakespeare's Portia. In doing it I am thinking of Genia Schwarzwald — of Frances Perkins — of Susan B. Anthony — of Alice Paul — of such lovelier and more feminine, yet equally individual women as Sarah Bernhardt — of Jane Addams with all her faults — of Nancy Astor — of Catherine the Great — and if you don't mind being put in with such a gallery, a good deal of yourself . . . I do so hope that I am not infringing on your ideas — that is the only thing that worries me about it . . ."

Dorothy did not object to sitting for her portrait with this distinguished group. When she came home for Christmas she gladly supplied Lewis with recollections of her youthful struggles and encounters. Early in the new year, she was off again on a lecture tour. Addressing the Wisconsin Women's Club in February 1932, she announced that her husband was busy with "the first of his novels that has featured a woman in the leading character since he wrote *Main Street* and I think it will be a dandy."

However, when *Ann Vickers* appeared the next year, Mary

Gawthorpe and Dorothy's other friends of suffrage days were outraged; the book was a caricature of feminism rather than a tribute to the sisterhood to which his wife had proudly belonged and in which she still claimed membership.

✖ 6
Danubian Magic

IN ALBANY, NEW YORK, Governor Franklin D. Roosevelt, confident of winning the Democratic presidential nomination in June, was assembling the brain trust that promised to give the country a new deal. But for most Americans it was still a season of bankruptcies, hunger marches, bank failures, and mortgage foreclosures. Even more ominous was the news from overseas. Britain, governed by a coalition under J. Ramsay MacDonald and with more than two million unemployed, had gone off the gold standard. The new Spanish democracy was threatened with civil war. Japan, emboldened by worldwide confusion and uncertainty, had launched an unofficial war against China by occupying Manchuria. The USSR was suffering a disastrous famine. And in Germany, Hitler won 11 million votes when he challenged Hindenburg for the presidency. Though defeated by a small plurality, it was evident that Hitler's hour was close at hand.

Increasingly disturbed by perils abroad, Dorothy, after only three months in America, again sailed for Europe in April 1932. She had arranged a rendezvous in Paris with her old mentor Fodor, who agreed to accompany her as auxiliary eyes, ears, and political counselor on a tour that would include Geneva, Berlin, East Prussia, Warsaw, Prague, Budapest, and Vienna. Lewis followed her to Paris and pleaded — not very coherently — that she cancel the trip and come to England with him. "Dorothy wouldn't even consider the idea," Fodor recalled. " 'You know me, Fodor,' she said. 'We are going on.' I don't think Red was ever very fond of me after that. He was angry, very angry, when he left us and went to London." It was a whirlwind trip, according to Fodor, during which their journalistic efforts were sometimes hampered by the red-carpet treatment accorded Mrs. Sinclair Lewis. Their attempts, for example, to find out how the German population was faring in the Polish Corridor (the slice of Prussia ceded to Poland by the Versailles treaty) were systematically thwarted by overattentive Polish officials.

Arriving in Vienna in late April, Dorothy again succumbed to what Vincent Sheean called her "extreme susceptibility to the Danubian pretension." She loved the mood and atmosphere of the city and its people. Strolling one afternoon in the Belvedere Gardens, she gazed at the venerable gray stone apartment house on Prinz Eugenstrasse, where she had spent her happiest days with Josef. She was taken with the notion of moving back to this beloved city, at least for a while. There seemed no serious obstacles. Lewis, wherever his ostensible home, would wander. Two-year-old Michael could flourish here as well as in America, while his mother pursued her work without an ocean between them, enjoying the contentment that came of cultivated society, opera, theater, and all the cozy diversions of Viennese life.

Genia Schwarzwald applauded the idea. In short order she found a sumptuous apartment with vast blue-tiled bathrooms at Wohllebengasse 9. Dorothy leased it along with a villa in Semmering for weekends. All this was well within the Lewises means. *Ann Vickers* was about to become a best seller, Doubleday would provide a $30,000 advance for the next book, Goldwyn had paid handsomely for the film rights to *Arrowsmith*, and Sidney Howard was preparing a dramatization of *Dodsworth*.

A special attraction in Vienna was the presence of congenial colleagues — Fodor, still representing the Manchester *Guard-*

ian; Whit Burnett of the New York *Sun* (who was also in process of launching *Story* magazine with his wife, Martha Foley); Bob Best, the attractive young U.P. man; and her good friends Frances and John Gunther, correspondent for the Chicago *Daily News,* who (unlike Sheean) shared her enthusiasm for what he called "the old lilac city." They made a place for her at their table in the *Journalisten Zimmer* of the Café Louvre, welcomed her as an associate member to the Anglo-American press club, and readily persuaded her that Vienna was an ideal base for reporting the European scene. Here, a year earlier, the failure of Austria's leading bank, the Credit-Anstalt, had triggered a worldwide financial crisis. Antagonism was growing between the liberal Social Democrats who controlled Vienna and the reactionary national government. Conservatives and socialists alike had long favored union with a still democratic Germany — Anschluss — as the answer to both countries' economic problems. But France had vetoed the proposal and now was determined to prevent the customs union that was under active discussion. Meanwhile native fascists — who had taught Hitler his first lessons in anti-Semitism and rabid nationalism — and their private army, the *Heimwehr,* were gaining ground, inspired by Nazi triumphs in Germany.

Dorothy omitted the taboo subject of politics when she set about persuading her husband, who was still in London, of the delights of their coming sojourn in Austria.

"My room is large and white and full of crimson brocade," she wrote from the Hotel Imperial, where she was staying, pending the move to Wohllebengasse, "and it looks out on the Ring where the trees are greener than trees in the electric light and I see two cafés with box trees surrounding them, and automobiles are tooting, and at my bedside is fruit and on this table are tulips and lilacs & who says Vienna is dead?

"All day through *the* loveliest country — Buchs — Laudeck — Innsbruck — Schwaz — Through country like this we shall walk to Venice in September . . ."

Dorothy cut short her stay in Vienna in mid-May, when she and Lewis returned to the United States. Like hundreds of other American parents, they were horrified by the news that the kidnaped Lindbergh baby had been found dead on May 12. "It makes me physically sick; makes me want to hurry home to Micky," Lewis wrote. "Well, we are hurrying — we'll be off a week from tomorrow. I know you too thought immediately of Micky at the news."

After an unusually brief stay at Twin Farms Dorothy again sailed on the *Europa* on August 23, 1932, this time accompanied by her husband, Michael, and the junior Fraulein Haemmerli. Lewis was, predictably, unhappy in Vienna, where he was an outsider in Dorothy's worshipful circle of native diplomats, politicians, artists, academicians, and journalists and irked by their incessant dialogue about the world situation. There was much entertaining both in the Vienna flat and in the Semmering villa, which Lewis described as "a cuckoo-clock house in aspect, with Ritz comfort in beds and bathrooms and kitchens and chairs and lights . . ."

In the autumn, Dorothy invited her sister Peggy for a visit with her five-year-old daughter Pamela. Lewis, seized with his usual restlessness, took Peggy off for a trip to Italy. On November 8 Dorothy wrote him a long gossipy letter full of the pleasures of Viennese life. She had given a party for Pammy complete with ice cream and *kugelhupf,* had been twice to the theater, had dined out with some of the most delightful people in town, entertained others including "a terribly charming little actress named Luise Rainer," had "looked in at the Argentine consulate on the floor above us, where a big party was going on and there met Count Salm [possibly Ludwig, ex-husband of the American heiress Millicent Rogers]; Micky had had a hair-cut and was 'handsome and very adorable.' "

As to her own state of mind, there are none of the protestations of "desperately missing" her absent husband that were customary in their correspondence. "It's probably just as well

I didn't go," she wrote. "You were cross with me and whenever I was with you I was lonely. Sometimes I think you don't see me at all, but somebody you have made up, a piece of fiction like Ann Vickers. So terribly lifelike that you almost convince me that's me, until suddenly my heart is crying outside a locked gate with the other 'me' inside looking in on the false one with you . . ."

The Lewises had planned a large house party at Semmering to celebrate Christmas 1932. One guest arrived before the holiday week — Baroness Hatvany. Better known as Christa Winsloe, she was the author of *Mädchen in Uniform,* the tragic story of a school-girl, Manuela, who falls hopelessly in love with one of her teachers and ultimately commits suicide by plunging down the well of a circular staircase. It was made into a film — one of the first with a frankly lesbian theme — which was shown in America in 1932. German-born Christa had many gifts. A talented sculptress and a witty ranconteur, she possessed a charm and sophistication that exemplified for Dorothy the magic of Central European culture.

When they first met in the 1920s, Dorothy had been more interested in her husband, Baron Laci Hatvany, an intimate of Josef's and a great charmer, who shared her passion for politics. But in December 1932 Christa's impact was suddenly overwhelming. In her diary Dorothy wrote:

> She stood there still in her hat and jacket; it was seven in the morning and I wore green pyjamas. "Hello," I said and went to shake her hands. It was six years since I had seen her. But instead we kissed. I thought she looked much older: much too heavy and tired. What was the sudden indescribable charm in that too-soft face, and the heavy-lidded eyes. (The upper lid is very arched, the lower straight). Anyhow immediately I felt the strange, soft feeling — curious — of being at home, and at rest; an enveloping warmth and sweetness like a drowsy bath . . .

Dorothy's attachment for Christa deepened during the hectic Christmas party. Among the guests were John and Frances Gunther; Edgar and Lilian Mowrer; Marcel and Marta Fodor; Peggy Wilson; Alexander Frere Reeves, a British publisher, and Patricia Wallace, daughter of the mystery story writer Edgar Wallace, whom Frere would soon marry; Virgilia Peterson, the lovely and brilliant literary critic, and her future husband, Prince Paul Sapieha of Warsaw; Nicholas Roosevelt, then minister to Hungary; First Secretary Haddow of the British legation in Vienna and his wife; and Baron and Baroness Hatvany. There were five children of assorted ages: Michael Lewis, Pamela Wilson, Diane Jane Mowrer, Johnny Gunther, and Dennis Fodor.

Fodor recalls a week of unadulterated pleasure enlivened by witty companions and his lovely Marta's gypsy songs performed nightly to her own guitar accompaniment. The sun seldom shone though there was plenty of snow. By midafternoon under gray skies, there was nothing to do but huddle indoors and begin serious drinking. Lilian Mowrer remembers the occasion as a housekeeping nightmare. Dorothy, who had acquired a Ford that she drove with abandon, spent hours commuting to Vienna to replenish the food and liquor supply. On December 24 she was determined to serve carp, a traditional Viennese Christmas Eve delicacy and a few days earlier had brought a huge live fish from Vienna, planning to store it in the pond which had unfortunately frozen over. Photographs of the house party show a resolutely merry group, riding a toboggan, making snowmen, and frolicking with the young. Lewis, who was at his best playing host, is said to have done less drinking than his guests.

On December 28 Dorothy turned to her diary in which she wrote at length during the following week:

> So it has happened to me again after all these years [she wrote recalling her attachment to Gertrude Tone and a "Sapphic" episode in Berlin]. To love

a woman is somehow ridiculous. *Mir auch passt es
nicht. Ich bin doch heterosexuel* [It doesn't suit
me. I am heterosexual]. . . . Well then, how account for this which has happened again. The soft,
quite natural kiss on my throat, the quite unconscious (seemingly) even open kiss on my breast, as
she stood below me on the stairs . . . What in
God's name does one call this sensibility if it be not
love? This extraordinary heightening of all one's
impressions; this intensification of sensitiveness;
this complete identification of feeling? It was so
when I read her book and suddenly felt that I *must*
translate it, because in its essence I might have
written it myself. *I* was Manuela, as she is Manuela
and everything that has happened to her has in
essence, and under other circumstances, happened
to me. This incredible feeling of sisterhood . . .

Curiously, this experience seemed to have had the effect of
unlocking Dorothy's erotic sensibilities in general, not merely
toward Christa. She recorded a walk, during the house-party
week, with the husband of a close friend of whom she had
long been fond but for whom she now felt an overpowering attraction (which she managed to curb). More surprising was the
impact on her relationship with Lewis. When the last guest had
left Dorothy followed Christa to Budapest, returning to Vienna
on January 2, where she wrote:

I came home on the night train. In the morning
I dropped into bed in the Wohllebengasse and
slept until 10. Then motored to the Semmering.
Above Glognitz the sun was brilliant. Suddenly I
was glad, glad, glad to be home with the party over.
Hal was in his room. When I came in he was glad.
I could see he was awfully glad. I stood a long time
in his arms, loving his familiar feel and smell, rub-
bing my face on his face. What are you going to
do? he said, and I said: First of all take a bath. So
he said: Stop in on your way down. I stopped in

in a dressing gown and nothing else and he said: Come to my bed. So I did and it was awfully good. Especially good, with me too tired to expect it to be and suddenly it was there and very wonderful . . . It would be nice to have a new child as the end-of-the party . . . I have been very, very happy. And all the time, every moment, I have thought of Christa.

7

"two quite different feelings"

THE POSTPARTY EUPHORIA ended when Lewis resumed heavy
drinking and Dorothy's hopes for a second child were dashed
by a miscarriage. It was a relief to see him off for London,
leaving her free to work on her magazine pieces and also to start
a novel (titled *The Tulip Box*, it was never completed). Weekends in Semmering were shared with many guests including
Marcia and Russell Davenport, Phyllis Bottome and her husband Ernan Forbes-Dennis, and, Lewis' friend, Broadway producer Philip Goodman and his wife Lily. Possibly under the
relaxing influence of strong wine, Dorothy unburdened herself
one evening to the Goodmans.

"Darthy is leaving Wredde," he wrote afterward to his crony
H. L. Mencken. "She wishes no alimony, but only to be rid
of him. Say what you will, the woman is all decency and dignity. Her stories are long, it is true, and that she is a lady journalist (worse, a lady foreign correspondent who is always privy
to wars that are being secretly made between countries whose
names she is unfortunately not at liberty at present to divulge)
is also true. But she's not without steel in her character, and
her inner self stands erect and proudly . . . Poor Wredde! I
fear it will be said of him that he couldn't remain a celebrity,
but had to become a mere notoriety. But of Darthy you must
revise many of your prejudices. She has her own ego and it
goes marching down the street behind a brass band at times, and
she is an energetic money maker; but she is honest and not
cheap, and she hates all of Wredde's vermin friends. More, she

tells him so. Her plan is to earn enough to support herself and her baby, and to give Wredde the rest of the earth in which to get drunk and make a public damn fool of himself. At least, all this was the earful Lily and I got last night. For all I know, as I write this they may be in one another's arms."

Physically any such reunion was, of course, impossible since they were separated by a large slice of the European continent and the English Channel. But distance once again renewed their affection. As the memory of his last days in Vienna faded, Dorothy was buoyed by the prospect of going to Italy with Christa in March.

She had written on the morning when she shared her husband's bed: "Obviously there are two quite different feelings. I don't love Hal any less. Rather more." Such indeed seemed to be the case. With her need for warmth and tenderness satisfied, she could offer more gentle understanding to her husband; also, it was urgent to prove to herself that Christa notwithstanding, she was a basically heterosexual woman.

In February she wrote to Lewis: "There's nothing real in life for me excepting you and what is part of you, our son . . . I was hysterical before you left, and I was a wreck after. It doesn't matter. I love you, love you, love you . . ."

Lewis responded in kind: "You seem to me in my mad life my one refuge and security. You see, I don't care a damn — not any more at least — for fame and all those amiable experiences, but only (and this is a not-too-easy contradiction) for you and Mickey on the one hand, and Freedom (whatever that empty thing may be) on the other . . ."

He had, he said, given up drinking spirits for the next seventy-seven years and when he was about to sail homeward on the small ship of his choice, the *American Farmer*, assured her, "I have thought of you every minute . . . My little darling! You're not so very big, you know. Neither am I. And you and I and Mr. Mickey are forever together. My darling!"

He wrote often and lovingly during the crossing. On March 4, 1933: "I interrupted the writing of this letter to go listen to the events from Washington on the radio — A miracle; Kaltenborn on top a car moving behind that of Prests Hoover and Roosevelt down Pennsylvania, instantly switching us to a man on top of the Willard Hotel, and the whole coming, clearly, to a ship at sea! . . . Europes are nice, but I prefer Vermont. I shall be there with you. It's true, isn't it, that there will be apple trees, and flaming lilies and the moon over the low mountains and you and me after dinner, sitting smoking on the terrace, and inside, when it becomes chilly, the fireplace and lamplight and lots of books? Love me, so we can go home."

Arriving in New York during the bank moratorium of March 1933, he was surprised to find neither panic nor rioting. He had begun work on a new novel about hotels and was seeing numerous old friends including Frank and Esther Adams. "I have never seen Esther look half so beautiful. Also, just when you are letting yours grow, she has bobbed her hair. She said 'Lord, how I miss Dorothy . . . !' I'm not so sure I shall see Gertrude Tone at all. Frank Adams told me she is now at Tony's every night, terribly soused. That is why she has never written to us. God what a thorough tragedy. Frank said he thought Franchot was in Hollywood . . . Not one word from you since London. Darling!"

"I have a very bad conscience that I haven't written," Dorothy replied on March 13. The reason was an unexpected assignment from a Jewish news agency for an up-to-the-minute report on what Dorothy called "the German inferno." Since January 30 Hitler had been Chancellor. When a fire on February 27 partially destroyed the Reichstag building and Hitler pronounced it a Communist plot, President Hindenburg by decree suspended free speech, a free press, and other liberties, leaving the Nazi storm troopers free to rampage. Hitler had not yet begun to exterminate the Jews but many were robbed, beaten, and murdered; they were excluded from public service, the universities, and the professions. On April 1, 1933, Hitler proclaimed a national boycott of Jewish shops. "It is really as bad as the most sensational papers report," Dorothy wrote to Lewis. "Hitler gets up and speaks about German unity and German loyalty and the new era, and the S.A. boys have simply turned into gangs and beat up people on the streets . . . and take socialists and communists and pacifists & Jews into so-called 'Braune Etagen' [brown floors] where they are tortured. Italian fascism was a kindergarten compared to it. It's an outbreak of sadistic and pathological hatred. Most discouraging of all is not only the defenselessness of the liberals but their incredible (to me) docility. And, my dear, in Berlin suddenly the old shop-worn ideas of civil liberties, democratic sanctions etc. seemed pretty good to me. I wanted to go around reciting the Gettysburg address. Edgar [Mowrer] is constantly threatened, but has no intention of leaving Berlin & doesn't think he is in actual danger . . . Oh Hal, oh my darling my dear, it's a long time and why did we ever quarrel, and why did you go back to spirits, and will we ever be happy and quiet again, and do you love me, and . . . and . . ."

On March 15, she bade farewell to Vienna and Semmering, sold her car to Gunther, and headed for Italy, where Christa, Micky, and Fraulein Haemmerli were awaiting her in Portofino. After a sentimental visit to Villa Galotti, scene of her sojourn with Lewis before their marriage, she wrote him from Torre di Giorgio:

"I have never felt so cut off from you emotionally as I have in all this time. I think for one thing that I was ill for a time after you left. I had that miscarriage and . . . I felt as though our marriage were somehow going on the rocks. And I had no emotional strength with which to try to pull it off. Your going back to drinking spirits was part of it . . . It seemed to me that our life together was falling into exactly the pattern of your life with Grace . . . Only, and this is the truth, and I suppose the only truth, I do love you, I love you too terribly . . ."

Lewis, who was crossing the American continent gathering material for his novel, replied from Del Monte, California: "Your feeling of lack of closeness and electricity in our letters, of distance not to be covered is partly imaginary. When we are in Vermont, I think it will all seem a bad dream. If I hadn't been bored by Semmering, if I hadn't been exasperated by Genia's intrusions, if I weren't such a damned Philistine, so Babbitt, that I comprehend neither music nor painting, you would never have felt shut off . . . You say you wonder whether the course of us may not, does not, run like that of mine and Grace — There is one difference, at least, which is pretty fundamental. She is mean, grasping, a son of a bitch. You are never mean, never grasping. You have faults. (Ever know that?) You are somewhat too inclined to run the show, both conversationally and domestically, but as I probably am so inclined also, we ought to be able to endure that in each other so long as neither of us is mean, and neither is . . ."

Before receiving this reassuring reply Dorothy apologized for her "unhappyish letter" — "I can't forgive myself for having been so angry with you. Could I *ever* have been angry with you? I love you so, I love you so —"

Eminent refugees from Hitler's Germany were arriving daily in Santa Margherita, a nearby village — among them Franz Werfel, the prolific novelist and playwright, best known in America at that time for his plays *Goat Song* and *Juarez and Maximilian,* which had been produced in New York by the Theatre Guild; Fritz von Unruh, a Prussian aristocrat whose antimilitarist writings had jolted the nation, particularly the officer caste with whom he had served in World War I; and Gerhart Hauptmann, Germany's most distinguished dramatist and recipient of the Nobel Prize for Literature in 1912.

"The roster of names of the writers and scientists who have left Germany reads like the German Who's Who," Dorothy wrote. "There's not a single important writer there any longer. Thomas and Heinrich Mann, Alfred Doeblin, Feuchtwanger — I would be entirely happy if it weren't for the German situation which strikes me very closely . . . Did you ever hear of anything more fiendish than the blackmailing of the whole world, by holding the German Jews as hostages. I lie awake nights thinking what one could do . . ."

In Portofino she completed a powerful indictment of Nazism titled "Back to Blood and Iron." "Before I left the atmosphere in Vienna had gotten so poisonous that it even drifted through closed doors into one's writing room, like a poison gas, a disease germ or a bad smell," she told Lewis. "It looks as though Austria would also go Nazi . . . I couldn't write, got too mad — down here, in a divine atmosphere of peace and ease, I finished the article. I think it is pretty good . . ."

Soon she was corresponding with the Vermont staff about opening the house and joyously anticipating sailing for home on the *Rex* on May 4. Lewis had apparently raised questions about her relationship with Christa: "Have no fears, I ain't thata way," Dorothy replied. "But I am somewhat otherwise and I miss my husband damn it frightfully. Your letters are like roses in December. And the thought of you across the sea *and* the continent is dreadful . . .

"It's terribly funny sharing a house with another woman. Somehow it reminds me of college days. There is something slightly absurd about it. But Christa is extremely good company — very easy going, very amusing . . . she's the most sympathetic woman I have met in years and years . . . she had the house going beautifully before ever I arrived. I have decided that what every worker needs is a wife . . . If I can't live with you in Vermont I had rather live with Christa here than anything I can at once imagine . . ."

Though she was on friendly terms with her newly divorced husband, Christa had no desire to return to Hatvan, his estate near Budapest, or to live under the hated Nazi regime in her native Munich, where she owned a house. "Christa has made up her mind to come with me to New York," Dorothy wrote. "I persuaded her, because for the moment there is absolutely no opportunity for her in Germany, or for anyone of her attitude of mind. Johnnie [Farrar] will look after her in N.Y. I am sure, since she is his author, and I've written Marcia [Davenport] and Esther [Adams], too. I've told her whenever she gets tired of N.Y. she can come to us. She will be working. Has a new play which sounds like Broadway to me. Please write a note to Christa and tell her you are glad she's coming. She is a little nervous about you and afraid."

These anxieties proved groundless. Christa was made welcome at Twin Farms, the first in a long succession of fugitives from Hitler's Europe whom Dorothy would shelter, and Lewis' reaction posed no problems. "Baroness Hatvany was instinctively akin to Red," Vincent Sheean wrote, "as only neurotics can be with each other; no sentence had to be completed really, because each knew what the other intended to say. I think they liked each other very much . . ."

In June, Dorothy learned from her agent that the lecture business was "on the up & up for next fall & winter — the first real steady improvement since the depression hit us . . . We are getting several engagements for the fall & more in prospect . . . P.S. I have a Club near here interested in Baroness Hatvany. I wish she might give me a subject — something on developments in Europe, women's place in them or something of that sort."

The catastrophic pace of events in Central Europe made another trip abroad seem essential before the end of summer. In August 1933 Dorothy left with Christa for Austria, where Chancellor Engelbert Dollfuss had suspended parliamentary government in March and local Nazis were staging huge demonstrations. Among many others, she called on her first Viennese neighbor, a socialist schoolteacher named Anton Murbacher. The result was a moving article, "A Wreath for Toni," * climaxed by Toni's death in the assault on the Karl Marx Hof through which the Dollfuss regime destroyed the Austrian Socialist Party in February 1934.

Upon her return to Vermont, Dorothy's heavy writing commitments necessitated solitude. From the Plaza in New York, she wrote to Lewis: "My piece, praise God, is finished. And I have not been out of this room for two solid days. Nine hours at the typewriter and the whole 6,000 words written down at one breath . . . no liquor and just two cigarettes . . .† I kiss you and Mickey and Christa. And Mrs. Currie. And Haemmerli and Agnes and Ella and Stub [the gardener] and Bongo and Mitzi [a white cat whose descendants still populate the Barnard, Vermont, area in large numbers] . . . and I wish the hell I were home and will be any minute."

When she returned to Twin Farms, Christa had left for Virginia Beach, where she was entertained by Lewis' first wife, now Mrs. Telesforo Casanova. In lieu of a diary, Dorothy had taken occasionally to writing long introspective letters, which she kept in her files instead of mailing them. One of these, addressed to Christa, is filled with the anxieties masked from the world by her poised manner. In non-Freudian terms, she described a classic conflict between id and super-ego: "I am neither a good worker, nor a good mother, nor a good wife, nor a good friend . . . Perhaps you have observed the *spaltung* [cleavage] in me, for I am one thing emotionally — optimistic, warm-hearted, easily *verliebt* [in love], strongly sensual, slightly brutal, deeply attached, responsible, self-confident, courageous, generous, inconsiderate, ruthless, vulgar — and something quite

---

* The article was an example of Dorothy's deft use of imagination to enhance fact. No one named Murbacher — and no schoolteacher — died in the clash, though many others did.
† A chain smoker all her life, Dorothy's periodic efforts to kick the habit are painfully familiar to fellow tobacco addicts.

otherwise intellectually . . . This self is profoundly pessimistic, conservative, self-disdainful, suppressed, critical, tender, of excessively disciplined sensuality (afraid of it) tentative, humble. Almost never in my life have I been able to bring this mess which is the original me plus the cultivated me (cultivated in the agricultural sense of the word) into harmony . . . part and parcel of all of me is a belief in life and in creation and a terrific discouragement with myself that I put nothing new, nothing unique into the universe. Hence this passion . . . to serve more creative natures . . . which lies at the root of my attachment for Hal, and also at the root of my attachment for you . . ."

Lewis had been talking of renting a house in England for the next six months. But instead he went to Chicago in the fall to collaborate on a play with Lloyd Lewis, drama critic of the *Daily News,* while Christa spent the early months of 1934 in New York with Dorothy. Lilian Mowrer, who was in America on a lecture tour and was also a guest for several weeks in the 90th Street apartment, recalls a very affectionate relationship between the two. Others regarded the friendship as special. "They were a couple," John Farrar said. "If you asked Dorothy for dinner, you asked Christa too. We loved having them. They were both marvelous company."

However, in March, Dorothy went with Lewis and Michael for a vacation in Bermuda. On her return she wrote to Christa, who was again off on a round of visits:

"I want to go to Europe to do some work, and I haven't made up my mind whether to leave in the next few days or whether to wait until after I have moved the family to the country. And then there is my health which is not good . . .* I weigh now only 63 kilos [about 138 pounds, not too little for her five-foot, seven-inch height] which makes my figure good, my face drawn and my temper execrable . . . The time in Bermuda was really lovely. Red was well, *gut gelaunt* [good-

* Diagnosed as diabetic, she had been on a rigid diet.

natured] and we had a good good time together. If my life were
otherwise the best thing for me to do would be to go up to Vermont early, spend a very quiet summer, resting and concentrat-
ing on my health, but the truth is that dear as Red is to me —
and he really is — life with him is nerve racking in the extreme
. . . Our family is well off. I was afraid we would be up against
it this month, but Dodsworth [starring Walter Huston and Fay
Bainter] is the most successful play of the season, and Hal is
drawing $800 a week out . . ."

Since she hated to miss the spring in Vermont, Dorothy decided to postpone her trip abroad. Two wings had been
added to the "new house" (known originally as the "Chase
House"), which was now a spacious U-shaped clapboard structure, shaded by ancient trees and a fragrant lilac hedge. An
enthusiastic and expert gardener like her father, Dorothy had
designed an impressive perennial border against a low stone
wall that marked the edge of a wide grassy terrace, with the
valley and Mount Ascutney as background. Guests were dazzled by a changing panorama of superb delphinium, dahlias,
roses, or Madonna lilies; they long remembered delectable salads
of raw *mange-tout* peas, miniature beans, carrots, beets, and
other choice produce. But the dilatory husbandry of her hired
hands was a constant source of exasperation, and Dorothy
usually spent her first days on the farm in a weeding orgy.
"I talked to Stub, who had his usual excuses," she wrote to
Lewis. "This time I was absolutely firm and said, 'Stub, there
is no use your arguing about this. I tell you, and I tell it to
you finally, those flower beds and the vegetable garden have
not been properly taken care of. I also tell you exactly what
is wrong and I expect you to remedy it. If you don't want to do
it my way, then find someone else to work for.' At which he
became very mild. So I hope (but don't really expect) that he'll
reform . . ." *

* Her premonition was correct. The Vermont response to such lordly com-
mands was seldom positive.

Having spent most of the summer of 1934 and the following winter under the Lewis roof, Christa left on a cross-continental tour in pursuit of the opera star Ezio Pinza, for whom she had formed an unaccountable (and unrequited) affection. Her ultimate goal was Hollywood, where she hoped to work as a scenarist. It was an unlikely prospect; though she was a gifted author in her native tongue, her written English was pure pidgin, punctuated by frequent lapses into German or French. The excerpts from her letters to Dorothy that follow are typical: "Of course there arne thousands of Italien soldiers and fishermen who look as well he [Pinza] does, and better . . . biutiful men — as I told you — they always bored me . . . Men for 'us' are onely good for a time but not a la longue. What a sujet . . . essentially nothing on earth can come between us — not a man — nicht von mir aus. Was vir gemein haben liegt auf einer andern Linie [not on my side. What we have in common is of a different order] . . . Wenn ich doch auft eine Stunde Wenigstens zu Dir hinschlupfen könnte un 'Dotto' sagen [If only I could be close to you for an hour and say 'Dotto'] . . ."

Not surprisingly, Dorothy found these singular communications unsatisfying. After a visit to her alma mater, Syracuse, for a lecture appearance, in another unsent letter to Christa she wrote:

"I stayed at the sorority house, and they were all awfully pretty and flattering, and after my speech a party and several of my old professors came . . . lovely, lovely Jean Marie Richards who in my youth was Dean of the girl's college and for me the epitome of all worldliness, elegance, culture & refinement; sixty now, elegant, old and as mocking as ever, and she thinks I'm fine and after all these years I was happy happy happy that she thought so . . .

"I have three small letters from you . . . but they are not letters to me, they are a cry into the circumambient universe. I feel that something between us has broken, and like all that love I wonder now if it was ever there . . . I had a strange dream last night. I dreamed I was putting out into a very rough sea in a frail ship, and the crew were all women. I was afraid, and woke up, sweating . . ."

In Christa's letters, which continued to drip with Teutonic sentimentality, there is no sign of waning affection. However, the correspondence lagged when, disappointed in her hopes of earning a living in Hollywood, she returned to Europe in 1935 to make her home in southern France. Dorothy came to her rescue with an allowance of fifty dollars a month in 1940 when France had fallen to the Germans and Christa could no longer draw funds from her Munich bank. Communications were totally cut off after November 11, 1942, when German forces moved into the previously unoccupied portion of France in retaliation for the Anglo-American invasion of North Africa. Dorothy had no further word of Christa until the war's end when a mutual friend, Helene Meier Graef, wrote from Munich on July 20, 1946, telling her that Christa had been living in Cluny, Saône-et-Loire, "with a French-Swiss girlfriend from Geneva, Simone Gentet . . . a rumour persists obstinately that she had been a spy. Christa once described her as a hysterical, dissolute, morphine addict and alcoholic, but she certainly knew nothing of Simone's other activities, should the rumour be true. Simone is supposed to have been convicted, and since the two lived together, Christa was suspected also and shot . . . we know with such absolute certainty that Christa was the most violent enemy of National-Socialism and that she would never have made the slightest compromise. On the contrary, we were always worried that the Gestapo would grab her and we still believed this is what happened to her because she had helped many Jewish friends to get out of the country . . . dear Mrs. Dorothy Thompson, you seem to me the only person who could shed some light into this darkness . . ."

Determined to clear her friend's name, Dorothy sought the

help of the French Embassy in Washington. In December, Ambassador Henri Bonnet, after checking with the French police, wrote: "Miss Christa Winsloe died on June 10, 1944 . . . She was not captured by the maquis but murdered by a man named Lambert, who killed her, falsely pretending that he was fulfilling orders from an underground movement. In fact, Lambert was nothing but an ordinary criminal . . ."

8
"Good-by to Germany"

DOROTHY WAS OFF to Europe once again in July 1934, leaving Lewis in charge of a household that included Michael and his nurse, Peggy Wilson and Pamela, Wells Lewis, Lewis' secretary Lou Florey, and an assortment of servants, several with offspring. Dorothy had decided that four-year-old Michael needed, above all, the companionship of contemporaries. But Lewis, who could not endure the presence of a single child for long, found the situation intolerable and soon fled. From Franconia, New Hampshire, he wrote to his wife:

"The household got to be just a little too much for me, Saturday. Wells, in all sweetness invited the registrar of Andover, one Dr. Eccles, who had been very helpful to him in entering Harvard (he has passed all his exams, by the way) to drop in at Barnard . . . Well Dr. phones and can he and his wife AND nine-year-old girl (in a house already simply lousy with children) come and stay Friday to Monday . . . I stayed long enough to welcome Eccleses, hordes of Eccleses (and very nice they proved to be) to explain that I had previous engage, here and beat it . . ."

Within a month he sent one family group off — Mrs. Waller, Dorothy's secretary, and her four young. "Between you and me, I have had, for an undomestic gent, rather a full measure of kids . . . this summer when I mean to be tranquil . . ." He promised to find a far more competent replacement for Mrs. Waller. In fact, he assured her he would have waiting for her when she returned "an assortment of three or four good secre-

taries who at least know enough about Germany etc. to be able
to spell names, and have them ready for you to make your choice
— if you want any of them — while you are writing your articles
and preparing lectures . . ."

Dorothy at this point was in London where she had an unexpected brush with British justice. Driving a borrowed car she
had run head-on into a bus in Trafalgar Square. She was rescued from an awkward situation by Dale Warren, Phyllis Bottome's editor at Houghton Mifflin whom Dorothy had met the
previous winter in Boston. Dale provided her with the services
of a friendly barrister gratis, a chivalrous deed that marked the
beginning of an enduring friendship.

The news that Nazi conspirators had murdered Chancellor
Dollfuss on July 25 made a quick trip to Austria imperative.
"My God things are exciting in this part of the world," she wrote
to Dale from Vienna, issuing at the same time a cordial invitation to visit Twin Farms that fall. In early August, oblivious to
the hazards she posed at the wheel to her own life and others,
she rented another car and headed for Berlin via Salzburg,
Innsbruck, and Munich, pausing en route to call on old friends
and to talk politics with chance acquaintances at inns and cafés.
Everyone she interviewed was either rejoicing or despairing at
the prospect of a Nazi triumph in Austria, which seemed inevitable despite the opposition of the new chancellor, Kurt von
Schuschnigg. Streets decked with the Nazi flag — the black
swastika in a white circle on a flaming red background —
greeted her when she crossed the German border. At Garmisch,
an American friend who had attended the Oberammergau
Passion Play told her, "These people are crazy. When they
hoisted Jesus on the cross a German woman next to me said,
'That is our Fuehrer, our Hitler.' And when they paid out the
thirty pieces of silver to Judas she said, 'That is Roehm* who

* Ernst Roehm was one of the old comrades Hitler executed in the great blood
purge of June 30, 1934.

betrayed the leader.'" In Murnau she visited a Hitler youth camp where an enormous banner bore the slogan: "WE WERE BORN TO DIE FOR GERMANY."

Dorothy vividly described — and possibly embellished — her experiences on this journey in her second *Harper's* piece, "Good-By to Germany." "When I reached Berlin I went to the Adlon," she wrote. "It was good to be there, like home. There was Fix in the bar, with his shining hair and his shining smile and his good Dry Martinis. There was the big porter who can always get anything you want — reservations when the airplane is sold out and money when the banks are closed. There was the manager who always remembers how many people there are in your family and what room you had last time. Oh! I was glad to be back! The French doors were open into the garden and the fountain was sparkling and the little lawn was as smooth as the finest broadloom, and a man in an apron was actually sweeping it with a broom. It was all the courtesy, all the cleanliness, all the exquisite order which is Germany . . . I was still in my room in the morning when the porter rang up from the desk. 'Good morning, madam, there is a gentleman here from the secret state police.' 'Send him up,' I said. He was a young man in a trench coat like Hitler's. He brought an order that I should leave the country immediately within forty-eight hours, for journalistic activities inimical to Germany . . . I packed my things after a while and went downstairs. I stood for a few minutes in the lobby. Lord, how familiar it was. In this lobby I had met my husband for the first time. Out there in the garden we had had that birthday party . . . The porter helped me with my luggage . . . I went into the bar. '*Auf wiedersehen, gnaedige Frau,*' said Fix . . ."

This account is both more and less dramatic than the reality. She had been in Berlin ten days before being ordered out. And she did not quietly pack her bags and depart unnoticed. The Nazis' highhanded treatment of critical journalists was a matter of diplomatic concern. Although he had not been officially ousted, the German Foreign Office had made life so difficult for Edgar Mowrer that he had reluctantly had himself transferred to Paris a year earlier. Around the same time the correspondent of *Paris Soir* was explicitly threatened with expulsion but the order was rescinded when the French government threatened to take reciprocal action against German journalists. During the Reichstag fire trials in 1933, two Russian correspondents were expelled; when the USSR in turn booted every German correspondent out of Russia, the ban was lifted.

In Dorothy's case, Ambassador William E. Dodd promptly dispatched Consul General Geist to the Foreign Office to lodge a protest. He was told that the reason for the order was primarily Dorothy's Hitler interview, published in 1932, and secondarily the reports she had written in 1933 describing and condemning Hitler's anti-Semitic campaign. He was also informed that no appeal was possible since the decision came "from the highest authority in the Reich which was at this time out of communication." She was given an additional twenty-four hours' grace but, rather than accept favors, decided to leave for Paris on the next train on August 25.

"Nearly the entire corps of American and British correspondents went to the railway station to see her off and wish her good luck," Frederick T. Birchall reported in the *New York Times*. "They gave her a bunch of American Beauty roses as a token of their affection and esteem. When the train carried her away she was leaning out of the window, a little tearful over such a demonstration of comradeship, the armful of roses almost hiding her, and she waved a cheerful farewell." This sendoff so impressed the sleeping car conductor that he insisted on giving her a compartment to herself, although she had only paid for a second-class sleeper that she should have shared with another passenger.

The expulsion of Mrs. Sinclair Lewis was front-page news in America. When reporters caught up with her husband in New

York, they found him in a sour mood. "Well what do you expect me to do about it?" he said. "After all, Dorothy has covered seven revolutions, so she ought to be able to take care of herself. She's no poor, weak, little woman who needs my help. I think she's perfectly capable of issuing all the statements that are necessary, and no doubt she will do so."

Less restrained in his reaction was her lecture agent Feakins, who, striking while the headlines were hot, placed an advertisement announcing the availability of "Dorothy Thompson (Mrs. Sinclair Lewis)," whose "lectures, highly informative and presented in the virile compelling style which characterizes her writing, place her before the largest and most discriminating of audiences. Subjects: 'The Crisis in Germany' 'This World Peace Problem.' Miss Thompson will speak on additional subjects after returning."

Dorothy did not come home immediately. Instead she went to Saarbrücken to gather material for articles on the future of the Saar Basin — the mining and industrial region rich in coal and iron ore that had been under League of Nations control since the end of World War I. She correctly foresaw that an intense Nazi propaganda effort would result in a German victory in the plebiscite held in January 1935.

In her own cabled report on her expulsion, Dorothy adopted a casual tone. "My offense was to think that Hitler is just an ordinary man," she said. "That is a crime against the reigning cult in Germany, which says that Mr. Hitler is a Messiah sent of God to save the German people — an old Jewish idea. To question this mystic mission is so heinous that, if you are German you can be sent to jail. I, fortunately, am an American, so I merely was sent to Paris. Worse things can happen to one."

Upon her return to America she continued to treat the experience as a minor episode in the life of an adventuresome reporter. However, she had the expulsion order framed and hung it on her wall as a proud trophy.

PART VI

ASCENDING COMET

🎵 1
"such a crowded life . . ."

AFTER HER DRAMATIC EXIT from Germany, Dorothy was deluged with speaking invitations, including one from the Herald Tribune Conference (later renamed the Herald Tribune Forum), where she appeared on October 4, 1934. This was a platform often graced by the most distinguished figures in the nation's public life, many of whom were friends of Helen Reid, wife of the newspaper's publisher Ogden Reid and impresario of the meetings. Diminutive, forceful, and soft-spoken, H.R., as she was known to her colleagues, had been a suffrage activist and remained a zealous champion of her own sex in the male-dominated world of journalism. Impressed by Dorothy's magazine pieces, she conceived the idea of making her a political columnist — a function until then a male monopoly.

"It was a great disappointment not to have had a word with you after your speech," she wrote to Dorothy on October 5, ". . . I shall keep on hoping that when you return to New York we may have a real talk over the luncheon table."

"You were no more disappointed than I," Dorothy replied. ". . . I was awfully ashamed to have rushed away as I did . . . But I have had such a crowded life in the last three months that I simply had to rush from one engagement to another . . ."

When they met during the next month, H.R. broached her proposal. Dorothy found it attractive. A regular column would provide a more dependable income than free-lance writing and could pay handsomely if syndicated. In a day when newspaper reporting was generally as impersonal as the editorial pages were dull and predictable, such individualistic columnists as Walter Lippmann, Mark Sullivan, Heywood Broun, and Westbrook Pegler wielded wide influence. Dorothy looked forward to joining this oracular company. In addition, she deluded herself with the notion that writing a column would be a less demanding task than reporting, something she could do quietly at home without being constantly on the move. After a lecture appearance in Akron on December 1 she was interviewed by a U.P. reporter who wrote, "Dorothy Thompson — more recently Mrs. Sinclair Lewis — is going to drop lecturing, cease to be a world traveler and go home to be a mother to little Michael Lewis. The woman who interviewed Hitler and was brave enough to say she thought him neurotic, also is brave enough to rearrange her career in favor of her 4-year old son . . ."

Although details remained to be worked out, Dorothy was confident of the outcome.* Aware that she lacked the expertise on domestic affairs that her new role would demand, she went to Washington in the spring of 1935 for an intensive course in the politics of the New Deal.

After a two-hour interview with Huey Long, she wrote to Lewis that he was "shrewd, fantastic and not altogether unlikeable . . . rushed off to see [Donald] Richberg [one of FDR's first brain trusters], whom I didn't like. Dry and unimaginative. Dined last night with [Senator Lester J.] Dickinson, who is too conservative for any use but a charming fellow as conservatives usually are. He introduced me at dinner, at the Shoreham, to an attaché of the German embassy (took some aplomb on both our parts) . . . Today I have been on the road since nine o'clock . . . saw [Joseph P.] Kennedy of the Security and Exchange Commission, who is extremely intelligent and informed, [Herbert] Feis in the foreign office (old friend) lunched with

* In a chronology of her life that she sketched out when she started her autobiography she wrote: "1935. Began career." She then had fifteen years of successful journalism behind her but evidently dated her real "career" from the time when she became an interpreter rather than a mere chronicler of events.

Jerome Frank, whom I like but he is another of the bright boys who knows a lot more about things and economics than about people. Then I spent a good two hours with [Isador] Lubin of the Bureau of Labor Statistics who is extremely able and gave me lots of very good information indeed. Then I saw Katharine Lenroot in the children's bureau apropos that Youth article that I haven't written but should. Tonight I go to dine at the Feis mansion with [William] Phillips [Undersecretary of State] of the foreign office I mean state department and others and hope thru Phillips to get to Mrs. Roosevelt.

"Tomorrow I see Hopkins and probably Tugwell . . . I have had one of the most interesting weeks of my life, but it leaves me more doubtful than ever I can ever write on any domestic subject for Lorimer [George Horace, the anti-New Deal editor of the *Saturday Evening Post*]. I've spent days in the relief administration going through reports, looking at pictures, talking with people. Some of the things they have done are so thrilling that I want to jump off immediately to see them closer at hand . . . It is all a new frontier, a new sort of pioneering. And yet I become increasingly convinced that this administration is on the rocks . . . there are several things I want to see in Philadelphia. Then I shall go to California directly and break the trip on the way back. And then spend three or four more days in Washington."

A Midwestern lecture tour in the fall of 1935 afforded an opportunity to assess FDR's opposition. In Topeka, she was invited to dinner by the leading contender for the GOP nomination, Alfred M. Landon, a veteran of Theodore Roosevelt's Bull Moose campaign and the only Republican elected governor west of the Mississippi in 1932. William Randolph Hearst, whom Dorothy still detested, had just endorsed Landon. In the journal that she kept during this trip, she wrote:

> Hearst has his chief sob sister out here . . . Adele-what-you-call-her [Adela Rogers St. John] with the

assignment, "Make Mrs. Landon the best loved
woman in the United States!" Very sick making
. . . I like him — Landon — better than Knox,
better than Hoover (though Hoover is more intelligent) better than Vandenberg from the little I
saw of him. Lots of sense. And would like to be
honest. But shrewd . . . He was tired to death.
Talked with an effort. The kind of man that you
instinctively trust (but I am a poor judge) — not
artistic, intuitive like Roosevelt. Not animated by
any real passion. But a good head, and a very
American type — middle western. Independent
and kind. We talked about Jimmie Sheean's book
[*Personal History,* published in January 1935]
which he had certainly read — about Raymond
Swing, whom he thought was a fine fellow. (He is
a good politician and knew whom I would like.)

Everywhere Dorothy's lectures drew impressive crowds. Jewish audiences, particularly, clamored to see and hear their very
Christian champion. Of a stop in Tulsa, she wrote:

Bnai Brith here and the Jews . . . It is very
early and my skin has that tight drawn feeling,
dry and gritty that a night in a sleeper always
gives. We go to a hotel and the coffee room.
Breakfast and more of the delegation. Eager, kind,
interested. I am smothered in eagerness and kindness. But they have rooms ready for me, and
flowers, and a pint of rye whiskey — Okla is dry
— cigarettes; thoughtfulness, hospitality, everything except leaving me alone "in my own temper." They want to talk about Hitler — the Jews
— the protestant revolt in Germany. I talk. I
feel like a phonograph record. Coffee, orange
juice, indigestion. Nerves getting jagged. Jumpy.
Would I like to be alone? I would rather be alone
than anything on earth. In my room. A bath.
Bed. Sleep. Clean clothes. My dress — I am getting jolly sick of this single afternoon-morning

black dress! Even the collars, the various collars
cannot alleviate its staleness . . . In the evening
the hall was jammed — 1700 seats and lots standing. Well, they like me. Afterward we went back
to the hotel . . . Questions — talk — and then the
train . . .

In Chicago she met with Gustav Stolper, the Austrian economist, who was there on business. Professorial in manner, articulate, knowledgeable, and conservative, he helped crystallize
Dorothy's economic views. With his wife Toni and three children, he had come to America in 1933, before the great flood
tide of intellectual émigrés, and achieved immediate success as
a consultant to major financial institutions. The Stolpers had
been Dorothy's houseguests when they first arrived but were
now established in their own comfortable home in New York.
From Rochester she wrote to Gustav:

"You were sweet to let me pour out my heart and all my
troubles as I did. I keep thinking about myself in relation to
you, and I realize that I have been a rotten friend. I got all tied
up with the difficult three ring circus of my life. Dear God I
am tired . . . Last night I had a wonderful crowd — a thousand
people and they all paid to come. But I am not sure that what
I say (with so much eloquence) is the right thing to say at all
— I need to talk with you . . ."

On the last lap of her trip, which took her through western
New York, scene of her childhood, her father's image returned
to her with special vividness. She wrote:

I sat on his knee and held my cheek against his. It
had a nice clean masculine smell. Only perched
on his knee, always ready to fly . . . He loved
Margaret most, because she was like mother. "A
clever child, Doro-thea, but not much comfort —
Maggie for comfort" (and *how* Peggy hated to be
called Maggie.) Why wasn't I a comfort? I loved

him so . . . Oh my dear father! I was never a
comfort to you and you live in me like the truth of
a thought. I wanted to grow up, amount to something, do something for you, make you proud of
me — and then suddenly you were dead.

Apparently determined to give comfort to her current family,
Dorothy went home for Thanksgiving.

Margaret Grierson Thompson with her baby daughter Dorothy in Clarence, New York, 1893. Standing are Reverend Peter Thompson and his spinster sister Henrietta, Dorothy's favorite aunt.

The Methodist church and parsonage in Hamburg, New York, where the Thompson family lived from 1901 to 1905, the longest stay of Dorothy's childhood.

Dorothy acquired a stepmother in 1903. The wedding party included: (1) and (2) the bride's parents, Dr. and Mrs. George Abbott, (3) Dorothy, (4) Miss Eliza Abbott, the bride, (5) Reverend Peter Thompson, the bridegroom, (6) Isabel Abbott, a cousin, (7) Peggy Thompson, (8) Willard Thompson, (9) Reverend Ward Platt, who performed the ceremony, (10) Mrs. Platt, and (16) another cousin, George F. Abbott, the future Broadway playwright and producer. Others are Abbott relatives and family friends.

Dorothy (seated at left) played guard on the 1911 girls' basketball team at Lewis Institute.

Celebrating a decorous Fourth of July 1912 in Chicago with Aunts Margaret and Hetty. In the fall, Dorothy entered Syracuse University.

Gertrude Tone, a wealthy and unconventional Niagara Falls, New York, matron, took Dorothy under her wing and encouraged her ambitions.

Barbara De Porte graduated from Cornell in 1917, then worked as a volunteer in the suffrage movement, where she and Dorothy met.

Sept. 1st

I shall never forget this evening in Rouen, the first evening in France. It is a beautiful city. Tall ships lie at anchor in the shadow of an exquisite cathedral where long ago "the Maid" was burned at the stake by the English – a city of quaint, crooked streets, and brilliant cafés. It lured us, so enroute to Paris we stopped off to spend a day and a night. At the hotel we struggled with our rudimentary French. "Une chambre, pour dieux, avec l'eau froid et chaud, confortable mais bon marché" – we muttered the phrase over + over on our way to the "Hôtel Dieppe". Then it was Asya who essayed the assault on the maître d'Hôtel – Asya with her amazing facility with any tongue. Two hours ago neither of us knew any French, so we started evenly. Now she is directing the chamber maid to call us, scolding the ticket agent, ordering a meal, enquiring directions without the slightest difficulty – to be sure no one is deceived for an instant – she brands herself a foreigner tout de suite but at least she makes herself understood. Alors–

Rouen

Opening page of the diary Dorothy kept on her first journey abroad in 1920 with Barbara De Porte. (See pages 42–43.)

In Rome, Barbara posed with a group of Italian Socialists. At her left is Joseph Schlossberg, the American labor leader who served as escort to the two young journalists during much of their trip.

Beatrice Sorchan, a worshipful friend, joined Dorothy on a walking tour in the Bavarian Alps during the summer of 1921.

Dorothy at twenty-eight. Photographed in Budapest.

Left, Rose Wilder Lane, a novelist and fellow publicity-writer at the Red Cross in Paris, became Dorothy's chief confidante after the marriage of her traveling companion, Barbara, in November 1920.

Right, Paul Scott Mowrer of the Chicago *Daily News* urged Dorothy to try her luck as a journalist in Vienna. She followed his advice early in 1921.

Below, Marcel Fodor initiated Dorothy into the mysteries of Central European politics.

Dorothy on an outing in the Vienna hills with Josef Bard, whom she married in 1922.

When poet Edna St. Vincent Millay visited Budapest in 1923 every male within range — including Josef — found her irresistible.

The Bards were favorites of the small Anglo-American circle in Vienna that included novelist Phyllis Bottome, wife of a British diplomat, and poet Louis Untermeyer.

In the salon of Frau Doktor Eugenia Schwarzwald, Dorothy mingled with Vienna's artistic and political lions.

At Eugenia's country home, Dorothy met Count Helmuth von Moltke, who became a devoted friend though thirteen years her junior. Scion of a renowned Prussian family, he later led and was executed for his part in an anti-Nazi conspiracy.

A page from Dorothy's notes on an interview with Sigmund Freud, probably in 1922 or 1923.

Raymond Gram Swing, leading contender for the Berlin post that went to Dorothy.

Sigrid Schultz, who followed Seldes as chief of the Chicago *Tribune*'s Berlin bureau.

Edgar Ansel Mowrer of t Chicago *Daily News,* brother Paul Scott Mowrer.

H. R. Knickerbocker (at left), who succeeded Dorothy as Berlin bureau chief for the Philadelphia *Public Ledger,* with the French army in 1939.

Dashing Floyd Gibbons, who covered two World Wars, reports by radio on the arrival of the Graf Zeppelin at Lakehurst, New Jersey, on August 6, 1929, using what was described as "the first transmitting set compact and light enough to be carried around."

nne O'Hare McCormick, the espected roving foreign corresondent of the *New York Times*.

William L. Shirer, a pioneer of broadcast journalism, reports the signing of the Franco-German armistice at Compiègne for CBS on June 22, 1940.

George Seldes, a Berlin colleague and subsequent Vermont neighbor.

John and Frances Gunther.

Dorothy in her Berlin apartment at Händelstrasse 8 in 1927.

Becoming Mrs. Sinclair Lewis at the Register's Office in London on May 14, 1928. The other bridal pair were identified as Mr. Henry George Wales, an American author, and Miss Amelie Lucie Boyer.

Mr. and Mrs. Lewis in high spirits after a quasi-religious ceremony in the Savoy Chapel.

Drawing of Sinclair Lewis by Constantin Aladjalov that appeared in Dorothy's translation of *PEP*, a satirical book about a German Babbitt. She dedicated the book, published in 1929, to her husband "in admiration and comradeship."

The "old house" at Twin Farms where the Lewises spent their first Vermont summer together.

Young Michael basks under the admiring gaze of his parents.

In the autumn of 1932 Dorothy moved her family temporarily to Vienna where this reunion took place. Left to right: John Gunther, Marcel Fodor and his wife Marta, Frances Gunther, Dorothy, Sinclair Lewis.

Christa Winsloe, author of *Mädchen in Uniform*, to whom Dorothy became deeply attached during her stay in Europe in 1932 and 1933.

Dorothy arriving in Paris after her expulsion from Germany in August 1934. The bouquet of American Beauty roses was a farewell token from her Berlin colleagues. The event was front-page news.

A broadcaster as well as a syndicated columnist, Dorothy reached a huge audience in the late 1930s. In the hope of softening her belligerent tone, her radio sponsors preceded her talks with the dulcet melodies of Phil Spitalny's All-Girl Orchestra.

Waiting for Dorothy to finish her broadcast. In foreground, left to right, Ethel Moses and her husband John, Dorothy's agent; Franklin P. Adams (F.P.A.); David Sarnoff, president of NBC. Behind Mrs. Moses' hat are Dan Golenpaul, producer of "Information, Please!" and his wife.

Dorothy again made headlines in 1939 by laughing aloud at a rally of the German-American Bund. The hatless man behind her is her press agent, Irving Mansfield.

At a rally after Russian armies invaded Finland in November 1939, Dorothy exchanges pleasantries with Herbert Hoover and Fiorello La Guardia.

Though they were bitter political antagonists after Dorothy deserted Willkie to support FDR in 1940, she and Clare Boothe Luce remained friends. Here they share the speakers' platform at a dinner on January 23, 1941, of "Union Now," an organization advocating union of the United States and Great Britain.

James Thurber in *The New Yorker*, May 16, 1936.

"He's giving Dorothy Thompson a piece of his mind."

A Scarsdale *Inquirer* cartoon in the late 1930s.

"And remember — no more Dorothy Thompson!"

Not the Big Apple but an ovation for Eleanor Roosevelt after a sparkling performance at the New York *Herald Tribune* Forum. Leading the applause are Mayor La Guardia and Helen Rogers Reid. Her rock-ribbed Republican husband Ogden seems to be having trouble registering enthusiasm for the Democratic first lady.

Attorney Morris L. Ernst, a devotee of FDR.

Max Ascoli, future editor of the *Reporter* and an authority on Italian fascism.

Gustav Stolper, economist and international financial expert.

Hamilton Fish Armstrong, editor of *Foreign Affairs*.

David L. Cohn, a charming southern gentleman, political liberal, and man of letters, was a favorite escort as well as a valued adviser.

Economist Alexander Sachs leaving the White House in August 1936 after a "long and mysterious conference with the President." An even less publicized meeting in 1939 presaged the development of the atom bomb.

Gardner Rea in *The New Yorker,* March 11, 1939.

"Has Germany answered Dorothy Thompson yet?"

The spacious "big house" at Twin Farms, scene of much hospitality and gala entertainments.

Michael with his half-brother Wells Lewis in the summer of 1941. At the wheel is Dorothy's secretary Madeline Shaw. A farmer's son flourishes a flag.

Dorothy and Michael at a cookout with her research assistant Herman Budzislawski, who turned out to be a Soviet agent.

Alexander Woollcott, another part-time Vermonter, helped launch Dorothy on her radio career.

Vincent Sheean and his wife, the former Diana Forbes-Robertson, perennial guests at Twin Farms.

Hilda, Baroness Louis de Rothschild.

A treasured friend -- Dame Rebecca West.

DOROTHY THOMPSON
237 EAST FORTY-EIGHTH STREET
NEW YORK CITY

Dearest Helen:

Thank you so much for your sweet note. Will you save November 8th — some time between 6 and midnight for my housewarming? I've moved into a very sweet little house which Hitler's victims have made into a very personal instrument for living that fits me like a glove & I'm absurdly happy in it — for the first time in New York —

You'll get a "regular" invitation to the 6 to midnight party, but this is personal.

Love,

Dorothy

Dorothy's rift with the *Herald Tribune* in 1940 did not impair her affectionate relationship with Helen Reid, to whom she sent a special, handwritten invitation to her Turtle Bay housewarming on November 8, 1941.

Dorothy in the living room of her new home.

A toast to the bride and groom. Dorothy and Maxim Kopf celebrate their wedding at Twin Farms on June 16, 1943.

Celebrants, left to right: seated, pianist Ania Dorfmann, ex-opera diva Alma Clayburgh, the bride. Standing, Beata Budzislawski, Winotou Zuckmayer, Rudy Rathaus, Maxim's best man.

DOROTHY THOMPSON

Bookplate designed by Maxim shows Dorothy *rampant* treading on Satan *couchant*.

Joyful wedding guests, Dale Warren and Esther Root Adams (Mrs. F.P.A.), feast on lobster salad.

Stung by unflattering comments on her shape, overheard after a lecture appearance, Dorothy went on one of her periodic crash diets. "I've lost 20 lbs. by sheer strength of character and feel *very* smug about it," she wrote on March 27, 1952, to David Sarnoff.

1893 Born
1900 mother died
1907 went to Aunts
1914 grad from college
1921 went to Europe
1928 married S.T.
1935 Began career.
1942 ~~Hadden~~ Found max
1949 Began decline
1956 Decided change life
1963 ?
1970 ...?

Milestones. Dorothy sketched out this chronology of her life when she began work on her autobiography in 1958.

An ardent gardener to the end, and always remarkably free of personal vanity, Dorothy sent this photo, taken during one of her last Vermont summers, to Dale Warren with the comment, "This is a very good picture of sweet peas."

⚘ 2
"God damn soul mates"

SINCE 1934, the Lewises' winter home had been in Bronxville at 17 Wood End Lane, where Lewis had bought a large, somber, half-timber "Tudor" house while Dorothy was abroad. She disliked the architectural style — a symbol of affluence in the twenties and thirties — and the location, a rich, sedate suburb neither city nor country. She added a butler to the ménage and hired as Michael's governess Mrs. Emily Walker Carter, a small, blunt Scotswoman who became the most faithful of family retainers. Among her duties was safeguarding the keys to the liquor closet during Dorothy's absences. Lewis' drinking remained a problem but he could still be a charming host when sober. During one such interlude, Dale Warren paid his first visit at Bronxville. He had not yet met Lewis, though his friendship with Dorothy had been cemented during a weekend at Twin Farms in September 1934.

Dale was unstinting in his admiration for Dorothy. In turn, his amiable, unaggressive personality made him a welcome companion for her. After visiting his home in Boston she wrote in her diary, "Why is it that bachelors like Dale always seem to be better housekeepers than anyone else. The tea was perfect. Dale looked pinker and nicer than ever. I think that I always see him in an Eton collar being 'a little gentleman' . . ." Their affinity was strengthened by the fact that their birthdays fell on the same day and were jointly celebrated for more than twenty years. Of his first Bronxville call, Dale wrote:

"I went with trepidation and also with considerable prejudice.

I had heard a great deal of talk about Red and a lot of it was not favorable." Greeting him at the door, Lewis said, "We are having two countesses for lunch. One of them is swell. I don't like a lot of Dorothy's friends — except big John Gunther — but I think I'm going to like you." The "swell" countess was Reine de Roussy de Sales, wife of the diplomatic correspondent of *Havas,* the French news agency, and *Paris Soir.* The other was Rosie Waldek,* an ex-Berliner. Also on hand were Avis and Bernard DeVoto (he was then an editor of the *Saturday Review*) and David Cohn, an attractive young bachelor who was the favorite "extra man" of numerous New York hostesses. A native of Greenville, Mississippi, where his Polish-born parents had settled in the mid-nineteenth century, he combined authentic southern charm with political liberalism and the versatility of a latter-day Renaissance man.

Dale remembers the afternoon as delightful; Lewis drank nothing but milk, did most of the talking (a feat when Dorothy was around), and provided expert advice to a young editor. On subsequent occasions, to his sorrow, Dale found Red "drunk as a skunk" and his wife distraught. Though Dorothy tried to ration his liquor supply, it was hardly possible to do so at their frequent parties where everyone else drank heartily. Nor was his temper improved by Dorothy's growing tendency to rehearse or replay her lectures on world affairs in her drawing room. Katherine Gauss Jackson (daughter of Dean Gauss of Princeton and an editor of *Harper's*) recalls an evening she spent with her husband Andrew and Herbert Agar and his second wife Eleanor Carroll Chilton, the novelist, at a party in Bronxville where wine, whiskey, and gin flowed abundantly. After dinner Lewis announced, "Those of you who want to discuss The Situation

---

* Née Rosie Goldschmidt, the daughter of a respected Jewish banker, she had divorced her first husband, a physician named Grafenberg, to marry Franz Ullstein, chief of a publishing empire. Again divorced, she married Graf Waldek, described by her acquaintances as "always invisible." During the early Hitler years she traveled with mystifying ease between the United States and Germany. A skilled journalist, she was, for a time, on Dorothy's payroll as a research assistant.

will go to the library. The rest of us will stay here and talk about books and the theater." Half of the group marched off, led by the hostess.

It was as much the need to escape from the friction at home as ambition that kept Dorothy on the road. But in February 1935 she interrupted her lecture schedule for a southern vacation with her husband. Disheartened by the fact that *Jayhawker,* the play he had written with Lloyd Lewis, had closed in three weeks and the failure of his latest novel, *Work of Art,* Lewis was quarrelsome and rude. In Jamaica he walked out on her. "What can a woman do under conditions like these except to try with all her will to make herself *innerly** independent, innerly free?" Dorothy wrote to him. "Oh Hal — you and I were made for each other — I feel that and I think you feel it . . . God damn soul mates. And then suddenly this feeling which seemed so solid is blown into atoms. And I sit in the dark . . ."

Certainly Dorothy and Red were not made to live with each other. But the intellectual rapport between them reasserted itself when she returned to Bronxville and Lewis, in due course, joined her there. He had decided to tackle a different kind of book, the satirical story of a fascist takeover in America to be called *It Can't Happen Here.* As had been the case with *Ann Vickers,* Dorothy would be his most important resource, and, for once, her knowledge of the irksome "Situation" would be an asset. She was delighted to help her husband sound the alarm about a threat she regarded as grave in a country where such demagogues as Senator Huey Long of Louisiana and Dr. Frank E. Townsend in California were attracting large followings.

Lewis worked diligently on the book all summer at Twin Farms, which was remarkably tranquil with fewer than the usual complement of guests.

Wells Lewis, now a Harvard freshman, was spending a year

---

* Dorothy often seemed to think in German; "innerly," a rarely used English adverb, was one of her favorite modifiers, as is the German *innerlich.*

abroad. From London, where he had arrived armed with a list of the Lewises' many British friends, he wrote on July 15, 1935: "Dear Father and Dorothy . . . I sat down and sent off about thirty letters of introduction, with a hand written copy of the form letter which Dorothy gave me. The response was immediate. All day Thursday I was bombarded by mail and telephone . . . Saturday I lunched with H. G. Wells [after whom he had been named] . . . Today, for lunch, I went to Rebecca Wests'. She couldn't have been kinder . . . Lunch Wednesday with Jonathan Cape, following a 'talk to make plans' with John Gunther . . . Letters from the country have come from [among many others] Joseph Bard, who is now in Dorset, telling me to come whenever I like . . ." Vincent Sheean was also in Europe, where he had married Diana, the lovely young daughter of the eminent actor, Sir Johnston Forbes-Robertson. One of the few frequent visitors at Twin Farms was George Seldes, Dorothy's one-time Berlin colleague, now a near neighbor and an expert observer of indigenous American fascism. In August, with Lewis' book done, Dorothy and Red sailed on the *Île de France* for a month's stay in Europe. It was their last trip abroad together.

When Dorothy had left for her Midwestern tour in the autumn of 1935, Lewis was rejoicing in the success of *It Can't Happen Here.* Since her schedule of one-night stands made correspondence difficult, she occasionally sent pages from her diary to Lewis in lieu of letters. There are few references to her husband or son in the journal. However, after her return on Thanksgiving Day she described the family reunion in a lengthy entry:

> Got into New York at one o'clock. Feakins had called off the lunch with N.B.C. vice presidents, or they called it off or something. I went to the Berkshire [where Lewis often stayed after a night in town]. No trace of Hal nor was he home, so I

called up Oyster Bay and Polly Howard [wife of
playwright Sidney Howard, who dramatized *Dodsworth*] told me he had started into New York. I
breakfasted and lunched on orange juice and
coffee. By and by he came. A little *blau* [tipsy],
ordered a whiskey soda, ate no lunch. After a
while we went home . . . Emily [Carter] and the
servants were all in the day nursery, a fire, nice
lights and Miko all dressed up in a blue sailor suit,
threw himself into my arms. I had brought him
(Hal and I) some toys, and we played with them.
He dragged me off from the others. "Come in
your room, Mummy, and play with me." We
played policeman for it seemed hours. Mike said,
"Tell me a story — about Georgio." I was horribly
tired, and said perhaps his father would tell one.
Hal, slightly exaggeré with drink, started a story,
very ironical. He talked over the child's head, and
for me. He wasn't interested, really in amusing
the little boy. Suddenly the boy threw himself on
the floor, put his head on his arms and started to
weep. Hal was upset and angry . . . stalked out
of the room. The child looked after him with a
pained and hostile gaze. I started the story. Soon
he roared with laughter. Hal came back evidently
determined to be a good father. We went in to
dinner. Mike had been allowed to sit up. He was
adorable . . . Hal left before dessert to lie down.
"Why does Daddy go away?" the child asked. "He
is tired." The child looked puzzled. Miss Nelson
[a replacement for Emily Carter, who was preg-
nant] took him upstairs and put him to bed, waiv-
ing the bath. I went up and sat on his bed. He sat
up in his little plaid dressing gown . . . I kissed
him, told him another incident in the endless epic
of Georgio, and he went to sleep. Miss Nelson
said after I had gone next day, he threw himself on
my bed and wept bitterly. Now and then he asks
suddenly for me, and is sad. He is terribly bound

to me . . . Hal did not come down and I had a
long talk with Nelson. She says he gets along much
better in school with the other children. The
teachers say he has an extraordinary mind but independent and intractable. Very imaginative, an
extraordinary sense of words. "It's shocking that
you go away," he said. "Simply shocking." I sat
in the library with the girls and later Hal came
down, somewhat soberer. Then he was charming,
and very wistful about my going away again and
full of self-mockery. I left with the girls and Emily
at 11 . . .

The evening, in Emily Carter's recollection, typified what was
amiss in Michael's relationship to his parents. "He was scared
to death of his father," she said. "And as for his mother, why did
she have to make up those terrible stories? They gave him
nightmares. But she wouldn't just read to him out of a book.
She was always bringing him toys — we had closets full of them.
What he wanted was for her to stay home. Still I never blamed
her for leaving. Really I was glad for her sake when she went
on all those trips — her life when Mr. Lewis was there was impossible, just impossible."

Yet Dorothy still regarded her marriage as permanent. Discussing her contract with the *Herald Tribune* in correspondence
with Helen Reid, she wrote on January 20, 1936: "I am going
to have a big personal problem in connection with this work
because it has been the custom of my husband and myself to
spend five months of the year on a remote farm in Vermont
which we really regard as our home. It is very essential for my
husband's work that this routine be disturbed as little as possible and it is also essential for my domestic happiness that I
should have some months of the year that I can spend as he
chooses to determine . . . I foresee some difficulties which are
exclusively my own problem, married as I am to a restless husband who loves to travel, prefers to travel with his wife, and

rebels against any restrictions on his freedom. However, he is himself very excited about the possibilities of this work and will be extremely pleased to have me turn my attention away from Europe to our own country in which he is more interested . . ."

🌀 3
Debut

WITHIN A MONTH, the business arrangements for Dorothy's column were worked out.* In the course of the negotiations, Dorothy called at the Reids' Madison Avenue mansion, bringing with her a large scrapbook of clippings to show the publisher. Subsequently she returned as a dinner guest. It was her introduction to the world of the really *rich* rich. Ogden was the son of Whitelaw Reid, an Ohio-born newspaperman who married Elizabeth, daughter of Darius Ogden Mills, a banking, railroad, and utility magnate who listed his occupation in *Who's Who* as "capitalist." In 1872, when he had become editor-in-chief of the New York *Tribune,* Whitelaw bought the paper from Horace Greeley's heirs and moved it into what was then the tallest building in New York.† In London, the Reids' son Ogden met his future wife Helen Rogers, a native of Appleton, Wisconsin, and a Barnard graduate who was serving as secretary to Whitelaw, then United States Ambassador to the Court of St. James's.

---

* An interoffice *Herald Tribune* memo dated February 3, 1936, reads:

"We need a contract with Mrs. Sinclair Lewis (Dorothy Thompson), (address to be had from Mrs. Reid) to do a column three times a week, approximately 1,000 words, on a general basis of fifty percent from the syndicate return, we to guarantee $10,000 a year, she participating to the extent of fifty percent after total billing amounts to $20,000. This last need not be in figures in the contract . . .

"Mrs. Lewis is to have an office in our building, is to have a secretary and is to have two months vacation. The contract is to be for one year giving us the option of renewing for three years at the same rate, under the same conditions. She is to start her column during the week of March 16th."

† A few years after the death of James Gordon Bennett in 1918 the Reids acquired the *Herald,* which had first been sold to Frank A. Munsey, and merged the two papers. The *Herald Tribune* expired in 1966.

Reared in the relaxed climate of La Follette Progressive Repub-
licanism, Helen was a political liberal whose views and friendships were not limited by partisanship. But her husband and
his family were hereditary, rock-ribbed Republican conservatives, although, as members of the eastern establishment, they
were international-minded and Anglophile. Ogden Reid's
cousin Ogden Livingston Mills had been a state senator, a
United States congressman, Undersecretary of the Treasury in
Hoover's administration, and was still, in 1936, a power in the
Republican Party.

Since her chief ideological bond with her publisher was their
common concern for the dangers of fascism, Dorothy might have
prudently launched her column with a discussion of foreign
affairs. However, the Italian invasion of Ethiopia and Hitler's
reoccupation of the demilitarized Rhineland were not the burning issues for most *Herald Tribune* readers. This was the time
when Roosevelt was seeking a second term, while Herbert Hoover, Ogden Mills, and other GOP stalwarts charged him with
leading America into socialism, bankruptcy, and tyranny, and
such old-line Democrats as Alfred E. Smith and John J. Raskob
in the newly formed Liberty League joined in the attack; more
violent thunder from the far right was orchestrated by the radio
priest Father Charles E. Coughlin from his Shrine of the Little
Flower in Royal Oak, Michigan.

Her column, titled "On the Record," was to appear three
times a week, alternating with the august Walter Lippmann.
Advance advertising described her as the advocate of a "new
liberal conservatism" — her own definition of her philosophy,
which matched that of her friend Gustav Stolper on whom she
leaned for advice. She was distressed to learn that he was going
abroad shortly after her debut as a columnist. "I feel crushed
that you are leaving on the twenty-first for a prolonged trip,"
she wrote to him. "What ever shall I do without you? I feel
absolutely deserted."

Stolper's influence is discernible in her first column, which appeared on March 17, 1936. The subject was the proposal, then being debated in Congress, to tax excess corporate profits — a distressing prospect to her well-heeled audience. In a modest opening paragraph she conceded:

"I, like 120,000,000 other Americans, will probably never grasp the truth about the money system. Professor Einstein also admits that he doesn't understand it . . ." Thus comforted, corporate executives and their wives were encouraged to read a thousand lucid and lively words about a potentially arid subject. Her critical conclusions placed her alongside such dissident Democrats as Lewis Douglas and James P. Warburg, who had been close advisers of FDR in the early New Deal years. They had repudiated what they called "the degenerate capitalism of the Republican twenties" but saw state monopoly as an equal evil. This would also be the stance of another adviser who joined Stolper on her economic brain trust, Alexander Sachs,* who had served in the first of the New Deal agencies, the NRA, subsequently returned to the banking house of Lehman Brothers, but remained an always friendly critic of FDR. She would also be in tune with the Republican standard-bearer Alf Landon, who was accused of "me-tooism" because he declined to condemn *in toto* the New Deal measures that FDR's supporters claimed, on plausible evidence, had raised national income by more than 50 percent and rescued some 6 million Americans from unemployment. Like other "moderate" critics he argued that it had been wastefully done, with much duplication of effort, inadequate study of visionary schemes, and a dangerous concentration of power in Washington. Within a few months the volume of her mail, pro and con, was clear evidence that her informative, often controversial column was becoming a fixture at many American breakfast tables.

---

* It was Sachs who in 1939 arranged the fateful meeting between Roosevelt, Einstein, and Leo Szilard that resulted in the Manhattan Project and the Atom Bomb.

"What did I do to-day?" she wrote to Lewis, who had gone to Vermont early in the spring. "Well, I went to the N.B.C. and had lots of pictures taken for publicity during the conventions [of 1936] and then I went to J. and H. Thorpe and picked out some linen for slip-covers for the Bronxville house, and some stuff to upholster the little chair in the red-and-white guest room in the Vermont house . . .

"I went to the office and found that a storm had broken out around my defenseless head about smorning's piece on the Supreme Court decision. From the reactionaries? From the upholders of the constitution and of the Old Deal? Not at all! From Betty Swing and the Woman's Party and the advanced feminists all of whom are pleased as punch with the old boys' decision that no states may make minimum wage laws for working women because they believe in Equality . . .* But a man from Farrar & Rinehart en route to Irita's [Van Doren] "Books" stopped me in the elevator and said 'Arent you Miss Thompson?' . . . and he said that was the swellest piece anybody ever wrote. And I got a telegram from Johnny Farrar and from W. W. Norton saying more or less the same . . . I decided that I would write another piece and answer the feminists, and telephoned around to the Woman's Trade Union League and the Ladies Garment workers and established that none of the women who really work at machines and not at making women's party propaganda are worried about their rights being invaded by the minimum wage law but that they are worried because already the wages of some laundry workers have been reduced from 31 cents an hour to 22 cents . . . When I got home little Nero had just come back from a party at school, very tired and happy, and I put him to bed and he didn't even ask for a story . . . And all the time I kept thinking of my darling husband . . . and wondering whether Stub ever *had* spaded up the flower

---

* The court had struck down a New York law establishing a minimum wage for women. The arguments pro and con were echoed in the debate about the Equal Rights Amendment in 1970.

beds, and whether he had properly sprayed the peonies . . . and that I love you more than tongue can tell . . .

DOROTHY LIPPMANN SULLIVAN"

Despite these wifely concerns, she spent little time at Twin Farms that summer. In June she covered the two presidential nomination conventions in Cleveland and Philadelphia in the dual capacity of columnist and NBC radio commentator. Afterward she went abroad convinced that it would be more useful to update her impressions of Europe than to report Landon's lackluster campaign or the "rendezvous with destiny" that Roosevelt had promised in his acceptance speech.

Banned from Germany, she was forced to rely for authentic news of the Third Reich on such friends as H. R. Knickerbocker and William L. Shirer. (The latter was then representing Universal News Service; a year later he joined Edward R. Murrow's team of CBS radio commentators.) In London, William Stoneman and other American correspondents chafed at the British government's silence about the romance of Edward VIII and Mrs. Wallis Warfield Simpson, for whom he would forsake his throne in December. Dinah and Vincent Sheean, living in Paris, were dismayed by the Anglo-French arms embargo against Spain, where the democratic government though allegedly aided by the USSR faced defeat as Hitler and Mussolini supplied far greater support to Franco. Jay Allen was already in Madrid and Sheean would soon follow. Deeply disturbed by the prospect of another fascist triumph, Dorothy eloquently supported the Loyalists in her column during the next year, for which she was labeled a Red and castigated by the American Catholic hierarchy.

She returned to Twin Farms in the autumn, leaving Lewis in New York, where he was busy with a WPA Federal Theatre production of *It Can't Happen Here.* Dorothy was unimpressed by the *Literary Digest* poll, which forecast that Landon would win thirty-two states with 370 electoral votes against sixteen states with 161 votes for Roosevelt — a monumental error that hastened the magazine's demise.

"I read Brother Landon's speeches," she wrote to her husband, "and observe that the Star of Destiny is not shining on the gentleman's brow. I should like to be for him, but I am neither old nor discouraged enough. Nor have I any passion for lost causes . . . Only for thee, only for thee! Come home, Sir, as quickly as possible . . . P.S. The second word down in the left hand corner is the Spanish of Gugelhupf."

Dorothy spent election night in the Iridium Room of the St. Regis Hotel in New York with Mr. and Mrs. Harry Hopkins, Colonel Lawrence Westbrook, a WPA executive, and her sister Peggy — an unswerving Democrat. Except for this clutch of New Dealers, everyone else in the room, including Dorothy, was wearing a Landon sunflower* and ignoring the returns that foreshadowed a Roosevelt landslide. At midnight, as Landon's telegram conceding the election was flashed on the screen, no one stopped dancing. Dorothy urged Hopkins and Westbrook to propose a toast to the President. When they declined on the ground that they might be lynched, Dorothy rose, rapped on her glass, lifted it, and then said in a resonant voice, "Ladies and gentlemen, I should like to propose a toast to the President of the United States, Franklin D. Roosevelt." The orchestra paused for a moment as she and her companions raised their glasses. Then the music started up and everyone else returned to the dance floor, stonily ignoring the interruption.

"I never saw such rotten sportsmanship," Dorothy said. "The decision was made, the people in the room would have to accept it, so why not with better grace?"

According to Westbrook, after she sat down she "publicly cast

* A politic gesture for a columnist on a very Republican paper. Although she had little enthusiasm for Landon, she was, as yet, no admirer of Roosevelt either.

off her sunflower — forever." If so, the gesture was not known to her publisher who, with his cousin Ogden Mills, was spending a melancholy evening in the *Herald Tribune* city room, awaiting along with other Republicans the returns from the rural areas that would surely reverse the trend. After Landon had conceded, according to one account, an editorial writer called out, "Well, Ogden, I see you still have those great Republican strongholds, Vermont and Utah!" He replied angrily, "This is no laughing matter. It is a national disaster." Shortly afterward Utah fell to the Democrats. James Farley had been proved right: only two states went Republican — Maine and Vermont. Roosevelt had gained the largest presidential vote in history.

4
"First Lady of American Journalism"

"FIRST LADY OF AMERICAN JOURNALISM" — so was Dorothy often introduced on the speaker's platform. It was an accolade she might have declined in favor of her respected friend, Anne O'Hare McCormick, the able roving correspondent of the *New York Times*. Dorothy had, however, a good claim to the title. An advertisement marking her first anniversary in the *Herald Tribune* boasted that her column was appearing in more than 130 newspapers:

"One reason why: unique among women columnists, men read her as much as women, men discuss her opinions as often as do women, men look forward to her tomorrow's comment on today's news — as frequently as women. Men ask her to address exclusively male meetings. She is the only woman ever to address the Harvard Club of New York, the Union League Club of New York. She was one of four to address the Senate Judiciary Committee on the Court enlargement proposal. She was the first — in the 169 years of its history — to address the New York State Chamber of Commerce."

By the summer of 1937 she was also on the way to becoming a radio star. Although still disdained by some intellectuals, the medium was beginning to attract distinguished writers, among them the sharp-tongued drama critic Alexander Woollcott. Dorothy Parker reproached him for this defection in a *Vanity Fair* article, writing, "Still he is faithful to the stage, although his bi-weekly outings with her wicked stepsister, the radio might be considered mild cheating . . ."

Woollcott conducted arch literary flirtations with both Dorothys — Parker and Thompson — and introduced the latter to his agent, thirty-one-year-old John Moses,* whose clients included the ventriloquist Edgar Bergen and his impudent puppet Charlie McCarthy. Relegating Feakins to the role of lecture agent, Dorothy entrusted her future on the air waves to Moses. In August she made her first appearance on commercial radio. Between sales pitches ("Particular people prefer Pall Malls" — then pronounced Pell Mells) her vibrant, well-modulated voice, impeccable, faintly Anglicized diction, and moving fervor soon won her a devoted audience. To insure that her potential be exploited to the full, Moses added to her payroll an imaginative young man named Irving Mansfield to serve as her press agent.†

Although she was carrying a backbreaking workload, she was unable to resist still another assignment that came to her from Bruce and Beatrice Gould, who had assumed the editorship of the venerable *Ladies' Home Journal* and were in the process of enlarging its scope far beyond the accustomed limits of the ladies' magazines. A column by Dorothy Thompson seemed an ideal component. Bruce had first met Dorothy in Berlin at a party given by the Knickerbockers in early 1931, and they had afterward seen each other intermittently. Prodded by Beatrice, he called her in 1937 to say, "I'm having trouble with my wife, she insists on having you in the *Journal.*" In the interest, she laughingly said, of the Gould's domestic tranquillity, Dorothy agreed, setting her own price of $1000 a column. Her association with the Goulds — and the column that appeared regularly for more than twenty years — was to prove one of the happiest experiences of her professional life.

---

* Dorothy later recommended Moses to Franklin P. Adams, and the result was "Information, Please!," the immensely popular quiz show conceived by Dan Golenpaul. It was launched in 1938 with Clifton Fadiman as master of ceremonies and F.P.A. as anchor man along with John Kieran, the *New York Times* sportswriter whose fund of nature lore amazed his listeners. A frequent guest was the irreverent pianist Oscar Levant.

† Mr. Mansfield's gifts as a publicist flowered after his marriage to the writer of racy fiction Jacqueline Susann.

Dorothy's audience in the late 1930s was matched by only one other woman, whose syndicated column "My Day" began appearing in January 1936 and whose writings were also featured in *McCall's*. "She and Eleanor Roosevelt are undoubtedly the most influential women in the U.S.," *Time* magazine asserted in a cover story about Dorothy.

The source of Dorothy's power was both the size of her constituency and its diversity. Her increasing preoccupation with the evils of Nazism and concern for its victims endeared her to a large Jewish audience and to a miscellaneous coalition of anti-fascists. Financiers and businessmen respected her cautious economic views. In her *Journal* column she tempered sophistication with a recurring note of simple piety, inspiring confidence in the church-going heartland of which she was herself the product.

It was the last constituency she addressed in a collection of moralistic essays published as *Dorothy Thompson's Political Guide*. One reviewer called it "a friendly want-to-be-helpful type of a book . . . It should do a lot for us next winter when the club season opens . . ." Ralph Thompson in the *New York Times* was less gentle. "A series of loosely connected sermonettes," he wrote, ". . . 'Political Guide' is my present nomination for the emptiest book of the month. Above all it manages to convey the impression that Miss Thompson prefers freedom to tyranny, liberalism to intolerance, peace to war, and her own point of view to anyone else's."

Dorothy took such criticism calmly. Writing "sermonettes" was her way of reaffirming her fidelity to her cherished father, whose values found little expression in her current way of life. She was, on the contrary, close to enacting the role of the glamorous "Dorothy" of her more worldly girlhood fantasies. Ethel and John Moses, who became close friends in the course of their business association, found her beautiful as well as brilliant. Her prematurely gray hair — a Thompson family trait — heightened the youthful glow of her rosy skin and the classic regularity of her features. "She was radiant," Ethel Moses said. "Slender — perhaps you'd say svelte. She had a beautiful bosom, and looked marvelous in low-cut or bare-shoulder evening dresses — great sweeping, gorgeous chiffon creations from Bergdorf's. I don't think she had time to eat — she seemed to be living on Dexedrine — John sometimes scolded her for guzzling pills. After her broadcast, she'd often dash off to deliver a speech, then go to a party, sit up most of the night talking and drinking Scotch without any hangover the next day."

Dorothy's husband was seldom with her on these nocturnal jaunts. One devoted escort was Peter Grimm, a tall, suave, and very successful real estate broker and man-about-town. More often she was seen with David Cohn, who admired Dorothy and, probably because it amused him, in addition to his own writing did research for her.

Since the frenetic pace of life made daily commuting to Bronxville burdensome, Dorothy, before starting her column, rented a small apartment to serve as an urban *pied-à-terre*. In April 1937, after an evening in town, Lewis decided to spend the night there. When he arrived he found David Cohn with her and accused them of being lovers (a suspicion shared by many of her friends). Lewis took a taxi back to Bronxville and, after giving the servants a full account of his wife's alleged infidelity, stormed out of the house.

Mark Schorer, Lewis' biographer, attributes the break to Lewis' resentment of his wife's success at a time when he was obsessed by "fear of creative exhaustion." (He had indeed published only one book, *The Prodigal Parents,* in the past two years, and that was mediocre.) This, too, was Dorothy's interpretation. "This business that you have built up now in your mind about me and you," she wrote, "about being the husband of Dorothy Thompson, a tail to an ascending comet, and what not, is only because you are for the moment stymied, and you have been that many times." Such reassurances failed to move him. He did not come to Twin Farms that summer but paid her a brief — and far from therapeutic — visit in New York when she was hospitalized in August with an intestinal ailment. In the fall, she closed the Bronxville house and moved with Michael into a spacious apartment at 88 Central Park West — an address slightly less prestigious than the avenues east of the park but with its own aura of upper-bourgeois comfort and elegance. Though she set aside a room for her husband, he never occupied it. Instead, after renting a place of his own, not far away at the Wyndham Hotel on West 58th Street, he left in October on a lecture tour.

Professionally and socially, Dorothy's life was full and exhilarating. But late at night when her last guests had left, she was often at her desk writing to Lewis, who showed no inclination to come home. She destroyed many of these notes but preserved a few in her files, marked in her own hand "unsent." "I feel that you are my husband and I will feel it till the day I die," she wrote. "I cannot treat you as one among many; I cannot endure the thought that our marriage is finally and permanently over . . . I try not to think at all, not to remember at all, to imagine you somewhere far off . . . on some distant journey from which you will return . . ."

At rare intervals Lewis appeared at one of Dorothy's parties and she reciprocated occasionally at his apartment, sometimes acting as hostess. At one of these gatherings Vincent Sheean's wife Diana, generally known as Dinah, met Dorothy's husband for the first time. They had much in common, since his current preoccupation was with the drama and she came of a distinguished theatrical family. "Red was charming to me," she recalled. "He made me feel important, which I wasn't. With Dorothy, I was more or less invisible, just 'Jimmy's wife.'"

Dinah was, in fact, ill at ease and usually silent when she and her husband visited the Central Park West apartment, where Dorothy surrounded herself with people who provided the expert talk on foreign affairs she most enjoyed and which was indispensable to her work. Singly or in groups they started dropping in around tea time, often staying far into the night in her comfortable living room where, on tables near well-cushioned chairs and sofas, bowls were heaped with cigarettes and sturdy kitchen matches; the supply of whiskey and soda was abundant and hearty sandwiches were served at all hours. The shared concern of all was the conviction that the spread of fascism would be halted only on the battlefield and that the United States eventually must join in the struggle, a view that set them apart from the vast majority of Americans at that time.

All her counselors were steeped in the problems of Europe. Hamilton Fish Armstrong, for example, had gone abroad in 1918 as United States military attaché in Belgrade, subsequently as a diplomat and journalist, had come to know the leading political figures of the day, and in 1928 became editor of *Foreign Affairs,* which he fashioned into a potent weapon against the tide of isolationism.* Count Raoul de Roussy de Sales, as diplomatic correspondent of the most important French papers, enjoyed almost ambassadorial status and was widely esteemed for his clear and liberal perspective on world affairs. Educated in Britain, he spoke impeccable English and played a far more than journalistic role as a champion of French patriotism and idealism.† Herbert Agar, a handsome Anglophile journalist, had spent four years in London as literary editor of *The English Review,* in 1934 won a Pulitzer Prize for his book on the American presidency, *The People's Choice,* and became, in the 1940s, a major advocate of aid to Britain. Other regular visitors were

---

* Of his cousin, the isolationist congressman Hamilton Fish, who became a favorite of the German-American Bund, Armstrong wrote, "I don't remember ever agreeing on any matter whatsoever with my cousin the Congressman."

† A typescript of a diary he kept from 1938 to 1942 is among Dorothy's papers and contains many references to her. Because the diary was only half intended for publication, a considerably edited version, with many personal comments deleted, appeared after his death, titled *The Making of Yesterday* (Reynal & Hitchcock, New York, 1947).

John Gunther, who had returned to New York after the publication of *Inside Europe*, the economists Gustav Stolper and Alexander Sachs, and Max Ascoli, the future editor of the *Reporter*, then a recent exile from his native Italy.

"Sometimes, Dorothy and I would go around the corner to an Italian restaurant — it had been a speakeasy — for dinner," Ascoli recalled. "Then we'd go back to her place and sit up, sometimes till four in the morning, talking with Dorothy writing away furiously on her golden pad. I was delighted to find a phrase or an idea of mine — mostly on fascism — in one of her columns — I was just writing for the *Yale Review* and other small-circulation magazines in those days and I was glad to have a wider platform." On one occasion Ascoli, who was en route to Europe when the Hitler-Stalin pact was signed in August 1939, sent her by clipper a shipboard diary that, in abbreviated form, became the text of an entire column (with credit to an anonymous friend).

In addition to this resident cabinet, Dorothy by cable and telephone tapped an overseas network of diplomats and journalists who had become her friends during her years abroad. These personal ties lent immediacy and authority to her writing. Ironically, the deep affection for the German people that had made her slow to accept the reality of Hitler's rise to power now filled her with the fury of a lover betrayed and enabled her not merely to inform but to stir her readers.

✌ 5
"we who are not Jews must speak . . ."

ON MONDAY, November 17, 1938, Herschel Grynzspan, a seventeen-year-old Jew, walked into the German Embassy in Paris and fatally shot Ernst vom Rath, the third secretary. A week later Dorothy appealed in Grynzspan's behalf to her radio audience. She was now appearing on the General Electric Hour, to which an estimated 5 million radio sets across the country were tuned at nine o'clock Monday evenings.

"I feel as though I know that boy," she said, "for in the past five years I have met so many whose story is the same — the same except for this unique desperate act. Herschel Grynzspan was one of the hundreds of thousands of refugees whom the terror east of the Rhine has turned loose in the world. His permit to stay in Paris had expired. He could not leave France, for no country would take him in . . . Herschel read the newspapers, and all that he could read filled him with dark anxiety and wild despair . . . Thousands of men and women of his race had killed themselves in the last years, rather than live like hunted animals . . . he got a letter from his father . . . he had been summoned from his bed, and herded with thousands of others into a train of box cars, and shipped over the border, into Poland . . . Herschel walked into the German embassy and shot Herr vom Rath. Herschel made no attempt to escape . . . every Jew in Germany was held responsible for this boy's deed. In every city an organized and methodical mob was turned loose on the Jewish population . . . But in Paris, a boy who had hoped to make some gesture of protest which would call atten-

tion to the wrongs done his race burst into hysterical sobs . . .
he realized that half a million of his fellows had been sentenced
to extinction on the excuse of his deed . . . They say he will go
to the guillotine, without a trial by jury, without the rights that
any common murderer has . . . Who is on trial in this case? I
say we are all on trial. I say the Christian world is on trial . . .
If any Jews, anywhere in the world protest at anything that is
happening, further oppressive measures will be taken . . .
Therefore, we who are not Jews must speak, speak our sorrow
and indignation and disgust in so many voices that they will be
heard . . ."

Dorothy followed up the broadcast with two columns in a
similar vein. Within a month readers and listeners spontaneously contributed $40,000. She set up an ad hoc organization,
the Journalists' Defense Fund, with a board that included
Hamilton Fish Armstrong, Heywood Broun, John Gunther,
General Hugh Johnson, Frank R. Kent [political columnist of
the Baltimore *Sun*], Alice Roosevelt Longworth, Westbrook
Pegler, Leland Stowe, Raymond Gram Swing, William Allen
White, and Alexander Woollcott. In Paris, Edgar Ansel Mowrer
with the help of the incorruptible French journalist, André
Géraud (known to an international audience as Pertinax) retained a brave and able Corsican lawyer, Moro Giafferi, to defend Grynzspan. Funds were also supplied to the World Jewish
Congress, which had taken on the task of locating widely dis-
persed witnesses to the ordeal of Grynzspan's parents in the concentration camp, and whose testimony would be the basis of the
defense.*

It was Dorothy's special talent to dramatize, through the tragic

---

* On March 16, 1939, Dr. Nahum Goldmann wrote to Dorothy, saying in part:
"The first amount of 100,000 francs which you have kindly remitted several
weeks ago has been expended . . . To ensure the continuity of the work . . .
I venture to request you to forward a new on account remittance of at least
$5,000 . . ." Events outdistanced the efforts in Grynzspan's behalf. After the
fall of France in June 1940 he was sentenced to a twenty-year penitentiary term
by a French court "under German supervision."

case of one individual, the disasters that still seemed remote to many Americans. Nineteen thirty-eight had been, in her words, a year of "horror walking," a year of continuous Nazi conquests of whose consequences she learned from eyewitnesses. William L. Shirer was in Vienna in March just before Hitler's triumphal entry and watched as storm troopers looted the Rothschild mansion, as young toughs heaved paving blocks into the windows of Jewish shops, and Jews were forced to their knees to scrub streets and toilets while mobs jeered and roared with delight.

"Over at the Cafe Louvre Bob Best of U.P. is sitting at the same table he has occupied every night for the last ten years," Shirer wrote. "Around him a crowd of foreign correspondents, male and female, American, English, Hungarian, Serb. All but Best in a great state of excitement.* . . . Marta Fodor is there, fighting back the tears, every few minutes phoning the news to Fodor . . ." Nearby, in a quiet bar off the Kärtnerstrasse, Shirer's colleague Edward R. Murrow saw a young Jew take an old-fashioned razor from his pocket and slash his throat. "Why does Germany want Austria?" Dorothy wrote in her column. "For raw materials? It has none of consequence. To add to German prosperity? It inherits a country with serious problems. But strategically it is the key to the whole of central Europe. Czechoslovakia is now surrounded. The wheat fields of Hungary, and the oil fields of Rumania are now open. Not one of them will be able to stand the pressure of German domination . . ."

As Hitler's campaign to rescue the Sudeten Germans mounted, Dorothy gave a rousing address at a pro-Czech rally in Madison Square Garden on September 26, 1938. "An enthusiastic audience but one which chiefly applauded when the word Russia

---

* Best subsequently defected to the Nazis and became one of their radio propagandists. After the war, when he was arrested, tried, and sentenced to a long prison term, Dorothy, who had known him well in her Vienna days, pleaded for clemency in his behalf, not because she condoned treason but because of the bitter personal frustrations that she felt had caused it.

was mentioned, thus revealing a communist majority," de Sales commented in his journal.* It was, in any event, too late to halt Hitler's sweep over Central Europe. On September 29, Chamberlain and Daladier signed the Munich pact, of which Dorothy wrote in her column:

"What happened on Friday is called Peace. Actually it is an international Fascist *coup d'état* . . . Germany is guilty of provoking what was nearly an all-European war. And the punishment for this guilt is that she received everything that she was going to fight the war over. This 'everything' is more than the Sudeten territories. It is more than a free hand in the east. It is the domination of Europe . . . In both Britain and France the facts have been suppressed by the exercise of government pressure on the controlled radio and newspapers. The people of England and France are confronted with a *fait accompli* without even being able to gain in advance possession of the facts on which it is based . . ."

Dorothy felt it her mission to insure that her own countrymen were not similarly kept in the dark. Other fine journalists were, to be sure, equally concerned. But none hammered away at the same theme with such single-minded persistence.† For a writer so obsessed, to hold a large audience was a considerable feat. When a collection of her columns, titled *Let the Record Speak*, was published in 1939, Lewis Gannett, reviewing it in the *Herald Tribune*, wrote, "I read five books yesterday and the best of them, the one which throws the most light on the onrushing newspaper headlines was the one you and I have already read . . . Most of this book consists of columns that Dorothy Thompson wrote at white heat, commenting

---

* The Communist line at this time, which backed the United Front against fascism, was reversed in August 1939 with the signing of the Hitler-Stalin pact.
† Margaret Case Harriman, writing in *The New Yorker*, estimated that of 238,000 words Dorothy wrote on international affairs in her column from 1938 to 1940, 147,000, or more than three fifths of the total, were devoted to attacking Hitler's regime.

on the foreign news of 1936–39. Miraculously they seem better today than when they were written . . . Winston Churchill's comments on the world crisis of the last three years, compared to Dorothy Thompson's, sound timid, faltering and sometimes wrongheaded . . . Churchill writes pungently; Dorothy Thompson write fireily. Sometimes she seems to write almost hysterically . . . Almost alone among the political commentators, Dorothy Thompson is not afraid of admitting that, like the rest of the human race, she is subject to emotion. She gets mad. She pleads; she denounces. And the result is that where the intellectualized columns of her colleagues fade when pressed between the leaves of a book, these columns still ring . . ."

In the *New York Times,* Charles Poore's praise was tempered by amiable irony. " 'Let the Record Speak' might as well have been called 'Let the Record Shout,' " he wrote. "And this is not because Miss Thompson's prose style sometimes produces with extraordinary fidelity the effect of having someone bellowing in your ear. It is because her book shows how often she has been prophetically right . . . there's a simple rule, widely used in discussing Miss Thompson's views of the world. When you agree with them, you say so. When you do not, you don't actually say so; you say, instead, that she is too emotional . . ."

The latter charge was frequently heard, for the weight of opinion in the United States opposed involvement in the troubles of Europe. Even after September 1939, when Hitler's armies had invaded Poland and France and England finally declared war, a *Fortune* poll showed that only 3 percent of Americans favored military involvement. A year earlier, Charles Lindbergh had given powerful aid to isolationists with a radio speech urging his countrymen to accept "the wave of the future" represented by Hitler's invincible Germany. Dorothy responded with a vigorous column of which de Sales wrote in his diary:

"Dorothy Thompson tells me that her article on Lindbergh (a good piece) in which she unmasks this sombre cretin and his

Nazi affinities has provoked such an avalanche of letters and insulting and threatening telephone calls that she is afraid. Lindbergh is still the national hero for lack of a better. No one but she has had the courage to commit the sacrilege of knocking him off his pedestal . . ."

Her challenge to Lindbergh and other isolationists had special importance at a time when rapidly growing anti-Semitic organizations were accusing Jews of trying to drag America into the war. Most vocal of these groups was the German-American Bund, which staged a Madison Square Garden rally on the evening of February 20, 1939. Some 19,000 supporters gathered to salute their leader Fritz Kuhn and to denounce war-mongering, Jew-loving Franklin Roosevelt. Traffic was closed off for two blocks outside the Garden, where a police army of some 1700 struggled to prevent a confrontation between the Bundists and an almost equal number of anti-Nazi protesters.

Driving uptown with Ethel Moses and Irving Mansfield after her broadcast, Dorothy — when she saw the melee — insisted that they get out of the taxi. Press card in hand, she talked her way through the police lines and the three found seats in the press section at the front of the auditorium. As a Bund orator warmed up the audience with an anti-Semitic diatribe, Dorothy responded by bursting into a resounding laugh. Flash bulbs popped as she continued her lusty guffaws amid cries of "Throw her out!" Some ten minutes later she departed under police escort — in fact she was late for a scheduled address to the United Chapters of Phi Beta Kappa at the Astor. But she had made her point. The episode was front-page news next day and the following week *The New Yorker*'s "The Talk of the Town" commented:

"It is hard to say how much of the Bund's fury against Dorothy Thompson was political and how much was the irritation of any group of solemn men confronted with a lady laughing in a superior and exasperating manner for reasons that are mysteri-

ous to them. Their feelings were probably not unlike the indignation and bewilderment of a Shriner who finds that his wife
is amused by his singular hat, and to that extent the engagement
at the Garden came down to a war of sex rather than ideology.
Regardless of why Miss Thompson's laughter annoyed the Nazis,
however, there can be no doubt that it had a healthy effect . . .
We live in merry times Dorothy. Take care of your larynx."

An irate reader sent Helen Reid a clipping of *The New
Yorker* item with a marginal note typical of the virulent anti-
Semitism then flourishing: "The drool printed to please
Yiddish advertisers is just about the abyss of nonsense. Let Roosevelt (Judenlieber) love 'em; your readers don't . . ." Pro-
Nazis often accused Dorothy of being Jewish (they had done
the same to Lewis after publication of *It Can't Happen Here*).
In reply she had her secretary mail a form letter addressed "TO
THOSE WHOM IT, ODDLY ENOUGH, CONCERNS." In
it she traced her lineage adding, "I consider this whole business
supremely irrelevant and it is only in order to settle malicious
gossip rising from pro-fascists who want to destroy everything
this country stands for, that I thus expose my own ancestry. I
consider the raising of this question un-American . . ."

❧ 6
Fruits of Fame

EARLY IN 1939 Louis Sobol, a Broadway columnist, included Dorothy's name on a list of ideal dinner party guests. In a jocular column she published a rival list, including sufficient descriptive detail to make it clear that these glamorous personages were well known to her: "Harold Nicolson . . . much more amusing than Anthony Eden; Clare Boothe Luce . . . can discuss politics, letters, fashion with equal vivacity and knowledgeability . . . ; Alice Roosevelt Longworth . . . has wit spiced with malice and warmed by humor; Beatrice Lillie . . . on the stage or off, the funniest woman alive; Mrs. Franklin P. Adams . . . looks like a ripe peach . . . ; Neysa McMein [the popular artist and magazine illustrator] . . . men adore her; Katharine Hepburn . . . a modest earnestness in the midst of so much good looks; Mrs. Ogden Reid . . . knows about everything and never reveals it; Ania Dorfmann . . . a concert pianist who really likes to play; Eve Curie . . . a young woman who has everything; Noel Coward . . . for his wit, his vibrance; Kip [Clifton] Fadiman — a man who makes a large part of his living by public speaking and never makes a public speech; Charlie Chaplin . . . if he will once again tell of his adventures hunting the wild boar; for a soupçon of learning, two college presidents, Robert Maynard Hutchins of Chicago and Stringfellow Barr of St. John's in Annapolis . . . both of them are marvelously good looking; my own favorite, Sir Willmott Lewis, the veteran correspondent of 'The London Times' in Washington; Sinclair Lewis can come to any of my parties and not because

it is his right. Nobody living talks better if he likes the party
. . . off the stage he is a marvelous actor." Of herself she wrote
self-deprecatingly, "As for Dorothy Thompson, she is terrible.
She always talks politics and has a horrible habit of holding
forth. Given the slightest opportunity she makes a speech, and
nothing that she says to herself in the cab on the way home
seems to cure her."

Dorothy did, in fact, often entertain such glittering company.
"Her parties were fabulous," Ethel Moses recalls. "Everyone
who was anybody in New York might be there — Henry and
Clare Luce, or Bob Moses [czar of the state's parks and other
public works] or dozens of other glamorous types." Dorothy
could well afford to be a lavish hostess. In 1939 her earnings
were at their peak. Her income from radio had jumped from
$13,000 in 1937 to nearly $60,000. Through the tactful intervention of John Moses, the revenues of her syndicated column
had climbed from $14,000 to $25,000 and her monthly piece in
the *Ladies' Home Journal* was yielding $12,000. In addition,
there were handsome lecture fees: "Dorothy Thompson was paid
$103,000 last year," *Time* magazine reported on June 12, 1939.
"Her business expenses were $25,000 and she contributed $37,-
000 in taxes, which left her $41,000 to live on. She gave 20
percent of that away . . ."

Shortly after the story appeared, Dorothy saw *Time*'s publisher Henry Luce at a dinner and reproached him for what she
regarded as an invasion of privacy. She could not deny, however, that the figures were reasonably accurate. Never before
had she had anything close to so much money "of her very own."
Though Lewis was a lavish spender when it came to dwellings,
travel, and his own wardrobe, he was often penny-pinching
about his wife's expenditures.

Dorothy enjoyed to the full the luxuries her own earnings
could now support. An equal pleasure was distributing largess,
a special satisfaction to a woman who as a poor minister's daugh-

ter and a novice writer in a strange city had been forced to be grateful for the generosity of rich friends. She seldom contributed to organized charities, preferring her individual philanthropies; among these she gave highest priority to Hitler's victims. Their plight had been one of her chief preoccupations since 1937, when she produced — with the aid of a research staff including Countess Rosie Waldek — a long scholarly article on the subject that appeared in the April issue of *Foreign Affairs*. The magazine's editor, Hamilton Fish Armstrong, credited the article with spurring the State Department to convene a conference of thirty nations at Évian in July 1938 to discuss the worldwide emigration and resettlement program she had outlined. Although there were those who thought Hitler would be delighted to have the democracies take the Jews off his hands at their expense, no large-scale resettlement plan was ever developed. The rescue effort remained the responsibility of private organizations and individuals.*

"It seems to me that in those years," Ethel Moses said, "whenever I saw Dorothy she had an envelope full of immigration papers in her handbag. She was always collecting affidavits of support for someone."

Her major concern was for cherished friends of her European days. Fodor, who had fled from Vienna to Prague after Hitler's conquest of Austria, was rescued by the Sheeans in a breakneck drive only hours ahead of the advancing German armies. With his family he was brought to America, installed temporarily at Twin Farms, and later established in Chicago, where Dorothy and John Gunther helped finance a chair for him as a lecturer at her old school, Lewis Institute, now part of the Illinois Institute of Technology.

Frau Doktor Eugenia Schwarzwald with her husband Hemme

---

* Dorothy repeatedly deplored the failure of the democracies to open their doors to refugees. After the war she tried, without success, to revive the resettlement plan when millions uprooted by Hitler sought a haven and could find none except in Palestine.

had taken refuge in Switzerland. When some of her former pupils at the Schwarzwald Schule hoped to set up a lectureship for her at the University in Exile of the New School for Social Research, Dorothy volunteered to underwrite the cost of $4000 a year. But there were other problems: Hemme was in failing health after several strokes; Genia was recuperating from cancer surgery.

"I realize that you are suffering from financial straits," she wrote to Genia, "having lost everything in Austria and only with Hemme's pension [from a British bank of which he had been an officer] as a certain security. This is something I cannot bear to think of. I love you dearly; and besides this, I am under eternal obligation to you, for I really think you saved my life in 1926. And my life is still dear to me and the debt unpaid. I would therefore like to ask you to accept from me a definite and regular contribution to the maintenance of your peace of mind. I would like to send you $100 a month — that is between four and five hundred francs — for as long as you need it and as long as my own earning power is approximately what it is at present."

Genia's failing health, in the end, precluded immigration. After her death in August 1940, her companion Marie Stiasny wrote to Dorothy: "You were so near her heart that it does not become me to thank you for everything you have done for her, but only through you was it possible that she survived and even enjoyed this last year of her life. A telegram you have sent her more than a year ago, telling her that you love her and want her and Hemme to come to America she always kept in her bed. I will put it in her coffin . . ." *

In addition to loans, affidavits, and gifts of money, Dorothy offered her favorites among the intellectual refugees a temporary home at Twin Farms and a number settled permanently in the area. She had begun investing in local farm property and

---

* Dorothy wrote a moving tribute to Genia titled "The Most Beautiful Kind of Courage" in her *Ladies' Home Journal* column.

had built three summer cottages on nearby Silver Lake (also known as Stebbins Pond). Soon a sizable colony of interesting émigrés were her neighbors.

She had decided to devote at least a third of her Vermont acres to commercial agriculture, a project inspired by memories of the happy months she had spent on the Heist farm near Hamburg, New York, during her childhood. Lewis had always regarded the notion as an impractical extravagance. Now she invested in a herd of cows and sheep, built new barns, an ultramodern henhouse to accommodate a thousand layers and several hundred future broilers, and a farmhouse for the hired tiller of the soil.*

This venture made a large dent in her income, as did the elaborate supporting services her arduous work schedule required. By her own estimate, she had written a quarter of a million words in 1938 and was committed to even more in 1939. Though she had an office at the *Herald Tribune,* she seldom went there, preferring to write her columns in longhand in bed, where she usually worked till noon. Speeches were occasionally dictated to a typist (so that she could do so when and where the mood seized her a half-dozen typewriters were scattered around the Central Park West apartment). She now had three secretaries, all, oddly, with the same (though differently spelled) given name: Madeleine Bourget Walker, a young French-born widow, Madeline Shaw, and Madelon Schiff. Between them, they sorted out and acknowledged the hundreds of letters that came to her each week, typed and retyped her columns and scripts, kept track of her appointments, and burrowed in files and libraries for facts she was too busy to dig up herself. The first draft of a typical column read, "In 1929–30 Finland spent blank percent of her total national budget on education and public health, blank percent went to defense, Sweden spent blank percent of her budget on education and social welfare,

* Lewis had deeded Twin Farms to her after their separation.

blank percent for defense. In the great states the figures are reversed . . ." In the case of that column the statistics precisely documented her thesis.

Occasionally, the facts were less obliging. A somewhat embarrassing episode occurred when, on the basis of an anecdote relayed to her by Ethel Moses, she reported that Jewish children were being subjected to widespread harassment by anti-Semitic schoolmates. The column prompted Fiorello La Guardia, New York's mercurial and ardently antifascist mayor, to institute an elaborate investigation, which established that the incident was an isolated one. "I am so fond of Dorothy," he wrote to Helen Reid, "and being a mere man am therefore biased and unable to give her a scolding. But do tell her to please give us a chance to give her the facts when something like this is handed to her."

It was not the only time that Mrs. Reid would be called upon to exercise her diplomatic gifts to quiet the tempests stirred by her favorite but sometimes impetuous columnist. However, considering the volume of Dorothy's output, there were surprisingly few slip-ups, thanks to her excellent memory and the loyal devotion of her staff, whose duties extended far beyond the secretarial. When his mother was otherwise occupied, it was one of the "girls" who escorted Michael to the dentist or to a new school; in Vermont, the resident secretary cheerfully took on such chores as helping to paint the boathouse or weed the garden. One ordeal they all dreaded on the annual summer safari from New York was a ride with Dorothy at the wheel. "The maids used to cower on the floor as Dorothy went zooming along, talking and driving a mile a minute," Madeline Shaw recalled.

Life with Dorothy was strenuous but never dull. Her energy and her success generated a vicarious pleasure for everyone in her orbit. When in June 1938 she received her fourth honorary degree, Helen Reid wrote: "For years and years I have intended to go back to a Columbia Commencement but it took your degree to get me there and I was glad and proud of the University for honoring you . . . You looked so lovely . . . When you said afterward you had some one waiting for you I decided it would be easier for you to make a getaway without trying to talk to one more person especially as you had plenty of men on your trail . . ."

🎋 7

Sons and Lovers

AN UNHAPPY CONSEQUENCE of Dorothy's multiple professional tasks and her absorption in world affairs was that she had less time than ever for Michael. While it was true that writing a column did not require as much travel as reporting (though she still often took to the road for lecture tours), the effect had been to convert her home into a workshop, where the entire household revolved around her continuous need for useful consultants and absolute isolation on "column days."

Dinah Sheean recalls a typical evening in the Central Park West living room when Dorothy was engrossed in talk with Jimmy, John Gunther, and several other important men. Michael walked in and tugged at his mother's sleeve. "It's time to go," he said. "Go where, Michael?" she asked. "To school." "Oh, darling, I can't possibly leave now. Fräulein will take you. Give me a kiss. I'll come see you next week." On the verge of tears, Michael left. It was a scene that would be often reenacted in different locales and with a changing cast of characters.

Even during summer vacations her new passion for agriculture left her with little leisure. Discussions of fertilizers and feed and chastisement of the farmer who never managed to show a profit consumed such hours as were not filled with debate about global matters with equally concerned adult guests. Dorothy's shortcomings as a mother had long worried her friends.

On August 28, 1937, Frances Gunther wrote in her diary: "Betty [Swing] talked of D's boy Michael, their visit to Vermont,

how she never left her boy John alone with Michael for fear
he might hurt or kill him — how he beat his nurse — how he
was a monster — a sadist etc. — how D ought to take him to a
psychiatrist — how terribly sorry she felt for D who had no
time to be with her child. I said Why feel sorry? She could be
with him if she wanted to. She'd rather be with her career.
Much better if she stayed home and minded her husband and
child instead of minding the nation . . ."

Dorothy was aware that her son was unruly and "difficult"
and consulted a variety of specialists about him in addition to
her physician, Dr. Cornelius Traeger, who for many years provided an indispensable crisis intervention service for the Lewis
family. On medical advice, after Michael had suffered a severe
case of pneumonia in the summer of 1939, she decided to send
him to boarding school in Arizona, an exile for which he never
fully forgave her.

"When she was home, she used to have Michael brought into
the living room around five and show him off to her guests —
he was handsome and very tall for his age," Madeline Shaw recalls. "But she never did the things other mothers do. She didn't
have time."

Yet the glory of motherhood was one of Dorothy's favorite
themes. "Society, at this moment, has a greater need of good
mothers than it now has of more private secretaries, laboratory
assistants, short-story writers, lawyers, social workers and motion
picture stars," she wrote. "It is a better thing to produce a fine
man than it is to produce a second-rate novel, and fine men
begin by being fine children."

"What do parents owe their young?" she asked in another
moralistic essay. "They owe their children a home free from
domestic strife and wrangling. They owe them an atmosphere
of family consideration and affection. But parents do *not* owe
their children every luxury, the indulgence of every whim and
fashion, complete lack of responsibility through childhood . . .

The spoiled child is a peculiarly American phenomenon, selfish, demanding, pampered far beyond the necessity of his years . . ."

Oblivious to her own sermons, Dorothy both pampered and neglected Michael. Meanwhile the youth who really engaged her maternal attention was Wells Lewis, now an exceptionally hand-some Harvard senior showing real talent for journalism and at work on his first novel. He continued to spend most of his vacations at Twin Farms and through him Dorothy established a cordial relationship with his mother Grace.

In June 1939, Grace, in financial straits, asked Dorothy for a $500 loan. "After reading the Thompson eulogy in this week's TIME, I feel as if I know you very well," she wrote. "That plus our happy encounter last summer in Vermont . . ."

A few days later, Wells added his plea: "Your help will be an incomparable mercy and would also, truly be a loan . . . I feel of course, that this is my problem, not yours. But as you know, I am broke at the moment. Next fall, with a job, I can turn over most or all of my income to Mother for paying off the loan . . . I am sorry that I should have just borrowed from you myself . . . If I had fully known of Mother's situation (most of her let-ters are deceptively cheerful) I should never have bothered you myself but sought elsewhere for the $100. It will of course be repaid as promptly as my July check arrives . . ."

Dorothy kept no record of her response but one can assume it was affirmative. Wells was one member of her circle who could count on her generosity. Another was Jimmy Sheean, who had returned from Spain in the spring of 1939 and, for a very modest rental, lived in the "old house" in Vermont from May through October with Dinah and their baby daughter. Dorothy had kept her husband's room in the big house exactly as he had left it but he came only for two uneasy weeks. "On many evenings he would say: 'Any more sitayashuns and I go to bed,' Sheean wrote. "And inevitably, unconsciously, fatally, Dorothy would be back at it within a few minutes. She meant no harm; she could not help it."

Dinah, who was also weary of listening to a dialogue from which she was excluded, spent happy hours with Lewis helping him rehearse his lines in the plays in which he would shortly make his stage debut — Thornton Wilder's *Our Town* and Eugene O'Neill's *Ah, Wilderness!* He appeared in summer stock in Ogonquit, Maine, and subsequently in Provincetown. There he met and formed a strange but durable attachment for an eighteen-year-old apprentice actress, Marcella Powers, and began to demand a divorce. Dorothy refused.

"Come home, come home," she wrote. "All sorts of men have crossed my life in the last ten years. Some of them liked me. One or two claimed they loved me. Lots of them I have liked, had real affection for. But you were my man . . . I am therefore, in a not very classic way, the very picture of Penelope . . ."

In fact, she was not pining for her husband in lonely chastity. Nor was there any reason why she should have. He had left her when she was still, at forty-six — as one man put it — "a magnificent animal," or, as another said, "the kind of woman you felt it would be fun to go to bed with." From time to time several did.* The current object of her affections was Fritz Kortner, a short, thick-set, heavy-jowled German-Jewish actor whom she had first met in the 1920s when he was a star of the Berlin State Theatre. They renewed their acquaintance in 1936 in England, where he had fled with his family. The following year he came to America and so persuaded Dorothy of his devotion and genius that in 1938 she provided an affidavit of support for his actress wife, two children, and his aged mother, plus a cash loan of $10,000. Although she deplored her husband's obsession with the theater, Dorothy decided to help the new "creative man" in her life by writing a play with him dealing with the plight of refugees in New York. The collaboration was complicated by the fact that Kortner, soon after his arrival in America, left for

---

* After these brief encounters Dorothy often sat down at her typewriter and wrote a detailed account of the experience. Her proper secretaries read and promptly burned the manuscripts.

Hollywood hoping to duplicate the success of Oscar Homolka, Erich von Stroheim, and Emil Jannings. Most of Dorothy's friends found Kortner rude and arrogant and were distressed at the prospect of an additional work burden for her. But in Wells Lewis' eyes she could do no wrong. "How is the play going?" he wrote in December 1939. "I was tremendously impressed by it, and by its theatrical possibilities, as well as being most charmed by Mr. Kortner."

Dorothy apparently did not discuss her theatrical venture with the friend who might have given her the soundest counsel — the drama critic Alexander Woollcott, a fellow Vermonter with a summer house on Lake Bomoseen. He had suggested in August that *The New Yorker* do a profile of her.* She was delighted by the prospect, unconcerned by the knowledge that the magazine's barbed portraits seldom flattered their subjects, and, in her reply, sketched out the image she wished to project.

"Rebecca [West] doesn't know me well enough to do the profile. Red does but wouldn't. I wish you would . . . I wish someone would say that I am a hell of a good housekeeper, that the food by me is swell, that I am almost a perfect wife, and that I am still susceptible to the boys. In other words, I wish someone would present me as a female. I am tired of being told I have the brains of a man. What man? But leaving that aside, I haven't. And I am *not* a very good journalist. Walter [Lippmann] and Edgar [Mowrer] and Johnnie Gunther and lots of my friends are *much* better and I know it. My strength is altogether female. I am good receptive audience and wise people tell me things, and I have wits enough to know (usually) who makes sense and who doesn't . . . I went to Europe to get away from a man; I stayed in Europe to be with another man; I left journalism to marry a third man; I re-entered it — in preference

---

* Simultaneously, Jack Alexander was at work on a piece about Dorothy for the *Saturday Evening Post.* Aided by Dorothy's sister Peggy, whom he rewarded with a $100 fee for her research assistance, he produced a lively portrait that ran in two long installments in May 1940, a month after *The New Yorker* profile.

to other kinds of work — because I could write a column and stay home. That's heresy which the feminists wouldn't like, but it's a fact. Work with me has always been a by-product and a secondary interest; I'd throw the state of the nation into the ash-can for anyone I loved . . ."

8
Political Schizophrenia

WIDELY ADMIRED THOUGH SHE WAS for her battle against fascism, Dorothy's unsympathetic, often hostile comments on FDR's domestic program drew the fire of liberals. "Miss Thompson hates not Roosevelt the less but Hitler and Mussolini the more" was the theme of a savage piece that appeared in *Ken*, a short-lived radical monthly, in May 1938. This charge was a grotesque exaggeration. Far from hating Roosevelt, Dorothy, when she came to know him, was susceptible to his charm and impressed with his statesmanship despite her objections to the New Deal; and for his wife she had an almost worshipful respect. A more reasoned and telling critique of her ambivalence appeared in the *Nation* on June 25, 1938. "Dorothy Thompson is that combination of small-town girl who makes good and woman of the world which is peculiarly American," Margaret Marshall, an astute political analyst, wrote. "She brought out of Europe a deep hatred of fascism . . . and she has performed an important service by her campaign against fascism and in behalf of its victims . . . She is the most interesting and dramatic personality among the columnists . . . Her writing is vigorous and has wide appeal. Her style is gusty and fresh. Each column reads like a tour de force . . . If Miss Thompson were to be judged on the basis of her comments on foreign affairs she would be set down as a liberal of good will who sees the totalitarian flood advancing over Europe and wishes to stop its course . . . But in relation to her comments on the American scene her columns on Europe appear in a different light . . . She is always choosing with great dramatic gestures between good and evil and in the name of freedom. She is always dealing in ultimate truths — and coming out on the side of immediate reaction . . . a good show. But it is just such good shows that cast doubt on the motives of our self-appointed anti-fascist Joan of Arc . . . To fight the New Deal as if it were communist is vicious. To fight it as if it were fascist is also vicious, and even more confusing because it is a more subtle and intellectually less discredited approach."

Among the columns that roused Miss Marshall's ire was one titled "The Right to Insecurity" in which Dorothy grudgingly agreed to pay her employees' social security taxes but smugly observed, "I was brought up to believe that there's only one thing absolutely certain in life and that is that one eventually dies. Never having had the slightest feeling of security, it's a luxury that I do not miss. I prefer exhilaration to certainty, risk to dullness, danger to boredom, work to a job, and independence to a pension . . ." "Unemployed and unemployables please copy" was Miss Marshall's comment.

George Seldes, Dorothy's Vermont neighbor and one-time colleague, whose own ideology had been moving steadily left-ward, mounted an even more pointed attack in his book *Lords of the Press,* coupling her with Walter Lippmann, who was also critical of the New Deal. In a chapter titled "From Reds to Riches," he accused her of political schizophrenia — the result, he said, of her recently acquired wealth and the influence of the rich, conservative friends and advisers who had supplanted the radical associates of her youth, "One of the bravest pieces of writing done in America since 1917 . . ." Seldes wrote, "was Dorothy's defense of Loyalist Spain and defiance of the Catholic hierarchy which supports the bloodiest movement in the name of Christ the modern world has seen . . . Miss Thompson is willing to fight against Fascism, but not willing to look at that phenomenon everywhere around her. She says she is willing to give her life for civil liberties but she sneers at the American Civil Liberties Union."

Dorothy was upset by Seldes' taunts. "My dear George," she

wrote ". . . You start by saying I was once a radical. You do not define what you mean by a radical but you certainly imply that I was once something which I am not now. That is not true. My political philosophy has remained extremely consistent since I have had one . . . I have never picked my friends for their political viewpoints. I have picked them for their brains, their character, their charm or for any of the thousands of reasons that one human being finds another human being sympathetic. I have never believed it was necessary to agree with anybody in order to like him. I am very fond of you, George, although I do not agree with you on many things, and at present am extremely annoyed with you . . ."

Dorothy's defense was strengthened by the fact that Seldes had inadvertently attributed some statements of Walter Lippmann's to her. She called her attorney Morris L. Ernst into action and corrections were made in the second edition although the book's thesis remained unaltered.

Seldes' criticism was, in fact, intemperate. To true believers in the New Deal she was no liberal. But she could justly call herself an "independent," who over the years would defend Mrs. Roosevelt when she was under attack by the Catholic Church, speak out for freedom of the press when *Esquire* magazine was threatened by censorship, and deplore Red-baiting attempts to prevent Bertrand Russell from lecturing at City College in New York. If she was critical of the New Deal's often floundering social and economic programs, and strongly opposed the plan to enlarge the Supreme Court, she had as company a good many intelligent Americans who could not be called reactionary. She had attempted to spell out her philosophy in a magazine piece titled "The Dilemma of the Liberal." The essay had little to do with liberalism as the term was understood by those who carried its banner in the America of that day. It was instead a discussion of her European experiences and the envy she had felt for young German Communists and Nazis who gloried in a "sense of belonging," false though their creed might be. This was what was missing in her present life, she wrote, evoking the secure world of her childhood in which the one basic need, in her father's view, was "to get right with God."

Among others, John and Frances Gunther found Seldes' article puzzling. "He says she [Dorothy] is conservative, bourbon, naturally a bit selfish but also troubled by poor —" Frances wrote in her diary. "I said no, she was genuinely troubled . . . Her loyalty to her bosses, all Right, Curtis, Hearst, Lorimer, Reid, kept her from development toward left, her natural tendency. If the Left gave her big important job, she would do it — good for her, good for Left — & could help them both (Dilemma of Left being it lacks just that type of Organizing Efficiency, Vitality, Push that D.T. has to nth degree)."

John's analysis was closer to the truth than Frances'. Dorothy's commitment to the Methodist creed of social justice was outbalanced by the conservatism of the self-made man or woman who feels more contempt than compassion for those less successful. She was comfortably at home among those Republicans concerned with defending their hard-won property, who exalted individual initiative and yet shared Roosevelt's stance on world affairs. However, as the election of 1940 neared, such moderates were not likely to control the GOP presidential nomination. The front-running candidate was isolationist Senator Robert Taft, whose views, Walter Lippmann wrote, "make Mr. Neville Chamberlain seem like a far-sighted and strong statesman."

For those of Dorothy's persuasion, what seemed a heaven-sent solution to this quandary presented itself in the person of Wendell Willkie. Though an enrolled Democrat, he had, as President of the Commonwealth and Southern Corporation, established himself as an effective anti–New Dealer by waging a vigorous and partly successful battle against the Tennessee Valley Authority. Tall, rugged, with a forelock that fell engagingly over his brow, Willkie was an outspoken supporter of the Allied cause. He was articulate, looked like a president, and was immensely attractive to women. As a businessman with a winning personality he seemed the ideal choice for those Republicans who abhorred the heresy of a third term and considered Roosevelt an incompetent executive but accepted the reality of the Nazi threat. Willkie spent a week at Twin Farms in the summer of 1939 with Dorothy and the Sheeans. All were impressed by his intelligence and charm. An enthusiast for mechanical gadgetry, Willkie afterward sent his hostess, in lieu of a bread and butter letter, a gleaming electric refrigerator to replace the venerable Lewis icebox. When she returned to the city, Dorothy shared her enthusiasm with Helen Reid, one of Willkie's early and most adroit supporters. "If the convention doesn't nominate him," Dorothy said, "I'm going out into the streets and do it myself."

PART VII

CRUSADE

❧ 1
Boadicea

Another Sun* by Dorothy Thompson and Fritz Kortner opened at the National Theatre on February 20, 1940, with a cast that included Kortner's wife Johanna Hofer and two very popular players — Celeste Holm and Leo Bulgakov. Brooks Atkinson called it "a drama that never starts marching across the stage." When the critics of New York's five other dailies were equally cold the play closed in a week. From Beverly Hills, Lewis sent words of comfort: "A lot of people will say 'never mind' but I can really say it factually, having had my own plays 'Hobohemia,' 'Jayhawker' and 'Angela' roasted plenty, and still going on tackling that most difficult of artistic forms with my new one . . . If you feel depressed, you must remember that it's just because you have had such amazing uniform success that a partial failure will seem worse than it is . . . I have always thought you were a far better dramatist than Kortner, for all his experience and ingenuity. Some day, you'll do another play — do it when you're off in the country and fresh and rested . . ."

Dorothy, however, had learned an expensive lesson. The production had cost her more than $30,000. Never again would she invest her talents or money in the Broadway theater. A month after the stage debacle, on March 23, she sailed on the *Manhattan,* bound for still-neutral Italy, accompanied by her secretary Madeleine Walker. There was a large bon voyage party. In her diary she wrote:

* The title was taken from Vergil's *Georgics:* "They change their home and pleasant thresholds to seek a country lying beneath another sun." Lewis had argued against the name on the ground that it was ambiguous, sounding like "Another Son."

> Flowers piling into the room when we went in.
> Boxes like little coffins. Odd who sends one flowers
> . . . Connie [Dr. Traeger] — the Basque delega-
> tion, Rumanian minister . . . The purser came
> down, and is my old friend from the *Leviathan.*
> He has moved me into an enchanting little suite,
> sitting room, bedroom and bath . . . home for the
> next eight days . . . I put Fritz [Kortner] and
> [his wife] Hanna's roses on my night table and gave
> half the other flowers to M. [Madeleine]. I thought
> about F. and why I cannot understand him . . .
> Will he think of me this evening — and if he does
> with what emotions — bitterness, resentment . . .

Anxieties about her faltering romance were soon obliterated by the pleasures of an ocean voyage. She wrote:

> I walked around the deck in the moonlight . . .
> the sea a soft swell and the wake silver — only the
> tremor of the engine on the ship — lovely,
> lovely . . .

It was luxurious to sleep almost without interruption for two days. Afterward she made a dramatic nightly entrance into the dining salon to her place of honor at the captain's table and speculated with her fellow passengers on what lay ahead. This was the season of the "phony war." Following the signing of the Hitler-Stalin pact in August 1939, German and Russian armies had dismembered Poland. Although Britain and France had responded by declaring war on Germany, there was still a military lull. Postponing comment on the European scene until she could report firsthand observations, Dorothy fashioned lively columns out of shipboard encounters with young Americans. Some were planning to join the volunteer ambulance corps in Britain; others were Jewish medical students en route to Europe, where they were forced to seek their education because of the quotas that were still enforced by American medical schools.

"We also have our modified versions of Hitler's racial laws," she observed, "only they are not enforced by the state but in a silent and unpublicized manner by our so-called free universities."

Since neither she nor her secretary spoke Italian, her first need when she arrived in Rome was for a translator. Through her European grapevine, she had learned that an old Vienna colleague, Sari Juhasz, had taken refuge in Italy with her Jewish husband and daughter after the Anschluss of 1938. Miraculously, the efficient Miss Walker located her address in Rome, and cabled asking her to call at the Excelsior.

"It was like a message from heaven," said the diminutive multilingual Hungarian journalist. "We were penniless. I was so shabby that the clerk at the Excelsior didn't want to show me up. Miss Walker had to come down to the lobby to get me. I hadn't seen Dorothy for eight years. I remembered her as always wearing very plain tailored suits. Now she swept into the room draped in beautiful filmy chiffon. Her hair was white. She looked like a snow goddess. She kissed me and said, 'Sari, what do you need most?' I said, 'Stockings.' She pulled open a drawer. There must have been a dozen pairs of nylons in it. She handed me six. I cried with joy."

Dorothy was granted an audience with Eugenio Pacelli, who, a year earlier, had been elevated to the papacy as Pius XII. She used the occasion to plead that he exert his influence to keep Mussolini out of the war. According to her account, Pius smiled enigmatically and said, "Now I know you are a Protestant, my child." "Why? Because I didn't kiss your ring?" "No," he replied. "Because you have such faith in the limitless power of the Catholic Church." It was a witty way to mask his continuing complaisance toward fascism. Elsewhere on her journey — in Ankara, Bucharest, and Belgrade — she was appalled by the fatalistic resignation of many of the statesmen she interviewed. She was also impressed by the fact that wherever the will to resist Hitler survived, the name of Franklin D. Roosevelt was a talisman of hope. Convinced that a change of America's leadership might be catastrophic at this critical time, she wrote a column proposing, in effect, that the 1940 election be called off with both parties uniting behind a coalition ticket, Roosevelt for President, Willkie for Vice President. The suggestion evoked a public rebuke from Paul Block, publisher of two important outlets for her syndicated column, the Pittsburgh *Post-Gazette* and the Toledo *Blade*. "Always strongly emotional, Miss Thompson seems to have lost her perspective on this trip," he wrote in an angry editorial. Her apostasy also prompted a cautionary message from Helen Reid: "Forwarding cable from Count de Sales QUOTE Your friends and faithful public unanimous in asking you to write human interest stories and background and keep off politics. Love Raoul UNQUOTE Heartily agree. Ship reporting delightful. Hope you will stick to plan of writing about nongovernmental people. Love."

The message reached Dorothy in France where the situation scarcely inspired less "political" reporting. At an evening spent with United States Ambassador William C. Bullitt, Eve Curie, newly returned from America, Laurence Steinhardt, United States Ambassador to the USSR, and her friends the Sheeans, the coming presidential election was high on the agenda. Denmark and Norway had fallen to the Germans, the collapse of France seemed imminent, and it appeared that Britain would be left standing alone, more than ever in need of Roosevelt's practical and moral support. In her rooms at the Meurice, Dorothy told the Sheeans that she planned to visit the Maginot Line. When she did so the following day, she received permission to fire three shells from a French artillery battery at the German lines. For this symbolic deed, General Hugh S. Johnson in his column dubbed her "a blood-thirsty, breast-beating Boadicea." Meanwhile, the invasion of the Low Countries had begun and, by the time Dorothy returned to America, German mechanized divisions had driven deep into northern France.

Shortly after the catastrophic events of May 28, when France had fallen and the desperate evacuation of British forces from Dunkirk followed, Dorothy dined at the Starlight Roof of the Waldorf Astoria with a group that included Leopold Stokowski and the young foreign editor of *Life,* Julian Bach. Later the party adjourned to her Central Park West apartment.

"All of us were barely controlling our tears," Bach said. "We envisioned a fortress America surrounded by fascist foes. It seemed unlikely that Britain could hold out. Dorothy leaned against the mantle piece and delivered a marvelous Churchillian speech, filled with unquenchable determination. She seemed to me to represent all that was best in western civilization — her brilliant mind, her magnificent voice, her leonine presence."

This spontaneous talk was a rehearsal for one of her most stirring addresses, delivered in Canada in July. Carried by short wave to Britain, it was replayed in a recording for the Prime Minister, to whom she addressed herself directly: ". . . around you Winston Churchill is a gallant company of ghosts. Elizabeth is there and sweetest Shakespeare. Drake is there, and Raleigh and Wellington. Burke is there and Walpole and Pitt. Byron is there, and Wordsworth and Shelley. Yes, and I think Washington is there, and Hamilton, two men of English blood whom gallant Englishmen defended in your parliament. And Jefferson is there, who died again the other day in France. All the makers of a world of freedom and of law are there . . ."

She delivered equally spirited talks on her regular radio program, some of them emanating from the General Electric building at the New York World's Fair in Flushing Meadow, remembered by the World War II generation as the last time, for many years, that they would see the flags of the United States, Britain, Germany, France, Italy, Japan, and the USSR flying side by side. Her sponsors, somewhat uneasy about her belligerent tone, tried to soften the effect by introducing her with such soothing melodies as "Love Sends a Little Gift of Roses" played by Phil Spitalny's All-Girl Orchestra.

Dorothy was, by this time, calling for universal conscription, convinced that the United States would soon be forced to enter the war. The Selective Service Act became law in September, but many Americans still opposed such mild measures as the agreement whereby Britain obtained fifty overage destroyers in exchange for ninety-nine-year leases to naval bases in English territory. The internationalist-minded *New Yorker,* which a year earlier had applauded her defiance of the German-American Bund, published in April 1940 a deftly hostile two-part profile by Margaret Case Harriman, who wrote of "Miss Thompson's talent for brooding over the welfare of mankind and at the same time inflaming it to further disasters . . . Her admirers say that hers is the dilemma of the voice crying in the wilderness, of every farseeing patriot who must holler to be heard . . . Other people alarmed by her belligerence in print, see her as a dangerous warmonger and incendiary . . ." Mrs. Harriman made it plain that neither she nor most of the people she interviewed were among the "admirers."

However, as bombs continued to fall on Britain, Americans listened with increasing concern to the voice of Edward R. Murrow, reporting the stoical courage of the English people and the heroic feats of the RAF. In August, when Dorothy appeared in Springfield, Massachusetts, at a rally sponsored by the Committee to Defend America by Aiding the Allies, she drew an overflow audience.

"Seldom has so large a cross section of Springfield been seen at one time," the Springfield *Union* reported. "There were leaders in the civic and social life of the city, hundreds of members of women's clubs and educators and industrialists were noted among the men. Side by side sat those who were evidently of foreign birth and those whose family history ran deep into the history of the city . . . [There were] people of all ages . . . Several parties arrived in trucks . . . There were many from surrounding towns, and there were a half dozen smart station wagons from the Berkshires . . .

"A concert by the Hampden County WPA band closed with everyone singing 'God Bless America,' then the band broke into a Syracuse University air, Miss Thompson's alma mater and . . . she appeared on the stage. From the moment she appeared this statuesque grey-haired woman held the audience in the hollow of her hand. She spoke forthrightly without mincing words and her voice was flexible enough to meet every demand made upon it . . . As the huge audience left the Auditorium and milled its way out, not a dissenting voice was heard . . . 'What a woman,' 'Great speech' and 'She knows what she is talking about' evidenced the approval of the great mass of listeners."

Other audiences were similarly moved. Yet even among those who approved her purpose, there were a few who objected to her style, as did her friend and fellow columnist Heywood Broun, who once observed: "Dorothy is greater than Eliza because not only does she cross the ice but breaks it as she goes. Moreover, she is her own bloodhound."

✌ 2
"To thine own self be true"

HELEN REID, in due course, persuaded Dorothy to retract her proposal for a Roosevelt-Willkie ticket. "I think my column about a third term was a mistake," she wrote to publisher Paul Block on June 7, 1940. "It was written from a feeling of expediency. I was, at the moment, sure that Roosevelt would be re-elected . . . It seemed to me that if Roosevelt won on the present set-up — the New Deal crowd — it would be a catastrophe . . . I doubt if Mr. Roosevelt will live through another four years of this kind of strain . . . the vice president would be of prime importance . . . I do think Roosevelt has a magic kind of leadership, and I saw no one else on the scene likely to get the nomination who has any capacity for leadership of the nature needed. As soon as I got back from Europe I saw that a change had occurred . . . [Roosevelt] is tired and defeatist. We need a new President. From my own point of view there is only one man on the scene, and that is Wendell Willkie . . . If Mr. Willkie is nominated I shall support him to the hilt . . ."

In June she went to the Republican Convention in Philadelphia as an ardent Willkie partisan. Laboring with equal zeal were Mrs. Reid, Irita Van Doren, and Clare Boothe Luce. One of Dorothy's effective weapons was Lewis' son Wells, who was in Philadelphia as a reporter for the Greenville, Mississippi, *Delta Democrat-Times,* where he had been working for the past year after graduating from Harvard in 1939.* On June 26 Dor-

---

* It was David Cohn who introduced Wells to Hodding Carter, the paper's publisher.

othy turned her column over to Wells, demonstrating that young men of military age shared her view of the European crisis.* Describing himself as a "nineteenth century liberal" who was considered reactionary by Reds and radical by Republicans, Wells voiced disgust with the inefficiency of Roosevelt's New Deal "henchmen," pronounced the Republican Party of Herbert Hoover "dead as the dodo," and acclaimed Willkie as "the executive to save this country (if it is still here to be saved next January) . . ."

A few days later Willkie's amateur backers triumphed. His nomination was hailed as a stunning victory for the eastern liberal wing of the GOP. But as the campaign progressed, it became evident that the old guard had by no means been routed or silenced. Willkie himself seemed to be floundering, calling the bases-for-destroyers deal "arbitrary" and "dictatorial," berating Roosevelt for an insufficiently vigorous policy in one speech, and in another charging him with carrying the country to the brink of war.

Dorothy confided her disappointment in the GOP campaign to Fodor, who spent the summer of 1940 at Twin Farms with his wife and son. For many hours they debated the overriding questions. Could Britain hold out? Would Willkie, if elected, really be free of the isolationists? How indispensable was FDR? And what was the proper role of a columnist tormented by such questions? Fodor — though a staunch Roosevelt supporter — assessed Dorothy's situation in realistic terms. She had fought for Willkie's nomination; she was employed by a Republican paper and now syndicated in more than 150 others that, with minimum exceptions, opposed Roosevelt. She could not, he argued, either prudently or rationally switch sides at this late hour.

Another friend, Morris L. Ernst, took a different view. A

---

* Wells volunteered for service in the United States army more than a year before Pearl Harbor.

volunteer adviser to the President, deeply committed to his re-election, he felt Dorothy's support could be a powerful aid in a race that might be closely contested. Reexposure to the Roosevelt charm, he thought, might tip the scales. While she was still abroad he wrote to FDR suggesting, for the record, that Miss Thompson might have gathered some useful intelligence that the President might like to hear at first hand. Roosevelt replied: "I shall be delighted to see Dorothy Thompson when she comes back. She has been here several times as you know. Do try to get this silly Willkie business out of her head."

The meeting that took place in the White House on the morning of October 1 was conducted on a lofty nonpolitical plane. Dorothy reported chiefly on the appalling military weakness of the neutral nations. The President was particularly interested in her analysis of Hitler's plans for the economic and political conquest of South America. When the interview ended, FDR said to Ernst: "Take Dorothy over to see the Old Man [his nickname for Secretary of State Cordell Hull] and tell him to show her a file I had started after a meeting with the Senate Foreign Affairs Committee in 1938 and titled, at my suggestion, 'Germanica Incorporated.' "

In person, Dorothy found FDR neither "tired" nor "defeatist." She was, on the contrary, overwhelmed by his magnetism, courage, and wisdom. Within a week she had made her decision and announced it on October 9 in a column titled "The Presidency."

"This column," she wrote, "has often criticized the Roosevelt administration, and sometimes very sharply . . . I have known Wendell L. Willkie for several years; he is a very good human being . . . But I shall support the President because I think he has assets on his side that nobody can match. The President knows the world. He knows it . . . better than any other living democratic head of a state . . . The range and precision of his knowledge, military, naval, political, his understanding of conflicting social forces, his grasp of programs — all these impress every person whose life has been spent in foreign affairs with whom he talks. No new President could acquire this knowledge in weeks or in months or in four years . . . the figure of the President looms above that of any statesman, except perhaps Winston Churchill whose stature grows under fire . . ."

At Republican breakfast tables across the country and in the office of the *Herald Tribune*'s publisher, the column was a thunderbolt. For the next few days, the paper devoted a half page to irate comments on the column, adding its own disclaimer: "Our disagreement with her conclusions as to the Presidency is as complete as that of our readers."

A well-timed speaking engagement in Buffalo took Dorothy out of the eye of the storm. However, she had left behind a second column on the presidency for publication on Monday, October 14. It was duly set in type but, on orders of the publisher, did not appear. "Herald Tribune Gags Dorothy Thompson," the liberal tabloid *PM*, edited by Ralph Ingersoll, proclaimed that afternoon. *PM* had readily obtained a copy of the column from one of her syndicated outlets, the Washington *Post*, and published an excerpt in which she documented her assertion that "the Axis desires the defeat of President Roosevelt."

Helen Reid, a born conciliator, struggled to repair the damage Dorothy had done to the *Herald Tribune*'s circulation: "Please add my name to that ever growing list of Americans who feel that so long as Dorothy Thompson remains a contributor to the *Herald Tribune* they do not care to have the paper enter their doors," a typical subscriber wrote. "Your paper has long been our watchword and it is with regret that we feel we can no longer read it."

"We sympathize fully with your point of view about Miss Thompson's work during the campaign," HR replied. "We all make mistakes at times and I feel that Miss Thompson's position in regard to the campaign was a serious one. But do you not think it might be worthwhile to consider what she did as an error of judgment rather than something that has entirely finished her usefulness in the world?"

Dorothy herself had no apologies to offer and never fully explained her eleventh-hour change of heart. Blithely quoting Polonius' admonition to his son, "To thine own self be true," she flung herself into the Democratic campaign with enthusiasm. According to Robert Sherwood, FDR's chief speechwriter, "The best suggestions in the assembled material came from Dorothy Thompson, who was still with the New York *Herald Tribune,* and from Dean Acheson who had walked out of the New Deal in its first year but was now giving strong support to the President." On election eve she joined Roosevelt, Hull, Carl Sandburg, and Alexander Woollcott in a two-hour radio marathon in which campaign speeches were mingled with Broadway and Hollywood entertainment.

Applause for her stand came from some surprising quarters. There was, for instance, an unexpected reaction from Mrs. Henry Luce, Sr., mother of the publisher of *Time.*

"My dear Miss Thompson," she wrote, "Your recent column in support of Mr. Roosevelt is greatly to be admired and applauded. Your honest and courageous stand will help to dissolve the doubts of many, though you yourself will suffer for it. There are, however, important occasions when one must choose one's path, however painful & lonely it is sure to be . . ."

"I cannot tell you what a comfort your letter was to me," Dorothy replied. "When one has made oneself so isolated and estranged, laid oneself open to such vicious attacks, and then had it even said 'Someone has certainly paid that girl a lot of money' — when one is publicly attacked in a most venemous way by a woman one has liked, admired and consistently defended against her catty women 'friends' — I am talking about Harry's wife, Claire — when one knows, and knew that a stand would bring one all this, and serious financial losses — then every kind cheering word goes right to one's heart. I am a woman, Mrs. Luce, and not at all insensitive — something you may find it difficult to believe. The truth is I cry my eyes out a lot of the time. However, I dry them up again, too . . . I wish you could persuade your powerful son, Mrs. Luce, we are voting ourselves into American fascism if we elect Willkie . . ."

Mrs. Luce's daughter-in-law Clare did not take Dorothy's defection lightly. They had, after all, worked side-by-side for Willkie's nomination. In her first political speech, Clare undertook to refute Dorothy's pro-Roosevelt columns and, recalling her belligerent words and gestures, dubbed her "the Molly Pitcher of the Maginot Line." Dorothy retorted by naming Clare "the Fisher body of politics." The public thoroughly enjoyed what the press labeled a confrontation between "two blond Valkyries on the prows of opposing ships of state," which was climaxed by a much-publicized radio debate.*

By the end of the year 1940 rumors that Dorothy's days with the *Herald Tribune* were numbered reached England, where Whitelaw Reid, heir-apparent to the publisher's chair, was serving as a volunteer with the RAF. He urged his mother to use her diplomatic powers to prevent the paper from losing a columnist he regarded as uniquely valuable. And as soon as the campaign was ended H.R. tried to steer her stormy protégée into tranquil nonpolitical waters.

"Dear Helen," Dorothy wrote, "You know, I *want* to act the way you desire . . . to 'write on unpolitical subjects' . . . 're-view a book' . . . do the sort of things that you told me, so charmingly, that, when I put my mind to it, I can do well. On

---

* Trude Pratt (later Mrs. Joseph P. Lash), one of Mrs. Roosevelt's political aides, persuaded Bernard Baruch to foot the bill for air time. The two contestants were so evenly matched that there was doubt about whether the investment was worthwhile for the Democrats. After the election, Clare sent Dorothy a gracious telegram and their friendship was unimpaired. The experience, Clare said, convinced her never again to engage in public debate with a woman because "differences of opinion between women are always treated by the press as inspired by personal dislikes."

the other hand, I do not see how a political commentator can avoid the major political questions of the moment . . ." An impasse had been reached; in the eyes of the publisher, Ogden Reid, Dorothy had committed a mortal political sin.

"I feel an unbridgeable hostility to me in the *Tribune,*" Dorothy wrote to Helen on January 23, 1941. ". . . I think we shall be happier divorced . . ." Her contract was not renewed when it expired in March 1941.

Financially, the break did her no immediate harm. John Moses negotiated an advantageous contract with Bell Syndicate and her readership across the country increased. The real loss was the *Herald Tribune* itself, which had given her precisely the audience she needed — essentially conservative Americans who would listen to her even when they disagreed, except when a sacred principle like the third term was at stake. In her new outlet in New York, the *Post,* she had no one to argue with. This was no longer the staid journal of Curtis days. The New York *Post* had been sold to Dorothy Schiff Backer, who was steering it on an erratically leftward course. Under the editorship of Ted O. Thackrey, the paper was building circulation among Jewish and black readers, and among liberals flirting with Stalinism. To this audience, the internationalism of Dorothy Thompson offered few surprises and her patrician tone on domestic matters was often irritating.

Dorothy anticipated no such problems when she wrote on January 29, 1941, to Mrs. Roosevelt:

"The *Herald Tribune* is not renewing my contract. They (or rather Ogden Reid) have never forgiven me for the election stand . . . I want you to know that I do not suffer financially by the change. You are so kind, that I feared you might hear of it and that it would worry you, so I want you to know this."

Roosevelt acknowledged her services with a rather heartless quip — "At least I kept my job," he wired. Some of her friends felt an offer of an ambassadorship would have been more appropriate. So far as we know Dorothy never sought any such token of gratitude. Her chief reward was ready access to the man in the White House, who for the rest of her days was enshrined in her private pantheon of heroes. In an eloquent article in *Life* she wrote of his third inaugural, "Standing there, watching him proceed to the inauguration altar, watching the eyes of the representatives of stricken nations follow him, a sense of the awful and beautiful significance of this man came over me. For I felt that every one of the ambassadors of lost nations and the lost democratic cause, and the lost cause of freedom was saying to himself, 'See, he too, was stricken, and stricken dreadfully. He, too, must have thought in black, black moments that all was over. But it was not true. For he recovered to preside over the greatest country under the sun, and to be the only man elected three times to that office, and out of the liability of his suffering, he made an asset, and deprived of his legs, he lived as a voice, a heart, and a mind.'

"Maybe the Ambassadors did not think that. But I thought it, watching him and them . . ."

❧ 3
"what one valiant woman can do . . ."

ONE OF DOROTHY'S FAVORITE POEMS was *Lepanto* by G. K. Chesterton — a rousing ballad that commemorates the sixteenth-century battle in which a Christian fleet led by Don John of Austria defeated the Turks and freed the Mediterranean from their control. To the bafflement of her less devout friends, she saw the struggle against Hitler as a comparable crusade against paganism in which victory would be speeded by a religious revival. In late August 1939 when the "war of nerves" was reaching a climax, she sent a 400-word cable to Harold Nicolson proposing that he use his influence as a member of Parliament to set up a worldwide day of prayer and meditation, with short-wave radio devoted to the great religious music of Germany, readings from the Sermon on the Mount, and appropriate chapters from the Old and New Testaments. "England's strength," she said, "is not appeasement with the enemy of peace nor war but a glorious Christian resistance. I mean this with all seriousness. I am not at all crazy. Love from Red who thinks I am."

Nicolson — replying graciously by letter on August 29 — assured her he did not think her crazy. "The conflict, if it comes, will be a moral conflict," he wrote, "and it is for that reason I have minded so terribly in the last few years that we have soiled our moral case by trying to appease the dictators . . . Dear Dorothy it is so welcome in this moment of terrible anxiety to get messages from you and Red . . ."

Within a few days it was too late for prayers. As German and Russian armies swept into Poland, England and France finally honored their commitments by declaring war. Dorothy, however, did not abandon her evangelical dream. It moved her in early 1941 to conceive of an organization to be called the "Ring of Freedom," which would bind together in a militant fellowship all true believers in the principles for which the Allies fought. As a first step she ordered from one of the city's best jewelers, Van Cleef and Arpels, a specially designed ring, showing two hands clasped over a globe; she then arranged to have inexpensive replicas mass-produced. As her deputy in this project she enlisted a young Zionist, Meyer Weisgal, whom she had first met when she became involved in the defense of Herschel Grynzspan in 1938. A talented organizer and fund raiser, Weisgal was serving as a personal representative of Dr. Chaim Weizmann and at the same time attempting to establish the Max Reinhardt Repertory Theatre in America. He had been an adviser during the Thompson-Kortner theatrical venture.

The ideal occasion for launching the new crusade presented itself on May 6 when a group calling itself The Committee of 1000 staged a dinner in Dorothy's honor at the Astor. Representatives of "Free France," "Free Italy," "Free Poland," and other countries then under Nazi domination paid tribute to her in a "roll call of democracy" and the President sent greetings. Before the dinner, Dorothy had sat for a bust by sculptor Jo Davidson. Mrs. Sara Delano Roosevelt presented it to her with the words, "No other individual so symbolizes the American qualities of courage, intelligence and a recognition of the dignity of man as does Miss Thompson." Wendell Willkie, who harbored no ill feeling about her political desertion and was now zealously supporting FDR, called her "the first to see clearly the threat of totalitarianism, not only in its military aspect, but in its economic, social and its revolutionary aspect." He then produced what must have been the highlight of the evening, a message from Winston Churchill: "Miss Dorothy Thompson has won a famous name. She has shown what one valiant woman can do with the power of the pen. Freedom and humanity are grateful debtors."

In response, Dorothy called for America to be placed on a "total war footing." She then went on to explain that she happened to own "a ring of curious design," that she would give a replica of it to anyone who subscribed to "Ten Articles of Faith," providing that he found two others to whom to present the ring. "It must never be purchased by the recipient but always come as a gift from one person to another."

In the audience was Count Raoul de Sales, who wrote afterward, "The ceremony took on rather quickly the air of a revival meeting. Dorothy made a singular speech in which she set forth her credo in ten points . . . a sort of refurbishing of several ideas which are not particularly new, such as love for one's neighbor, the socialist society, equality of work, national independence etc. The idea of distributing the rings is to create a kind of freemasonry among the partisans of the new society. This stems from the Oxford Movement, the Ku Klux Klan, and primitive Christianity. Practically, it is a question of making war . . ."

Oblivious to this interpretation, Dorothy was exhilarated by the response to her appeal. Letters and several thousand dollars poured in, and a subsequent meeting in Town Hall was well attended. There was, to be sure, a considerable problem of financing still to be solved. Dorothy, however, was full of confidence. She cabled Chaim Weizmann in London asking for the loan of Weisgal's services for six months, wrote to David Dubinsky, suggesting that he raise $10,000 in the needle trades, deposited $500 of her own in the Ring's account, and departed in late July on an even more exciting venture — a visit to embattled England.

Just how the trip was arranged is cloudy; certainly the British government was eager to have her, but it was important, also, to her credibility that she appear as a private citizen. She was greeted at the airport only by a BBC underling and by James Drawbell, the young and charming editor-in-chief of the *Sunday Chronicle,* which had been publishing her columns. In his recollection, Dorothy strolled off the plane without any clear idea of where she would be staying or what she would do in England. She readily accepted Drawbell's offer to act as her guide. He installed her in a suite at the Savoy, which soon had to be exchanged for a larger one. When her presence became known she was deluged with visitors, for her Montreal broadcast after Dunkirk had made her a celebrity in Britain. "We held a day and night reception for every government in exile," Drawbell said. "We had to hire three secretaries to handle the mail and phones. At one point Dorothy asked me 'Who's paying for all this?' When I said the *Chronicle* — which was true — she seemed quite satisfied."

Drawbell mapped out a whirlwind tour — visits to the most devastated towns, bomb shelters, RAF bases, and a broadcast from Plymouth; speeches to working women and to the military brass; a visit to the Queen and to Prime Minister Churchill. The schedule exhausted him but Dorothy was never too weary to bounce to her feet and deliver an impromptu inspirational speech or to sit up till early morning talking.

"I was an exhilarated wreck when she left," Drawbell said. "She was charming, delightful and also a prima donna and a monster." * After her departure on August 23, Mollie Panter-Downes wrote in her London notes for *The New Yorker:* "Just underneath Wednesday's Court Circular announcement that the Premier [Winston Churchill], on his arrival in London, had

---

* Drawbell produced a book, *Dorothy Thompson's English Journey,* out of his notes and her broadcast scripts and columns. The English edition — small because of the paper shortage — sold out quickly when it appeared in January 1942 and arrangements were made for publication in the United States. This Dorothy refused to permit on the ground that she might be suspected of being a British agent. She was adamant despite Drawbell's pleas; there were those who thought that one would worry about such an accusation only if it were true. Dorothy in subsequent years tried to make amends by offering bountiful hospitality to Drawbell.

been received in audience by the King was a solitary paragraph to the effect that Miss Dorothy Thompson had left. This respectful treatment was in keeping with the general reception accorded to the lady . . ."

Some private comments were less deferential. William Stoneman of the Chicago *Daily News* recalls with wry amusement an evening when she joined a group of old London hands, allegedly to be briefed, did most of the talking herself, and drank more than her fair share of Scotch, apparently unaware that it was a collector's item. Indeed, even in the hard-drinking circles in which she moved, Dorothy's consumption of alcohol — increased probably by the unhappiness of her private life — caused comment. So too did her habit of answering her own questions rather than listening. At forty-eight, her hearing, which would soon be seriously impaired, was beginning to fail. As is common among the deaf, she found it easier to talk than to listen. These weaknesses did not lessen her effectiveness in public — she was too professional to drink more than she could handle before a speech, and like other spellbinders she was stimulated by the sound of her own voice and the response of an audience. When she addressed a Carnegie Hall rally on her return from England, Thomas Lamont, sitting in the front row, whispered to Peter Grimm, "She speaks like an angel."

By the end of the summer of 1941 many of Dorothy's constituents in the Ring of Freedom had joined forces with another New York group calling itself the Fight for Freedom Committee. This was a faction, led by her friend Herbert Agar, the detective fiction writer Rex Stout, and Harold K. Guinzburg of Viking Press, which had repudiated the "short-of-war" policy of the Committee to Defend America by Aiding the Allies, chaired by William Allen White, editor of the *Emporia Gazette*. In the autumn, the Ring and Fight for Freedom agreed to coordinate their efforts within an umbrella agency to be known as Freedom House. Dorothy was elected co-chairman of the new organization and soon became its president. "Few people could equal her as a speaker," says George Field, who, as executive director, steered Freedom House through an often stormy course. "She could run with an idea. She was an evangelist. Once, when I complimented her on a particularly beautiful speech, she nodded as though she knew it. 'And every word was true," she said."

In October, Dorothy joined Wendell Willkie and Mayor La Guardia to address a Madison Square Garden audience that cheered the speakers' call not only for support of Roosevelt's foreign policy but for America's entry into the war. Sentiment in the country was, however, still divided; in September, renewal of the Selective Service Act had passed in the House of Representatives by only one vote.

The debate, of course, became academic after December 7, 1941. And it was not Dorothy Thompson or Freedom House or even Franklin Roosevelt — but the Japanese bombs that fell on Pearl Harbor — that forced America to take up arms against Hitler. However, the many individuals and organizations that had championed the Allied cause had accomplished something of real significance. They had convinced many Americans that the war into which they were finally drawn was being fought for a just, even a holy cause. This was not the patriotic hysteria of World War I, whipped up by inflated propaganda about Kaiser Willy and the atrocities committed by grotesque "Huns." The bombs falling on Britain and the enslavement of millions of men and women in the conquered countries as forced laborers in Germany or in death camps made clear the meaning of a Nazi victory. Thanks to those who had reported and analyzed the ugly reality day after day, the men who entered the armed forces as conscripts or volunteers and their families understood the nature of the enemy.

✥ 4
"Far & forgotten . . ."

"THERE IS A BIG DINNER to honor D. Thompson tonight," John Gunther wrote to Frances (from whom he was now divorced) on the evening of the tribute to Dorothy in May 1941. "I am going with HFA [Hamilton Fish Armstrong]. Red is upset and furious that Dorothy should be 'honored.' "

Lewis was in fact wholly out of sympathy with his wife's messianic role, which, in his eyes, contrasted ironically with her unwillingness to liberate him from their marriage. "You are now the most prominent advocate in the whole country not only of Freedom but of generosity to those who differ with us," he wrote. "Are you going to deny your entire faith by holding an unwilling ex-associate?"

When Dorothy rejoined that she still believed he would return to her one day and that she had, throughout their marriage, promised never to divorce him, Lewis replied bitterly: "You have become the Supreme Being, and you alone can decide what is right and just . . . Forget the . . . praise of you as a prophetess and be the girl for whom I did every damn thing it was in my power to do. If you get a divorce, life will be a lot saner for Micky, for me and for you . . ."

This had been his thesis for many months, most of them spent as an itinerant actor and lecturer with Marcella Powers as his companion. No longer did he derive a vicarious satisfaction from Dorothy's achievements as he had still done a year earlier when he wrote:

"Of your columns lately, I have particularly liked your attack on Chicago's music czar . . . and your tribute to Heywood Broun even though I thought that in this last you, like all his old acquaintances, did too much credit to that eloquent sentimentalist. You unintentionally did a dirty trick to a gang of females at the White House, in the Infantile Paralysis broadcast. Mrs. Roosevelt was competent but refained and an Episcopal Sunday School teacher; then come two dreadfully ragdoll-minded provincial females; then Mary Pickford drooled; and suddenly into this bunch of amateurs steps a Professional — clear, sure, convincing, dramatic, moving — Miss Dot Thompson. It was hard on all those gals, dear . . ."

Within a few weeks he was using her intellectual gifts as a weapon against her. "The strangest aspect of your great brilliance, your power of analysis of masses of men outside yourself, is that you never — analyze your motives, or your feeling and relationship toward anybody near you," he wrote. "You have continued to declare that you veritably love me, that no one else so greatly cherishes me, even while by a thousand omissions you demonstrate that your attitude toward me is not love nor even very lively affection, but rather a mixture of nostalgia, amusement at such humor as I may have, admiration of me as a workman, and above all, hurt pride . . ."

Dorothy replied at length but left the letter in her file marked "unsent." "It is not true," she wrote. "That I miss your charm and your funniness and your wit . . . I loved you for something in you enormous, indignant, wounded, creative and powerful . . . when I said 'I wish I had never set eyes on you' I was only saying that I wish I had been spared this excruciating pain . . ."

Different though the circumstances were, she was reliving the humiliation of the long months when Josef Bard had sought a divorce and she had resisted. Now there was the added anguish of a son who seemed to be reacting with the classic symptoms of the offspring of warring parents. Tall beyond his years, he frightened his playmates by a passion for knives and firearms and learned little at a succession of private schools. "The awful thing is Mickey," Dorothy wrote. "I don't dare to say it. But he seems utterly unreal to me. He doesn't seem like my child . . ."

When she asked Lewis to share the responsibility and expenses of their son, Lewis accused her of wandering "through a great fog of self-pity . . . and hysteria."

"I don't think that you really believe that I am 'hysterical,' " she replied. "Hardly by nature, at least. As for my self pity — no it's not quite that. I am terribly, terribly sorry for all three of us." She proposed that they set up a trust fund that either of them could draw upon if their incomes fell below a specified level. "As I told you, I am not concerned about the present, but I *am* concerned for the future. I am no longer young, and I no longer have the health which I have been blessed with all my life. [She had recently undergone surgery, probably a hysterectomy.] I cannot for very long, stand the pace that I have gone for the past two years. Also, my main income is from radio broadcasting and there is not a chance that this will continue much longer . . . I am willing to put into such a common trust whatever you are willing to put into it. I am trying to sell the Bronxville house. I would be willing to put in the entire return from that, and meanwhile to put in twenty-five thousand dollars that I have saved . . ."

As had happened during her first marriage, all the world knew that her husband had become seriously attached to another woman; this time, there was a son to be considered. Lewis had introduced Marcella Powers to Wells as his future stepmother. When Michael was scheduled to spend a vacation in California with his father, Dorothy wrote: "Be a sweet man and do not introduce Marcella to Mickey — if she is still with you — as his future Ma. He would not like it, and he is sensitive, aggressive, difficult, jealous, and very very nice . . ."

Before sailing for England in July she wrote to Lewis, "If you wish to divorce me, I shall not contest the suit. I shall keep still ⸲ . . . I will not go into court and make a case against you. I would fight through all courts and all eternity for the exclusive custody of Michael. That is my only condition . . ." In London, she told Drawbell that the first suite to which she was assigned in the Savoy was the same one in which she and Lewis had spent their wedding night. Whether this was fact or illusion, the hotel was filled with memories of her husband.

Upon her return, her lawyers counseled that, if she was indeed willing to go through with a divorce, it would be preferable to be the plaintiff in the proceedings. Other factors may have influenced her. In her public role, Lewis had become something of an embarrassment to her. Ostensibly because of his pacifist beliefs, but surely also as a subconscious act of hostility to his wife, he was threatening to join the isolationist America First Committee. In November she filed suit for divorce in Woodstock, Vermont, charging "willful desertion." She wrote at once to Wells Lewis to tell him of her decision. "I am of course infinitely sorry to hear about the divorce," he replied from Fort Bragg, North Carolina, where he was in training as an infantry private. "More for Father's sake, almost entirely, because for you I am convinced that it is a necessary thing. Yet it has been inevitable, in spite of your pious hope for a wise old age for Papa. He will just get more and more himself: with a certain grandeur in all that he does, but hard on wives, children and such. By the by: I would save my commiseration for Marcella, not Father. It is she who will end up on her ear, not he . . ." *

On January 2, 1942, the decree was granted. In one of her rare diary entries in this period Dorothy wrote: "Always those years of intense pleasure & blackest pain. Still the crazy con-

---

* Wells's prognostication was wrong. Lewis provided handsomely in his will for Marcella, who became a successful literary agent after his death.

viction that he loved me & it would all add up to something. But it was so quickly over for him, or maybe it never began. On that first day he said 'I will buy us a house in Vermont this shape and looking down a valley. And he did. And insofar as we were ever happy we were happy there. Now, to sit in the Woodstock Courthouse, charging desertion — and to feel nothing at all, literally nothing but faint distaste. To have felt too much is to end in feeling nothing. Four years of loneliness & agony & work, all anodynes. The last terrible remembering in London . . . But now it is the ratification of something that has been over & done with & not even Michael, any more, reminds me of him. 'Far & forgotten like a scene in a cameo.' "

PART VIII

"FRUIT-BEARING AUTUMN"

🦋 1
Command Post

ALTHOUGH THE FAILURE of her marriage to Lewis left a wound that never entirely healed, the years immediately after her divorce were — in the words of Horace — the "fruit-bearing autumn" of Dorothy's life. Her prestige and influence were at their height, America had finally joined the battle against Hitler, and in her personal life she achieved a degree of emotion equilibrium.

What might have been a tragic incident ushered in this mellow interlude. When Vincent Sheean, who had been reporting on the battle of Britain, returned to America early in 1941, he moved with Dinah and their two daughters into Dorothy's Bronxville house, which was vacant and still unsold. On a snowy February night, random sparks — probably from an unscreened fireplace — were whipped to a roaring blaze. The Sheeans awakened in time to escape from the second-story bedrooms but the house was gutted.

Relieved that her friends were uninjured, Dorothy took the loss philosophically. Instead of sequestering the proceeds of the insurance in the trust fund she and Lewis had discussed, she bought a town house at 237 East 48th Street. This was one of the remodeled brownstones she had yearned for twenty years earlier, when she visited Beatrice Sorchan's mother, Mrs. Walton Martin, who had then begun to acquire the square block that became Turtle Bay Gardens. The upkeep would be no problem; her column, in the hands of Bell Syndicate, was flourishing, the *Ladies' Home Journal* had increased her stipend to $1500 a month, she received $1000 or more for a single appearance on the lecture platform, and she again — after a hiatus of several months — had a commercial radio sponsor.

She was also blessed with an exceptionally skilled and devoted staff to operate the combination home and office she planned to establish. Madeline Shaw, blond, pretty, and indefatigable, was now the number-one secretary, replacing Madeleine Walker, who had married Hillis Clark, a magazine editor, and was expecting a child. Emily Carter had been summoned back, following the death of her husband in 1939, to serve as housekeeper, general factotum, and sometime confidante. "I really could have gotten a better-paying job," Emily said. "But Mrs. Lewis was very possessive about the help. She wouldn't hear of my working for anyone else. And I suppose she was right. We really understood all her ways." Equally familiar with her employer's exacting tastes were Marie, the cordon bleu French cook who presided in the kitchen, and her Czech chambermaid-waitress, Maria Schneider. As social and professional emergencies required, domestic and secretarial reinforcements were mobilized.

In the spring of 1941, Dorothy added to her retinue a research assistant, Herman Budzislawski, the former editor of the liberal-left weekly *Weltbühne* in Berlin. Budzi — as he was known in the household — was initially assigned the duty of monitoring and digesting the foreign-language press and broadcasts. A skillful journalist and dialectician, he made himself indispensable in short order. Although Dorothy usually did her writing in bed in the morning, sometimes she rehearsed the next day's column in an after-dinner monologue delivered to whatever audience was at hand. The less hardy guests and staff members slipped away unobtrusively. But Budzi stuck it out to the end. Next morning he would present her with a neat typescript — an edited version of the previous night's talk — ready, with only minor revisions, to go to press. "Budzi was such a harmless little fellow," Madeline Shaw said. "I liked him though not everyone did."

Chief among the dissenters in Dorothy's entourage was her other bilingual aide, Countess Hilda von Auersperg. Daughter of a princely Austrian house, aristocratic in manner, witty and urbane, her lack of empathy for Budzi was both a matter of style and politics. Although she was passionately anti-Nazi, Hilda, like many of Dorothy's conservative refugee friends, regarded communism as a menace second only to fascism. "I never trusted him," Hilda recalled. "His whole point of view was the straight party line. But Dorothy was very naive about some things and she wouldn't have listened if I'd said anything against Budzi."

Hilda regarded her high-powered employer with admiration and affection tempered by humor. She was, for example, amused one morning when she arrived around ten to hear Dorothy, barely awake as the curtains were drawn, exclaim, "I have it! The key to everything is the farm problem." There followed a great flurry of activity — a breakfast tray planted on the bed amid masses of newspapers, notes, and clippings as Dorothy dictated the column she had been composing in her sleep.

So far as Budzi was concerned, Dorothy, at the moment, had no reason to worry about his pro-Soviet sympathies. She had found much to admire in the USSR during her visit in the 1920s, and after the German invasion in June 1941, the Russians were America's beleaguered and heroic allies. In addition to serving as a fact-finder and sounding board for her ideas, Budzi was useful in countless ways. Among other services, he introduced her to a gifted interior designer, Geo Bergal, who, with infinite attention to detail and at minimum cost, converted her old-fashioned house into what she described to Helen Reid as "a very personal instrument for living that fits me like a glove." The décor — largely "Bauhaus modern" — was custom-made for a very special occupant.* In the vestibule visitors con-

---

* De Sales in his diary characterized it as "style Munich 1910." The phrase was crossed out in Dorothy's copy.

fronted a door on whose glass panels a Dutch artist, Joep Nicolas, had painted in silver eight sketches depicting the lady of the house, writing, dispatching her column to the paper, greeting guests, debating the issues of the day over cocktails and dinner, listening to chamber music, and finally asleep with a guardian angel hovering overhead. An exotic gadget in the library, with its ceiling-high shelves housing some 3000 books, was a concealed hinge which, when a button was pressed, swung open to reveal the guest bathroom. The living room was dominated by a black leather couch some eight feet long, equipped with folding armrests similar to those in airplane coaches.* In contrast to the rather severe black-and-white color scheme in most of the house, Dorothy's bedroom was a bower of femininity — all pale green satin and ivory with a huge mirror over the fireplace. A secretary's cubicle led to her study, which — after Pearl Harbor — took on the air of a command post. Walls papered with maps, an illuminated globe, and a short-wave radio enabled her to follow the progress of the war on land, sea, and air.

Her preoccupation with the war and her passionate belief in its importance increased her intimacy with Private Wells Lewis, who spent his furloughs either at her town house or Twin Farms and kept in close touch with her by letter. "Dearest Dorothy," he wrote from Camp Stewart, Georgia, "I have just written a lot of comforting lies to mother and my current girl friend; but you are the only one of my relatives to whom I can't send such balderdash. In fact — do let me know what is happening . . . About Europe and the world I feel so much that I will write you nothing but wait until we can sit opposite each other, with a highball apiece . . . as we have done so often in the past, sometimes talking about very sorrowful things, but always in a way that has brought me untold pleasure . . ."

---

* Max Ascoli, after his first view of the mammoth couch, remarked, "Now Dorothy can sit all the fat-asses in New York in a row and lecture them all at once."

As she had done before when she passed a milestone in her life Dorothy decided in January 1942 — the month when her marriage to Lewis was finally ended — to resume keeping a diary "for thoughts and events." The journal petered out after only a half-dozen entries, but they provide at least a glimpse of the comings and goings at Turtle Bay.

January 1   Wells is here, and last night in the melancholy that always follows drinking broke into a rather bitter protest against his life in the army, its inactivity, rigidity . . . He wants officer's training in the marines, cavalry or best in the intelligence service.* Dr. Parker [Dr. Valeria Hopkins Parker, a leader of the "social hygiene" movement] called yesterday to interest me in "vice" . . . Prostitution I told her, is the price some women pay for the virtue of others . . . Max [Ascoli] came in this afternoon and we talked at length about the foreign and internal policy about which he is as critical and skeptical as I . . . We drank tea in the kitchen & Marion† came to take him to train & see house.

On January 3, the day after she had been to Woodstock for her divorce, she wrote:

Rather haggard after two nights on the train that backed and filled like Dumbo. Wrote a column in the morning. Fodor came in for lunch — unchangingly optimistic. Too optimistic. Liberals are God's children. They blink with pleased an-

---

* Thanks in large part to Dorothy's intercession with influential Washington friends Wells became an officer candidate in June 1942.
† Ascoli had married Marion Rosenwald Stern in 1939. "I wanted Dorothy to be my best man at the wedding," he said, "because I thought she could out-talk all the Rosenwalds." She declined the honor but came and was a sparkling guest.

ticipation on the edge of the precipice. Emmy Rado [a refugee working for OSS] came in the afternoon about Paul [Scheffer] * and I spent an hour trying to find where he is.

Ham [Armstrong] called me & told me Raoul de Sales has T.B. It is stinking. The most civilized mind, the freest spirit, the wisest judgement — and he is going to be out when we need him most . . .†

January 4   By telephoning all over the place I've found Paul [Scheffer] is at Sulphur Springs [where a group of diplomats were interned]. Called J. Wheeler Bennet [a British writer on foreign affairs], Emmy and Eleanor [Lansing Dulles, an old friend]. He's under the State Dept. & from El I gather will never be freed. I want him in protective custody where we can get at him. Unlike Ham [Armstrong] and John [Gunther] I don't altogether trust him. He's playing some game — to send him back to Germany is insane. He knows too much, is too intelligent. I don't think he's a hero. He'd sell out. Then why not to us?

Mickey is darling. I motored him and Den [Dennis Fodor] out to school; much slush. I didn't leave the car. Many goodbyes & God bless us — and that darling baby-manly face.

In the evening I worked on a memo for D. [Colonel "Wild" Bill Donovan, head of the OSS, an old friend].

January 5   The Ladies Home Journal editorial has to be

---

* Scheffer, the German journalist whom Dorothy had first met in Russia in the 1920s, was Washington correspondent for the *Frankfurter Zeitung*. When the United States entered the war he was interned as an enemy alien and threatened with deportation. Widely respected for his expertise in Soviet affairs, he was also mistrusted as a German nationalist who never repudiated Nazism.

† De Sales died in December 1942, a loss deeply felt not only to Dorothy, who had leaned heavily on his counsel, but also by the many other admirers of his intellect and integrity.

written this morning . . . Went to lunch with Agars, Gdsmiths [Arthur J. Goldsmith, a Freedom House board member] and [George] Field (whom I will never learn to like) & discussed Freedom House. Had to fight to invite anti-Nazi Germans . . . Agreed to organize the "opening" party Jan. 17th. Wrote end of memo to B.D. [Bill Donovan] in afternoon. Louis Bromfield & Arthur [Root of Dartmouth] came in at six and we agreed with pleasure. Bud. came for supper, Madeleine [Walker Clark] for the night. Over whiskey we discussed the Globe in chess terms interrupted by Wells who slightly drunk is playing the piano at 2 A.M. Oh yes, wrote a column this evening.

The diary was neglected for two weeks while she was off on a lecture tour. On January 19 she resumed:

Days are grueling. This morning I rose at ten, wrote until noon. B. [Budzislawski] came in & we lunched together discussing until 3 the probable internal situation in Germany . . . E.E. [Ernestine Evans, a journalist and old friend now with the Office of War Information] & Budz again . . . Bill Paley [President of CBS] called — Joe Barnes [former foreign editor of the *Herald Tribune* now in a top post with the Office of War Information] came in for half an hour & we tried to work out a scheme . . .

Ernestine Evans, who lived nearby in an apartment on 48th Street, became one of Dorothy's frequent visitors. An ebullient woman with a fertile brain, which was, unfortunately, as disheveled as were her person and dwelling place, she lavished ideas on her many literary friends, but never managed to finish any of her own books. It was her lively mind that hatched the "scheme" for a weekly short-wave broadcast that Dorothy delivered in German over CBS. She chose as her format letters or conversations addressed to an imaginary friend named Hans. This was an alias for Count Helmuth von Moltke, with whom she had kept in contact until America's entry into the war and who represented in her mind all that was best in the German character. Dedicated to the concept of a peaceful federation of European nations, his view was the antithesis of the Nazi philosophy. Von Moltke was now the leader of a group of young idealists known as the Kreisau Circle (named after the von Moltke family seat), which had drawn up a liberal and enlightened program for Germany to be implemented after Hitler's downfall. However, the Kreisau Circle was a discussion rather than an action group, opposed to violence, prepared to await Hitler's inevitable defeat and then establish a new nation dedicated to the ideals of Christian socialism.* Dorothy's broadcasts consisted of a dramatic running account of the mounting Nazi atrocities, compelling evidence of the inevitability of Allied victory, and reiterated pleas to "Hans" and his friends to back up their words with deeds.†

In the spring of 1942 Dorothy devised still another instrument for achieving victory. This was a project known as the Volunteer Land Corps, which had the twin goals of easing the shortage of farm labor and exposing effete city youth to the benefits of rural life. The idea was an offshoot of Camp William James, a project designed to provide a "moral equivalent for war" through work on the land. Spurred by Dorothy, President Roosevelt had given his blessing to the venture, which was launched in 1941 at Tunbridge, Vermont, under the direction of Professor Eugen Rosenstock-Huessy. In mid-May 1942, leaving Hilda Auersperg to read her letters to "Hans" on the air, Dorothy departed to take personal command in Vermont, where some 600 city boys and girls had been recruited by a vigorous publicity campaign. Lodged with local farmers they worked at

---

* Like all the plots against Hitler the Kreisau scheme was doomed to failure. Along with other conspirators, von Moltke, who had played no part in the assassination attempts, was executed in early 1945.
† At Ernestine's suggestion, some of these broadcasts were published in a book, *Listen, Hans!* (Houghton Mifflin, Boston, 1942).

GI pay of fifty dollars a month as substitutes for the hired hands who had gone to war. On weekends, groups gathered at Twin Farms in Barnard for a giant cookout, to help write the Corps's newsletter, and to listen to an inspirational talk by the presiding genius of the venture. Dorothy conveyed her enthusiasm to her friends. Alexander Woollcott invited some of the young corpsmen to a picnic at Lake Bomoseen, and contributed fifty dollars to the cause and what he called "500 words of Green Mountain prose" to the newsletter. Eleanor Roosevelt sent a $500 gift from the American Friends Service Committee and the concert artist Ania Dorfmann came for a weekend and stayed to be photographed by *Life* playing the piano for the young farmers.

Meanwhile, Wells Lewis, newly commissioned as a second lieutenant, was staying at the Turtle Bay house in New York and shopping for his officer's uniform. He also managed to pay a brief visit to Vermont in the course of the summer. From Camp Pickett, Virginia, he wrote to Dorothy in September, "We have moved to a new camp: a dreary dump some 1,000 miles from anywhere, but with better training facilities. The move is supposed to have been secret, however, so don't mention to anyone where I am . . . My lightning glimpse of Twin Farms' incredible beauties has made the panorama of camp and station all the more depressing: the damn wood barracks, sawdust streets. I wish we'd go overseas . . ."

𝕏 2
"Sudeten Vermont"

THROUGHOUT THE HITLER YEARS Dorothy not only entertained distinguished refugees in her home but persuaded many to settle permanently near Twin Farms. So considerable was the influx that John Gunther dubbed the Barnard area "Sudeten Vermont." In addition to these imported friends there were other congenial neighbors, among them the painter Sanford Ross, the Arctic explorer Vilhjalmur Stefansson, and his wife, Evelyn, a talented sculptor who lived nearby in Bethel. Hospitable as always, Dorothy never lacked for companions to share the sunset and martinis on her terrace. She was also in the summer of forty-two redoubling her efforts to make her acres fruitful. She added to her flocks and herds and fumed at the red tape required by the War Production Board when she demanded lumber for new barns and sheds. In this bucolic setting, Dorothy, who periodically went on crash diets, enjoyed the produce of the land to the full. "She would make a big fuss if her saccharine bottle wasn't on the table," Madeline Shaw said, "and then put away six ears of corn and three slabs of huckleberry pie." Not surprisingly, her once svelte figure grew corpulent. Dennis Fodor, then a boy of fourteen, says his chief recollection of Dorothy was the feel of whalebone when he touched her.

Temporarily, at least, Dorothy had stopped worrying about her weight. She was surrounded by people who admired and loved her whatever her shape. There were the Fodors and Dale Warren, an ever-sympathetic guest. To the relief of Dorothy's

American friends, who were embarrassed by his wife's proximity during her liaison with Fritz, the Kortners had vacated the old house.* They were replaced by the devoted Budzislawski and his wife and daughter. A few miles away was Backwoods Farm, now the home of the German playwright Carl Zuckmayer, his wife Alicia, and their daughter Winotou (named after a character in a James Fenimore Cooper novel). Dorothy had presided masterfully over their immigration in 1938, when she not only sponsored them but secured a letter from President Roosevelt giving them the status of "welcome guests" of the United States. When Zuckmayer, knowing almost no English, had found it impossible to make a living as a writer in Hollywood or New York, he turned to year-round subsistence farming in Vermont and, miraculously, succeeded.

"Dorothy loved coming to our house," Winotou recalled. "Over at Twin Farms all they talked about was politics, politics, politics. But at our place they gossiped about people, they laughed, drank wine and my father played the guitar and sang German ballads." Another ornament of her circle was Princess Anna Schwarzenberg, whom Dorothy had installed in one of her small cottages when she arrived as a penniless refugee from Vienna.

On a July morning, along with Dorothy's breakfast tray, Emily brought what seemed an odd message from Budzi. He was expecting a visitor, a painter named Maxim Kopf, who was eager to do Dorothy's portrait and wanted to spend a week or so at Twin Farms making preliminary sketches. It was essential that he gain a full understanding of his subject. Could he be lodged close to her in the "big house" rather than at the Budzislawski's? Dorothy demurred. She had never heard of the man and had no desire to sit for a portrait. But Budzi's wishes pre-

---

* Hilda Auersperg was not disturbed. "European wives don't mind that sort of thing," she commented. "They know these affairs won't last. They look forward to a peaceful old age."

vailed. Kopf arrived in August and was installed in one of Dorothy's comfortable guest rooms.

An Austrian by birth, Maxim had grown up in Prague and served in a Czech regiment of the Austrian army in World War I. His career as a painter had taken him twice to Tahiti and once before to America, where he worked in the studio of stage designer Joseph Urban in 1923. Returning to Prague, he achieved considerable success, particularly for his portraits of celebrated actresses. When Czechoslovakia fell to Hitler in 1939, he fled to Paris, where he lived with a group of writers and artists, some of whom were avowed Communists. It was there that he had met Budzislawski, who was putting out an underground edition of *Weltbühne.* Maxim disclaimed any party affiliation and was generally regarded as a nonpolitical Bohemian. However, with the outbreak of war in 1939, he was arrested as a suspected spy and locked up in the Paris prison *La Santé.* After the French surrender he managed to reach Morocco, where he was interned for some months by the Vichy police but finally released.

Along the way, Maxim had been married three times. Wife number one is remembered only as an anonymous "peasant girl." Number two was Mary Davos, a star of the Prague stage who launched him as a painter of theatrical celebrities. His third and current wife was Lotte Stein, a popular Jewish actress who had also fled Prague after the Nazi takeover. Lotte's American cousin, Martha Valentine, undertook the arduous task of rescuing the Kopf family. First, she found a foster home in Washington for Lotte's son by a prior marriage. A year later she had secured for Max and Lotte the precious visas and affidavits of support and passage to America from Lisbon.

They traveled separately but the family was reunited in 1941 in an apartment Martha found for them near her own on Amity Street in Brooklyn. Unknown in this country and without influential patrons, Maxim barely eked out a living doing portraits from cheap photographs for working-class neighbors for twenty-five or thirty-five dollars apiece.

Despite the rigors he had endured, Maxim at fifty was a lusty, handsome six-footer, genial in manner, given to bawdy humor, and with a taste for fleshy women. Before the portrait was done, Dorothy was convinced that she had found the great love of her life — a latter-day incarnation of the dark-eyed, dashing Giulietti to whom she had longed to lose her virginity in 1920. Returning to New York, Maxim, who by his own admission spoke seven languages badly, wrote a letter she carefully preserved, though it was, on the surface, one of the least memorable communications she had ever received:

"I did not fall asleep as I was expecting after I left Vermont for New York — I had a wonderful time in your place and liked everybody so much and tried to overcome a kind of *nostalgie* on entering the dining car to weep over a plate of soup — the dinner was lousy — Long live your cuisinier, long live your ice box — But anyhow I brought your picture and the flowers safe to New York, where Lotte was already waiting for me — *Thank you so much for all.* This sentence includes more than it says. Yours Maxim. Give my love to Boudzs."

Madeline Shaw, who routinely opened Dorothy's mail, had no trouble sensing that her employer was being thanked for favors more precious than *blanquette de veau* or fresh raspberries. Nor had the budding romance escaped the sharp eye of Emily Carter. "The woman was sex-star-rved," she said in her rich Scottish burr. "What else could she have seen in that stallion of a man?" The Goulds, who met Maxim for the first time at a small dinner party in Turtle Bay in the fall, reacted more sympathetically. They were struck by Dorothy's unusually deferential attitude toward this jovial guest. "She's going to marry that man," Beatrice said afterward to Bruce.

𝕏 3
Attending to Life Itself

AFTER A STRENUOUS but satisfying summer Dorothy faced a series of annoying events when she returned to the city in the autumn of 1942. She had, by her own account, proposed marriage to Maxim and he had accepted. Aware that her position demanded a mate more distinguished than an unknown, impoverished painter, she determined to make him famous. At considerable expense, she arranged an exhibition of his works at the Wakefield Gallery and persuaded his eminent countryman Jan Masaryk to preside at the opening. Though Maxim was not a painter of the first rank, the show received a good press. Flattering comparisons were made with the work of the great expressionist Kokoschka. But sales were negligible. His canvases, described by one critic as "macabre configurations," were not, it seemed, what the rich wanted to hang on their walls.

Much more unsettling than this evidence that her patronage could not bring instant fame to her protégé was the discovery that Lotte Stein showed no inclination to part with Maxim. Dorothy had exchanged roles with Eileen in the Bard triangle of the 1920s; she was now the "other woman," loved by and coveting the husband of a clinging wife. She decided on direct action — not the face-to-face confrontation that had been Eileen's tactic but a letter whose imperious tone infuriated Lotte. Not only did she refuse to seek a divorce, she threatened to make the letter public. Realizing that she was in serious trouble, Dorothy retained the renowned lawyer Louis Nizer to arrange for a divorce and the return of the damaging letter.

She had had more than her fill of unpleasant publicity within the past year. One odd episode had landed her name and picture in the papers under the headline "Dorothy Thompson Is Bitten in Café Row." According to the published account, she had gone to the theater with an unnamed "escort" (probably Maxim) to see *Café Crown,* a comedy whose setting was the favorite rendezvous of Yiddish writers and actors in New York. After the show, Dorothy and the "escort" went to have a look at the original — the Café Royale. There a drunken blond woman created a disturbance by shouting "Heil Hitler." She was removed but lurked at the entrance and, when Dorothy left, kicked and bit her.

"Why should people be interested in my personal affairs?" Dorothy asked an interviewer later. "Some woman almost bit my finger off the day Singapore fell. And the incident almost crowded Singapore off the front page. People should be discouraged from prying into the intimate lives of public persons . . ."

Dorothy had another similar grievance. Katharine Hepburn and Spencer Tracy were costarred in a film called *Woman of the Year,* a giddy comedy about a delightful but shrewish lady columnist who is obsessed with world affairs and foreign men. She is finally tamed by an all-American sportswriter. Press agents encouraged the impression that the picture was based on the career of Miss Dorothy Thompson. Asked what she thought of the film, Dorothy called it "a sickening travesty and thoroughly unconvincing." Most people found it a beguiling, featherweight farce, but it was not a self-image Dorothy relished.

She was also disturbed when her beloved house made her the target of criticism. With the thought, she said, that it might be helpful to Geo Bergal, she had encouraged *Look* magazine to photograph the interior. Shortly after the article appeared, Dorothy published a column denouncing American materialism and calling for all-out sacrifices in behalf of the war effort. The ironic contrast between her elegant dwelling and Spartan preachments prompted Bernard DeVoto to compose a blistering essay that appeared as the editor's "Easy Chair" in *Harper's Magazine.* Obviously, he said, in order to live up to her principles, the owner must now be planning to sell her luxurious house, "put the proceeds into bonds to help the war effort, and conduct the literary life henceforth by an oil lamp at a kitchen table in a hall bedroom somewhere on Second Avenue . . ."

Dorothy was stung by this attack from an old friend. "My dear Bennie," she wrote, "In all good humor (because I love you dearly) I feel called upon to take my typewriter in hand to speak with some asperity about your recent asperities in Harper's . . . The house is a manifestation not of gadgeted luxury but of hard-working living. The notable thing about it is, that in taking it I made a change from the really conspicuous waste of the villa in Bronxville, once presented me by my husband, to a house totally eliminating waste . . ." Right or wrong, this was one argument she could not win. DeVoto — an indefatigable controversialist — sat down at *his* typewriter and dashed off a 2000-word rejoinder. Dorothy pleaded guilty to being "the eternal Protestant with an ineradicable Puritan strain" and invited DeVoto to come for a drink when he was next in New York.

Presently, a more ominious invasion of her privacy was in prospect. The threat came, unexpectedly, from the English novelist Phyllis Bottome, an intimate of her Vienna days. The friendship had cooled over the years as Dorothy did not share Phyllis' consuming interest in Adlerian psychoanalysis, while Phyllis deplored what she regarded as the rightward drift of Dorothy's political views. However, with the outbreak of war they became comrades in arms united in the battle against Hitler.*

* Phyllis' prime contribution to the cause was her novel *The Mortal Storm,* which was made into a powerful anti-Nazi film. First published in 1937, the book was reissued in 1945 by Faber & Faber, London.

"My Darling Dorothy," Phyllis wrote on February 9, 1943. "I am sending you this study before I bring it out in a little book of six studies, taken in each case from intimate friends of my own, each of whom in one way or another is now well known in the world . . . My six are Adler; Dorothy; Ivor Novello [a British actor, composer, and playwright whose most famous work was the World War I theme song "Keep the Home Fires Burning"]; Ezra Pound; Mrs. James Roosevelt [mother of FDR]; David and Margaret Bottome [her grandparents] . . . I have for a long time greatly disliked anything I saw written about you, feeling that they were either spiteful or twisted away from truth in one way or another. I do not think that the enclosed is spiteful or irrelevant and it would be what I should write of you dead or alive, so that I hope you will not feel hurt by it or that I have gone at this task of love without deep thought and sincerity . . ."

Why Phyllis expected there would be a market for this oddly assorted collection is mysterious; equally puzzling was her apparent hope that the manuscript would not distress a woman looking back on the loss of two husbands and maneuvering to acquire a third.* Although she paid tribute to Dorothy as a fighter for freedom, the bulk of the essay was devoted to psychological probing neatly aimed at the subject's rawest nerve.

"Her fairy godmother at her christening had given her splendid equipment for life," Phyllis wrote, "a perpetual ardour; an impeccable memory; an eye for every salient fact; a sparkling courage; and absorbing powerful senses trained to observe and express; but the one mischievous cross-grained fairy who attends each child's christening took away from Dorothy the quality needed for creation — the power to attend to life itself . . .

"Dorothy has made two marriages, both of which were fail-

---

* Dale Warren, who was her editor at Houghton Mifflin, rated Miss Bottome as a "difficult author." Josef Bard, when he learned of this episode, commented, "She was the worst friend Dorothy and I had."

ures . . . Joseph Bard was . . . brilliant, he was a considerate, unselfish and most entertaining host . . . and he believed that he could be a great philosophical thinker — if only Dorothy could be a little quieter . . . Dorothy loved Joseph with all her heart; but she saw no reason why she should be quieter . . . So Joseph departed with someone he thought quieter than Dorothy . . . the light-hearted girl never looked out of Dorothy's eyes again . . . Almost before Dorothy had had time to understand the reason of her first great defeat, the greatest American novelist of his time asked her to marry him. Sinclair Lewis too had been defeated in marriage . . . physically also he was not a whole man . . . But all that he had suffered appeared as a wonderful opportunity to Dorothy's crusading nature . . . Sinclair wanted to have a home . . . where there was a certain amount of ready-made peace. Dorothy had never really had a home, and did not know exactly how to make one . . . She slept at home; answered and made telephone calls at home; and sometimes ate there; but she was her best and most constant self almost anywhere outside of it . . . the price of satisfying Sinclair would have been to give up being Dorothy . . ."

In response Dorothy wrote to Phyllis that she was "hurt, angered and shocked by your essay pretending to be an analysis of my personal life and public work . . . the fact that I am to a certain extent a public character does not connote that I have no right to a private life . . . With all your interest in psychology, you seem to have overlooked completely that I have a child, an adolescent son, who suffers enough as it is from having two parents who are much in the public eye, and would be taunted beyond endurance by having the relations of his mother and father analyzed and, as it were unmasked. Joseph is happily and permanently married. No resentment which might conceivably remain in my own heart could possible induce me to make public my estimate of his morals and behavior. I would not desire to hurt him or to hurt his wife, who is a sensitive and charming woman . . ."

Although she based her complaint largely on the sensibilities of her son and former husband, Dorothy must have been most wounded by the portrait of herself as a woman who lacked "the power to attend to life itself." She was, in fact, giving her private life a good deal of attention in these months, with the result that, through Mr. Nizer's intervention, Lotte Stein was finally persuaded to seek a Reno divorce. Meanwhile, Dorothy remained adamant about Phyllis' essay and succeeded in having it withdrawn from the collection.

On April 13, 1943, Dorothy Thompson and Maxim Kopf announced their engagement. They were photographed in the apartment where he had been living at 310 East 44 Street, both unsmiling, with uplifted chins in a pose suggesting a lofty moral purpose. The accompanying news story gave a brief account of Dorothy's career and prior husbands. Mr. Kopf was described as "a leading artist of Prague." No mention was made of any previous marriages.

From North Africa, Lieutenant Wells Lewis sent a congratulatory V-mail letter: "Dearest Dorothy: Just heard of your engagement to Maxim Kopf whom father writes me of as 'A fine fellow, good painter, good outdoor man, with humor.' I'm so very happy for you!"

℥ 4
The Prince Consort

FOR A WEEK Twin Farms had seethed with activity. Aromas from Marie's kitchen gave promise of vast and delectable casseroles, huge cakes, and giant platters of cookies. The choicest produce of the garden was tenderly gathered to be fashioned into mammoth salads. The punch bowl, polished to a gleam, was ready for the festive *Bohle* — the well-spiked wine punch beloved of Central Europeans.

Early on June 16, 1943 — Dorothy's third wedding day — a trainload of New York and Boston friends arrived: Henrietta Ely, Alex Sachs, Doctor Connie Traeger, Peter Grimm, Ania Dorfmann, ex-opera diva Alma Clayburgh with an unexpected French maid in tow, red-haired Rumanian author of travel books Anita Daniel, Esther Adams, Geo Bergal, and Ernesta Barlow.* In a dither of excitement was Dale Warren. "It was the wedding to end all weddings," he wrote. "I arrived promptly, weighted down with 1) 14 live lobsters from Charles Street, 2) a wedding present which was an antique scroll reading 'God Protect us from Tyrants Abroad and Traitors at Home,' 3) a Grant Woodish print which I had captioned 'Mr. and Mrs. Kopf Emerge from the First Universalist Church, Barnard, Vt.' 4) a sizeable royalty check from Houghton Mifflin, 5) a 10 volume de luxe set of Willa Cather, likewise from Houghton Mifflin, 6) a blood certificate (or whatever you get married with) which I had been told to pick up in Wood-

---

* Ernesta (Mrs. Samuel) Barlow is a sister of the writer Catherine Drinker Bowen. Dorothy was often a guest at the Barlows' musical evenings in their Gramercy Park home.

stock . . . Among those who made quick work of the lobsters were Peggy and Howard Wilson and Rudi Rathaus [a Polish friend of Maxim's] . . . and a hungry photographer from *Life* magazine. The Zuckmayer guitar worked overtime."

Following the church ceremony in Woodstock the party gathered on the broad lawn facing Mount Ascutney to toast the bride — radiant, if portly, in a demure print dress, and the stalwart groom who towered becomingly over her. Anita Daniel vividly recalls Maxim and Zuckmayer, stripped to the waist, regaling the company with a simulated wrestling match, a snake dance led by Budzi, the discovery of a soup tureen filled with fresh caviar, donated by Alma Clayburgh, which Anita and Zuck consumed by the spoonful. She also remembers Peggy and Howard Wilson standing primly on the sidelines as the scene grew increasingly boisterous, more than a little bemused by this explosion of Sudeten Vermont gaiety. Dorothy, however, was merry as she had not been for years; Maxim had, it seemed, revived her youthful joie de vivre.

"He treated her like a teenage girl, and she loved it," one friend said. "He never missed an opportunity to pat her bosom or pinch her bottom." Another recalls seeing the brawny Maxim toss his squealing bride to the ceiling in an exuberant moment. Certainly his lusty masculinity satisfied a deep physical and emotional need. And she found his ribald humor amusing.* Not all of Dorothy's circle warmed immediately to

---

* "She was always talking about the marvelous bed-life they had," Dinah Sheean recalled. "When we make love the whole house shakes," Dorothy told a startled friend. The last statement may well have been an echo of a famous line of Marie Stopes, the British birth control and sexual freedom pioneer of the 1920s who remarked of her most successful union, "When my husband and I make love we roll on the floor like puppies and the whole house shakes." A quip attributed to Dorothy, which may be apocryphal, typifies her uxorious mood: A visitor was shown into the 48th Street house one afternoon and started up the stairs. A woman's voice from above called, "Go away whoever you are. I'm fuckin' busy and vice versa." Even in her correspondence Dorothy sometimes adopted Maxim's earthy style. After a severe illness, she wrote to Grove Patterson, editor of the Toledo *Blade,* ". . . my general condition can only be described by my husband, whose language is sometimes dreadful, but in his words, I feel like a match that has been 10 days in the piss pot . . ."

Maxim. "He was uncouth," says Emily Carter, recalling an occasion when, as she was serving dinner, Maxim patted her midsection and compared it with the mound of Jell-o she was passing. "I nearly dumped the dish on his head," Emily said. "Dorothy lost plenty of friends because of him." One such might have been a titled European friend of Dorothy's who came to call at 48th Street shortly after the marriage. Maxim thrust his head out of a second-floor window to see who had rung the doorbell. The lady identified herself. "Oh I'd have known you anyhow," he said. "You're the one with the great big tits."

But for Dorothy, such crudities were outbalanced by the great gap in her life that Maxim filled. He had lifted from her the blight of that special loneliness which is the lot of the "extra woman" in a society that holds sacred the sexually balanced dinner table. Because she was a celebrity and one who wielded power, she had no dearth of invitations. And even at fifty she had seldom lacked willing escorts. They were, however, more ornamental than emotionally satisfying — sexually neuter bachelors, some young enough to be her sons, or worldly widowers who found her charming but were on the prowl for far wealthier widows whom they would ultimately marry. She could still include these courtiers in her entourage but she was no longer dependent on them. It must have warmed her heart to receive an invitation from Eleanor Roosevelt for "you and your husband" to dine on June 7, 1944, at the White House.

Determined that this marriage would succeed, Dorothy spared no expense to minister to her husband's needs, comfort, and success. A large and handsome studio was built for him in Vermont and half of the top floor in Turtle Bay was converted into his workshop. She energetically solicited portrait commissions, though with little success. Maxim's brush did not flatter his subjects; of his portrait of Dorothy he remarked when it was completed, "My God, I've made her look like George Washington."

Though he contributed little to the family income, Maxim performed admirably in his role of prince consort, seizing every opportuniy to bolster his wife's ego. He designed a bookplate for her that shows Dorothy *rampant,* treading on Satan *couchant,* and adorned the ceiling of the 48th Street library with frescoes on similar themes. He was solicitous of her health and tried to reduce her martini and Scotch consumption (a foredoomed effort since his large body seemed to have a bottomless capacity for alcohol and both looked forward to the nightly cocktail ritual). Although Dorothy's global monologues bored him, he tolerated them good-naturedly, retreating when he could to the solitude of his studio, and, on a few occasions, departing for a short trip abroad with his old Bohemian cronies. Dorothy herself was frequently absent on speaking engagements and when she was at home was often closeted for hours with important advisers or incommunicado on "column day" — the inexorable metronome that governed the rhythm of her life.

Her inattention seldom troubled Maxim, a sincere artist who found his real fulfillment in painting and sculpture. He gladly reciprocated for the worldly ease his wife provided by serving as the sturdy oak on whom she could lean in the large and small crises that punctuated her life, many of them caused by the peccadilloes of her fifteen-year-old son. Maxim, who had been a roistering youth himself, proved a sympathetic stepfather. In one of her few diary entries during these years, Dorothy wrote, after she and Maxim had visited Michael at military school: "I have never felt more tenderly toward my son than in the last year. I see that adolescence is a terribly difficult time for a boy and especially one so sensitive and overgrown as he . . . I am both too strict and too indulgent with him, as the result of trying to play a double role of mother and father . . . But I also think that Maxim's presence has uncramped my feelings, by sharing the responsibility. Everything is easier & more natural . . ."

✿ 5
"How is he? Why don't I hear? . . ."

ONE THEATER OF THE WAR that Dorothy watched with special anxiety was Italy. Wells Lewis had taken part in the landings at Salerno in September 1943 but she had no direct word for many weeks afterward, when Allied troops were meeting with stubborn German resistance at Cassino. In October, he was finally able to write: "Dearest Dorothy: The enclosed award [the Silver Star] resulted from an incident in the Sicilian Campaign. I am, of course, very pleased; but I wish you wouldn't mention this fact to anyone (should there be the occasion) except possibly Mickey. The reason being that I don't want Mother to hear of it. She thinks I'm still with Headquarters Battery (I'm a Line Commander now) probably at some seaport & far removed from shot & shell; & should she think otherwise, she would worry much more than the occasion warrants. I hope you worry about me too; but your sense of how important this war is for all of us, is some compensation . . ."

In the next twelve months, only two letters from Wells reached Dorothy. Both dealt chiefly with the indignation that he and his men felt at John L. Lewis' threatened coal miners' strike in the midst of war. Dorothy was equally outraged, and applauded when Roosevelt, in response, proposed to take over the mines and operate them under military protection (a step that proved needless when Lewis secretly reached an agreement with Secretary of the Interior Harold L. Ickes). This tough stance by a president heavily dependent on labor support was one of many factors that convinced Dorothy of his heroic stature. Following the triumphant Normandy landings in June 1944, his continued leadership seemed to her more than ever indispensable, and she supported his bid for a fourth term without reservation.

It was an ugly campaign. The GOP standard-bearer, Thomas E. Dewey, did not attack either FDR's social objectives nor the conduct of the war but described the administration as a group of "tired old men." It was, as Robert Sherwood wrote, "a charge not easily refuted, for those in highest authority were unquestionably tired and getting no younger day by day." Rumors about the President's failing health were supported by photographs taken in July before his departure for a Pacific tour that showed him looking frail and haggard and, as always in these years, seated. Roosevelt had, in fact, since the Tehran Conference in 1943 stopped wearing the painful, heavy leg braces that enabled him to stand.

Dorothy had seen the President on several occasions and spoke frankly of his physical disabilities in a broadcast that was widely hailed as the most effective speech delivered by any of his supporters during the 1944 campaign. In a voice vibrant with emotion she said, "They say he is tired. And I say you *bet* he's tired. Churchill is tired; Stalin is tired. Marshall, Eisenhower and MacArthur are tired; Nimitz is tired; Admiral King is tired. And G.I. Joe is tired — so damned tired that he has red rims around his eyes and premature lines in his young face . . . Every mother of a man overseas is tired — tired from that never-ending worry: How is he? Why don't I hear? . . . And if in the President's face, printed like scars of battle is the record of crises endured and overcome, could anything better become the leader of our nation? I love that face — so full of weariness and gaiety, of spiritual suffering and indomitable confidence . . ." *

By a bizarre coincidence, on the same day that Dorothy spoke with such feeling of the President and the anguish of soldiers'

---

* After the broadcast, a half-million copies were mailed out in response to requests. It was later published as a booklet, *In Support of the President* (Overbrook Press; Stamford, Connecticut, 1944).

mothers — on October 29, 1944 — the boy who had evoked her deepest maternal feelings, Wells Lewis, was dead. Serving as aide-de-camp to Major General John E. Dahlquist, he was shot and instantly killed by a sniper's bullet. She did not receive the news until November 13 and canceled her scheduled broadcast that evening. Sinclair Lewis, who was in Chicago and had an almost pathological aversion for public displays of emotion, called his ex-wife's action a publicity stunt. In truth, no gesture of hers was ever more heartfelt.

Three days later, on November 16, she wrote to the Zuckmayers, "It is hard for me to explain what this boy meant to me. He was the most blessed by the gods and yet unfortunate child I have ever known. He had superlative good looks and talents and a most superlative brain, and was torn between two gifted and bitterly hating, bitterly quarrelling parents. I know that because I loved him, and he loved me, he felt security with me that he found nowhere else, and out of that grew a very great influence that I had over his whole development. In some ways he was closer to me than Michael, since a maternal possessiveness and exaggerated sense of responsibility seems to divide us from our children, somewhat. I never felt it was my business to 'bring up' Wells, but only to love him and give him a home. Perhaps because of that I brought him up more than anyone else did. He came to me on all occasions — his children's toys and his civilian clothes are in my house. He was going into politics by way of journalism when he came home. I looked forward to his career, as to a completion and very great improvement on my own. He was in a most intimate, complicated and infinitely comforting way something of my own. I make myself recriminations that I did not do more — do something active and positive to get him out of the hell in which he fought uninterruptedly for two years but neither my own convictions nor his would allow me to do so. My grief is in every cell and I do not want it assuaged. It is part of me forever and it is what remains to me of him . . ."

PART IX

"LIFE WITHOUT
THE ENEMY"

1
"twilight of the Gods . . ."

DOROTHY KEPT UP a sporadic correspondence with John Gunther's ex-wife, who had emigrated to Palestine after their divorce. Early in 1945, Frances sent her several poems of her own composition, expressing her hopes for a peaceful reconciliation of the warring nations. "I like them all," Dorothy replied, "especially the last, 'Earth.' Maxim and I are going to Europe. Soon — now — It is high time for me. But I fear it is not yet time for your verses. We are inextricably tied to the enemy. We cannot imagine living without the enemy. We are in mortal fear of what would happen to all of us without an enemy. That terror — of life without the enemy — is what terrifies *me*."

With victory in sight it was becoming evident that the problems of peace would be, in many respects, more intractable than those of war. Two great dilemmas loomed ahead: first, the question of how to deal with defeated Germany, second, the future relationship of the Allies to the USSR. Memories of the Hitler-Stalin pact, the Russian attacks on Poland and Finland, and the great purges had persuaded most Americans that Stalin's Russia was not to be trusted. Dorothy, on the other hand, was still convinced that the heroic defenders of Stalingrad had neither expansionist postwar aims nor international revolutionary aspirations. Possibly influenced, but certainly encouraged by her research aide Budzislawski, she set great store by Moscow's action in May 1943 dissolving the Third International, thus allegedly assuring the autonomy of Communist parties in other countries. In her column on February 18, 1944, she wrote:

"Security for the Soviet Union means peace . . . Twenty-five years of bitter experience have convinced the Soviets that wherever there are strongly reactionary governments, under the domination of powerful imperialist or cartel-monopoly interests, militarism or other institutions traditionally hostile to the Soviet Union, there is danger of encirclement and eventual attack by anti-democratic forces that will openly or secretly support hostile governments in the future . . . The Soviets want permanent peace with the western powers . . ."

Appearing as a panelist on the radio program "People's Platform" shortly afterward, she developed the same theme and supported the idea of a European Federation but did not demur when one speaker suggested that the union of culturally distinct groups within the USSR might be a model for the future protection of small nations by the great powers. "It sounds to me rather like the 'protection' offered by Scarface Al Capone," another panelist commented. Dorothy's friend Gustav Stolper reacted vehemently. "After I heard your last broadcast and read your last article my first impulse was to convey my shock and indignation in a telegram," he wrote. ". . . My shock is occasioned by your conclusions which — as I confidently wish to assume are unconsciously reached — for some time have been faithfully following the line of the fellow travelers."

Dorothy's views on the "German question," as well as her confidence in Soviet intentions, placed her at odds with her most knowledgeable friends and advisers. She condemned the Allied demand for unconditional surrender on the ground that, as she wrote in October 1943, "there is an enormous anti-Nazi movement in Germany waiting for the opportunity to break out." William L. Shirer and other future historians would document that there was no widespread resistance to Hitler and that the major conspiracies against him — all doomed to failure — were motivated by the prospect of military defeat rather than repudiation of Nazi ideology.

While her concept of the German people as the victims rather than the perpetrators of Nazism was a delusion, there was a rational basis for her opposition to such Draconian proposals as the Morgenthau Plan, which called for reducing Germany to an agricultural nation after the war. Dorothy set forth her position persuasively in a long preface to the collection of her short-wave broadcasts published in 1942 as *Listen, Hans!* Although scholars might quibble over details, her analysis of German history and psychology — composed at white heat — was a tour de force.

"We must stop making political judgements of worldwide importance on the basis of our likes and dislikes," she wrote, "that the Prussians are wicked and disagreeable and the Austrians nice — especially those highly cultivated Austrians whom most diplomats meet. When the Nazis invaded Austria, the Austrian population behaved with a savagery toward Jews and other minorities that put the Prussians in the shade. The historic fact is that the Austrian Empire was exactly as expansionist as the Prussian, though it preferred to use Reich Germans to fight for it, and to marry its way around rather than fight at all . . ."

Dorothy argued that Germany had had many histories — as the Holy Roman Empire, the Confederation of the nineteenth century, the Weimar Republic, and Hitler's Third Reich — that it was never a nation of "pure blood," that Germany must now accept the ethic of the Western peoples and become a nation-state in a nonaggressive European framework of nation-states.

"Here we have the Dorothy Thompson whom I have always admired," John Chamberlain wrote in the *New York Times,* "the Dorothy Thompson who does not confuse writing with oratory . . . The Catos among us will denounce her for not wishing to see our modern Carthage obliterated and its fields strewn with salt. But who among us has the inhumanity to recommend the destruction of 80,000,000 people? We cannot beat the Nazis by doing things which only a Nazi could do. The 'other Germany' must be found, even if it figuratively involves cutting Nazi tissue out of 80,000,000 brains by some as yet undiscovered super-surgery. Dorothy Thompson has some ideas about effective social surgery that are worth listening to here. And, happily, she has ceased to write at the top of her voice."

But it was not merely the supporters of Morgenthau and his British counterpart Sir Robert Vansittart who found Dorothy's attitude toward Germany unrealistic. Her good friend Shirer, for example, reached an agreement with her to discuss anything but Germany when they met because their positions were so irreconcilable. Max Ascoli also deplored her stand. "When we see each other, I am afraid we are going to quarrel rather badly on the German question," he wrote on August 21, 1944. "I think that in the many years of our friendship, this is the first and only instance when, on a fundamental political problem, we failed to see eye to eye. For my part, hating sometimes my own ideas and their practical conclusions, I have reached the point where I believe in a Carthaginian peace."

Another old friend, Ben Ames Williams, a popular novelist and short story writer, found that they were at opposite poles: "I look back on those sunny days when I used to drive about New England in the days before the fall, and drop in at Barnard, and listen to Red and talk with you —" he wrote. "I look back on them with wonder that the world ever had time and space and facilities for so much fun . . . I dunno how much you could tolerate me anyway. Sure, we're both on the same side. But I'm deathly afraid of a part of you . . . I'm not at the Stout extremity but I'm nearer to him than to you. I think maybe I should give Germany a chance to justify herself by works . . . under due safeguards. Lippmann says fifteen years; I think maybe thirty-five years . . ."

Inevitably, Dorothy was in conflict with fellow board members at Freedom House, particularly Rex Stout, who also headed the Society for the Prevention of World War III, a coalition of the most vocal opponents of a "soft" peace. (Dorothy, in turn, was Vice-Chairman of the Association for a Democratic Germany headed by Dean Christian Gauss, Reinhold Niebuhr, and others who believed that a large reservoir of anti-Nazi sentiment survived in the Third Reich and could be mobilized after the war.) Her disagreements with Freedom House reached a climax in the course of a dispute that followed the untimely death of Wendell Willkie in October 1944. George Field had conceived the idea of dedicating a new Freedom House building to the protagonist of "One World." Dorothy favored an alternate and more costly memorial proposed by Willkie's devoted aide, Russell Davenport — an international library. Field nonetheless went ahead, secured the blessing of Mrs. Willkie, Irita Van Doren, and a majority of the board, and began fund raising. In December, Dorothy, returning to New York from a lecture tour, found herself outvoted thirteen to one at a board meeting. Field had had the temerity to prepare a news release, in advance, announcing the Willkie Memorial Building. Dorothy resigned as President. Afterward, in the hope of avoiding a public controversy, she issued a mild statement, vaguely charging Freedom House with having departed from its original principles and deploring an organization whose "policies are eventually made not by the board and often without consultation, but by the employed staff, with the Board merely ratifying their actions . . ." Her ideological differences with her colleagues were, however, well known.

A few months earlier she had left the advisory council of the Writers' War Board on the ground that she could not subscribe to a statement which declared that "In our attitude toward Germany and the postwar world we should be guided not by sentiment ('After all there must be lots of decent Germans') not by assumption (This time they've learned their lesson) but by bitter experience gained in two wars, the first of which we lost politically through our failure to recognize the German Will-to-Aggression."

By the end of 1944, these arguments were no longer abstractions. France and Belgium had been liberated and, in early 1945, American, British, and French forces were surging into Germany, while the Russians, after driving through Poland, were within thirty miles of Berlin.

In late April 1945 Dorothy donned a WAC uniform and with Maxim, for whom she had wangled accreditation as a war correspondent, flew overseas to be on hand for the climactic closing days of World War II. When they arrived in Europe, the German armies in Italy had surrendered and Mussolini, captured in flight, had been killed by partisans. Within the following week, Hitler lay dead in his bunker in bomb-shattered Berlin and Truman and Churchill declared the war in Europe ended on May 8. Less than a month after it had mourned Roosevelt's death on April 12, the world celebrated V-E Day while representatives of fifty nations gathered in San Francisco to write the United Nations Charter.

Landing at Ciampino airport, Dorothy had an unexpected reunion with Fodor, who was serving on the public relations staff of General Mark Clark, commander of the 5th army. The Kopfs were added to the general's press entourage for a tour of Berchtesgaden, Salzburg, Vienna, and a salt mine where Göring's looted art treasures were hidden.

Through firsthand observation and interviews she learned of the intransigence and brutality of the Soviet conquerors. In weekly broadcasts over the Mutual Network and in cabled columns she reported on her disillusionment with the Russian allies. After a harrowing visit to a newly liberated death camp she fashioned a moving article whose sophistication foreshadowed Hannah Arendt's reflections on "the banality of evil" during the Eichmann trial in 1961. "The Germans are in many

ways *like us,"* Dorothy wrote. "That is what is terrifying about
the concentration camps, with their millions of victims murdered en masse by the most modern and hygienic methods . . .
They are in many ways *like us* — these people in whose country
victims descended to cannibalism . . . While they did so the
administrators of the camps lived in pleasant and civilized villas
. . . Nothing to me, in visiting these camps, was so shattering
as the sight of the homes of the SS administrators — of the men
who, in a modern bureaucratic manner, according to card cata-
logues, dossiers and files, gave the orders which resulted in
tortures, carefully calculated famine and corpses piled like cord-
wood when the crematories were too full. Their homes were
civilized. I pulled out of the library of one of them the lyric
poems of Goethe . . . On the piano of one of them I found
the lovely *lieder* of Schubert and Hugo Wolf . . . the Nazi concentration camps themselves were testing places of mass reactions. Does the world realize that some of the worst crimes in
these camps were committed by the inmates? . . ."

The devastation wrought by war, not only on cities but on the
human spirit, struck her with particular force when she returned
to Berlin for the first time since her expulsion in 1934. "I met
the remnant of old friends," she wrote. "They were glad to see
me, as I was glad to see them, and proud of them, too, for they
had been among the resisters . . . They had held together
during the war, in many groups, with many others . . . but
that, they told me was over now since none of the conquerors
knew how to discover and use that community . . . These were
all highly civilized people; the unbridgeable chasm between myself and them was the chasm which would exist between people
who had been to hell and those who had not . . . one could
participate remotely in that twilight of the Gods when the city
came crashing down and the Russians, savage with combat, came
through the shelters with flashlights at night, picking their
women and dragging them out and by day plundering the shops,

with the Berlin mob joining them, women fighting each other for strings of sausage or jars of marmalade . . . women of the kind called 'nice' led out weeping to be raped and returning at dawn drunken, laden with bottles and exuberant because rewarded with the contents of a liquor shop. It is one thing to look at the pictures of Hogarth or of Goya and another to be participants in the pictures. It is one thing to believe that man can be wicked and another to come to the final awful conviction that God is dead . . ."

✺ 2
"Put forth Thy wrath upon the heathen who knew Thee not"

THE KOPFS WOUND UP THEIR VOYAGE in May in the Holy Land, where Dorothy was accorded an enthusiastic welcome by Jewish leaders, deeply grateful for her unflagging championship of Zionism. Of her many appeals in behalf of the cause, one of the best-remembered was a column published in the *Herald Tribune* in 1939 when a British White Paper proposed drastic limitation of Jewish immigration. "The 'Arab rebellion' in Palestine," she wrote, "is actually limited to . . . rebel gangs . . . more or less directed by the Mufti and the Higher Arab Committee . . . The Jews in Palestine numbered 75,000 in 1919. They now number about 450,000 . . . They have developed beautiful agricultural settlements, built fine cities . . . And they have not ousted any Arabs. On the contrary whereas there were 600,000 Arabs in 1919, there are now 900,000 . . . Palestine has become a problem by reason of the incitation of the Arab population by Arabian nationalists operating with terrorist gangs and assisted by Italian and German propaganda, and Britain has decided that the safest thing for her to do is to come to terms with the Arab leaders . . ."

Her position was equally forthright in 1943 when she contributed a glowing essay to a volume commemorating Dr. Chaim Weizmann's seventieth birthday. Unequivocally endorsing the concept of a Jewish national home, she wrote: "The best place to send people, or allow them to go, is the place to which they want to go. The Jews of Europe want to go to Palestine. They want to go to the one place on earth where they will not be received out of charity or bad conscience but joyfully — where they will not only be admitted but welcomed. I know that the Arab situation creates a woeful problem. But I also know that the Arabian world is an empty and neglected world. It is an impoverished world, not because it is overcrowded, but because it is backward. From a long view the exclusion of the Jews will do nothing whatever for the welfare of the Arabs. They had far better emulate the agricultural and industrial example of modern Jewish Palestine . . ."

In the course of their 1945 visit the Kopfs were guests of honor at a reception given by the future foreign and prime minister Moshe Sharett, visited a kibbutz, were photographed strolling through the streets of Tel Aviv, admiring the sunset from the seaside Café Pilz, and in the Hadassah Hospital, where Dorothy was briefly confined with an attack of enteritis. In the interest of objectivity, Dorothy also interviewed a number of Arab leaders. Their names are not recorded but it is probable that she was entertained in Jerusalem by Vincent Sheean's friend George Antonius, a Christian Arab, and his charming wife Katie. Born in Syria, educated in Alexandria and at Cambridge, Antonius had been in the British government service for years, first in Egypt and then in Palestine. A leading intellectual spokesman for the Arabs, he predicted that his people would never be reconciled to the partition of the country, which was then imminent. The gravity of the problem was apparent during Dorothy's stay. Initially the Jewish response to Arab attacks on their settlements had been purely defensive. But now organized groups of Jewish extremists had begun to counter terror with terror and frightened Palestinian Arabs were fleeing their homeland in large numbers.

When she returned to the United States, Dorothy spoke at several Zionist meetings but her zeal for the cause had been undermined. Over the years, she offered a variety of explanations for her change of heart. According to Vincent Sheean, she claimed that while she was hospitalized in Jerusalem, Jesus of

Nazareth appeared to her in a vision, holding out his arms to the dispossessed Palestianian Arabs. To Fodor, Dorothy said that her faith in the validity of Zionism was shaken when she overheard a Jewish soldier in British uniform say, "Their war is over, ours begins."

Whatever the immediate trigger, Dorothy began, in her column, to voice concern for the Arab refugees and dismay at the tactics of the Jewish terrorists. Meyer Weisgal, her closest friend in the Zionist movement, was in Palestine at the time. Weisgal, who subsequently became chancellor of the Weizmann Institute of Science in Rehovoth, wrote in his memoir: "I got a cable from New York asking me to intervene with Dorothy and get her to desist from her attacks on the terrorists. I answered that I could not pass judgment before I received a telegraphic summary of what she had written. I got it, and cabled back that I could not in all honesty repudiate her; she was sincere in what she wrote, no matter how noble the motives ascribed to some of the terrorists . . . Weizmann was deeply and irrevocably committed against the Jewish terrorists; his was the warning and moral voice; and his was the moral authority. Dorothy was not Jewish, she could not speak with that all-commanding directness. She was bound to be misunderstood; the result was that her utterances against Jewish terrorism were violently resented by the leadership of the Zionist Organization of America . . .

"The attacks upon her became outrageous. She was accused, among other things, of having lined her pockets with the fees of Zionist organizations. This stung her deeply, and here I was able to support her protest. She had taken nothing for herself. Like most speakers in public demand she was under contract with an agent, and agents are perhaps the least generous of spirits — it is an occupational disease. All monies accruing to her from public lectures [to Zionist groups] went into a trust fund, which I controlled, for the German-Jewish refugees who came into her orbit."

Dorothy's repudiation by her former admirers led Weisgal to

recall a Seder service in his New York home in 1942 that Dorothy attended along with Jo Davidson and Dr. and Mrs. Weizmann. Reading the service, Dr. Weizmann made a great point
of including a sentence that had been deleted from the revised
text: "Put forth Thy wrath upon the heathen who knew Thee
not." Dorothy asked, "Chaim, what's this all about?" and he
replied, "This is for you, my dear."

Dr. Weizmann did not interpret this rather ambiguous comment. But Weisgal wrote, "In the light of what was to happen
to Dorothy some years later, his words were prophetic."

Nowhere was her position more unpopular than at the New
York *Post,* presided over by editor Ted O. Thackrey and his
then wife, publisher Dorothy Schiff. On November 30, 1945,
the *Post*'s Readers' Forum led off with a letter from Rex Stout
under the boldface heading FEELS THOMPSON'S COLUMN DOESN'T
BELONG IN POST.

Among the few voices raised in her defense was *The New
Leader,* which commented editorially: "Rex Stout and his 'all-
Germans-are-bad' boys are engaged in an organized drive to gag
Dorothy Thompson. In this campaign Stout has resorted to
character assassination and vituperation reminiscent of the methods of Fascists and Communists . . ." But Stout's charges struck
a responsive chord among the *Post*'s readers. Angered by her
attitude toward Germany and her objections to the Nuremberg
war crimes trials that began in September 1946, they found her
sympathy for the Arabs intolerable. (To what extent readers
spontaneously conveyed their reactions to the publisher is un-
clear. Dorothy was convinced — and Weisgal agrees — that
American Zionist groups mounted an organized campaign
against her.) In response to a cautionary letter from Thackrey,
Dorothy wrote on November 3, 1946:

"I cannot imagine that anyone with a knowledge of my past
would believe that I am vastly more disturbed by persecutions
of Germans than of Nazi victims . . . I am concerned, however,

that persecution should cease and *prosecution* take its place . . .
I am greatly perturbed about the behavior and propaganda of
some Zionists, or self appointed leaders or spokesmen for the
Zionist movement, specifically the [Peter] Bergson [also known
as Hillel Kook] and Ben Hecht group [supporters of the Jewish
extremists]. These people are the worst contributors to anti-
Semitism in America in my mind . . . I do not see, also, how
anyone could misunderstand the powerful plea I made to the
United Nations to open the allied countries to the displaced
European Jews.* There are Zionists, however, who did not like
that column. They don't want any alternative except Palestine . . .

"I was in Palestine in May, 1945, and I assure you, Ted, that
the situation there is *not* the way it has been presented by many
of the Zionists. It is one of the most complicated and difficult
problems on earth today . . . It is true that I have shifted many
attitudes in the past, but I have shifted them according to the
facts and new knowledge of facts, or what I have reason to believe are facts . . . Why, Ted, in all good nature don't you give
me credit for having predicted with considerable prescience, the
chaos of the United Nations arising over the veto power and
the struggle bound to develop by quadrapartite occupation between the Great Powers over Germany?"

She had, in fact, been one of the first commentators to foresee
these and other postwar problems. She was correct also in pre-

---

* Dorothy's friend Morris Ernst, who also favored this immigration scheme,
wrote in his memoir: "Active Jewish leaders decried, sneered and then attacked
me as if I were a traitor. At one dinner party I was openly accused of further-
ing the plan of freer immigration in order to undermine political Zionism."
Ernst attributed this opposition to what he called "the fanatical emotional
vested interest in putting over the Palestinian movement" and to the exigencies
of fund raising. "To raise millions is not too hard so long as solicitors can say,
'These bedeviled Jews of Europe have nowhere else to go but Palestine,'" he
wrote. But this argument became academic when neither America nor any other
nation opened its doors to the remnant of European Jewry. Israel, in the end,
was the only place where they could hope for a life of dignity and usefulness.
And as this became apparent, the idea of a Jewish state drew the support of
many Jews and non-Jews who had never previously been pro-Zionist.

dicting unending conflict in the Middle East, and, within a few years, the United States government's program for reconstructing a democratic Germany would closely parallel her ideas. The issue in 1946 was not whether she was right or wrong; hers was a failure not so much of judgment as of sensibility. With world opinion jolted by the horrors revealed at Nuremberg, it was not the moment to advocate sympathy for Germans or Arabs, particularly to a preponderantly Jewish audience.

"It was a good letter," Thackrey said to me many years later, "perfectly good pragmatic reasoning." But the *Post,* he pointed out, was then a shaky enterprise competing with the much better established *World Telegram, Evening Sun,* and *Journal.* The Thompson problem was debated at length in the office of the *Post*'s publisher and in the end the decision went against her, as she wrote to Weisgal on March 5, 1947:

"The Post is dropping my column. It is a personal blow — for one thing financial. A full quarter of the income from my column comes from my New York outlet; I am under no illusions whatever about the probability of my finding another outlet in New York. Helen Reid will hardly take me on, with all the political writers already appearing now, and hardly, also, close upon the heels of the death of Ogden. (Like an insult to his memory! Thus do the dead live on). Roy Howard does not want to build up the column section of his paper; the Sun (ha ha) considers me too liberal . . . I am crushed at the thought that this campaign has been instituted by 'liberals,' against a writer in a 'liberal' newspaper, whose intolerance of an opposing or differing view leads them to character-assassination, and career-assassination. It has been boundless, going into my personal life . . . I am not writing you, Meyer, to ask any aid or any intervention. Please believe that. Since it is pressure I despise, I do not want to counter it with other organized pressures. I just felt like telling you. I am very, very fond of you." *

---

* Around the same time the *Post* parted company with another uncongenial columnist, Victor Riesel, who was welcomed by Hearst. Years later, when it had

For Dorothy, the bitterest blow was the discovery that Zionists equated criticism of their policies with anti-Semitism. "I refuse to become an anti-Semite by designation," she said, recalling not only her long record of benevolence to Jewish refugees, her steadfast battle against Hitler, and, perhaps, the fact that she had once been ridiculed for walking out of a dinner party where an anti-Semitic joke was told with the comment, "I will not remain in the same house with traitors to the United States." Indeed, in her personal and public life, Dorothy's stance had always been — and remained — the antithesis of even that casual anti-Semitism typified for example in the pages of *Time* magazine, which in the days before Hitler commonly wrote, "Fannie Hurst, Smart, Semite Novelist" or "Smart Jew David Lilienthal" and identified the premier of France as "Léon Blum, lean, spidery, Socialist and Jew" or "Jew Blum." Nor did she share the feelings of her friend Harold Nicolson, whose attitude was typical of the British and American upper class when he wrote in his diary: "Although I loathe anti-semitism, I do dislike Jews."

"Dorothy was never anti-Semitic," said Anita Daniel, whose differences with her on the issue of Zionism never impaired their friendship. "And to accuse her of having been bought — as some did — was shocking. I never knew anyone of more absolute integrity."

"Dorothy's conscience was certainly never for sale," Ted Thackrey said. "And it was fantastic to call her an anti-Semite."

"I speak as one among many of your Jewish friends," Helen Woodward wrote. ". . . As you may remember, I do not always agree with you, but this attack is stupid . . . I know that you had a special attitude toward Jews. I was familiar with that attitude because it was like my husband's. You both seemed to think that Jews were better than other people and so expected more of them."

---

become New York's only evening paper, the *Post* was sufficiently secure to expose its readers to the views of conservative William Buckley.

Dorothy replied gratefully, "I think I coined the phrase 'Jews are like everybody else but more so.' I've become accustomed to the fanatic nationalism and self assertion of the Goyim against their weaker fellows. When Jews do it, it makes me think 'What a world where *even* the Jews have gone crazy —' "

❧ 3
"Nichts bleibt mir erspart"

"Nichts bleibt mir erspart" — "Nothing is spared me" — Dorothy wrote the Zuckmayers when she realized that her son was determined to become — of all things — an actor. Where Michael was concerned nothing ever seemed to work out according to her nobly conceived but feebly implemented designs. She had agreed with Emily Carter that the unruly boy needed discipline, but when he protested the austerities of the military academy to which she sent him in 1945, she weakened and transferred him to a less rigorous private school in New York where he proved equally resistant to learning. "Michael again flunked geometry," she wrote his father in June 1947, "passing his other subjects — having dropped Latin — with only fair grades . . . he is still entirely short of certain necessary credits for college entrance; he has not a single math credit and only one instead of four necessary language credits."

In 1947 she sent him to a summer school in Woodstock, hoping it would accomplish more than had a succession of private tutors. In 1948 she was forced to abandon hope of a conventional academic career for her son. Innocent of even a high school diploma, he was enrolled in the Royal Academy of Dramatic Art in London, to which he had been admitted through the good offices of Diana Sheean. Dorothy allayed her misgiving about turning her unpredictable eighteen-year-old offspring loose in a strange land by drawing up a written contract concerning money and deportment to which they both subscribed.

The Sheeans had been divorced in 1945, and the following

year Jimmy became a summer tenant of the old house at Twin Farms. Dorothy was enchanted to have him back and to resume their global dialogues, which they continued by letter during his absences on lecture tours or on travels abroad. She was even more pleased when Jimmy decided he would like to buy the place, thus insuring his permanent proximity.* In early 1948, she was equally gratified when a rapprochement between the warring Sheeans seemed imminent.

"I also hope Dinah will re-marry you," she wrote. "Your mutual jealousy should be overcome. Yours of Dinah, which I have had the opportunity to observe is very silly. Dinah's of your women friends is rather more understandable — to me anyhow . . . Dinah knows perfectly well that you are not in love with me and never have been. But she feels, I think, some sort of close relationship between us, rather like that of a protective older sister toward a younger brother. That can also intrude into the allness of a relationship. Maxim, at first, resented our friendship very much. I had to make it clear to him that I don't feel the slightest maternal feeling for him, Maxim, and it is precisely because I do not feel any that I cherish him so eminently as a husband. All other men I have greatly loved — Josef and Red — made a mother out of me and by so doing killed the lover in me . . . To go back to you and Dinah — quite impersonally, I believe that every marriage made originally in love can be made happy by understanding and perseverance. I believe that if ten years ago I had had as much wisdom as I have today (which isn't much) I could have restored, or rather fulfilled, the never-fulfilled meaning of my marriage to Red . . ."

Lewis, at this time, had taken up what was to be his final residence, Italy. Dorothy cabled him on December 10, 1948:

* This dream was not fulfilled. Sheean had no talent for managing the money he earned through his books and lectures. When he failed to meet his mortgage payments, Dorothy, to prevent foreclosure by the bank, repossessed the house.

"THROUGH INTERVENTION DINAH SHEEAN MICHAEL HAS OPENING IN ROYAL ACADEMY DRAMATIC ART LONDON AND TO TAKE IT MUST BE IN LONDON JANUARY SIX . . . HIS OVERWHELMING INTEREST IS THE THEATRE . . . I BELIEVE HE WILL LEARN VASTLY MORE THROUGH PURSUING HIS METIER THAN IN PRESENT STAGNATION AM GOING TO LET HIM GO AND AM ALSO ARRANGING TUTOR FOR HISTORY LITERATURE MODERN LANGUAGES . . . SURE YOU WILL WANT GET IN TOUCH WITH HIM AND HOPE YOU APPROVE . . ."

Dorothy went to Boston to see Michael off on the *Media* but was stricken with pneumonia and spent Christmas in Massachusetts General Hospital. In London, Dinah Sheean lavished on Michael her boundless capacity for affectionate attention to her friends and their offspring. For the first time, a warm relationship developed between Dorothy and "Jimmy's wife," as the latter kept the anxious mother posted about her unpredictable son's doings. Professionally, the news was good: Michael had talent and was mastering the actor's art. But his leisure, alas, was not spent with tutors but with female playmates and in inordinate drinking.

Other London friends of Dorothy's opened their doors to Michael, among them Baroness Moura Budberg, Rebecca West, and her husband Henry Andrews. Michael's presence afforded Rebecca an opportunity to reciprocate for a considerable favor Dorothy had done her the preceding year. Following the publication of her brilliant book *The Meaning of Treason, Time* magazine made her the subject of an adulatory cover story that included a résumé of both her professional and personal life. The latter, inevitably, mentioned her long liaison with H. G. Wells, father of her son Anthony, a subject Mrs. Andrews wished obliterated from the record, though it was common knowledge on both sides of the Atlantic. Dorothy, by a personal appeal to Henry Luce, succeeded in having the offending paragraphs deleted. The omission struck many readers as grotesque. But Mrs. Andrews was grateful and glad to do what she could to keep an eye on Michael. He presented a familiar problem since her relationship with her own son was far from serene. Over Christmas 1949 Michael visited his father at Villa La Costa in Florence. Lewis gave Dorothy a cheerful account of the visit in a letter written on January 1, 1950. Christmas dinner had been very pleasant, he said. But as he had not fully recuperated from pneumonia and needed a complete rest he had sent Michael off on a tour of Italy with an old friend of Lewis', Jamie Campbell.

Echoing, perhaps consciously, past comments on his own performances, he wrote: "Mike does impersonations — somewhat too many of them — with a flair and variety which would seem to indicate that he really will be a good actor. And he is extraordinarily good looking now. Whether he will ever take off so much as one hour and just Read a Book, I have no idea . . .

A wonderful new year to you.

EVER

H"

Back in London, Michael continued to work hard at the Academy and to sow increasingly wild oats elsewhere. To the dismay of his mother and her friends he announced his intention of getting married. The bride of his choice was a pretty, amiable, and sensible young Alsatian woman, Bernadette Nansé, who had been working as an *au pair* girl in the home of one of Baroness Budberg's friends. The objection was not to his choice of a bride but to the idea of marriage for a youth of twenty with no means of support except his mother. Nor were Bernadette's parents pleased with the prospect of an actor as son-in-law. Maxim, who had gone abroad in the spring of 1950 on one of his periodic furloughs from matrimony, took Michael with him on a tour of Spain and did his best to convince his stepson that he was not ready to assume responsibility for a wife.

Meanwhile Lewis' health had deteriorated sadly and he was nearing his final illness when Michael went to Rome to spend another Christmas with him. It proved a disastrous visit of which Dorothy received a blow-by-blow account from Lewis' current secretary, Alec Manson, who offered the far from comforting opinion that Michael was "in a worse condition than last Christmas . . . He has no idea what he wants either now or in the future. His only firm thought at the moment, appears to be a desire to remain an actor and to marry when he is over 21 . . ."

This report helped to make December 1950 one of the most distraught months of Dorothy's life. In mid-January 1951 she wrote to Dale Warren:

"On the 22nd Max and I went to Twin Farms where we celebrated an outwardly merry, but for me, most miserable Christmas, for I was beset by a nameless anxiety about Michael, who had also left on the 22nd to visit his father in Rome. I had no idea how ill Red was. Michael himself was in a highly nervous state, Red (this time understandably) irascible . . . at any rate their encounter was, as usual, mutually embarrassing and Mike, as usual, made himself difficult, so he was packed off a week before he expected to be and was back in London on the 29th. But the combination of everything landed me in Roosevelt Hospital on January 3rd, as near a breakdown as I ever hope to be. Mike, whose course at RADA was ended, came home January 5th, by air, and on January 10th the news of his father's death came . . .

"Red's death hit me a much heavier blow in the solar plexus than I would have imagined. At such moments all the old pains, hurts, joys, regrets, feelings of failure etc. come back in a wave . . ."

❧ 4
Journalist or Propagandist?

REJECTED AND EVEN OSTRACIZED by her once-devoted Jewish constituency, Dorothy was eagerly embraced by the opposing camp — the small circle of Americans concerned, for reasons variously compassionate, political, or economic, with the plight of the displaced Palestinian Arabs and bitterly critical of America's pro-Zionist policy, which culminated in the instant recognition of the state of Israel in May 1948. Encouraged by these new advisers, she reached the view that a religious state was inherently wrong and that the existence of Israel would lead to endless trouble in the Mideast. Dorothy's old friend Vincent Sheean, who had refused to discuss the Mideast with her in her pro-Zionist days, now became a valuable counselor.

"I was fed up to the point of imprudence," she wrote him, "by a whole series of mendacious propaganda tricks etc. and decided to correct a few things in the public prints; about the British selling arms over the embargo (to the Arabs); and of the fact that Arabs had been abominably treated — introducing the remark that there had been at least one Arab Lidice. You, my friend, were the authority, though I had heard it before, but since you got it from the U.S. Embassy in Cairo and it had, according to them been relayed to the State Department, I took a chance on its accuracy especially as I was unable to get from the State Dept. either confirmation *or denial*. But you can imagine how the fur flew. I am now officially an 'anti-Semite' . . ." While Sheean was checking the facts, an eyewitness arrived in New York and confirmed the truth of the incident.

Jewish terrorists had massacred some 250 Arab civilians in 1948 at Deir Yaseen. The incident — deplored by Israeli leaders and more than matched by Arab atrocities — would become a propaganda weapon for keeping open raw wounds between Israel and the Arab world.*

Dorothy's new position was quietly encouraged by Arabists in the State Department whose chief concern had always been the safeguarding of American oil resources in the Arab countries. Roger Tubby, of the Middle East Division, visited Twin Farms in 1950. Afterward Dorothy wrote to John Wheeler, her editor at Bell Syndicate:

"On November 8th I am planning to fly for a month to the Middle East, to look into the Arab situation. Confidentially, I am being sent, without other payment than expenses; I was offered (and refused) a fee, by the Near East Relief — and at the special request of the State Department who sent a member of the Middle East division here to see me — that I go. I have made it clear that I will not go as a propagandist for any point of view, but as an objective observer and analyst. I shall try to go to Israel, though it is dubious whether Arab Palestine or the Arab countries will receive me if I have a visa from Israel, or Israel in the opposite case. I shall visit Egypt, Jerusalem, Bethlehem, Transjordan, and Lebanon, at least. I believe it is a great journalistic opportunity and that the editors who subscribe to my column should be advised of the trip (without, I think, mentioning auspices; both the N.E.R. and the State Department want strictly unofficial reports) . . ."

She instructed her lecture agent to tell potential clients that "Dorothy Thompson is taking no lectures between November 10th and Christmas. During this time she will be in the Middle East. She has important contacts throughout the whole area,

---

* Twenty-four years later — in 1972 — Arab groups made the Deir Yaseen incident the theme of a demonstration at the United Nations, protesting the proposals of King Hussein of Jordan for a possible solution of the Arab-Israeli problem.

which she visited five years ago. En route she will make brief stops in London, Paris and Rome. She will thus have fresh and timely material for lectures after Christmas." Sheean, who sometimes saw himself in the role of mediator between Arabs and Jews, wired Dorothy from Pittsburgh, where he was lecturing: "Bon voyage give my love to the Grand Mufti of Jerusalem and to President Weizmann."

Returning from a tour that included Lebanon, Syria, Egypt, Iraq, Jordan, and Iran — but not Israel — she reported to Dale Warren that she had "worked like a slave" and now felt "quite competent to write an 'Inside the Middle East' a la Gunther."

To Ben Hibbs, editor of the *Saturday Evening Post,* she wrote that she had "met the prime ministers of all the countries I visited . . . was briefed in extended sessions by members of our own embassies and legations everywhere, met the Shah of Persia, saw many business men, collected examples of communist propaganda in Arabic and made a special study of social and economic movements in the Arab world . . ."

Although she offered to write "on spec" and promised "not to advocate but merely to *describe* and as far as possible to avoid mention, even, of Israel by more than passing reference . . ." Mr. Hibbs was not interested. There were, in fact, few outlets for Dorothy's reports on this subject, apart from her own column, since the only large group of American readers greatly concerned about what she called "the seething Middle East" were Jews whose prime interest was the future of Israel rather than the plight of her foes. Thus the only periodical in which she could place a lengthy article was *Commentary,* published by the American Jewish Committee. Dorothy's piece appeared in the March 1950 issue in tandem with a contrary view presented by Harvard historian Oscar Handlin. Under the title "America Demands a Single Loyalty," Dorothy focused on the threat to the status of American Jews inherent in the Zionist concept that all Jews were citizens of Israel; she also attacked the idea of

"cultural pluralism" and the renewed emphasis on Jewish identity that had been stimulated by the creation of the state of
Israel.

Her piece was, very largely, an echo of the thesis espoused by
Rabbi Elmer Berger, spokesman for a coterie of wealthy reform
Jews who had seceded from the American Jewish Committee in
1943 to form the American Council for Judaism, which was anti-
Zionist and unalterably opposed to the concept of "Jewishness"
as anything other than a religious faith.*

Rabbi Berger became a board member of a new organization,
American Friends of the Middle East, which Dorothy agreed to
head in June 1951. Dedicated in its opening statement to bringing peace to the Middle East by helping "Moslem, Jew and
Christian to regain, in the heritage of the past, the well-springs
of their life today," the organization attracted to its board a
number of distinguished citizens — among them Reverend
Harry Emerson Fosdick, President Virginia Gildersleeve of
Barnard, and Dorothy Kenyon, a liberal attorney — with no motive other than helping to bring peace to the Holy Land and
enlightenment to the Arabs. However, to a sophisticated eye,
the board was heavily weighted with pro-Arab, anti-Zionist partisans. Possibly for this reason, the *New York Times* failed to
report the opening press conference on June 22 — a gratuitous
act of censorship. To make amends, a lengthy letter from Dorothy to the editors appeared on July 29. In it she said, "The
American Friends of the Middle East is not directed against
Israel, but it is determined to try to see to it that the problems
and achievements of other Middle Eastern states are not ignored."

John Gunther mailed a clipping of the letter to Frances, who
sent a contribution to the new organization from Jerusalem in

* The split occurred when the AJC, which had been founded to combat anti-
Semitism in America and had opposed political Zionism, became increasingly
concerned with the plight of displaced Jews abroad and joined in the demand
for large-scale Jewish immigration to Palestine.

the hope that it would further "friendship and kinship between the Arab States and Israel." AFME embarked on a program of scholarships and cultural exchanges, but its major role soon became criticism of America's pro-Israel policy and defense of the Arab position. For these purposes it had ample funds at its disposal, one source being the Arabian American Oil Company — ARAMCO. Dorothy was obviously aware of this tie.* But it is possible that she did not know that major support for AFME's budget, which in due course rose to over $1 million annually, came from foundations that were CIA conduits.†

She was indignant in October 1952 when the New York *Post,* which still followed her activities with special interest, asked her to confirm or deny three recent items that had appeared in Walter Winchell's column:

> April 21 '52. Dorothy Thompson and Vincent Sheean are taking instructions from Archbishop Fulton J. Sheen.

> May 2 '52. Dorothy Thompson is flouncing around the Arab countries as the guest of the Egyptian gov't. The Syrians will decorate her any day. When she returns to the U.S. she will intensify her pro-Arab propaganda.

> May 11 '52. The N.Y. Times confirmed our report that Syria would decorate Dorothy Thompson, who has been doing propaganda for the Arabs. The citation (according to the May 3rd Times) was for "defending the Arab cause in the U.S."

Dorothy replied: "Item No. I is 100% untrue on both counts. I have never taken instructions from Msgr. Sheen (or any other Catholic) and neither has Vincent Sheean, as I know because he is my neighbor and close friend. Anyhow V. Sheean was born

---

* On September 9, 1953, William A. Eddy, a director of AFME employed by the Trans-Arabian Pipe Line Company, wrote to Dorothy to complain about AFME's failure to distribute her columns promptly to ARAMCO. "If they do not believe this to be their business, then it is just another reason for me to doubt that Aramco should continue any generous support to the organization . . ."

† This came to light in 1967 when AFME was named as one of eleven organizations receiving covert CIA funding.

and brought up in the Catholic Church; he has left it but never as far as I know formally. He wouldn't have to 'take instructions' — just go back.* Item II. I don't know what 'flouncing around' is intended to convey. I went to the Middle East last year in two capacities — as a working journalist and President of the American Friends of the Middle East . . . The organization paid part of my travel expenses and I paid the rest. We were not invited by any Arab government but in Egypt neither of us [DT and Dr. Garland Evans Hopkins, Vice President of AFME, who accompanied her] were able to pay our hotel bills. Item III. I was decorated by the Syrian government . . . for 'efforts to promote friendly feelings in the USA for the Arab countries . . .' I don't know what Mr. Winchell means by 'making propaganda for the Arabs!' If he means that I am an agent for Propaganda or anything else he is opening himself to a charge of libel for under the law I should register as such or incur punishment."

Winchell was not, however, the only one to deplore what was becoming an obsessive concern with the Mideast situation. Some important papers refused to publish her most partisan columns. The Washington *Star* periodically threatened to cancel her contract and several others did so. "We were losing papers all the time," said Virginia Shaw, who had replaced her sister as Dorothy's secretary after Madeline's marriage in 1948 to Richard Green. "But it was a matter of principle with Dorothy. She would never give in to pressure."

Old Near East hands among the foreign correspondents also applauded her stand. "She saw that the seeds of World War III were being sown here and she was one of the few commentators brave enough to speak up," said George Weller of the Chicago

* The source of this rumor was the fact that Maxim Kopf was taking instructions from Monsignor Sheen. He had embarked on a series of religious paintings and, in the view of his more cynical friends who had never noticed any symptoms of piety in him, was probably doing research at the best possible source.

Daily News. "She wrote it as she saw it; she was deeply moved by the plight of the refugees."

In November 1956 she departed on her last trip under AFME auspices, accompanied by Maxim and Virginia Shaw. This was at the height of the crisis precipitated when President Gamal Abdel Nasser announced the nationalization of the Suez Canal. In Cairo, Dorothy interviewed Nasser, pronounced him the handsomest man she had ever met, became one of his firm admirers, and later wrote an enthusiastic introduction to his memoirs. In Saudi Arabia the party was put up at an elegant hotel, operated by ARAMCO, and lavishly entertained by Ibn Saud. There were splendid quarters also (though equally ineffectual plumbing) at a government guest house in Karachi. Miss Thompson was guest of honor in Athens at a dinner given by King Paul and Queen Frederika. Maxim and Virginia, who were not included in the invitation, went sightseeing.

"Maxim never minded that sort of thing," Virginia said. "He had a lot of inner strength. He could laugh at the idea of his being 'Mr. Dorothy Thompson.'"

In the course of this trip Dorothy received what was, in effect, an ultimatum from John Wheeler. "Mr. [Benjamin] McKelway, editor of the Washington *Star,* has just called," he wrote, "and has made what I feel is a legitimate protest. He feels, and I agree with him, that you should not be President of American Friends of the Middle East, which is recognized as an organization sympathetic to the Arabs, and a newspaperwoman, too. It means you are trying to carry water on both shoulders.

"What has further aggravated the situation is that the organization has mailed out copies of some of your columns, which are favorable to the Arabs, as propaganda. Mr. McKelway has one of them . . .

"Here is what I strongly urge. You make up your mind whether you want to be a newspaper woman or a propagandist for the Arabs . . ." When she returned in April she resigned as president of AFME. But she never fully recovered from the slightly paranoid state that frequently afflicts partisans in the Arab-Israeli controversy. Regarding herself as the persecuted victim of a Zionist conspiracy, she became increasingly suspicious and intolerant particularly of "fuzzy-minded liberals," whom she blamed for her exclusion from the *Post* and the leading papers of other cities. In dropping her column the *Post* had behaved no differently from the *Herald Tribune,* which had also parted with her for political reasons. But in 1940 she was at the peak of her career and could take the setback in stride. By the 1950s she was weary and out of sympathy with the society in which she lived, increasingly nostalgic for the world of simple Christian values in which she had grown up. "Politically, she was like a great ship left stranded on the beach after the tide had gone out," said one friend.

5

"pawing the air"

IN THE OUTLINE FOR HER MEMOIRS Dorothy wrote, "1949 — Began Decline." She had, by this time, ample evidence that her fame and influence were waning. For example, on a trip to Germany with Rebecca West in 1948, she was introduced to Kenneth Ames, a young British reporter based in Berlin. "Trying to be tactful I told Miss Thompson how much I had enjoyed her short stories," he recalled. " 'I am afraid,' she replied coldly, 'that you have confused me with that Parker woman.' " It was a common error, distressing to a journalist whose name, only a few years earlier, had been a household word. Even editors who had long respected her found many of her political essays unpublishable. Frederick Lewis Allen of *Harper's,* who suffered when he turned down the work of any sincere author, must have agonized over the letter he wrote her on March 20, 1950: ". . . we all have a feeling that you have been feeling your way through a whole jungle of ideas . . . so that the result is not quite coherent — intellectually I mean . . . before Peter Viereck's book came out, we ran some nuggets of his in the magazine, and so in a way we have done our duty about the theoretical basis of conservatism . . . I feel really abashed in sending back to you any manuscript at all!"

Dorothy could still write with freshness and charm when her subject was personal and concrete. One of her best efforts was an elegiac piece that she titled "Good Night, Sweet Prince," which appeared in *Life* shortly after the questionable suicide of her friend Jan Masaryk in March 1948 following the Communist coup in Czechoslovakia. She was, by this time, an ardent Cold Warrior, embittered not only by ruthless Soviet expansionism in Eastern Europe but by the belated discovery that her long-trusted employee Budzislawski was not only a Russian sympathizer but a Soviet agent.*

She still read prodigiously, traveled widely in America on her lecture trips, and went abroad every two years. But — partly because of her growing deafness — she no longer listened attentively, assessing most situations in the light of her own preconceptions. Where her sharp reportorial eye and ear and her enthusiasm had once illuminated her columns, they were now often dull and ambiguous.

"Of late you have been giving the impression of one who is pawing the air," Paul Bellamy, editor of the Cleveland *Plain Dealer,* wrote to her on December 6, 1949. "You rightly say that now is a very uncertain period in the world's history and that most dogmatic people are fools. But on the other hand we expect our writers to be a little more sure of themselves than our readers, and it seems to me you have wobbled around so much in recent years that I can't put my finger on you any more, because I can't categorize you as being for tough treatment of the Germans or soft treatment, tough treatment of the Russians or soft treatment, tough treatment of the Chinese or soft treatment . . . I like a writer to nail his standard to the mast and fight for it, if necessary. I don't like columnists whose output too often consists of wringing his hands and crying 'Ain't it awful, Mabel?' "

Although her politics were veering steadily to the right, her course was erratic. In 1948 she cast a protest vote for Norman Thomas out of equal distaste for Truman, Dewey, and Henry

---

* Budzi departed in 1948 for East Germany, where he joined the faculty of the University of Leipzig. Dorothy described the experience in a *Saturday Evening Post* article, "How I Was Duped by a Communist" (April 16, 1949). In it, she correctly stated that party operatives had also infiltrated the staffs of other important political columnists.

Wallace, and in 1952, possibly at the urging of Diana Sheean, who was an ardent worker in the Democratic camp, she volunteered her help to Governor Adlai Stevenson although she was on friendly personal terms with General Eisenhower.

"I think you will become President," she wrote to Stevenson in August. "At least, at this date I hope so. This is not because I am a Democrat. By temperament and training I belong to the (diminishing) unorganized part of American society.

"I wonder whether I could be of any use to you? I do not mean, in the obvious way, as a campaigner, nor even giving you what boosts I can in the public prints. I mean rather occasionally calling your attention to information, ideas, and formulations that come from better or more knowledgeable minds than my own. I am a lonely worker and get most of my information from reading, for which I have a great deal more time than you; probably more than most assistants around you.

"The carefully nurtured and promoted opinion about General Eisenhower is that 'he knows Europe.' I do not think this is so. The General undoubtedly knows European political geography, its resources of manpower, and the economic foundations (or lack of them) for European support. Also, he is a man of considerable intuition, which is a help. But there is nothing to indicate that he understands the cross currents in the European mind, the sources of European *malaise,* the reasons for European rejection of what they think to be 'Americanism,' and the widespread spiritual 'neutralism.' These can be understood even partially only by someone who is thoroughly acquainted with European history, philosophy, and culture. Eisenhower never reads a book — or rather, he reads purely as an anodyne, mostly 'westerns.' I am aghast when I think of the superficiality of most of the advisers he is bound to attract to himself . . .''

Stevenson responded warmly, ". . . I, too, share the common view that you are the best informed American on Europe, and hence I should most eagerly welcome anything you cared to send me . . . I have *my* manifest disadvantages as a candidate too! But, at least I have read omnivorously and always, and have my first 'whodunit' still to read . . ."

The correspondence continued in this cordial vein over the summer. Yet in October she endorsed Eisenhower in a column titled "A Vote Against Trumanism." This reversal shocked — among others — Dorothy's meek sister Peggy, an unswervingly liberal Democrat. "Dearest Dorothy," she wrote, "How you vote doesn't concern me or anyone else, but your column with its wide influence really distresses me because, to this particular one of your ardent admirers, the one thing that has always stood out as a firm basis for your political ideas was your faith in the superior over the mediocre. In one of your recent columns you showed Stevenson to be superior Presidential material, Eisenhower mediocre. And now you tell your readers to choose the mediocre, apparently having no faith that the superior man can give the country good government . . ."

Dorothy scrawled a hasty reply: "I have *not* come out for Eisenhower — I want a change of Party. I think Stevenson will win, so I'm not jumping on a band waggon —"

This prediction must have been based on a reading of tea leaves. In the autumn of 1952, there was scarcely an observer of the political scene — from the lowliest precinct captain to the most sophisticated pollster — who was not aware that an Eisenhower landslide was inevitable.

PART X

LION AND CHILD

❦ 1
"a time to laugh . . ."

A FREQUENT GUEST at Twin Farms in the fifties was the gifted young Italian-born writer, Niccolo Tucci, whose wife Laura worked at the *Reporter* as secretary to Max Ascoli, its editor and Dorothy's old friend. Tucci enjoyed the hospitality extended to him and his family, although as a political liberal, he was often distressed by his hostess' conservatism.

"You are a lion and a child, an incendiary of certainties and a victim of doubts . . . Great and absurd as only noble people can afford to be . . ." he wrote after an evening of talk in which he had been alternately stirred by what he called her "beautiful outbursts" and irked by what seemed to him flaws in her vision. Those who knew her best concurred in his judgment.

Certainly it was the child — everything that was simple and earthy in her nature — that found comfort and satisfaction in the least intellectual of her husbands, a simple, unpretentious man who wrote, when he set sail in March 1950 on one of his holidays from domesticity, "My dearest on earth, It nearly broke my heart when I could not find you and was terribly nervous to miss my girl. At last I found you standing on the peer. I saw you, I saw your face and I saw the most beautiful expression on your face and I knew again thousand times stronger how much I love you and how close we are to each other. Then I said to myself, why you fool do you go without Dorothy and I think I'll never do it again —"

Maxim, said Dorothy, was "absolutely reckonable" — a quality she had never encountered in Sinclair Lewis or Josef Bard.

Confident of being cherished, Dorothy could write, "I *love* being alive" despite her professional disappointments. Life with Maxim was fun, when she had time to share it. There were splendid entertainments at 48th Street — a succession of dinner parties and musical evenings at which one might hear Yehudi Menuhin, Ania Dorfmann, and rising younger concert artists who welcomed Dorothy's patronage. More than 200 guests were invited for a two-shift New Year's Eve party in 1952 (cocktails six to eight or supper nine to midnight), and the list of acceptances included a decent sprinkling of important names.* It was not, however, the glittering assemblage of theater and literary folk whom Sinclair Lewis' name had drawn to parties in Bronxville nor the luminaries of the political and diplomatic world who gathered in the days when Dorothy Thompson's column was a power to be reckoned with and its author a darling of the establishment.

Even more agreeable than city life were the summers at Twin Farms, scene of frequent festive gatherings. Here in 1946, Dorothy staged a gala wedding breakfast for Emily Carter and Louis Haberman and celebrated the marriage of her son on his twenty-first birthday, June 20, 1951. As usual, Michael's will had prevailed over his elders'. And, for a few years, it seemed that he had been right. "Michael has had since last June a job with the Barter Theatre in Abingdon, Virginia," Dorothy wrote on March 5, 1952, to Rebecca West, who had commiserated with her about her son's precocious plunge into matrimony. ". . . Michael is blissfully happy, both with his job and with his girl, who is a wonderful sport. I must say that I like her enormously, and think that Michael did the smartest thing in his life when he married her. She has even got a job with Barter — handling the musical programs — and because of her sweet temperament,

---

* The printed invitation read: "Mr. and Mrs. Maxim Kopf (Dorothy Thompson) request the pleasure of your company . . ." Though she had been married for nearly nine years a good many New Yorkers, apparently, might have been puzzled by an invitation from Mrs. Maxim Kopf.

humor, and general good sportsmanship, is apparently the idol of the troupe . . . Michael is positively a comfort at present, and the kids are actually earning enough to live on, even without Michael's income from his father's estate, which has not yet been completely settled since the executors have so far been unable to unload that enormous place in Williamstown, which Red bought. This is certainly a turn of the wheel which I had not contemplated . . ."

Dorothy rejoiced further in 1954 and 1957 over the advent of two grandsons, John Paul Sinclair Lewis and Gregory Claude, and installed the family in a city apartment near her 48th Street house. Having always wanted a daughter, she became deeply attached to her daughter-in-law Bernadette — usually called Bennie. However, Michael's earnings in the theater did not keep pace with his responsibilities as a father. With her own income reduced, Dorothy worried about her grandchildren, to the point of parsimony. Bennie was wounded when Dorothy canceled her order for a layette at Best's, insisting that the same items could be bought more thriftily at Sears.

She also instituted economies at Twin Farms, where either she or Maxim did the shopping in person at local supermarkets after careful study of the advertised bargains. But these innovations did not mar the pleasures of her Vermont summers. Her annual birthday fiesta on July 9 took on more than ever the air of a national holiday. Often it was a joint celebration with Dale Warren and Ania Dorfmann, whose birthdays fell on the same day. Maxim contributed the gaiety of his presence and, sometimes, a venison goulash. When the huge chocolate birthday cake was cut, and her health toasted, Dorothy joyfully made her unvarying response, "Well, I made it again." A few familiar faces were missing in the gathering but there were a host of new and equally admiring friends — James and Peta Fuller, who had moved into Backwoods Farm when the Zuckmayers returned to Europe; Lisa Sergio, the handsome Italian-born radio commentator and lecturer who was living in Woodstock with Ann Batchelder, presiding genius of the *Ladies' Home Journal* food pages; Willy Schlamm, the one-time editor of the left-wing paper the Vienna *Weltbühne,* who had become a resident intellectual on the staff of *Fortune* and was within easy reach at his country seat in Rutland. There were congenial tenants in the summer cottages Dorothy had built on Silver Lake — among them Lolo Heineman, daughter of a wealthy refugee, now married to Dr. Stanley Sarnoff, Ely Culbertson, the bridge expert, and Agatha Young, a successful novelist. There was also an abundance of friendly indigenous neighbors who might raise an eyebrow over some of the "goings on" at Twin Farms but seldom declined its hospitality. Hilda von Auersperg had married Baron Louis de Rothschild in 1946, established her own splendid summer residence in nearby East Barnard, and could be counted on to add luster and an assortment of interesting houseguests.

While her newspaper columns increasingly mirrored what she called her "unhappy love affair with the world," her *Ladies' Home Journal* pieces continued to express her delight in life's pleasures and an unshaken faith in a divine guiding presence. Among the *Journal's* readers she still had devoted followers who flooded her with fan mail whether she wrote on progressive education (which she sternly disapproved), dieting (her own sporadic ventures), geniuses she had known, or child rearing. In 1952, the management of the *Journal* expressed its esteem by installing an ultramodern kitchen at Twin Farms. Although she was abroad while the work was in progress, Dorothy supervised from afar with her accustomed zest for the details of domestic décor. "I find the contrast between the darker blue and the white too sharp. The wall yellow is beautiful, but I don't like the red splatter linoleum," she wrote from Paris to Margaret Davidson, the *Journal* editor in charge of the project. "It is not the right color in contrast to the counter top, so I have

substituted the cream splatter . . . the butler's pantry floor
. . . should have two coats of shellac, no varnish, and the man
who scrapes it should also wax it with a heavy polisher and *paste
wax* . . ."

When she returned to Vermont that summer she wrote to
Beatrice Gould: "The kitchen is really a delight — *all* the
kitchens — for the L.H.J. compelled me to finish the job they
started. The LHJ kitchen lies between two appendixes: the
Butler's Pantry, which is a real room — the dining room of the
'help' where all the dishes are kept and washed, cocktails or tea
prepared etc. — and the Summer Kitchen, where the washing
machines and deep freezers are housed, all the vases kept, and
the flowers arranged. This had degenerated into a catchall. It
is now more or less worthy of its LHJ neighbor. Nothing is so
sweet as unearned increment."

The freezer she mentioned was a thirty-cubic-foot model
crammed with the produce of her farm — veal, lamb, pork,
every known vegetable, raspberries, strawberries, and peaches.
The overflow was canned and stored on shelves in the cellar,
which by autumn held 250 quart or pint jars of corn, succotash,
tomatoes (whole and puréed), mincemeat, sauerkraut, dill, mus-
tard, bread-and-butter pickles, fruit, boiled cider, jams and
jellies. Seasonally, some of this abundance was transferred to a
smaller freezer and storage shelves in New York. Dorothy described this treasure in luscious detail in a *Journal* essay in 1954,
revealing an awesome fund of agricultural lore. Calling the
piece "The Farm Problem and Me," she ruefully conceded that
her effort to run a commercially profitable farm was indeed
"Dorothy's Folly" but added that she would continue to farm
for consumption, not for profit, and gave others explicit instructions on how to do likewise. ("Buy two cows whose barn records
show they average 24 pounds per day . . . don't buy her if the
butterfat content of her milk is under 5 percent.") Apart from
the joys of the table, there were spiritual rewards, she said.

"Now . . . were I on the farm I would go down to the cool egg room to buff, grade and pack some 300 eggs in an hour. Work? I find nothing so restful! Nothing more calculated to take one's mind off H-bombs, Indochina, congressional committees and all the things that plague and stimulate my mind . . ."

"Grading eggs," Dorothy told Hilda Rothschild, "is my idea of Nirvana."

A collection of her *Ladies' Home Journal* pieces published in 1957 in a book titled *The Courage to Be Happy* bears witness to the broad range of her interests, her appreciation of poetry, music, and painting, and a warm humanism. In these personal essays one senses the qualities that made her an engaging and magnetic presence — the antithesis of the strident, egocentric evangelist who could overpower and exhaust her dinner companions. One piece, for example, "The Baby in the Kitchen," is a witty comparison of the rigorously aseptic regime under which her own infant was reared — in the days of Dr. Emmett Holt — and the relaxed schedule enjoyed by her grandsons in the Age of Spock. Past grievances long forgotten, she eulogized Edna St. Vincent Millay, who died in 1950, in an essay titled "The Woman Poet." "She spoke for every woman who has ever broken her heart," Dorothy wrote, ". . . as long as hearts love and mouths laugh, and flowers blossom, and the rain washes the pane, and the young spring breaks, and hearts being hungry search for solace and minds for insight, and the ear for song — these will not let you die! Nor, so long as I live will I."

With Maxim at her side Dorothy even enjoyed the thriftier way of life she had now adopted. In a letter offering hospitality to her Syrian friend Katie Antonius, she wrote: "Our schedule is this: My dear Emily comes in at 8:30, sends up breakfast to our rooms, and cleans the house. We don't have any formal lunch. Neither Max nor I likes to interrupt our work to go downstairs and sit at table . . . I never leave my room — I work largely in bed — until my urgent work is done, usually not until 3, and I always work until around 5. Emily, having sent ice etc. to the bar leaves at that time. And Maxim and I, after a leisurely cocktail, unless we are out or have guests, cook our own dinner and even wash the dishes . . . Maxim, like most artists loves to cook and does it very well. Incidentally, he does the shopping most of the time . . . I, who find domestic donkey work a *relaxation* am a very good kitchen maid! What we both loathe is making beds, vacuuming carpets etc. which is done for us. Emily, of course is available if there is a party . . ."

Returning from the Mideast early in 1957 Dorothy decided that more drastic changes were in order. Her reasons were various. Maxim, after recurring bouts of lumbago or sciatica, found the climb to his fourth-floor studio onerous. Although her earned income was dwindling, Dorothy had invested her savings shrewdly and had no real need to economize. But she had become increasingly conscious of Michael's limitations as a wage earner and determined to accept the rearing of her grandsons as her prime responsibility, which, she felt, she could discharge only by leaving them a substantial inheritance. Both 237 East 48th Street and the main house in Vermont with its accompanying outbuildings and land were sold. As a city dwelling, Dorothy bought a seven-room cooperative apartment at 25 East End Avenue. In Vermont, she proposed to settle into the "old house." Maxim was pleased with the northern light and the river view of the new city apartment but depressed by the loss of his splendid studio in Vermont.

While these complicated dual redecorating and moving plans were under way Dorothy departed to lecture in Oklahoma City. On her return, severe abdominal pains sent her to the hospital for surgery. A mass of intestinal adhesions and scar tissue was removed. With the assurance that no malignancy had been

356 Dorothy Thompson: a legend in her time

found, Dorothy spent her convalescence in the new apartment and managed to compose a cheerful essay about her operation for the *Journal* in January 1958. "I am tired, but I feel lighter — younger — in the knowledge that life can always begin again at any age . . . The operation was successful; the patient even lives, and a new year begins — happy, I hope, for us and for you too."

In high spirits she was off in February for a festive weekend at Harvard arranged in her honor by Stephen R. Graubard, a young historian who had become a summer tenant of one of the small Vermont houses and a steadfast admirer. Highlight of the occasion was a dinner at Leverett House attended by, among others, Professor and Mrs. McGeorge Bundy and Professor Henry Kissinger. Although he was aware that her star was setting, Graubard recalls her on this occasion as still "a Persona. She was radiant. She had courage, guts and she was a great raconteur. But basically," he added, "I think of her as a very simple person. She was not really in step any more with the hectic rhythm of New York. Vermont was her place. I remember a Sunday when she gave a talk in the Unitarian Church in Woodstock. As part of the ceremony a little girl in a starched dress walked down the aisle holding a lighted candle. To me Dorothy was that child . . ."

For several essays grouped in her book as "Elderly Reflections," Dorothy chose as text a familiar passage from Ecclesiastes 3: "To everything there is a season, and a time for every purpose under heaven . . . A time to weep, and a time to laugh; a time to mourn, and a time to dance . . . I am looking *forward* to being old," she wrote. "I know (as much as I know anything) that as long as I live I shall write. If public and publishers cease to be interested I shall write anyhow, perhaps only because formulating one's thoughts comes to be a habit impossible for most writers to abandon . . . the luxury of such late efforts, as I contemplate them for myself is that they are performed without external ambition, without desire for praise or fear of blame. One joy of old age is that in it we lose such ambition — the ambition for applause, recognition, popularity; the fear of an endangered 'career'; the pain of the slight . . ."

✌ 2
"A time to weep . . ."

FOR THE FIRST TIME in more than a decade there was no birthday party at Twin Farms on July 9, 1958. The Kopfs had also been missing from the annual celebration of Independence Day at the Rothschilds' Ellis Farm. A month earlier, Maxim and Dorothy had settled into the one-time Sheean house in reasonable comfort, although Maxim was not happy with the small shed that had been converted into his workroom. With Bernadette abroad visiting her parents, Dorothy was in charge of the grandsons, who were boarded in Woodstock with their nurse since Dorothy was no more than ever tolerant of the continuous presence underfoot of even the most cherished children. Although liquidating the house and farm where she had spent thirty summers was a sad business, Dorothy went about it with verve. Unwanted belongings and livestock were auctioned off at a costume party where Dorothy, garbed as Little Bo-Peep, led one of her prize calves into the living room. In mid-June Maxim suffered a heart attack. He was successfully treated at the Hitchcock Clinic in Hanover and permitted to return home, with a warning against overexertion, which he largely ignored.

Michael, on tour with a road company, came to Vermont for the holiday weekend. On Friday July 4 Maxim complained of feeling "lousy." After consulting the local doctor, Dorothy drove him back to Hitchcock Clinic. Though he appeared to rally from this second heart seizure he lived only until Sunday night. He was buried in Barnard and his grave marked by a huge boulder of blue limestone.

Dorothy seemed dazed at the funeral. "The day after Maxim

died, she was suddenly an old lady," Michael recalled. For two weeks after his death, she suspended her column. During the next month she struggled to resume it but her heart was not in the task. In her farewell column on August 22, 1958, she wrote: "This column has set an endurance record of continuous comment on major public affairs surpassed only by those written by David Lawrence and Walter Lippmann. During one third of my life — 21 years — 'On the Record' has been written three times a week, and for the last 17 years, 50 weeks annually. For almost as long a time I have contributed a monthly essay to the *Ladies' Home Journal* . . . When I became a young foreign correspondent for the Philadelphia *Ledger,* I received but one instruction: Get the news accurately. If possible get it first. Don't let your likes or dislikes obscure the facts, and remember the laws of libel and slander.*

"As a reporter and columnist I have tried to heed that advice. Yet I long ago realized that no matter how one strives for objectivity no one can fall out of his own skin. The very facts one selects as of eminent importance are choices and, like all choices, personal . . ."

Instead of commenting on the day-to-day news she had decided finally to undertake an autobiography. The task, she knew, would be much harder than writing a column. "It will require bringing into consciousness forgotten knowledge," she said, "facing up, with the benefit of hindsight, to errors of judgment too numerous to be pleasant, but errors that have by no means been mine alone . . ."

According to Meyer Weisgal, one of the "errors of judgment" that she now admitted was her turnabout on the question of Israel, which they discussed far into the night on his last visit to Twin Farms shortly after Maxim's death. Weisgal urged her to

---

* Throughout her long career as a journalist and polemicist Dorothy was involved in only one libel action. This occurred in 1950 when, on somewhat flimsy evidence, she charged an employee of the American legation in Berne with being a Nazi sympathizer. The case, which was actually directed not so much against Dorothy as against her informant, was dropped.

use her influence to advance a peaceful resolution of the conflict. In his memoir, *Meyer Weisgal . . . So Far,* he wrote, "This was one of the rare occasions in our friendship when she was absolutely silent for a long, long time. When she spoke at last it was to say slowly, 'Meyer, what you have said has touched me very deeply. I want to think about it . . . What you have told me will not be forgotten . . .' " She did not live long enough to take any action that might have mitigated the anger of those who never forgave her defection from the Israeli cause.

Accompanying her last column was a message to editors from Bell Syndicate: "No journalist of modern time has been so much written *about* as Dorothy Thompson. For a time she reached more readers than any commentator on serious political affairs in the United States. A double feature article about her appeared in the Saturday Evening Post, a double issue Profile in the New Yorker, she was the cover picture of Time, with attendant article and her life and career have been featured in many other publications. Articles by her have appeared in three anniversary collections of the best works of American magazines, significantly publications reaching very different audiences: The Saturday Evening Post . . . Ladies' Home Journal . . . and Foreign Affairs . . . Miss Thompson has, at all times, been highly controversial. Sometimes her enemies have seemed to outnumber her friends. She has lost outlets for persistently holding opinions contradictory to the dominant ones. But even her enemies or opponents have always been compelled to recognize and admire her honesty, strength of character, and disregard of possible injuries to her career . . ."

"It seems like burying an old friend," John Wheeler wrote to Dorothy.

"Oh, no," she replied. "Not the burial of an old friend. The momentary reaction seems to be that a major institution has fallen, but I never wanted to end my days frozen in marble pillars! I am really looking forward to the 'opus' — although not without trepidation!"

✣ 3
Am I Really a Writer?

DOROTHY'S RETIREMENT as a columnist and her proposed autobiography were prominently reported in *Time* and *Newsweek*. Eight publishers promptly expressed interest in the book. None was more enthusiastic than Dale Warren of Houghton Mifflin, who had encouraged such a project for years. There were, to be sure, already eight volumes of her writings in hard covers on library shelves.*

But all were compendia or expanded versions of newspaper columns, magazines pieces, or radio talks. She had made a few abortive attempts to produce a genuine book. One titled *The Moral Crisis of Our Time,* an extended sermon dealing with the evils of materialism and the need for spiritual regeneration, was never completed. The other was a third attempt at an autobiographical novel, *As the Hart,* taken from Psalm 42. "As the hart panteth after the water brooks, so panteth my soul after thee, O God." After reading the opening chapters, Warren had assured her it was going to be "a remarkable piece of work" but also ventured some tactful caveats:

"Will the reader who responds nostalgically to the idyllic and idealistic quality of this first section be able to keep pace with Harriet [the heroine] when she goes on to a world far more exciting and far less pretty? And will the 'sophisticated' reader who wants a 'sophisticated' novel have the capacity to immerse

---

* *The New Russia* (Holt, 1928); *"I Saw Hitler!"* (Farrar & Rinehart, 1932); *Refugees: Anarchy or Organization?* (Random House, 1938); *Political Guide* (Stackpole, 1938); *Once on Christmas* (Oxford University Press, 1939); *Let the Record Speak* (Houghton Mifflin, 1939); *Listen, Hans!* (Houghton Mifflin, 1942); *The Courage to Be Happy* (Houghton Mifflin, 1957).

himself in this very spiritual and also very special world . . . ?
. . . You recreate this world so vividly that in sections it almost
reads like non-fiction . . . Father at this stage, seems a little too
good to be true . . ."

Dorothy was beset with the identical problem when she began
to rework the same material in the first person. She had chosen
as epigraph for her book Goethe's words, "That man is happiest
who can reconcile the end of his life with its beginning." This
was to prove a formidable undertaking. As a result, she never
tackled the "more exciting and less pretty" parts of her story but
wrote and rewrote an account of her pious childhood and youth,
determined to find a unifying theme in the character of her
saintly father. She contemplated a trip to England and Ireland
to track down his surviving relatives and instituted a search for
the Thompson or Grierson family tartan. (None was found.)
She also picked up the strands in her network of friends but
made no use of the many letters they returned.*

It was not, however, merely nostalgia that slowed her progress
on the manuscript. Her energies were diffused by her desire to
erect a fitting monument to Maxim. With the help of Ala Story,
who had handled some of his shows, she planned a traveling exhibition of his major works. Subsequently she undertook and
financed an elaborately illustrated memorial volume.

In the autumn of 1958 she sublet her East End Avenue home
and rented a small apartment in Hanover, New Hampshire,
hoping that freedom from city distractions and easy access to the
Dartmouth library would speed the progress of her book. But
it was cold and lonely and she was harassed by the lack of an
experienced secretary to deal with her still voluminous mail and
to keep her intricate financial records in order. She went to
New York in November to see old friends and her family. Staying at the Cosmopolitan Club, she suffered a recurrence of ab-

---

* By corresponding with Mary Gawthorpe, with whom she had not been in touch
for years, she learned that Gertrude Tone had died in California on April 17,
1953.

dominal pains and was rushed to the hospital for more drastic surgery than the previous operation. Although she was again assured that there was no malignancy, friends and family found her, in her sixty-fifth year, greatly aged when they visited her at the Alden Hotel on Central Park West, where, after leaving the hospital, she set up temporary quarters not far from her son's home, with Emily Haberman in attendance. Faith Waterman, one of the ablest of her past secretaries, was recruited to handle correspondence, filing, and research for the book. On January 1, 1959, Dorothy began another diary, in a hand still clear and legible but one that betrays a weariness of mind and spirit:

> 1958 is over — the year of Maxim's fatal illness and my own severe one. Since I did not die (a consummation which, since July, has seemed devoutly to be wished) I suppose I have not, to use Maxim's words "rounded the full circle of my life." The selling of Twin Farms, the moving too — at least I have put my affairs in order as far as the children are concerned. But it will take the rest of my life to "digest" (again Maxim's words) this past terrible year. Just now, however, I am trying to digest my childhood. I still wonder whether my book is worth the writing and whether, indeed, I decided to do it as an excuse for giving up the column. It will be a terrific test of whether I am really a writer, independent of day to day news . . . I had early dinner with the family at the Oak Room — Kids, Peg & Howard, Willard & Mary. My party. The bill (with tips) came to $100. Oysters for six, soup roast beef & 2 vegs, dessert for 6. Bad service.

Jan. 3   Mrs. Titoch came in at 10 to hang the skirt of my grey Chinese silk dress — the material given me by Mrs. Wellington Koo.* How long have I worn it

* In making the presentation on August 23, 1949, Madame Koo wrote: "I cut out and kept the article you wrote about China and against the policy of the

and on how many lecture platforms has it trailed! Well, it won't any more, though requests still come in for speeches. Working again on accounts. I miss Ginny [Virginia Shaw] but what I don't miss is "Please sign these checks for me" . . . At least I know now and month by month where my money is going and can adjust my life to something approaching a budget. A day of self-recrimination. Why, why, why did I keep up that rat race so long — never time with Maxim except when I was too tired to be to him what he wanted and needed — not even (except on Sats and Sundays) an uninterrupted breakfast that meant so much to him. Now I am alone — more alone than I have ever been in my life, having had less than half a marriage . . .

Jan. 5   Most of the day with doctors . . . I want to feel well enough and have enough energy to get on with the book which now seems my only reason for living . . . Hilda [Rothschild] came for dinner this evening. She is always humorous and relaxing . . .

Jan. 6   Anita [Daniel] came for lunch. She always delights me by her incomparable capacity to enjoy life despite the cares & sorrows she has endured. Like Hilda, she really cheers one up.

Jan. 8   How long is this business going to last — of being exhausted by *everything* (except sleeping!). I don't think it's the operation (or only or chiefly) I have lived like an overwound watch spring for years . . .

Jan. 9   Rose late, bathed, dressed carefully and went to lunch with E. Cuneo [an old friend, board chairman of the North American Newspaper Alliance]

United States State Department." This was shortly after the United States had issued a white paper (August 5) announcing the cessation of aid to the Nationalists.

at 21. Champagne (instead of cocktails) a fabulous tournedeau, wonderfully cooked zucchini, coffee and, as always, excellent and stimulating talk . . .

Jan. 10   . . . I went to Hilda's for cocktails and to Tucci's for supper . . . V. Sheean was at Hilda's and I suggested half banteringly he take me to the opera . . . He asked what I would like to see & I said "Puccini — something light & melodious." He made a *mou* but agreed . . .

Jan. 11   . . . Michael & B. dropped in for a drink between his matinee and eve. performance. He lost the part he read and was accepted for on Broadway . . . leading man wouldn't play with anyone taller than he. What such casting considerations have to do with acting is beyond my comprehension. The American theatre, as I wrote long ago is "Heartbreak house" . . .

Jan. 12   Mrs. Horowitz came at 6 (Anita's sister) and will make over the S. Arabian pearls — God knows I tried to give them to AFME who couldn't dispose of them. If I lost them AFME would get $3,000 from the insurance company. I may just as well have them & wear them.*

Jan. 13   Lunched with Helen Reid at the Passy — beautiful lunch of sole and that very rare thing, tender, young, beautifully cooked string beans. Sole in white wine with grapes. Talk desultory, after so many years . . . She dropped me at Esther Adams' . . .

Jan. 15   Michael had got me tickets for JB & Gielgud, the two things I most wanted to see. But I had to cancel today's matinee I have a real grippe, but finished the L.H.J. article — or nearly . . .

* The pearls were among several costly gifts Dorothy received from grateful Mideastern potentates. Although she was no longer president, she cherished her association with AFME to the end.

Jan. 16   Willard came for lunch, distressed about
Peggy . . .*
Hilda came at 3 to say au revoir. She has been a
really devoted friend. Bill Ormerod dropped in
[Chief of the British Information Service, a popular man-about-town, and one of Dorothy's favorite
escorts in the years of her separation from Lewis]
. . . I love him if only because he was the very
first of my friends to welcome and receive Maxim,
and I recalled the dinner at the Lotus Club in our
(M's) honor. The English are slow to make friends
but have more fidelity to them . . .

On January 18, preceded by several crates of reference materials for her book and accompanied by her maid Traudl, Dorothy departed for a visit with her old friends the Wallace Irwins
in Southern Pines, North Carolina. She was installed in a charming guest cottage — an ideal setting for solitary reflection and
writing. But she was plagued by a bronchial infection and still
bogged down in childhood reminiscences.

January 22   I wrote about Tonawanda . . . I don't know what
all this has to do with my "life and times." But
certainly my life had its essential pattern fixed
before I was twelve. Odd that I really never knew
what I wanted to "do" with my life except live it
— and not work from 9 to 5 in an office at a "job."
Journalism was only a means to an end — to see,
to learn, if possible to *be*. The means swallowed
the end and the search for freedom became a
(voluntary) slavery. I find today that the "success"
I had means nothing to me, whatever. I wonder
exactly what went wrong . . .

The stay at Southern Pines was darkened by the painful final
illness of Wallace Irwin and Dorothy's continuing poor health.

* Peggy Wilson, suffering from Parkinson's disease, which she battled heroically
until her death in 1971, had gone to Cleveland to look after her daughter, whose
first baby had arrived prematurely.

She was far from robust when she returned to Vermont to spend the summer with Bernadette and the grandsons. Lisa Sergio proved a devoted friend as did Paul Scheffer, the German journalist who had been crippled by a hip injury during his internment and was now living in Woodstock. Her intimates were concerned — as they had been for years — about Dorothy's increasing consumption and diminishing tolerance for alcohol. She also continued to chain-smoke cigarettes at a suicidal rate.

Lunching one day with Scheffer in Woodstock, Dorothy suddenly collapsed and was rushed to the nearest hospital in Randolph, suffering a heart attack. With her health now seriously impaired, she realized that she could no longer live alone and decided to share the apartment of her recently widowed friend Tish Irwin in Washington. Often bedridden, she nonetheless continued to write her *Journal* pieces and to work on the book, aided by Fodor, a widower now. They talked of her early days abroad, with a stenographer present to record names and dates.*

In the summer of 1960, she summoned strength to visit Sauk Centre, Sinclair Lewis' birthplace, for a great celebration in his honor, taking with her Bernadette, six-year-old John Paul, and three-year-old Gregory Claude. Dorothy had undertaken to write a piece for the *Atlantic Monthly* based on the experience, although she knew it would be a painful ordeal. As it turned out, this was her finest prose work, convincing proof that she was "a writer, independent of the day to day news." Where her recollections of Maxim Kopf were filled with sentimental self-reproaches that never quite rang true and her attempts at autobiography were clouded by nostalgia, she found her ideal subject in the man who, as she wrote, "for a few years had been the center of my existence, had fathered my only child, and caused me more grief than joy, but whom, after more than twenty years, I could never put out of my mind." In this essay, titled "The

---

* Dorothy preserved a transcript of these notes. They are diffuse and cryptic but helped to jog Fodor's memory when I saw him in Paris in the winter of 1971.

Boy and Man from Sauk Centre," she wrote, with utter honesty and clarity, with a total lack of vanity, and with a magnanimity that was her noblest quality.

Of Lewis' strangely insensitive reaction when he received word of his son's death in 1944, she wrote: "Lewis bragged that he had heard the news just before he went to lecture and had never 'been better in my life' . . . My sister [who was with Lewis at the time in Chicago] was not shocked. She knew only too well that Lewis' reaction to frustrations and grief was to hit out at those who cared most for him, and often at those for whom he cared most. That was always the trouble: never knowing whether he really cared at all for anybody or anything except his work. Neither was I shocked when I heard the story some time later. I commented only that he must have felt perfectly dreadful. He repressed his emotions to a point unbearable for those who wished to share them . . ."

In her concluding paragraphs she assessed Lewis' place in American letters: "He does not live as do those few stupendous novelists revealing the human condition for all places and times. He never really penetrated the soul. He was not a poet of either verse or prose. But he is an ineradicable part of American cultural history in the twenties and thirties, and no one seeking to recapture and record the habits, frames of mind, social movements, speech, aspirations, radicalisms, crusades, and Gargantuan absurdities of the American *demos* during those twenty years will be able to do without him . . ."

In this memorable essay, it would seem, she finally fulfilled her lifelong desire to "serve" a creative man.

4
"Good-bye to a lifetime"

WEARY AND SUFFERING from a multitude of physical ailments, Dorothy was heartsick when she learned in the winter of 1960 that Michael had found a new love and was determined to end his marriage to Bernadette. On December 21, 1960, she flew off on her last trip abroad, thriftily traveling economy class despite her frail health. Bound for Lisbon to spend Christmas with Bernadette and the boys, she carried with her, sorrowfully, her son's divorce decree. Michael and the Sheeans saw her off at Idlewild International Airport. "She looked harassed, distracted and the signs of great illness were upon her," Sheean wrote. "At the very last moment when her flight was called and she dived nervously into the appropriate doorway, I had the feeling that she really did not know one of us from the other . . . There was an irresistible sense of farewell . . ."

Bernadette too was shocked by her mother-in-law's appearance when she met her at the Lisbon airport. "I hardly recognized her," she said. "She seemed to have withered away." Yet foreign sights and sounds proved, as always, a tonic. On a stop in Lisbon during World War II she had told an interviewer that she found the city "so calm, yet so colorful and gay — a wonderful city to live in and even die in."

On this, her last visit, she lunched and dined several times at the American Embassy residence where, according to Ambassador C. Burke Elbrick, "she captivated our guests . . . her mind was sharp and her wit keen . . ."

On January 2, Bernadette found her gasping for breath in her hotel room, calling feebly for oxygen. At the Anglo-American hospital the doctors pronounced her condition grave. Michael, who was rehearsing with Alfred Lunt and Lynn Fontanne in *The Visit,* flew over but left after four days when she showed a surprising improvement. Mrs. Elbrick recalls her last meeting with Dorothy:

"A cluster of silver curls on top of her head was held in place by a pretty blue velvet ribbon. Masses of cushions supported her and she looked like a Queen receiving her Court. She welcomed me warmly with a swift gesture of her hand. It was a sunny, cheerful room with high ceilings and an open window facing a patio with luxurious tropical foliage. She was in a gay conversational mood and her wit and charm kept me interested and amused. The clinical atmosphere of her surroundings had not altered her spirits until the nurse entered balancing a tray of diluted soup for her dinner at 5 P.M. She winced and expressed the view that no one could be expected to have an appetite at such an uncivilized hour. She removed the dry piece of toast from the saucer and spread the pâté de foie gras which my chef had prepared for her. She smiled as she savoured it and rolled her eyes with approval. After one nibble she put it down on the tray.

"She spoke animatedly on many subjects but mostly about the book she planned to write . . . She also spoke of her son and her great admiration for his first wife [Bernadette, who] was sweet, thoughtful and attentive . . ."

Morris R. Nelson, Jr., a young member of the embassy staff who spent considerable time with her, remembers Dorothy as "someone who seemed to be at peace with herself . . . When she spoke of past problems it was in a matter of fact manner . . . without malice or cynicism . . ." With Bernadette, Dorothy discussed the possibility of renting a villa in Portugal where she could be near her grandsons and could live inexpensively. She found the prospect attractive. In late January, over her doctors' objections she left the hospital and moved back to a hotel. Declining to ride in the ambassadorial limousine or Bernadette's Volkswagen, she preferred to have Mr. Nelson escort her in his car.

"It was pouring rain," Bernadette said. "I drove to the hotel with the nurse and we waited — I think maybe an hour. Where was my mother-in-law? Finally she arrived. 'We went on a little sightseeing tour,' she said. 'After all I've been in Lisbon for a month and I've seen almost nothing of the city.' "

Around eight o'clock that evening — January 30, 1961 — she dismissed the nurse. After ordering up a full-course Portuguese dinner she persuaded Bernadette to go home to her children. Next morning she was dead. The dinner tray was untouched. She had been sitting up in bed reading and apparently was reaching for the telephone when she was stricken with her final heart attack.

A simple funeral service was held of which Mr. Nelson wrote to me: "It was drizzling in sunny Lisbon. The service was held in the English church where one of the English romantic poets had been buried. There was only a handful of people gathered in front of the church . . . [My wife and I] sat in the last row, and I remember hoping — without presumption — that we could in some way be the surrogate for her public and the many friends who knew her well during her life . . ."

In accordance with her wishes, her body was shipped to Barnard to be buried beside that of Maxim. It was drizzling again on the cold May afternoon when she was finally laid to rest. At the graveside were Michael and Bernadette, her sister and brother, the devoted friends of her last days, Hilda Rothschild and Vincent Sheean, and a few Vermont neighbors. "It was like saying good-bye to a lifetime," Sheean wrote. In death, Dorothy achieved one of her goals — security for her family. She had set up trust funds for Michael and for her two grandsons in a will executed just before she left for Lisbon; her estate, including her real estate properties, books, manuscripts, and literary rights, was valued at $634,000.

There was no eulogy at her grave; she had wanted none and it is unlikely that the most articulate of her friends could have found the right words. She left behind a kaleidoscope of images, shaped by the eye of the beholder. In the memory of her childhood and college friends she was preeminently an evangelist, deeply committed to the Christian ethic. To her fellow journalists, she was a respected virtuoso of her craft. Dale Warren (who was prevented by illness from attending the service in Vermont) remembered her as a companion of unequaled wit, talent, and charm who had, above all, the gift of laughter. Meyer Weisgal called her "the most striking woman whose path ever crossed mine . . . a victim of both her emotions and her capabilities; a true victim in the classic sense." For those who had read her column and listened to her broadcasts in the years before America's entry into World War II, she was a voice of rare eloquence and courage.

But there were also those who remembered her as too self-centered for the small deeds of love on which enduring human relationships are built, domineering, arrogant, and fickle in her loyalties. She was all these things — gentle and ruthless, carnal and devout, lavish and parsimonious, sternly logical and unpredictably swayed by emotion. Yet within this contradictory nature, there was a sufficient touch of greatness to make her a unique phenomenon.

ACKNOWLEDGMENTS
NOTES AND SOURCES

Acknowledgments

Grateful acknowledgment is made to the following for their help:

Esther Root Adams
Kenneth Ames
Max Ascoli
Julian Bach
Josef and Eileen Bard
Beatrice Sorchan Binger
Marguerite Jarvis Bourne
Baroness Moura Budberg
Dorothy Burlingham
Whit Burnett
Cass Canfield, Sr.
James F. Carr
Lillian Cohn
Anita Daniel
A. R. Decker
Dorothy de Santillana
Avis DeVoto
James Drawbell
Peter Drucker
Eleanor Lansing Dulles
Ambassador and
  Mrs. C. Burke Elbrick
Morris L. Ernst
John and Margaret Farrar
George Field
Dennis Fodor
Marcel Fodor
Maude Franchot
B. H. and Abby Friedman
Peta Fuller
Bruce Gould

Stephen Graubard
Madeline Shaw Green
Peter Grimm
Barbara De Porte Grossman
Jane Gunther
Winotou Guttenbrunner
Emily Carter Haberman
Dr. Gordon Hoople
Ruth Hoople
J. Winifred Hughes
Katherine Gauss Jackson
Sari Juhasz
Dr. Lawrence Kubie
Mrs. Henry Goddard Leach
Isaac Don Levine
Bernadette Nansé Lewis
Michael Lewis
Anita Loos
Mr. and Mrs. Bleeker Marquette
John S. Mayfield
Countess Freya von Moltke
Ethel Moses
Edgar Ansel and Lilian Mowrer
John and Evelyn Nef
Morris R. Nelson, Jr.
Harriet F. Pilpel
Henry and Virginia Pleasants
Ernie Reed
Whitelaw Reid
Dr. Eugen Rosenstock-Huessy
Baroness Louis de Rothschild

Dr. Friedrich Scheu

Sigrid Schultz

Alan U. Schwartz

George Seldes

Lisa Sergio

Virginia Shaw

Vincent and Diana Sheean

William L. Shirer

Dr. Regina Stix

Toni Stolper

Shepard Stone

William Stoneman

Alice Tarnovski

Ted O. Thackrey

P. Willard Thompson

F. Jerome Tone

Louis Untermeyer

Martha Valentine

Dale Warren

Faith D. Waterman

Edward Weeks

Meyer Weisgal

George Weller

Dame Rebecca West

Agatha Young

Carl and Alicia Zuckmayer

Notes and Sources

The present repositories of unpublished documents are indicated by these initials:

Libraries

H	Houghton Library of Harvard University, Cambridge
HRR–L of C	Library of Congress, Helen Rogers Reid Papers
SU	George Arents Research Library of Syracuse University
T	Library of the University of Texas, Austin

Private Collections

CZ	Mr. and Mrs. Carl Zuckmayer, Saas-Fee, Switzerland
JSM	John S. Mayfield Collection, Syracuse, N.Y., and Bethesda, Md.
MvE	Mary von Euler, literary executor of Frances Gunther, Bethesda, Md.
TS	Toni (Mrs. Gustav) Stolper, New York, N.Y.

Names that recur frequently are abbreviated as follows:

BDePG	Barbara De Porte Grossman
DT	Dorothy Thompson
MKS	Marion K. Sanders
RWL	Rose Wilder Lane
SL	Sinclair Lewis

In a number of instances, the content has made it possible to fix the year in which undated letters were written. These conjectured dates are enclosed in parentheses, as (1927).

Foreword (Pages vii–viii)
Page
vii In an interview January 31, 1971, Mrs. Leach identified DT's "useful" New York and Philadelphia friends from 1917 to 1920.
viii "rattling good company." Dame Rebecca West to Dale Warren, January 18, 1965, JSM.

I: THE GIRL FROM SYRACUSE

Chapter 1 (Pages 3–10)
Page

3 Part of a never-completed autobiography. Only the first two chapters, titled "Childhood" and "College Days," were drafted, SU.

4 Married "beneath her." DT learned this from a cousin she visited in Pittsburgh in 1935 and entered it in her diary, SU.

4 On July 9, 1893. In articles about her, DT's birth date was often listed as 1894. However, 1893 is the year that appears in her school records and in her own notes for her autobiography.

5 The white clapboard church. The congregation outgrew the church and replaced it with a larger brick structure in 1928.

6 Interview with Marguerite Jarvis (Mrs. Thomas) Bourne, Hamburg, N.Y., October 16, 1971.

9 Family intimates whispered. Interview with Willard Thompson, New York, N.Y., October 23, 1970.

Chapter 2 (Pages 11–15)

11 Consumed with envy. DT described the experience in an essay, "The Moments that Educate," *The Courage to Be Happy* (Houghton Mifflin, Boston, 1957), p. 72.

12 According to DT's brother Willard, Eliza was a great consumer of Viava, a tonic with a high alcohol content much favored by teetotalers. One letter from Eliza (erroneously attributed to Margaret Grierson Thompson in the SU catalogue) urges Peggy to "tell Papa this Dr. thinks I ought to take malt and molasses substance, without any extras added . . ." SU.

13 "The founding Lewis." Letter to MKS from Mollie Cohen, Associate Professor Emeritus, Illinois Institute of Technology, October 1, 1971.

13–14 A transcript of DT's academic record and other data on Lewis Institute were furnished by F. R. Eckford, Registrar, Illinois Institute of Technology, and Mrs. Maureen Coutts.

15 At a church social. DT diary entry 1935, SU.

Chapter 3 (Pages 16–20)

16–20 Information on DT's college days was obtained from her autobiography and from the following interviews with her contemporaries at Syracuse: Miss Ruth Hoople, November 2, 1970; Miss J. Winifred Hughes, November 2, 1970, and October 15, 1971; Dr. Gordon Hoople, October 15, 1971.

17 The most dramatic of these. Fulsome accounts of the event appeared in the Syracuse *Journal* before and after Commencement day, May 31, 1937.

Chapter 4 (Pages 21–25)

21–25 For detailed and explicit information on the women's suffrage movement, the most complete and dependable source is the six-volume (1881–1922) *History of Woman Suffrage,* published by the National American Woman Suffrage Association. I have drawn particularly on Volumes V and VI, edited by Ida Husted Harper.

22 Hated organizing work. Letter from DT to Mr. Wright, June 11, 1920, SU.

22 On summer weekends. Gertrude Tone told this incident to Barbara De Porte, who recalled it when I interviewed her in London, September 3–7, 1971.

22 "How much that family . . ." DT diary 1935, SU.

23 Gertrude is described. Letter to MKS from Maude (Mrs. Edward E.) Franchot, February 7, 1971. Also interview, New York, N.Y., October 6, 1971.

24–25 Interviews with Barbara De Porte (Mrs. Meir) Grossman, London, September 3–7, 1971.

Chapter 5 (Pages 26–30)

27 The Social Unit proposed. *The Social Unit in 1920,* a presentation by Wilbur C. Phillips, Executive, and the discussion; transcript of a conference held in Cincinnati, October 23–25, 1919, SU.

27 Attracted a group. Interview with Dr. Regina Kronacher (Mrs. Tom) Stix, New York, N.Y., October 24, 1970.

28 Acquired the reputation . . . Letter to MKS from Mr. Bleeker Marquette, former executive of the Cincinnati Better Housing League and of the Public Health Federation, January 18, 1971, who wrote, "Mrs. Marquette describes her as good looking, quite slender and very popular with the young men. She was very demanding of the maids at the boarding house . . . I can subscribe to most of that myself. She was regarded by the Social Unit people as a very bright young woman, alert and very much on the job . . ."

Chapter 6 (Pages 31–34)

31 Assessing the startling changes. Alfred C. Kinsey, Wardell B. Pomeroy, Clyde E. Martin, and Paul Gebhard, *Sexual Behavior in the Human Female* (W. B. Saunders, 1953, Pocket Book edition, 1965), p. 299.

32 When a young Bryn Mawr graduate. Interview with Beatrice Sorchan (Mrs. Walter) Binger, New York, N.Y., February 3, 1971.

32 Mrs. Walton Martin. Mabel Alice Detmold, *The Brownstones of Turtle Bay* (East 49th Street Association, New York, 1964).

33 And none was more concerned. Letter to MKS from Barbara De Porte Grossman, May 31, 1971.

34   Barbara's passport troubles. Interviews with BDePG, London, September 3–7, 1971.

II: COMING OF AGE IN THE TWENTIES

Chapter 1 (Pages 37–40)

37   "It's been an amazing . . ." DT to B. Sorchan, June 26, 1920, SU.

38   "Dorothy met the leaders . . ." Letter to MKS from BDePG, cited above.

39   Pawning an elaborate dressing case. Letter from DT to Dr. Eugen Rosenstock-Huessy, October 22, 1940, SU.

39   Kay Boyle. Kay Boyle and Robert McAlmon, *Being Geniuses Together* (Doubleday, New York, 1968), p. 43.

Chapter 2 (Pages 41–48)

42 fn.   Among these fantasies. *Saturday Evening Post,* November 10, 1934.

46   "He offered me a job . . ." DT to B. Sorchan from Rome, September 26, 1920, SU.

Chapter 3 (Pages 49–54)

49   "I want to stay forever . . ." DT to B. Sorchan from Rome, letter cited above, SU.

51   "The crew had a wonderful reception . . ." The festivities were reported in the *New York Times,* July 18, 1920. The bas relief plaque was by the sculptor Onorio Ruotolo.

Chapter 4 (Pages 55–58)

55   Most of the bold revolutionaries. According to the *Dizionàrio Enciclopèdico Italiano 1956,* Giulietti was imprisoned during the fascist regime but survived and was elected a deputy in the Italian parliament in 1948 as an independent on the Republican list. He died in 1953 at the age of 74.

55   "We are staying here . . ." DT to B. Sorchan from Milan, October 22, 1920, SU.

56   "The Last Day." Undated typescript, SU.

56   The two were so moved. This experience is described in "An Ideal Citizen for an Ideal State" by Barbara De Porte, an unpublished typescript. DT is not named but the "Gentile friend" mentioned is DT, SU.

57   "This understandably upset Dorothy . . ." Letter to MKS from BDePG, cited above.

57   "By the way, Barbara . . ." DT to B. Sorchan from London, November 13, 1920, SU.

Chapter 5 (Pages 59–62)

61   Even the men who found her attractive. Interview with Isaac Don

Levine, whose long friendship with Rose Lane began in 1921, New York, N.Y., November 16, 1971.

61 Found her "brighter and more attractive . . ." Paul Scott Mowrer, *The House of Europe* (Houghton Mifflin, Boston, 1945), p. 391.

62 A story she later wrote. "The Top Floor at Madame Tusson's," unpublished typescript written by DT in Berlin in 1926, SU.

III: "A BLUE-EYED TORNADO"

In addition to the books specifically cited, the following have been valuable reference sources for this and subsequent chapters: Ilsa Barea, *Vienna* (Knopf, New York, 1966); Otto Friedrich, *Before the Deluge* (Harper, New York, 1972); Dorothy Gies McGuigan, *The Habsburgs* (Doubleday, New York, 1966); Albert Speer, *Inside the Third Reich* (Macmillan, New York, 1970); Karl R. Stadler, *Austria* (Praeger, New York, 1971); A. J. P. Taylor, *From Sarajevo to Potsdam* (Harcourt, Brace, New York, 1966).

Chapter 1 (Pages 65–71)

66 "Coffee in Vienna . . ." *Public Ledger,* Philadelphia, Sunday, January 8, 1922. Microfilm copies of a number of DT's early *Ledger* pieces are at SU.

66 In a more earnest vein. "The Tailor Made Homes of Vienna," *Public Ledger,* October 29, 1922; "New Vienna," undated typescript, SU.

67 The help of a teacher. DT, "A Wreath for Toni," Harper's Magazine, July 1934.

67 A roundup. Undated typescript, SU.

67 Marcel Fodor. Unless otherwise stated, all information attributed to Fodor is based on interviews with him in Paris, February 18–25, 1971.

68 fn. A few years later. Introduction by John Gunther to Fodor's *Plot and Counterplot in Central Europe* (Houghton Mifflin, Boston, 1937). The book reports many examples of Fodor's collaboration with Gunther, one of the most dramatic being an account of their coverage of the attack on the Karl Marx Hof in Vienna on February 12, 1934.

70 "A letter from father." The only letter from DT's father at SU was written two days after she sailed for Europe on June 21, 1920.

71 Her mother's grave was isolated. I visited this melancholy spot with Marguerite Jarvis Bourne on October 16, 1971.

Chapter 2 (Pages 72–78)

72 "I am at this moment . . ." DT to Rose Wilder Lane, September 24, 1921.

73 A standing invitation. A handwritten and probably unpublished portrait of Genia and her circle by DT is in the files at SU.

73 "I have a new fur coat . . ." DT to RWL, letter cited above.

74ff. All statements attributed to Josef and Eileen Bard are, unless otherwise indicated, based on interviews with them in London, February 10–16, 1971.

75 DT's comments on the peace ladies were made in two letters to RWL, one written on July 15, 1921, the other undated, SU.

75 Went off with Josef. Letter to RWL from DT, August 13, 1921.

75 A long weekend. An unpublished typescript by DT titled "Make Your Own Baedecker" provides a lively account of this excursion. SU.

76 "If I were more courageous . . ." DT to RWL, September 3, 1921, SU.

77 Problem of Dorothy's nationality. The timing of Dorothy's wedding was unfortunate, since the Expatriation Act of 1907 was still in force, providing that "any American woman who marries a foreigner shall take the nationality of her husband." Some eight months after her marriage, that law was repealed by the Cable Act, passed in September 1922, which provided that "a woman citizen of the United States shall not cease to be a citizen of the United States by reason of her marriage . . . unless she makes a formal renunciation." However, for those who had previously lost their citizenship the new law set up rules similar to the requirements for naturalization of any alien, including residence for at least a year within the United States. Except for a brief home leave, Dorothy did not touch her native shores again until 1928. Since she never, so far as is known, applied for a Hungarian passport — which would have been of little use — she was in effect stateless until November 1926, when on a visit to London she persuaded the American consul general to issue a temporary passport to Dorothy Thompson Bard, which he stamped "valid for one week." This was an irregular procedure, probably done because he assumed that she was stranded in Europe and intended to sail for home on the next ship. Instead she returned to Berlin where she was then based and induced the consul general there to extend her passport for two years — a triumph of charm over bureaucratic regulations that were clearly violated. The day after her marriage to Sinclair Lewis, on May 15, 1928, she hastened again to the consulate in London and had her passport genuinely validated in the name of Dorothy Thompson Lewis. She never explained how she managed her extensive travels over four years without valid papers, although she did tell an interviewer that she once used a red seal from a coffee can as a substitute for an official stamp. The passport mentioned above is in JSM Coll.

77   Threatened with eviction. Letter to Beach Conger, chief of the *Ledger*'s Berlin bureau, from DT, February 24 (1922), SU.
78   "I like marriage . . ." DT to Mary Gawthorpe, undated, SU.
78   "I note that the institution . . ." Gertrude Tone to DT, August 6, 1923, SU.

Chapter 3 (Pages 79–84)
79   "I thought my newspaper . . ." DT to Mary Gawthorpe, undated, SU.
80   "Seiner Kaiserliche . . ." From notes by DT and M. Fodor during discussions of her autobiography in Washington, D.C., in 1960, SU.
80   Ferenc Molnár. Typescript, SU.
81   "I think Molnár . . ." DT to Beach Conger, undated, SU.
81   Later she spun. "The Last Days of the Hapsburgs," typescript, SU.
82   A number of other journalists . . . Interview with Toni Stolper, New York, N.Y., October 30, 1970.
82   "Caught in the midst of the crowd . . ." "Nemeth: A Story of Post-War Vienna," typescript by DT, SU.
82   Her companions became. *The New Yorker*, April 24, 1940, p. 24.
82   "Things were rather exciting . . ." DT to Beach Conger, undated, SU.
83   "My love," he wrote. Josef Bard to DT, August 20, 1922, SU.

Chapter 4 (Pages 85–87)
85   "Wholesome, hearty . . ." Louis Untermeyer, *Bygones* (Harcourt, Brace, New York, 1965), p. 68.
86   In her diary. Entry made December 1935, SU.
87   The tensions. Interview with John Nef, Washington, D.C., October 15, 1970.

Chapter 5 (Pages 88–95)
89   "The bubbling, blazing days . . ." John Gunther, *A Fragment of Autobiography* (Harper, New York, 1962), p. 5.
89   Astounded to discover. Paul Scott Mowrer, *House of Europe*, p. 428.
90   An easy camaraderie. Gunther, *Autobiography*, p. 6.
90   Frederick Kuh. Kuh is quoted in Leo Lania, *Today We Are Brothers* (Houghton Mifflin, Boston, 1942), p. 183.
93   Continued to assure him. DT to Josef Bard, January 25 (1927), SU.
93   She described it. Introduction by DT to Zuckmayer's *Second Wind* (Doubleday, Doran, New York, 1940).
93   "She couldn't have understood . . ." From an article by Zuckmayer written after DT's death, translated from the German by his daughter, Mrs. Win Guttenbrunner, CZ.
94   Walked alone. *The New Yorker*, April 20, 1940, p. 29. A slightly

different version appeared in "Rover Girl in Europe" by Jack Alexander, the *Saturday Evening Post,* May 25, 1940, p. 113.

94   Not precisely what happened. DT's penchant for self-dramatization is not unusual among celebrities who are also writers. For example, when an interviewer asked why so many exaggerated anecdotes were published about Gloria Steinem, the women's liberation crusader of the seventies, her mother, an ex-journalist, replied, "Oh, Gloria likes a good story just the way I do," *New York Times,* May 2, 1972.

94   Interviewed Sigmund Freud. DT did not save the clipping of the piece (assuming it was published). However, she preserved her handwritten notes, which include a detailed description of Freud's office and the statement that "he would not undertake to psychoanalyze the world. 'I never take a patient unless I can offer some hope,' " SU.

94   "We were all working . . ." Interview with A. R. Decker, Stony Point, N.Y., June 12, 1971.

95   "The only woman 'newspaper man' . . ." Letter to MKS from George Seldes, September 9, 1971.

Chapter 6   (Page 96–103)

96   "There was a big chintz couch . . ." Interviews with Lilian and Edgar Ansel Mowrer, Wonalancet, N.H., October 20–21, 1970.

98   "I am ashamed . . ." Undated and possibly unsent letter, DT to Josef Bard, SU.

98–100   These are excerpts from letters written in January and February, 1927, SU.

101   "Nights now for me . . ." DT to RWL, erroneously dated January 10, 1926. The year was 1927. DT not infrequently slipped up on dates, SU.

102   "Sister, mother, guide . . ." Gertrude Tone to DT, May 20, 1927, SU.

102   "Oh Dorothy . . ." Jean Starr Untermeyer to DT, January 19, 1927, SU.

Chapter 7   (Pages 104–107)

104   In a mosaic. The Mowrers found shards of this mosaic in the rubble that had been Händelstrasse 8 when they revisited Berlin after World War II.

104 fn.   Von Maltzan. Edgar Ansel Mowrer, *Triumph and Turmoil* (Weybright and Talley, New York, 1968), p. 169. DT's comment was entered in her diary, September 28, 1927.

104   Von Moltke. Peter Drucker, who served as an assistant to Chancellor Brüning in the late days of the Weimar Republic, was a contemporary of von Moltke and knew him well. He describes him as "a nice boy . . . he had great courage and total incompetence [as a conspirator] . . . He really wanted to lead the life of a retired gentleman on his estate . . . but he felt the very heavy burden of his name . . . His mother, Daisy, was one of those women born to be a Sargent portrait, South African, of English-Scotch descent, a Christian Scientist, totally vapid, always trailing a cloud of chiffon scarves . . ." Interview with Peter Drucker, New York, N.Y., October 12, 1970.

105   Vincent Sheean's recollections of his first meeting with DT were relayed to me in a letter from his wife, Diana, January 7, 1971, and subsequently amplified in the course of interviews, September 11–15, 1971, in Leggiuno-per-Arolo, Italy.

106   "Good old work . . ." DT to Josef Bard, February 14 (1927), SU.

106   She wrote magnanimously. DT to Phyllis Bottome, January 27 (1927), SU.

107   In late May she experienced. DT to RWL, January 17 (1928). Of her verse she commented, "And I wrote this sonnet, which is not a good sonnet, but which I like, anyhow," SU.

IV: NEW HORIZONS

Chapter 1 (Pages 111–116)

112   At heart, provincial. Telephone conversation with Anita Loos, New York, N.Y., December 27, 1971.

114   Vivid memories of an afternoon. Interview with Sigrid Schultz, New York, N.Y., January 26, 1971.

114   "Just now I begin . . ." DT to Peggy Wilson, August 1 (1927), SU.

114   "And bring Sinclair along . . ." Josef Bard to DT, July 27 (1927), SU.

114   Her London flat. Eileen Agar to DT, August 1 (1927), SU.

115   In her diary. September 9, 1927, SU.

115   Dorothy recorded. September 21, 1927, SU.

115   "H. has kept his word . . ." September 28, 1927, SU.

115   "Long figure, leaning . . ." September 21, 1927, SU.

115   "It isn't quite the same . . ." DT to RWL, January 17, 1928.

Chapter 2 (Pages 117–123)

118   *The New Russia* (Henry Holt, New York, 1928).

118   "The first Soviet celebration . . ." *The New Russia,* pp. 7–9, 54.

119   Life was strenuous . . . DT to SL, November 11, 1927, SU.

119   "You go gallivanting . . ." SL to DT, November 4, 1927, SU.

120   "Hal, I miss you . . ." DT to SL, November 8, 1927, SU.

120   "Anyway, at least . . ." SL to DT, November 5, 1927, SU.

120   He had dinner . . . SL to DT, November 5, 1927, SU.

121   PEP. Lion Feuchtwanger, *PEP, J. L. Wetcheek's American Song*

Book, English version by Dorothy Thompson, drawings by Constantin Aladjalov (Viking, New York, 1929).

121 Much as he yearned. SL to DT, November 14, 1927, SU.

121 "Russia is stirring . . ." DT to SL, November 16, 1927, SU.

122 "I want to come home . . ." DT to SL, November 21, 1927, SU.

122 "You speak of buying . . ." SL to DT, November 14, 1927, SU.

123 "Quite a gay dog . . ." DT to SL, November 8, 1927, SU.

123 "A pompous old bore . . ." Vincent Sheean, *Dorothy and Red* (Houghton Mifflin, Boston, 1963), p. 79.

123 The tragic story of Rayna Prohme is recounted in Sheean's *Dorothy and Red*, p. 74 ff., and at much greater length in his *Personal History*, first published in 1934 (Houghton Mifflin, Boston; Sentry Edition, 1969), p. 262 ff.

123 Dorothy's "indomitable courage . . ." Sheean, *Dorothy and Red*, pp. 73, 77.

Chapter 3 (Pages 124–130)

124 "No, darling, I shan't . . ." RWL to DT, January 21, 1928, SU.

124 "I shall always . . ." RWL to DT, January 10, 1928, SU.

124 Persuaded her employers. In response to her persuasions, Samuel Dashiel of the *Ledger's* Paris office wrote to DT on January 20, 1928: "It certainly is hard to see Berlin copy coming under some other person's name if any. I have heard very favorably of Knickerbocker and if you say he is all right it seems to me he ought to get the job . . . Someone told me that Swing was very fond of working in Germany and I was wondering if he would apply for the job," SU.

125 "I feel humble . . ." DT to SL, March 9 (1928), SU.

128 Recalling the experience. Interview with Baroness Moura Budberg, London, February 15, 1971.

129 "Well, I have finished . . ." DT to SL, April 27, 1928, SU.

V: MRS. SINCLAIR LEWIS

Chapter 1 (Pages 133–141)

133 "I hope Hal . . ." Junius Wood to DT, April 28, 1928, SU.

134 A guest list, SU.

134 Was not in London. Interview with Dame Rebecca West, London, February 11, 1971.

135 The only surviving wedding guest. Telephone conversation with Anita Loos, New York, N.Y., December 27, 1971.

136 "Entering upon the phase . . ." Sheean, *Dorothy and Red,* p. 97.

139 She developed the "woman's angle." Diary entry, May 29, 1928, SU.

141 "We have all followed . . ." H. R. Knickerbocker to DT, August 22, 1928, SU.

Chapter 2 (Pages 142–149)

142   "You girls go . . ." Peggy Wilson reported this conversation to her brother Willard from whom I garnered it on October 23, 1970, in New York, N.Y.

143   "But it was not all work . . ." Sheean, *Personal History*, p. 321.

143   "I saw between Dorothy and Red . . ." Sheean, *Dorothy and Red*, pp. 134–35.

146   In her memoir. Sara Mayfield, *The Constant Circle* (Delacorte, New York, 1968), p. 139.

146   "By her own admission . . ." *The Constant Circle*, p. 189.

146 fn.   I queried. Sara Mayfield to MKS, January 5, 1971.

146   "Really it is too irritating . . ." DT to RWL, February 28, 1929, SU.

146   Old friends rose. John Gunther to DT, December 10 (1928), SU.

147   "Is there anything on earth . . ." DT to the Gunthers, February 22, 1929, MvE.

147   "I had no idea . . ." Floyd Gibbons to DT, September 4, 1929, SU.

148   "Red was not drinking . . ." Sheean, *Dorothy and Red*, p. 156.

148   "Darling, you are going to . . ." RWL to DT, December 29, 1929, SU.

Chapter 3 (Pages 150–158)

150   Dr. Moreno's "therapeutic theater." *New York Times*, November 9, 1938.

151   They had reached an agreement. "It was a marvelous sort of 1930s arrangement," one of Franchot Tone's intimates said after the actor's death. *New York Times*, September 19, 1958.

152   "Woman, I'll have you . . ." SL to DT, November 9 (1929), SU.

153   "Hal & I have taken . . ." DT to the Woodwards, February 21 (1930), SU.

154   "Not quiet weeks . . ." Sheean, *Dorothy and Red*, p. 172.

154   "Actually a moment . . ." *Dorothy and Red*, p. 181.

155   "She rang a bell . . ." *Dorothy and Red*, p. 181.

155   "Here I am . . ." DT to Helen Woodward, October 9 (1930), SU.

157   Letter to Letitia Irwin. November 26, 1930, SU.

Chapter 4 (Pages 159–168)

160 fn.   Harcourt, Brace. The subject is discussed in several letters from DT to SL, SU.

160   "The head of an eighteenth century . . ." DT, *"I Saw Hitler!"* (Farrar & Rinehart, New York, 1932), p. 15.

162   "They were suddenly proud . . ." Christopher Isherwood, *The Berlin Stories* (New Directions, New York, 1945), p. 179.

163   A diary entry. Berlin, February 3, 1931, SU.

163   "Oswald Villard wants you . . ." SL to DT from London, February 12 (1931), SU.

164   "How *can* I take . . ." DT to SL from Berlin (1931), SU.

164   "Little Dotty . . ." SL to DT from London, February 10, 1931, SU.

164   "I found things . . ." DT to SL (1931), SU.

166   Checking in at the Adlon. Interview with John Farrar, New York, N.Y., January 19, 1971.

166   For seven years. DT, *"I Saw Hitler!"* pp. 1–14 *passim.*

168   "Formless, almost faceless . . ." DT, *"I Saw Hitler!"* p. 13.

168   "I butted in . . ." SL to DT, February 8, 1932, SU.

Chapter 5 (Pages 169–173)

169   In her diary . . . April 15, 1932, SU.

170   But in 1931. DT's tax return enclosed with letter of March 29, 1932, from Bernard L. Ernst, SU.

170 fn.   In 1932. Handwritten worksheet by DT, SU.

170   "Your own Rawdon Crawley." SL to DT, October 17, 1930, SU.

171   "I am terribly homesick . . ." Diary, Berlin, February 1931, SU.

171   "I have reached Phyllis . . ." SL to DT, November 15, 1931, SU.

172   Addressing the Wisconsin. The clipping, dated February 25, 1932, which she sent to SL included a particularly hideous photo of DT. Above it she typed: "It's not either Ruth Judd. Nor Ruth Snyder [two recently convicted murderesses]. Someone even sent her a valentine!" SU.

173   Friends of suffrage days. Barbara Grossman recalled this reaction, which MKS shares.

Chapter 6 (Pages 174–181)

174   "Dorothy wouldn't even . . ." Interviews with Marcel Fodor, Paris, February 18–25, 1971.

175   "Extreme susceptibility . . ." Sheean, *Dorothy and Red,* p. 241.

176   "The old lilac city." John Gunther, *The Lost City* (Harper, New York, 1964), p. ix.

176   "My room is large and white . . ." DT to SL (1932), SU.

177   "It makes me physically . . ." SL to DT from London, May 1932, SU.

177   "A cuckoo-clock house . . ." SL to Frere Reeves, quoted in Mark Schorer, *Sinclair Lewis: An American Life* (McGraw-Hill, New York, 1961), p. 576.

177   "A terribly charming . . ." DT to SL, November 8, 1932, SU.

178   In her diary. December 28, 1932, SU.

179   Dorothy gave her own account of the party in her column in the New York *Herald Tribune,* December 25, 1940: "Something had drawn us back to Europe and I dragged the family toward Austria . . . To be near Vienna and yet in the country induced us to take a chalet in the mountains two hours away . . . nearby was a hotel to which, for overnight guests, was attached a villa . . . When we rented the villa for a week and invited a potpourri of American and European friends to spend Christmas with us, we hardly thought that they would all accept. They came from Germany and Hungary, from England and from spots in between. They were married and unmarried and engaged to be married. There were children and nurses and every room in the villa and every bed in the chalet was taken . . ."

179 Determined to serve carp. Interview with Lilian Mowrer, Wonalancet, N.H., October 20–21, 1970.

Chapter 7 (Pages 182–194)

182 "Darthy is leaving Wredde . . ." Goodman to H. L. Mencken, February 3 (1933), quoted in Schorer, *Sinclair Lewis*, p. 579.

183–184 The two letters from SL were written February 18 and February 24, 1933, SU.

184 "I have never seen Esther . . ." SL to DT, March 11, 1933, SU.

185 "It is really as bad . . ." DT to SL from Vienna, March 13, 1933, SU.

185 "I have never felt . . ." DT to SL from Portofino, March 25, 1933, SU.

186 "Your feeling . . ." SL to DT, April 9, 1933, SU.

186 Dorothy apologized. DT to SL, March 26, 1933, SU.

187 "The roster of names . . ." DT to SL, March 26, 1933, SU.

187 "Back to Blood and Iron." *Saturday Evening Post,* May 6, 1933.

187–188 "Have no fears . . ." and "Christa has made up her mind . . ." DT to SL, March 30, 1933, SU.

188 "Was instinctively akin . . ." Sheean, *Dorothy and Red,* p. 238.

188 The lecture business. William B. Feakins to DT, June 21, 1933. In this letter he also urged prompt payment of a $150 commission due him. SU.

189 "A Wreath for Toni." *Harper's Magazine,* July 1934.

189 fn. The article was. Interview with Dr. Friedrich Scheu, editor of the *Arbeiter Zeitung* and a scholar specializing in the history of Vienna in the twenties and thirties, Vienna, March 2, 1971.

189 Entertained by Lewis' first wife. Christa Winsloe to DT, August 1933, SU.

190 Regarded the friendship. Interview with Margaret and John Farrar, New York, N.Y., January 19, 1971.

190 On her return. DT to Christa Winsloe, March 31, 1934, SU.

191 An enthusiastic and expert gardener. The following communication is reproduced for the entertainment of fellow gardening enthusiasts.

DEAR STUB:

I have gone over the whole place in the two days I have been here, and I am fundamentally dissatisfied with the way it looks. I am going to put down in black and white exactly what is wrong with it, so that you can remedy it. Because I don't want to see the same faults when I come next time.

1. The flower beds: Not one of the flower beds has been properly prepared for the spring and summer. Last summer I protested again and again to Bill and also to you about the way you weeded. It is absolutely silly to spend anybody's time and our money putting men to work *pulling out weeds*. The only thing to do is to turn the soil completely over and take out the roots. Also the flower beds should, in the process, be built up so that the water will drain. All this takes more time to start with, *but* it saves repeating the same operation all summer.

2. The vegetable garden. The vegetable garden is full of grass roots. They will all grow again, and again you will spend my money and somebody's time pulling weeds. I thought you would have learned last summer from your expensive experience with the annual flower bed how soil ought to be prepared. You must get the weed roots out *before* you plant. Unfortunately it is now too late to do anything about this.

3. The general aspect of the place. You dig out weeds and leave piles of them over night or for several days. They look like hell. No gentleman's place ought to look like that. Your men ought to work with wheelbarrows and put the stuff they dig out into them and cart them away before they quit for the day. At the vegetable garden, for instance, there are heaps of rotting weeds and papers (paper containers that plants came in) all around the garden.

4. The edges on vegetable beds. A vegetable garden is a garden. The only reason we have a vegetable garden is for beauty and pleasure. It costs about five times as much to grow vegetables with the wages we pay as it does to buy them. The vegetable garden ought to be as neat as the flowers. That means that a) the edges must be straight and clear. The main garden ought to be marked off from the pasture, absolutely straight and clean. The same of the asparagus bed, the raspberry patch, and the garden up the hill.

5. The roadways. The grass needs to be scraped out of them. The roadway back of the house needs to be cleaned up. Josef is doing that now. He tells me you said that was unnecessary, he could spray poison on it. Under no circumstances do that. The poison if it hits the woodbine will kill that, too. Also if one ever wanted to put a

grass border next to the wall, the poison would make it impossible to grow grass there. Poison can only be used on open roadways.

Please do not try to do things in such a hurry. Once they are properly done you will save yourself days and days of work all summer. Go down to the Moons on some day off and look at the way a gentleman's garden ought to look. That estate is run by one man and two little boys, as far as the whole gardens are concerned.

I have complained every summer about gas bills. You use the motors too much, and run to Woodstock too much. That's not what we are paying you for. Make a list once and for all of the tools or anything else you need, and then either get them at once, or get Fernand to bring them up. I am very serious about what I am saying. There are three men working full time on this place. About Joseph's work I know, because he has worked for me before, under close supervision, and I observed him yesterday. I want a lot better results from the rest of you.

Except for this last paragraph I am giving a copy of this memo to Josef in German, so that he, too, will see what I want.

DTL

192   A visit to her alma mater. DT spoke on "The Crisis in Germany" in Lincoln Auditorium, Syracuse University, on December 20, 1934. The advance publicity for this appearance made much of Dorothy's nomination as a "Woman of the Year" by Mary Roberts Rinehart, who wrote in the January 1935 issue of *Pictorial Review* that she was chosen, "Because she is the woman journalist at her best. She thinks and works like a man but remains very much a woman; and because she has made a success of her marriage with Sinclair Lewis, and that, I fancy, with that brilliant and temperamental person, would be a career in itself for any woman." Syracuse *Journal*, December 12, 1934. This encomium, at a time when the tensions in the Lewis marriage were common knowledge to their friends, is another example of DT's gift for myth-making.

192   In another unsent letter. December 21, 1934, SU.

193   An allowance of 50 dollars. Christa named this sum in a letter from Cagnes, September 4, 1940, SU. Though DT kept no copy of her reply, it was a request she was unlikely to refuse.

Chapter 8 (Pages 195–199)

195   From Franconia. SL to DT, July 17, 1934, SU.

195   Within a month. SL to DT from the Berkshire Hotel, New York, N.Y., August 15, 1934, SU.

195   He assured her. SL to DT, August 18, 1934, SU.

196   Dale provided. Interview with Dale Warren, Boston, Mass., June 13, 1972.

196 "My God things are exciting . . ." DT to Dale Warren, August 16, 1934, SU.

198 Birchall reported. *New York Times,* August 26, 1934.

198 When reporters caught up. U.P. dispatch, August 26, 1934.

199 Placed an advertisement. New York *Herald Tribune,* August 27, 1934.

199 Her own cabled report. Distributed by NANA (North American Newspaper Alliance), August 26, 1934.

199 Proud trophy. This is the text of the expulsion order, as published in the *New York Times,* August 26, 1934:

> BERLIN, AUG. 24, 1934.
> OFFICE OF THE SECRET POLICE,
> PRINZ ALBRECHT-STRASSE, 8.

It has come to the attention of the authorities that you have recently again arrived in Germany.

In view of your numerous anti-German publications in the American press, the German authorities, for reasons of national self-respect, are unable to extend to you a further right of hospitality.

To avoid formal expulsion you are therefore requested to interrupt your sojourn in Germany as quickly as possible and leave the domain of the Reich immediately.

Signed by proxy [the signature is undecipherable].
To MRS. DOROTHEA LEWIS,
HOTEL ADLON,
BERLIN.

VI: ASCENDING COMET

Chapter 1 (Pages 203–208)

203 "It was a great disappointment . . ." HRR–L of C.

203 "You were no more disappointed . . ." DT to Helen Reid, October 24, 1934, HRR–L of C.

204 "Shrewd, fantastic . . ." Undated letter to SL from DT from Stoneleigh Court, Washington, D.C., SU.

205 In the journal. This diary, kept sporadically during the lecture trip, is at SU.

207 "You were sweet . . ." DT to Gustav Stolper, November 20, 1935, TS.

207 Dear God, I am tired. In addition to her strenuous schedule, Dorothy found American hostelries, in the pre-Holiday Inn era, debilitating, as she noted in a diary entry titled "Pet Abominations in American Hotels":

1) The telephone girl who says good morning instead of repeating the number and then gets it wrong.

2) The manager who wakes you out of a sound sleep to ask you if your room is all right.

3) Linen which smells of chloride.

4) Half burnt out and dim electric light bulbs.

5) Bedside telephones which you have to sit on the bed to answer. Hundreds have done so before you and the bed sags on that side. Tables so small that you can't take notes at the phone.

6) Dry ink bottles and rusted pens.

7) Canned orange juice.

8) French boudoir prints.

9) No pins or needles to thread.

10) Toilet seats with no covers in bathrooms too small to hold a chair or stool. So there is no place to sit and wipe one's feet.

11) Insufficient writing paper.

12) Tea balls, cheesecloth bags of tea, served on the side of the pot of water which has long since ceased to boil. (Should be death penalty for this.)

13) Neighbors radios.

14) Heat. Temperature 76–80 degrees.

Chapter 2 (Pages 209–215)

209 Among her duties. Interview with Emily Carter Haberman, St. Petersburg, Fla., February 24, 1972.

209 In her diary. January 9, 1936, SU.

209 "I went with trepidation . . ." Dale Warren, "Notes on a Genius: Sinclair Lewis at His Best," *Harper's Magazine*, January 1954.

210 fn. Née Rosie Goldschmidt. I am indebted to Toni Stolper for this information on Countess Waldek.

210 An attractive young bachelor. From Lewellyn Jordan, *A Biographical Sketch of David L. Cohn*, M.A. thesis, July 1963, Mississippi Collection, Library of the University of Mississippi, Oxford.

210 A party in Bronxville. Interview with Katherine Gauss Jackson, New York, N.Y., April 18, 1972.

211 "What can a woman do . . ." DT to SL (March 1935), SU.

212 A lengthy entry. November 28, 1935, SU.

214 In Emily Carter's recollection. Interview with Emily Carter Haberman, St. Petersburg, Fla., February 24, 1972.

214 "I am going to have a big personal problem . . ." HRR–L of C.

Chapter 3 (Pages 216–222)

216 Called at the Reids'. Interview with Whitelaw Reid, New York, N.Y., April 21, 1971.

217 "I feel crushed . . ." DT to Gustav Stolper, March 7, 1936, TS.

221　Dorothy spent election night. Robert E. Sherwood, *Roosevelt and Hopkins* (Harper, New York, 1948) , pp. 86–87.

222　"Well, Ogden, I see . . ." Arthur M. Schlesinger, Jr., *The Age of Roosevelt: The Politics of Upheaval* (Houghton Mifflin, Boston, 1960) , p. 642.

Chapter 4 (Pages 223–229)

223　An advertisement. Newark *Evening News,* December 10, 1937.

223　Reproached him. Dorothy Parker, "A Valentine for Mr. Woollcott," reprinted in *Vanity Fair,* edited by Cleveland Amory and Frederic Bradlee (Viking, New York, 1960) , pp. 290–91.

224　Introduced the latter. Interviews with Ethel (Mrs. John) Moses, New York, N.Y., December 4, 1970, and January 9, 1972.

224　"I'm having trouble . . ." Telephone conversation with Bruce Gould, Hopewell, N.J., June 15, 1972.

225　"She and Eleanor Roosevelt . . ." *Time,* June 12, 1939.

225　*Dorothy Thompson's Political Guide* (Stackpole, New York, 1938) .

225　Ralph Thompson. *New York Times,* August 15, 1938.

226　After giving the servants. Interview with Emily Carter Haberman.

226　Mark Schorer. Schorer, *Sinclair Lewis,* p. 629.

226　"This business . . ." DT to SL, April 29, 1937, SU.

227　She was often at her desk. Interview with Louise Eagan Garfield, one of DT's temporary secretarial staff at this time, New York, N.Y., June 6, 1972.

227　"Red was charming . . ." Interviews with Diana Sheean, New York, N.Y., and Woodstock, Vt., September 1970.

228 fn.　Hamilton Fish Armstrong, *Peace and Counterpeace: From Wilson to Hitler* (Harper, New York, 1971) , p. 11.

229　"Sometimes, Dorothy and I . . ." Interview with Max Ascoli, New York, N.Y., December 3, 1970.

229　An entire column. "Diary Between War and Peace," New York *Herald Tribune,* September 9, 1939.

Chapter 5 (Pages 230–236)

230　"I feel as though I know . . ." Broadcast, November 14, 1938.

232　"Over at the Cafe Louvre . . ." William L. Shirer, *Berlin Diary* (Knopf, New York, 1941, Popular Library Eagle Books Edition) , pp. 78–79, 85.

232　"Why does Germany want . . ." New York *Herald Tribune,* February 18, 1938.

233　"What happened on Friday . . ." "Obituary for Europe," New York *Herald Tribune,* September 21, 1938.

233 fn.　Margaret Case Harriman. *The New Yorker,* April 27, 1940, p. 24.

233 *Let the Record Speak* (Houghton Mifflin, Boston, 1939). Gannett's review was published August 25, 1939.

234 Poore's praise. *New York Times,* September 2, 1939.

234 A *Fortune* poll. De Sales diary, September 18, 1939, pp. 133–34, ms. at SU.

234 Dorothy responded. "Col. Lindbergh and Propaganda," New York *Herald Tribune,* September 20, 1939. Also "Colonel Lindbergh's Imperialism," New York *Herald Tribune,* October 18, 1939, and October 20, 1939.

235 Some 19,000 supporters. The meeting was front-page news in all New York papers on February 21, 1939.

235 "The Talk of the Town." *The New Yorker,* March 4, 1939, p. 11.

236 Anti-Semitism. The annotated clipping is in the HRR papers, L of C.

Chapter 6 (Pages 237–243)

237 A rival list. "On Party Material," New York *Herald Tribune,* March 29, 1939.

239 The magazine's editor. Introduction to an expanded version of the article published as a book, *Refugees, Anarchy or Organization* (Random House, New York, 1938), p. xi.

239 fn. Dorothy repeatedly. DT both wrote a column (April 29, 1939) and appeared as a witness in support of the bill sponsored by Senator Robert F. Wagner and Congresswoman Edith Nourse Rogers to admit 20,000 German refugee children to the United States. Like virtually all other proposals to provide a haven to those dispossessed by Hitler, it was defeated.

240 "I realize . . ." DT to Eugenia Schwarzwald, May 31, 1939.

240 "You were so near here . . ." Marie Stiasny to DT, August 8, 1940. DT wrote a moving tribute to Genia, "The Most Beautiful Form of Courage," *The Courage to Be Happy* (Houghton Mifflin, Boston, 1957), p. 5.

240 In addition to loans. One refugee whom DT did not sponsor, on the ground that she was overcommitted, was Meir Grossman. Meyer Weisgal, when I interviewed him in New York, N.Y., on October 1, 1971, suggested as a possible reason the fact that Grossman was aligned with the "revisionist" Zionist faction, inspired by Vladimir Jabotinsky and opposed to the policies of Dr. Chaim Weizmann, whom DT revered. Barbara Grossman discounted this theory. "It was just a matter of what life had done to Dorothy," she said. Interview, New York, N.Y., October 24, 1972.

241 The first draft. *The New Yorker,* April 27, 1940, p. 28.

242 "I am so fond of Dorothy." Fiorello La Guardia to Helen Reid, July 25, 1940, HRR–L of C.

242 "The maids used to cower . . ." Interview with Madeline Shaw (Mrs. Richard) Green, Wilton, Conn., November 8, 1970.

242 Helen Reid wrote. June 2, 1938, SU.

Chapter 7 (Pages 244–249)

244 Frances Gunther wrote. Diary, MvE.

245 "Society at this moment . . ." "If I Had a Daughter," *Ladies' Home Journal*, September 1939.

245 What do parents. "To Live and Create Life," *Dorothy Thompson's Political Guide*, p. 117.

246 Wells added. Wells Lewis to DT, June 12, 1939.

246 "On many evenings . . ." Sheean, *Dorothy and Red*, p. 291.

247 A cash loan. Undated letter from DT to Mr. George P. Klein, Department of Taxation and Finance, Albany, N.Y., SU.

248 "How is the play going?" Wells to DT from Lowell House, Harvard University, December 14, 1939, SU.

248 In her reply. DT to Alexander Woollcott, August 14, 1939, H.

Chapter 8 (Pages 250–254)

251 "The Right to Insecurity." New York *Herald Tribune*, May 11, 1938.

251 *Lords of the Press* (Julian Messner, New York, 1938) , "From Reds to Riches," pp. 347–58.

251 "My dear George . . ." DT to George Seldes, December 13, 1938, SU.

252 An "independent." "In Defense of Mrs. Roosevelt," New York *Herald Tribune*, April 29, 1938; "The Appointment of Bertrand Russell," New York *Herald Tribune*, March 27, 1940; letter of January 12, 1944, to Mr. William J. Cronin protesting the postmaster's decision in the *Esquire* case, SU.

252 "The Dilemma of a Liberal." *Story*, January 1937.

253 "He says . . ." Frances Gunther's diary, January 1, 1937, MvE.

254 "I'm going to do it . . ." Sheean, *Dorothy and Red*, p. 312; several other friends also recall this pronouncement.

VII: CRUSADE

Chapter 1 (Pages 257–263)

257 Brooks Atkinson. *New York Times*, February 24, 1940.

257 Lewis sent words. SL to DT, February 27, 1940, SU.

257 *fn.* The title. SL to DT from Beverly Hills, February 12, 1940, SU.

258 "Flowers piling . . ." Diary, March 23, 1940, SU.

259 "We also have . . ." Diary, March 27, 1940, SU.

259 "It was like a message . . ." Interview with Sari Juhasz, Vienna, March 2, 1971.

260　An angry editorial. Pittsburgh *Post Gazette,* May 16, 1940.

260　A cautionary message. Helen Reid to DT, April 15, 1940, HRR–L of C.

260　Told the Sheeans. Vincent Sheean, *Between the Thunder and the Sun* (Random House, New York, 1943), p. 120.

260　Hugh S. Johnson. New York *World Telegram,* October 23, 1940.

261　"All of us were barely . . ." Interview with Julian Bach, New York, N.Y., November 3, 1971.

262　The Springfield *Union* reported. August 28, 1940.

263　Heywood Broun. Quoted in Jack Alexander's *Saturday Evening Post* piece "The Girl from Syracuse," May 18, 1940.

Chapter 2 (Pages 264–271)

265　Took a different view. Interview with Morris L. Ernst, New York, N.Y., October 22, 1970.

266　"I shall be delighted . . ." FDR to Morris Ernst, May 18, 1940, T.

266　When the interview ended. Morris L. Ernst, *So Far So Good* (Harper, New York, 1948), p. 143. The FDR-Ernst correspondence is at T.

267　"We sympathize fully . . ." Helen Reid to Mrs. Robert Nehrbas, November 20, 1940, HRR–L of C.

268　"The best suggestions . . ." Sherwood, *Roosevelt and Hopkins,* p. 195.

268　An unexpected accolade. Undated letter from Mrs. Henry Luce, Sr., from Haverford, Pa., to DT, SU.

268　What a comfort. DT to Mrs. Luce, October 26, 1940, SU.

269　He urged his mother. Interview with Whitelaw Reid, New York, N.Y., April 21, 1971.

269　"You know, I *want* . . ." DT to Helen Reid, November 10, 1940, HRR–L of C.

269 fn.　Trude Pratt. Interview with Trude Lash, New York, N.Y., February 4, 1972.

269 fn.　Convinced her never again. Letter from Clare Booth Luce to John Mayfield, published in *The Courier,* Syracuse University, Library Associates, September 1963. Also published here is the telegram from Mrs. Luce to DT that says, in part: "well the champs are still the champs congratulations on the magnificent job you did for what you believe to be the right thing . . ." DT's handwritten reply is scrawled on the telegram: "I forgave all when you swatted Ham Fish. *Nothing unites people more than a common hatred.*" The words italicized have been crossed out. I am indebted to John S. Mayfield for decoding them for me.

270　A rather heartless quip. I have found no copy of this message; however, it has been repeated to me so often in identical language that I believe it was sent.

271   An eloquent article. "There was a Man," *Life,* January 27, 1941.

Chapter 3 (Pages 272–277)

272   One of Dorothy's favorite poems . . . *Lepanto* was one of many poems DT knew by heart and loved to recite. She referred to it in several columns, notably one published February 23, 1938, titled "The Last Knight of Europe," which leads off:

> Dim drums throbbing, in the hills half heard,
> Where only on a nameless throne a crownless prince has stirred,
> Where, risen from a doubtful seat and half-attainted stall
> The last Knight of Europe takes weapons from the wall . . .

"Thus once, when chivalry seemed dead in Europe, and all Christendom was capitulating to the infidel, did a 'nameless prince' — Don John of Austria — move alone, and is celebrated in Chesterton's great ballad 'Lepanto.'

"Men rose and followed that gallant prince. But who will follow the man who Monday rose and renounced his doubtful seat, as British Minister for Foreign Affairs [Anthony Eden, who resigned from the cabinet on February 20, 1938]."

273   One of the city's best jewelers. *Meyer Weisgal . . . So Far* (Random House, New York, 1971), p. 196.

273   At the Astor. The meeting was reported at length in the New York *Post,* May 7, 1941.

274   She cabled. Undated copy of cable to Chaim Weizmann, Dorchester Hotel, SU.

274   Wrote to David Dubinsky. July 1, 1941, SU.

275   In his recollection. Interview with James Drawbell, London, September 8, 1971.

275   "Just underneath Wednesday's . . ." Mollie Panter-Downes, *London War Notes, 1939–1945* (Farrar, Straus and Giroux, New York, 1971), p. 169.

276   Old London hands. Interview with William Stoneman, Paris, February 22, 1971.

276   "She speaks like an angel." Interview with Peter Grimm, New York, N.Y., January 8, 1971.

276–277   The most complete available account of the history of Freedom House, including DT's involvement, is Aaron Levenstein, in collaboration with William Agar, *Freedom's Advocate* (Viking, New York, 1965).

277   "Few people could equal . . ." Interview with George Field, New York, N.Y., December 15, 1971.

Chapter 4 (Pages 278–282)

278   "There is a big dinner . . ." John to Frances Gunther, MvE.
278   "You are now . . ." SL to DT, July 1942, SU.
278   "You have become . . ." SL to DT, July 1941, SU.
278   "Of your columns lately . . ." SL to DT, January 8, 1940, SU.
279   "The strangest aspect . . ." ST to DT, January 28, 1940, SU.
280   "Through a great fog . . ." SL to DT, February 12 (1940), SU.
280   "I don't think you really . . ." DT to SL, undated (1940), SU.
281   The America First Committee. Schorer, *Sinclair Lewis*, p. 679.
281   "Infinitely sorry . . ." Wells Lewis to DT from Camp Stewart, Georgia, November 26, 1941, SU.
281   Dorothy wrote. Diary entry, January 3, 1942, SU.

VIII: "FRUIT-BEARING AUTUMN"

Chapter 1 (Pages 285–293)

285   "Fruit-bearing autumn." Horace, Book IV, Ode 7.
286   Sometime confidante. Interview with Emily Carter Haberman.
287   "I never trusted him." Interview with Hilda, Baroness Louis de Rothschild, Cambridge, Mass., January 11, 1971.
287   A gifted interior designer. According to George Field, Bergal also decorated Freedom House and declined a fee for his services.
287   "A very personal instrument . . ." Handwritten note from DT inviting Helen Reid to a housewarming, November 8, 1941, HRR–L of C.
288 *fn.*   Max Ascoli. Interview with Max Ascoli, December 3, 1970.
288   Black-and-white color scheme. I am indebted to A. B. H. and Abby Friedman, who bought the house from DT in 1957, for a conducted tour of 237 East 48th Street on December 3, 1971. They recall DT as firm and gracious throughout the transaction. She asked, and got, her price, $85,000. She called with a gift of bread and salt after they moved in, but burst into tears, on a subsequent visit, when she discovered that Maxim's ceiling fresco in the library had been painted over. Otherwise, the Friedmans have largely preserved the original artifacts.
288   From Camp Stewart. Wells to DT, December 9, 1941, SU.
289 *fn.*   Ascoli. Interview with Max Ascoli.
290 *fn.*   Scheffer. Shepard Stone, whom I interviewed in New York, N.Y., on October 31, 1970, remembers Scheffer as a fascinating raconteur, who thought, erroneously, that the Nazis might have some of the answers to curbing Communism, with whose evils he was obsessed, following his tour of duty in Moscow. Scheffer is a leading character in *Wir Lügen Alle*, Olten, Walter Verlag, 1965, by Margaret Boveri. I am

grateful to Daphne A. Ehrlich of Houghton Mifflin, Boston, for a translation of the passages pertinent to his relationship with DT.

292 fn. Like all the plots. William L. Shirer, *The Rise and Fall of the Third Reich* (Simon & Schuster, New York, 1960, Fawcett Crest Book edition), p. 1392.

293 A picnic at Lake Bomoseen. Alexander Woollcott to DT, July 16, 1942, SU.

293 A $500 gift. Eleanor Roosevelt to DT, February 20, 1942, SU. This was one DT venture of which Mrs. Roosevelt approved; another was DT's support of the school lunch program that was commended in "My Day" on several occasions. She was, however, irked by DT's criticism of the New Deal. Joseph P. Lash kindly made available to me some sharp comments by Mrs. Roosevelt on a DT column, "On Borrowed Time," dealing with the National Youth Administration, W.P.A., and other relief agencies. Although her letter to DT (February 28, 1939, SU) was couched in tactful phrases, to another correspondent she called the column "utter nonsense" (Eleanor Roosevelt to Allen T. Burns, August 11, 1939, Franklin D. Roosevelt Library, Hyde Park, N.Y.).

293 From Camp Pickett. Wells Lewis to DT, September 7, 1942.

Chapter 2 (Pages 294–297)

294 Dubbed the Barnard area. ". . . we are going down to the Sudeten Vermont territory tomorrow and will have lunch with Jimmy [Sheean] and will certainly see Dorothy . . ." John to Frances Gunther, July 30, 1952, MvE.

295 Presided masterfully. Carl Zuckmayer, *A Part of Myself* (Harcourt, Brace and Jovanovich, New York, 1970), pp. 330–34, and an interview with Alicia Zuckmayer, Bern, Switzerland, February 23–24, 1971.

295 "Dorothy loved . . ." Interview with Winotou Zuckmayer, Guttenbrunner, Vienna, March 2, 1971.

295 Another ornament. A charming addition to the circle some years after the war was Helmuth von Moltke's widow, Countess Freya, who shared a house in Norwich, Vermont, with Professor Rosenstock-Huessy.

295 On a July morning. Interview with Emily Carter Haberman.

296 Maxim Kopf. Material on Maxim Kopf is derived from DT's essay, "My Husband, Maxim Kopf," in *Maxim Kopf* (Praeger, New York, 1960), and an interview with Martha Valentine, New York, N.Y., December 12, 1971.

297 A letter. Maxim Kopf to DT, August 12, 1942.

297 "That stallion . . ." This was an exaggeration of the usual feminine response to Maxim. DT's Vermont neighbor Agatha Young described him as "a magnificent male," in an interview, New York, N.Y., October 8, 1970. On the other hand, Esther Adams found him "intolerably crude . . . all those four-letter words . . ." Interview with Esther Root (Mrs. Franklin P.) Adams, New York, N.Y., February 2, 1971.

297 "She's going to marry . . ." Telephone conversation with Bruce Gould.

Chapter 3 (Pages 298–303)

298 By her own account. Interview with Lisa Sergio, Washington, D.C., October 16, 1970.

298 A good press. Reviews quoted in *Maxim Kopf,* pp. 13–18.

299 Bitten in Café Row. New York *Post,* February 12, 1942.

299 "Why should people . . ." Regina Kurlander in the Cleveland *Plain Dealer,* May 15, 1942. DT had her dates slightly mixed. Singapore fell on February 15, 1942.

299 "A sickening travesty . . ." Cleveland *Plain Dealer,* May 9, 1942.

299 To photograph. *Look,* April 7, 1942.

300 A blistering essay. *Harper's Magazine,* December 1942.

300 "My dear Bennie . . ." DT to Bernard DeVoto, December 2, 1942, SU.

300 Dashed off. Bernard DeVoto to DT, December 11, 1942, SU.

300 "The eternal Protestant . . ." DT to Bernard DeVoto, undated, SU.

301 "Sending you this study." A copy of the ms., which runs to twenty-six typed pages, is in the files at SU.

302 "Hurt, angered . . ." DT to Phyllis Bottome, February 24, 1943, SU.

303 Persuaded to seek a Reno divorce. Although every effort was made to handle the matter discreetly, it was generally known that DT paid Mrs. Stein a substantial sum. According to Martha Valentine the figure, originally $30,000, was finally reduced to $15,000. DT set forth her own version of the divorce in a letter written August 30, 1949, in response to an inquiry about an alleged relative of Maxim's: "Lotte Stein was a well-known German Jewish actress who fled to Prague. There she was unable to continue her profession after the Czech government closed the acting profession to persons without Czech citizenship. My husband, who was free, married Mrs. Stein, after she had divorced her husband for professional reasons, in order to give her Czech citizenship and a passport, on the understanding that the marriage could be dissolved without contest by either party. She continued to live (in my husband's apartment) with her husband and son. He left Prague before she did. Later, when he demanded a divorce, she made a lot of trouble . . ." SU. Though such marriages of convenience were common in the Hitler years, this was

obviously not Mrs. Stein's view when the question of divorce actually came up.

303   Announced their engagement. New York *Herald Tribune,* April 14, 1943.

Chapter 4 (Pages 304–307)

304   "It was the wedding . . ." From "I Visit Twin Farms," unpublished ms. by Dale Warren.

305   Vividly recalls. Interview with Anita Daniel, New York, N.Y., January 8, 1971.

305   "Like a teenage girl . . ." Interview with Peter Drucker, New York, N.Y., October 12, 1970.

305   His squealing bride. Interview with Dorothy de Santillana, Boston, September 21, 1970.

305 fn.   "When we make love . . ." DT made this remark to Cass Canfield, Sr., who recalled it when I interviewed him on September 18, 1970, in New York, N.Y.

305 fn.   "Go away . . ." This quip has also been attributed to Dorothy Parker. DT's letter to Patterson was written October 24, 1949, SU.

306   An invitation. Eleanor Roosevelt to DT, June 2, 1944, SU.

307   A bookplate. JSM.

307   One of her few diary entries. February 15, 1945, SU.

Chapter 5 (Pages 308–310)

308   "The enclosed award . . ." Wells to DT, October 29, 1943, SU.

309   "A charge not easily refuted . . ." Sherwood, *Roosevelt and Hopkins,* p. 820.

309   The most effective speech. FDR acknowledged DT's help more effusively after this campaign than he had in 1940, writing on November 27, 1944: ". . . I cannot delay any longer telling you how much I appreciate your valiant support. I know that it took courage and a resolute spirit to oppose the powerful interests which it was necessary for you to oppose . . ." SU.

310   "It is hard for me to explain . . ." CZ.

IX: "LIFE WITHOUT THE ENEMY"

Chapter 1 (Pages 313–320)

313   "I like them all . . ." DT to Frances Gunther, undated, MvE.

314   "People's Platform." Broadcast, February 26, 1944. I am indebted to John M. Patterson of the Columbia University School of Journalism for securing a tape recording of this broadcast from the Milo Ryan Phonoarchives of the University of Washington, Seattle. The other panelists were William Henry Chamberlain, author of *The Russian Dilemma;* Michael Williams, editor of *Commonweal;* Henry

Pratt Fairchild, New York University sociology professor; and Lyman Bryson, moderator. The subject was "What Is Russia's Foreign Policy?"

314 Gustav Stolper. Toni Stolper, *Ein Leben, Gustav Stolper 1888– 1947* (Tübingen, 1960), p. 430.

314 Confidence in Soviet intentions. Illustrative of the cordial feelings of many Americans toward the USSR at this time is a letter from Ambassador Andrei Gromyko to DT, dated March 30, 1944, in which he thanks her for transmitting "on behalf of the War Loan Committee of Newton, Massachusetts, bonds of the United States Third War Loan amounting to $1675.00 and intended as a gift to Marshall Josef Stalin," SU.

314 "An enormous anti-Nazi movement . . ." New York *Post,* October 8, 1943.

315 "We must stop making . . ." DT, *Listen, Hans!* (Houghton Mifflin, Boston, 1942), pp. 26–28.

315 John Chamberlain. Chamberlain's review was published November 28, 1942.

316 Ben Ames Williams. Letter to DT from Ben Ames Williams, August 6, 1944, SU.

317 Association for a Democratic Germany. The organization shut up shop in January 1951 for the sensible reason that it had achieved its goal with the establishment in West Germany of "as stable a democratic state as most of the rest of Western Europe," SU.

317 Found herself outvoted. Interview with George Field, New York, N.Y., December 15, 1971.

317 Ideological differences. Levenstein, *Freedom's Advocate,* pp. 65–66.

317 Writers' War Board. DT to Clifton Fadiman, August 10, 1944, SU.

318 "The Germans are . . ." "The Lesson of Dachau," *Ladies' Home Journal,* September 1945.

319 "I met the remnant . . ." DT, "Rendezvous in Berlin," *Saturday Review of Literature,* March 15, 1947.

Chapter 2 (Pages 321–328)

From April 25, 1920, until May 14, 1948, when the State of Israel was created, England governed Palestine under a League of Nations Mandate. During World War II, the Axis powers exploited the Arabs' hostility to the Jews and a number of their leaders, notably Haj Amin el Husseini, the grand mufti of Jerusalem, collaborated actively with Hitler and Mussolini. I have been unable to discover a truly "objective" account of events in the Holy Land and hence have drawn on two diverse interpretations: James Parkes, *Whose Land: A History of the Peoples of Palestine* (Taplinger, New York, 1971), an updating of *A History of Palestine from 135 A.D. to Modern Times* (Oxford University Press and Victor Gollancz); and Fred J. Khouri, *The Arab-Israeli Dilemma* (Syracuse University Press, 1968). Both authors are scholars; however, Parkes's sympathies are with Israel, while Khouri writes from the Arab perspective.

321 "The 'Arab rebellion' . . ." New York *Herald Tribune,* May 19, 1939.

321 A volume commemorating. *Chaim Weizmann: Statesman and Scientist,* edited by Meyer W. Weisgal (Dial, New York, 1944), pp. 21–30.

322–323 Jesus of Nazareth. This theory was relayed to me in a letter from Diana Sheean, who commented, "This seems to me terribly likely as Dorothy was so deeply Christian . . . it has the ring of truth to me," April 10, 1972.

323 Dorothy began. Although she expressed concern about Soviet maneuvers in the Middle East, all the columns datelined Jerusalem May 1945 are sympathetic to Jewish aspirations. Starting with a column titled "The Palestine Tragedy," New York *Post,* July 9, 1946, her emphasis was increasingly on Jewish acts of terrorism against Arabs, "Zionist zealotry," and the Machiavellian tactics of the USSR.

323 "I got a cable . . ." *Meyer Weisgal . . . So Far,* pp. 197–98.

324 "Words were prophetic." *Meyer Weisgal . . . So Far,* p. 197.

324 *The New Leader.* December 15, 1945.

325 fn. Dorothy's friend. Ernst, *So Far So Good,* p. 176.

326 "A good letter . . ." Interview with Ted O. Thackrey, New York, N.Y., April 13, 1972.

327 "An anti-Semite by designation." *Meyer Weisgal . . . So Far,* p. 198.

327 "I will not remain . . ." *The New Yorker,* April 20, 1940, p. 24.

327 *Time* magazine. John Kobler, *Luce* (Doubleday, New York, 1968), pp. 60–61.

327 "Although I loathe . . ." Harold Nicolson, *Diaries and Letters 1939–1945* (Collins, Fontana Books, London 1970), p. 473.

327 "Never anti-Semitic." Interview with Anita Daniel, New York, N.Y., January 8, 1971.

327 "Your Jewish friends." Helen Woodward to DT, December 11, 1957. DT's reply is undated, SU.

Chapter 3 (Pages 329–333)

329 "Nichts bleibt mir . . ." DT to the Zuckmayers, July 21, 1950, CZ.

329 A written contract. Done half in jest according to Madeline Shaw who witnessed it. Dated December 20, 1948.

330 "Hope Dinah will . . ." DT to Vincent Sheean, February 28, 1948, SU.

331   An adulatory cover story. *Time,* December 8, 1947.

331   Dorothy, by a personal appeal. Dame Rebecca cabled her thanks, December 1, 1947. DT again referred to the incident in a letter to Harold Ross, February 17, 1950, SU.

333   A blow-by-blow account. Alec Manson to DT from Rome, December 30, 1950. SU.

Chapter 4 (Pages 334–341)

334   "I was fed up . . ." DT to Vincent Sheean, January 27, 1949, SU.

334   An eyewitness. DT to Vincent Sheean, February 10, 1949, SU.

335   Wrote to John Wheeler. November 5, 1950, SU.

335   Instructed her lecture agent. DT to Harold R. Peat, October 17, 1950, SU.

336   Wired Dorothy from Pittsburgh. November 14, 1950, SU.

336   Reported to Dale Warren. January 15, 1951, SU.

336   The *Saturday Evening Post.* DT to Ben Hibbs, December 22 and 29, 1950, SU.

337 fn.   The split. There is a well-documented account of the bitter controversies between pro-, non- and anti-Zionist Jewish groups in Naomi W. Cohen, *Not Free to Desist: A History of the American Jewish Committee 1906–1966* (The Jewish Publication Society of America, Philadelphia, 1972).

337   Sent a contribution. Frances Gunther to DT, from Jerusalem, October 1 and December 20, 1951, SU.

338   To confirm or deny. Bennett Schiff to DT, October 21. DT's reply is handwritten on the back of his letter (for subsequent transcription by her secretary), SU.

338 fn.   This came to light. The disclosure and its consequences were reported in the *New York Times,* February 17, 1967; an A.P. dispatch, March 23, 1967; and the Washington *Post,* May 1, 1969.

339   "We were losing . . ." Interview with Virginia Shaw, New York, N.Y., January 29, 1971.

339   "The seeds of World War III . . ." Interview with George Weller, Rome, March 11, 1971.

340   An enthusiastic introduction. Gamal Abdel Nasser, *Egypt's Liberation* (Public Affairs Press, Washington, 1955).

340   An ultimatum. John Wheeler to DT, December 8, 1956, SU.

341   "A great ship . . ." Interview with Stephen Graubard, Cambridge, Mass., January 12, 1971.

Chapter 5 (Pages 342–345)

342   A young British reporter. Interview with Kenneth Ames, Vienna, March 3, 1971.

342   Peter Viereck's book. *Conservatism Revisited* (Scribner's, New York, 1949).

342   *Life.* Published as "Jan Masaryk Found One Answer," *Life,* March 22, 1948, and condensed in *Reader's Digest,* June 1948.

344   To Governor Adlai Stevenson. August 1, 1952, SU.

344   Stevenson responded. August 5, 1952, SU.

345   Endorsed Eisenhower. "A Vote against Trumanism," Boston *Daily Globe,* October 24, 1952.

345   Sister Peggy. October 26, 1952. DT's reply was handwritten on the back of Peggy's letter, dated 10/29/52, SU.

X: LION AND CHILD

Chapter 1 (Pages 349–357)

349   "You are a lion and a child . . ." Niccolo Tucci's letter is undated, SU.

349   "My dearest . . ." Maxim to DT, from aboard the *DeGrasse,* March 12, 1950, SU.

349   "Absolutely reckonable." From a mimeographed letter, August 12, 1958, DT sent to their friends after Maxim's death, SU.

350   Splendid entertainments. An unpublished ms. by DT, "How to Give a Party and Like It," is a dawn-to-dusk guide, complete with menus, recipes, and logistical instructions on how to give a sit-down supper for twenty-four with the aid of one transient maid. DT regarded the formal dinner as too constricting and called cocktail parties "the nadir of entertainment," SU.

351   Bennie was wounded. Interview with Bernadette Lewis, New York, N.Y., April 30, 1971.

352   "Unhappy love affair . . ." *The Courage to Be Happy,* p. 117.

352   Dieting. A fan letter from a plump reader prompted DT to write, "Good for you! The women I have known who have been absolutely irresistible to men have almost all without exception been fatties. One of them is Moura Budberg, the great love of Maxim Gorky; the last great love of H. G. Wells . . ." August 29, 1952, SU.

352   "I find . . ." DT to Margaret Davidson, March 31, 1952, SU.

353   "The Farm Problem and Me." *Ladies' Home Journal,* July 1954.

354   Katie Antonius. November 24, 1953, SU.

355   More drastic changes. DT to Dale Warren, April 14, 1957, SU.

356   "Elderly Reflections." *The Courage to Be Happy,* pp. 111–36.

Chapter 2 (Pages 358–360)

358   A costume party. Emily Haberman showed me a snapshot of this singular event; unfortunately, the quality is not adequate for reproduction.

359 "An old lady." Interview with Michael Lewis, Barnard, Vt., October 5, 1970.

359 Farewell column. Chicago *Daily News,* August 22, 1958.

360 "Has touched me . . ." *Meyer Weisgal . . . So Far,* pp. 199–200.

360 Accompanying her last column. Undated mimeographed news re-lease, SU.

360 "Burying an old friend . . ." John Wheeler to DT, August 18, 1958. DT's reply is handwritten on the back of his letter, SU.

Chapter 3 (Pages 361–368)

361 Prominently reported. *Time* and *Newsweek,* September 1, 1958.

361 Eight publishers. Atlantic Monthly Press, Doubleday, Devin-Adair, Harper's, Houghton Mifflin, McGraw-Hill, Rowohlt Verlag (Hamburg), and Simon & Schuster.

361 Warren had assured her. March 9, 1948, H.

362 "That man is happiest . . ." Johann Wolfgang von Goethe, *Kunst und Altertum.*

362 (None was found.) Letter to DT from Letitia Irwin, November 2, 1958, SU.

362 fn. By corresponding. Mary Gawthorpe to DT, June 8, 1960, SU.

367–368 "The Boy and Man from Sauk Centre," *Atlantic Monthly,* November 1960, reprinted as an appendix to *Dorothy and Red.*

Chapter 4 (Pages 369–372)

369 Heartsick. Interview with Alice Tarnovsky, who served as DT's part-time secretary while she was living with Mrs. Irwin, Washington, D.C., October 16, 1970.

369 "She looked harassed . . ." Sheean, *Dorothy and Red,* p. 326.

369 Bernadette too. Interview with Bernadette Lewis. New York, N.Y., April 30, 1971.

369 "She captivated . . ." Letter to MKS from Ambassador Elbrick, September 14, 1971.

370 "A cluster . . ." Quoted in Ambassador Elbrick's letter.

370 "At peace with herself . . ." Letter to MKS from Morris R. Nelson, Jr., November 28, 1971.

371 "Good-bye to a lifetime." Sheean, *Dorothy and Red,* p. 327.

372 As a companion. Dale Warren recorded his impressions in "Off the Record with a Columnist," *Saturday Review of Literature,* June 10, 1944, and "I Remember Dorothy," published in *The Courier,* Vol. IV, No. 2, Summer 1964, Syracuse University Library Associates, and reissued as a pamphlet.

372 "A true victim . . ." Letter to MKS from Meyer Weisgal, March 14, 1971.

INDEX

Index